FileMaker® 9 DEVELOPER REFERENCE

Functions, Scripts, Commands, and Grammars, with Extensive Custom Function Examples

Bob Bowers
Steve Lane
Scott Love

800 East 96th Street, Indianapolis, Indiana 46240 USA

FileMaker 9® Developer Reference: Functions, Scripts, Commands, and Grammars, with Extensive Custom Function Examples

ISBN-13: 978-0-7897-3708-3
ISBN-10: 0-7897-3708-6

Library of Congress Cataloging-in-Publication Data:

Bowers, Bob, 1969-

FileMaker X developer reference : functions, scripts, commands, and grammars, with extensive custom function examples / Bob Bowers, Steve Lane, and Scott Love. — 1st ed.

p. cm.

ISBN 0-7897-3708-6

1. FileMaker (Computer file) 2. Database management. I. Lane, Steve, 1965- II. Love, Scott, 1967- III. Title.

QA76.9.D3B67393 2007

005.75'65—dc22

2007024413

Printed in the United States of America

Second Printing, December 2007

Trademarks

All terms mentioned in this book that are known to be trademarks or service marks have been appropriately capitalized. Que Publishing cannot attest to the accuracy of this information. Use of a term in this book should not be regarded as affecting the validity of any trademark or service mark.

Warning and Disclaimer

Every effort has been made to make this book as complete and as accurate as possible, but no warranty or fitness is implied. The information provided is on an "as is" basis.

Bulk Sales

Que Publishing offers excellent discounts on this book when ordered in quantity for bulk purchases or special sales. For more information, please contact

U.S. Corporate and Government Sales
1-800-382-3419
corpsales@pearsontechgroup.com

For sales outside of the U.S., please contact

International Sales
international@pearsoned.com

This Book Is Safari Enabled

The Safari® Enabled icon on the cover of your favorite technology book means the book is available through Safari Bookshelf. When you buy this book, you get free access to the online edition for 45 days.

Safari Bookshelf is an electronic reference library that lets you easily search thousands of technical books, find code samples, download chapters, and access technical information whenever and wherever you need it.

To gain 45-day Safari Enabled access to this book:

- Go to http://www.quepublishing.com/safarienabled
- Complete the brief registration form
- Enter the coupon code TYDQ-Y8JC-WWCG-H2CQ-K9Q5

If you have difficulty registering on Safari Bookshelf or accessing the online edition, please email customer-service@safaribooksonline.com.

Associate Publisher
Greg Wiegand

Acquisitions Editor
Michelle Newcomb

Development Editor
Laura Norman

Technical Editor
Jay Welshofer

Managing Editor
Gina Kanouse

Project Editor
George E. Nedeff

Copy Editor
Geneil Breeze

Indexer
WordWise Publishing

Proofreader
Kathy Bidwell

Publishing Coordinator
Cindy Teeters

Book Designer
Anne Jones

Composition
Nonie Ratcliff

Contents at a Glance

Table of Contents

VII Appendix

About the Authors

Bob Bowers, CEO of Soliant Consulting, is a columnist and contributing editor for *FileMaker Advisor* magazine and has coauthored five books: *Advanced FileMaker Pro 5.5 Techniques for Developers*, *Advanced FileMaker Pro 6 Web Development*, *Special Edition Using FileMaker 7*, *Special Edition Using FileMaker 8*, and *FileMaker 8 Functions and Scripts Desk Reference*. At the 2002 FileMaker Developer Conference he was awarded the FileMaker Fellowship Award. Widely recognized as one of the leading educators for database and FileMaker Pro technologies, he is authorized by FileMaker, Inc., to teach the Professional Training Foundation Series. Bob is also a proud dad of two young children, an avid musician, a die-hard Cubs fan, and an accomplished woodworker.

Steve Lane, vice president of Soliant Consulting, served as a special projects developer at Scott Foresman, a leading K-6 Educational publisher. He has written for *FileMaker Advisor* magazine, and coauthored four books: *Advanced FileMaker Pro 6 Web Development*, *Special Edition Using FileMaker Pro 7*, *Special Edition Using FileMaker 8*, and *FileMaker 8 Functions and Scripts Desk Reference*. He has led training classes in FileMaker technologies all over the country and is also authorized to teach the Professional Training Foundation Series. He regularly speaks at the annual FileMaker Developer Conference where in 2003 he was awarded the FileMaker Fellowship Award for "pushing the boundaries of FileMaker Pro." When not writing about technology, Steve is likely to be found being chased about by his children, or grumbling over the fingerings of J. S. Bach. Or just grumbling.

Scott Love, chief operating officer of Soliant Consulting, served at Ziff-Davis Interactive as an online managing editor, served at Apple Computer as its web publishing technology evangelist, and led the technical marketing team at Macromedia. He has written dozens of feature and review articles on database and Internet/web topics for a wide range of computer publications including *Macworld* magazine and *FileMaker Advisor*. He has coauthored three books: *Special Edition Using FileMaker 7*, *Special Edition Using FileMaker 8*, and *FileMaker 8 Functions and Scripts Desk Reference*. He is also an authorized Professional Training Foundation Series instructor and a regular speaker at the FileMaker Developer Conference. In 2006 he was awarded the FileMaker Excellence Award "for developing outstanding technical and training resources for FileMaker." Scott lives in the California Bay Area where his penchant for gardening can be indulged year round.

Dedication

To FileMaker: the company, the people, the tool, the vision.

—Bob Bowers, Steve Lane, Scott Love

Acknowledgments

Nowhere is the tired maxim "it takes a village" more true (and the villagers more tired) than in the creation and production of a book.

Each of the authors has had to rely, not only on his wits and cunning, but especially on the efforts of his fellow authors. In the long marathon of writing and revising, we've found that when one member of the team gets a little winded, the others keep up the pace. Each chapter has benefited from the attention and feedback of several rather different outlooks and personalities, hopefully to the overall betterment of the book.

To Allen Goetsch, our unflappable project manager, our warmest thanks. The term "herding cats" has cropped up from time to time, but we imagine Allen is secretly envisioning a herd of something more like armored porcupines. Allen kept us organized and on track through the inevitable flow of submissions, revisions, table-of-contents changes, and debates over formatting, style, and design.

Many other colleagues also made important contributions to the mammoth task of mustering and checking our data. In particular, we'd like to thank David Galson, Jim Medema, TG Ricker, Caspar Harmer, David Kinel, Andrew Ofisher, and Arnaud Dazin for their fact-checking and editing; Jan Jung and David Boor for their design and quality assurance acumen; and certainly David Simerly for contributing the book's new material on AppleScript.

Acknowledgments wouldn't be complete without a tip of the hat to the talented and hard-working crew at FileMaker, Inc., without whom these great tools would not exist and prosper. We'd particularly like to thank Jay Welshofer, Rick Kalman, and Kevin Nathanson, seasoned product managers all, who steered us straight and provided guidance on many points large and small.

And finally, of course, the "production" part of bookmaking, that vexing little step from scrappy Word documents to something polished and glossy that fits just right in your hand. In this case the thanks is due once again to a highly skilled, quietly patient Que team, this time headed by our acquisitions editor, Michelle Newcomb, our development editor (again!) Laura Norman, and George Nedeff, our very patient project editor. Their pride in their work shows in every facet of the book you're holding. It's our good fortune to work with them again.

We Want to Hear from You!

As the reader of this book, *you* are our most important critic and commentator. We value your opinion and want to know what we're doing right, what we could do better, what areas you'd like to see us publish in, and any other words of wisdom you're willing to pass our way.

As an associate publisher for Que Publishing, I welcome your comments. You can email or write me directly to let me know what you did or didn't like about this book—as well as what we can do to make our books better.

Please note that I cannot help you with technical problems related to the topic of this book. We do have a User Services group, however, where I will forward specific technical questions related to the book.

When you write, please be sure to include this book's title and author as well as your name, email address, and phone number. I will carefully review your comments and share them with the author and editors who worked on the book.

Email: feedback@quepublishing.com

Mail: Greg Wiegand
Associate Publisher
Que Publishing
800 East 96th Street
Indianapolis, IN 46240 USA

Reader Services

Visit our website and register this book at www.quepublishing.com/register for convenient access to any updates, downloads, or errata that might be available for this book.

INTRODUCTION

Welcome to FileMaker 9 Developer Reference

Just the Facts

This is the book we've always wanted on our desks. Just as a writer always needs a dictionary nearby, we've found over years of developing FileMaker solutions that it'd be great to have a quick set of reminders within reach. It's impossible to recall each function's syntax or every script step's attributes. Although we use the Let( ) function every day, the exact output of RelationInfo() can be a little less fresh in our minds. This desk reference contains notes on all the script steps and calculation functions in FileMaker; provides lists of other facts such as error codes, port numbers, and XML grammars; and offers a library of useful or instructive custom function examples. We hope this book provides invaluable assistance to like-addle-minded developers everywhere, regardless of your experience with FileMaker.

Help Is a Function Key Away

Before going any further, we'd like to congratulate the tech writers, engineers, and product managers at FileMaker, Inc., for an excellent help system and electronic documentation. If you've never used FileMaker's help resources or website, you're missing a wealth of information. Both are fantastic places to learn, refresh your memory, or uncover areas of FileMaker you had no idea were there.

Sometimes, though, it's nice to leave what's on your screen unchanged, keep your work and your reference material separate, and be able to turn to actual paper. (It's hard to take notes in the help system, for example!)

Some of this book may overlap a bit with the help system, especially in cases where there's really nothing more to add: for example, as in the Abs() function. Where we hope this book does prove useful is in the additional information and examples we provide, the fact that it's collected all here on paper, and that it's more accessible during those times when you may not be in front of FileMaker or a laptop.

This desk reference is intended to be just that—a reference. It should serve beginners and experts alike and isn't intended to be read from cover to cover. Rather, the intent is that you'll look up functions you've forgotten, dog-ear useful pages, take notes, and find it a handy tool for building solutions quickly in FileMaker.

How This Book Is Organized

FileMaker 9 Developer Reference is divided into seven parts, each of which can stand on its own.

Part I: FileMaker Specifications

Part I covers the nuts and bolts of FileMaker's product family:

- Chapter 1, "FileMaker 9 Product Line," provides an overview of all FileMaker products and what purposes and audiences they serve.
- Chapter 2, "New Features of FileMaker 9"; Chapter 3, "Overview of FileMaker 8.5 Features"; and Chapter 4, "Overview of FileMaker 8 Features," provide an overview of the main features added to FileMaker Pro and FileMaker Pro Advanced in versions 8, 8.5, and 9.
- Chapter 5, "Specifications and Storage Limits," details the various hardware and software specifications for each product and other pertinent load statistics.
- Chapter 6, "Field Types and Import/Export Formats," reviews FileMaker's field data types and the details of supported import/export formats.

Part II: Calculation Functions

Part II details all FileMaker Pro calculation functions, syntax, and usage:

- Chapter 7, "Calculation Primer," reviews the layout and functionality of the calculation dialogs.
- Chapter 8, "Calculation Signatures," lists by category of the syntax and the output type for each calculation function.
- Chapter 9, "Calculation Functions," provides a complete description of each calculation function, lists examples, and in many cases offers additional comments on usage.

Part III: Custom Functions

Part III offers real-world examples of custom functions:

- Chapter 10, "Custom Function Primer," introduces the mechanics of creating custom functions, including how to build functions that use recursive logic.
- Chapter 11, "Useful Custom Functions," presents a collection of custom functions the authors have found useful or representative.

Part IV: Script Steps

Part IV reviews FileMaker's script steps and their options in detail:

- Chapter 12, "Scripting Primer," provides an overview of the mechanics of ScriptMaker and of working with script parameters, script results, and script variables.
- Chapter 13, "Script Step Reference," lists in alphabetical order all script steps in FileMaker Pro, their options, and notes on usage.

Part V: FileMaker Connectivity

Part V provides reference materials covering some of the major ways to connect to a FileMaker solution:

- Chapter 14, "FileMaker XML Reference," details FileMaker's XML grammars and provides a Custom Web Publishing command reference.
- Chapter 15, "FileMaker API for PHP," documents FileMaker's external API for PHP connectivity.
- Chapter 16, "JDBC/ODBC and External SQL Connectivity," reviews how to prepare a FileMaker solution for access from external applications via ODBC or JDBC, and how to configure a DSN for connecting a FileMaker solution to an ODBC data source.
- Chapter 17, "AppleScript Integration," provides an overview of the AppleScript object model for FileMaker.

Part VI: Quick Reference

Part VI provides quick reference to commonly needed FileMaker facts:

- Chapter 18, "FileMaker Error Codes," provides a complete list of all error codes.
- Chapter 19, "FileMaker Keyboard Shortcuts," lists shortcuts for both Mac and Windows.
- Chapter 20, "FileMaker Network Ports," lists information useful for IT/infrastructure support.
- Chapter 21, "FileMaker Server Command Line Reference," provides syntax and examples for administering FileMaker Server from a command line.

Part VII: Other Resources

Part VII helps you discover other ways to learn about FileMaker:

- Appendix A, "Additional Resources," presents a list of additional resources we have found helpful in FileMaker development.

Special Features

This book includes the following special features:

- **Cross-references**—Many topics are connected to other topics in various ways. Cross-references help you link related information together, no matter where that information appears in the book. When another section is related to one you are reading, a cross-reference directs you to a specific page in the book on which you will find the related information.
- **Notes**, **Tips**, and **Cautions** can be found in various spots throughout the book.

Note

A note contains information that offers additional details about the topic being discussed. These notes give you added insight into the discussion, but aren't absolutely essential to understanding the given topic.

Tip

A tip provides you with additional information that goes beyond what you might ordinarily know about a certain topic. Often, these tips contain helpful hints from our personal experience working with FileMaker over the years.

Caution

Pay special attention to cautions. They are provided to help you avoid certain pitfalls, or to reiterate a specific point that could trip you up if you aren't careful.

- **Icons**—In certain chapters we also refer to information that might pertain only to a certain platform. The following icons alert you to the usage for the item they appear with:

  Windows only

  Mac OS X only

  Web only

If more than one icon appears in a location, then the usage applies to each platform represented.

Typographic Conventions Used in This Book

This book uses a few different typesetting styles, primarily to distinguish among explanatory text, code, and special terms.

Key Combinations and Menu Choices

Key (and possibly mouse) combinations that you use to perform FileMaker operations are indicated by presenting the Mac command first in parentheses followed by the Windows command in brackets: (⌘-click) for Mac and [Ctrl+click] for Windows, for example.

Submenu choices are separated from the main menu name by a comma: File, Manage, Value Lists.

Typographic Conventions Used for FileMaker Scripts

Monospace type is used for all examples of FileMaker scripting. FileMaker scripts are not edited as text but are instead edited through FileMaker's graphical script design tool, called ScriptMaker. As a result, scripting options presented visually in ScriptMaker need to be turned into text when written out. We follow FileMaker's own conventions for printing scripts as text: The name of the script step comes first, and any options to the step are placed after the step name, in square brackets, with semicolons delimiting multiple script step options, as in the following example:

```
Show All Records
Go to Record/Request/Page [ First ]
Show Custom Dialog [Title: "Message window"; Message; "Hello, world!"; Buttons: "OK"]
```

Who Should Use This Book

We hope that anyone who develops FileMaker systems will find many aspects of this book useful. It's a book we, the authors, use in our day-to-day work, but that doesn't mean its use is limited to experts. This reference material is meant to be convenient and accessible to everyone.

PART I

FileMaker Specifications

CHAPTER 1

FileMaker 9 Product Line

Overview of FileMaker Products

The FileMaker product line is composed of a number of distinct pieces. Understanding their different strengths, capabilities, and requirements is an important part of your FileMaker knowledge base. This chapter provides a quick overview of the purpose and profile of each piece of the FileMaker software suite, along with relevant operating system requirements.

FileMaker Pro 9

FileMaker Pro is the original, all-in-one database design, development, deployment, and access tool. Users of FileMaker Pro have access to a full suite of database design tools and can create their own databases from scratch, with full authoring privileges. FileMaker Pro can host databases, sharing them across small groups of users, via FileMaker network sharing or Instant Web Publishing (IWP). A copy of FileMaker Pro is required to open and use FileMaker databases created by others, unless you're using IWP.

If you are an advanced developer or are working to build a complex system, we recommend FileMaker Pro Advanced. If you want to share your databases with more than a few FileMaker users at a time, you'll need FileMaker Server. If you need to share your databases with similar numbers of users via the Web or ODBC/JDBC, you'll need FileMaker Server Advanced.

Operating system requirements are as follows:

Mac: Mac OS X 10.4.8 or greater

Windows: Windows XP Professional, Home Edition (Service Pack 2), Windows Vista Ultimate, Business, Home Edition

FileMaker Pro 9 Advanced

FileMaker Pro Advanced is the successor to FileMaker Developer. FileMaker Pro Advanced includes all the features and functionality present in the regular FileMaker Pro software but has a series of additional features aimed at application developers. These include tools for debugging scripts; the capability to design custom functions, custom menus, and ToolTips; the capability to perform file maintenance; a Database Design Report that can help document a system; and a set of tools that lets you create a variety of "runtime" executable solutions. FileMaker Pro 9 Advanced also includes many new features that speed development, such as the capability to copy and paste fields, tables, and script steps.

We strongly recommend FileMaker Pro Advanced for any FileMaker developer who is serious about designing high-quality database systems. The extra tools are well worth the additional cost and, by using Advanced, developers can extend the functionality of their systems to end users by utilizing ToolTips and custom menus.

Operating system requirements are as follows:

Mac: Mac OS X 10.4.8 or greater

Windows: Windows XP Professional, Home Edition (Service Pack 2), Windows Vista Ultimate, Business, Home Edition

FileMaker Server 9

FileMaker Server is the tool of choice for sharing FileMaker files with more than a handful of concurrent FileMaker users. Whereas the peer-to-peer file hosting available in FileMaker Pro and Pro Advanced can host no more than 10 files for no more than 5 users, FileMaker Server can host as many as 125 files for as many as 250 concurrent FileMaker users. FileMaker Server can also perform regular, automated backups of database files, handle automatic distribution of plug-ins to FileMaker clients, and log various usage statistics.

If you want to share your databases with more than a few users, you'll want to invest in FileMaker Server.

FileMaker Server 9 also includes both the FileMaker API for PHP and XSLT publishing capabilities. What was referred to as Custom Web Publishing in prior versions is now included in the "base" server.

Operating system requirements are as follows:

Mac: Mac OS X 10.4.9 (Intel & Power PC based Macs), Mac OS X Server 10.4.9 (Intel & Power PC based Macs)

Windows: Windows 2003 Server Standard Edition (Service Pack 2), Windows 2000 Server (Service Pack 4), Windows XP Professional (Service Pack 2)

FileMaker Server 9 Advanced

FileMaker Server Advanced is required to host databases via Instant Web Publishing (IWP) or to connect via ODBC/JDBC to external SQL sources. FileMaker Pro and Pro Advanced can perform hosting for IWP or ODBC/JDBC for a small number of clients. For more than five connections, organizations will need to install FileMaker Server 9 Advanced: It can host up to 250 combined FileMaker and ODBC/JDBC connections, and up to 100 IWP connections.

Note that the installation for both Server and Server Advanced is identical. Advanced features are unlocked via serial keys and do not require additional installation.

Operating system requirements are as follows:

> Mac: Mac OS X 10.4.9 (Intel & Power PC based Macs), Mac OS X Server 10.4.9 (Intel & Power PC based Macs)
>
> Windows: Windows 2003 Server Standard Edition (Service Pack 2), Windows 2000 Server (Service Pack 4), Windows XP Professional (Service Pack 2)

CHAPTER 2

New Features of FileMaker 9

FileMaker Pro/Advanced 9

This chapter presents a broad overview of the many new features and benefits that have been added to the FileMaker 9 product line. If you're thinking of upgrading from a previous version, it will give you an idea of the benefits that await you; if you're already using FileMaker 9, use the overview that follows to ensure you're taking full advantage of all the newest version has to offer.

Conditional Formatting

As its name suggests, conditional formatting is a tool for controlling various aspects of the appearance of fields, buttons, and text objects on a layout. In past versions of FileMaker Pro, this could be achieved only through cumbersome workarounds that typically required stacking multiple calculation fields on top of each other. The addition of conditional formatting to FileMaker Pro 9 provides a lot of value for little effort.

To specify conditional formatting for an object, either right-click the object, or—with the object selected—choose the Format, Conditional menu item, which brings up the Conditional Formatting dialog shown in Figure 2.1.

You can specify as many different conditional formatting options as you need. For instance, you might want a customer's name to appear in bold text if he has an invoice over 30 days due, and in bold, red text if the customer has any over 60 days due. Many of the most common conditions (equal, not equal, greater than, between, and so on) are offered as preset choices, but you can also make the condition as complex as you need by providing a formula as the condition.

For each condition you set, you also specify a format to apply to the object. All the typical text attributes, such as font, size, and style can be assigned. Additionally, the object's fill color can be controlled, which is a particularly nice feature.

Conditional Formatting for "BalanceDue"

Conditional formatting allows you to dynamically change a layout object's formatting whenever one or more conditions are met. (You can use the Self function to refer to the content of the corresponding layout object in a calculation.)

Condition	Format
Value is > 10000	Bold, Fill Color

Add Delete

Condition

Value is | greater than | 10000

Format

Bold Underline Text Color:
Italic Strike Thru Fill Color:

Sample
Automate sophisticated tasks without programming.

More Formatting...

Cancel OK

Figure 2.1

The Conditional Formatting dialog provides control over many aspects of a field's appearance, including font, text color, style, and fill color.

Auto Resize Layout Objects

Another major layout enhancement to FileMaker Pro 9 is the ability to have objects automatically resize and/or move as a user resizes the window. This behavior is controlled by *anchoring* an object to the sides of the window; the anchors are set using the Object Size palette, shown in Figure 2.2. Objects can grow as large as necessary but will not shrink to less than their original size.

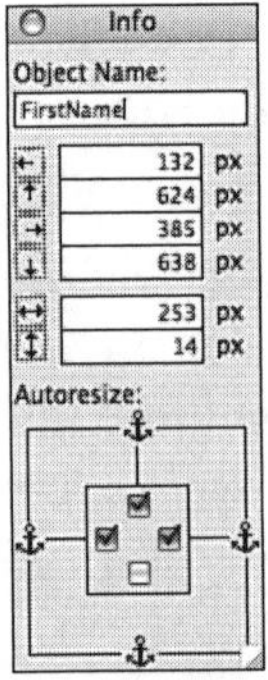

Figure 2.2

Layout objects can be anchored to the sides of the window, which causes the object to resize as the window expands.

If an object is anchored, for instance, to the top, left, and bottom edges of the layout, as the window is expanded, the object resizes to keep the same fixed distance between the object's edges and the top, left, and bottom of the layout: It appears to grow taller but not wider. In past versions of FileMaker Pro, every object behaved as if it were anchored to the top and left sides of the layout.

Objects contained in a portal or tab control behave as if they are anchored to the object they are contained within, rather than the entire window. If the portal or tab control isn't resizable, the objects they contain won't resize either, regardless of their anchor settings.

Portals that are vertically resizable (meaning they have been anchored to both the top and bottom of the window) either add more rows as the window expands, or each row expands proportionally. This behavior depends on the anchoring of the objects contained in the portal: If any object in the portal has a bottom anchor set, the portal rows each expand proportionally; otherwise, the row height is kept constant, and more rows are shown.

External SQL Data Sources

For many developers and users alike, the most significant new feature in FileMaker Pro 9 is the ability to integrate with External SQL Data Sources (ESS). ESS represents a vast improvement and simplification in FileMaker Pro's capability to interact with other database products. Tables from certain external data sources can be placed as occurrences on the Relationships Graph, at which point they can be used just like any native FileMaker table.

ESS has many practical uses. For instance, in organizations with large, enterprisewide database systems, FileMaker can access this data seamlessly, obviating the need to store data redundantly in FileMaker and to build data transfer mechanisms. Similarly, say a small business uses a MySQL-based shopping cart on its website and needs to pull order information into FileMaker Pro. Using ESS, the appropriate MySQL tables can be placed on the Relationships Graph, and then layouts and scripts can be created for interacting with the shopping cart data.

To connect to an external data source, you must first set up a Data Source Name (DSN) on the machine. ESS in FileMaker Pro 9 supports the following data sources: Oracle 9g, Oracle 10g, Microsoft SQL Server 2005, and MySQL 5.0 Community Edition.

Note

See Chapter 16, "JDBC/ODBC and External SQL Connectivity," for more information on DSN setup.

In a multiuser deployment, only FileMaker Server needs to be configured with a DSN to communicate with the external data source. No configuration is required at the FileMaker client level; FileMaker Server performs all queries against the data source and returns data to the client as if it were regular FileMaker data.

When you create a reference to an ESS table, a *shadow table* is created in the FileMaker file. You can't make changes to the schema of the ESS table, but you do have the ability to add unstored calculation and summary fields to a shadow table. As an example of when this would be useful, say you created a reference to an InvoiceItems table stored in Microsoft SQL Server. This table would have fields for such things as Quantity and Price, but would not typically have a field that returned the ExtendedPrice, because that's derived data. In FileMaker, you could add a calculation field to the shadow table for ExtendedPrice.

ScriptMaker Enhancements

There are several changes and features in FileMaker Pro 9 relating to the ScriptMaker.

Finding and Organizing Scripts

First, scripts can now be organized into groups. This makes them easier to find, certainly, and it also makes it easier to manage the script clutter that accumulates in a solution over time. In addition, you can now search for scripts within ScriptMaker. For solutions with many hundreds of scripts, this has the potential to save a developer a lot of time.

Editing Window

Another ScriptMaker enhancement is that the script editing window is no longer a modal dialog. This has three benefits for developers. First, you don't have to close a script before running it, which saves time while writing and debugging scripts. Second, you can have multiple script windows open simultaneously. This again saves time, especially if you need to copy and paste script steps from one script to another, or if you have a complex set of subscript calls that you're working with. Finally, the nonmodal script editing window makes it possible for multiple developers to be editing scripts at the same time. In past versions, only one developer at a time could be editing scripts in a file, which was a significant impediment to team development.

Script Debugger (9 Advanced Only)

In FileMaker Pro 9 Advanced, there are also enhancements to the Script Debugger. The new Script Debugger interface, shown in Figure 2.3, provides feedback on the error code generated by the last executed script step. You can also have script execution pause when errors are encountered.

Also notable is the ability to authenticate a script. In previous versions of FileMaker, you could use the Script Debugger only if you were logged in as a full-access user, which made it difficult to track issues that were related to privilege set restrictions. Now, when logged in with a lower level privilege set, a developer can use the Script Debugger by providing his password as authentication.

Data Viewer (9 Advanced Only)

New features have also been added to the Data Viewer in FileMaker Pro 9 Advanced. Now in addition to being able to specify a set of variables, fields, and expressions to watch, the Data Viewer automatically monitors any fields or variables referenced by the currently running script.

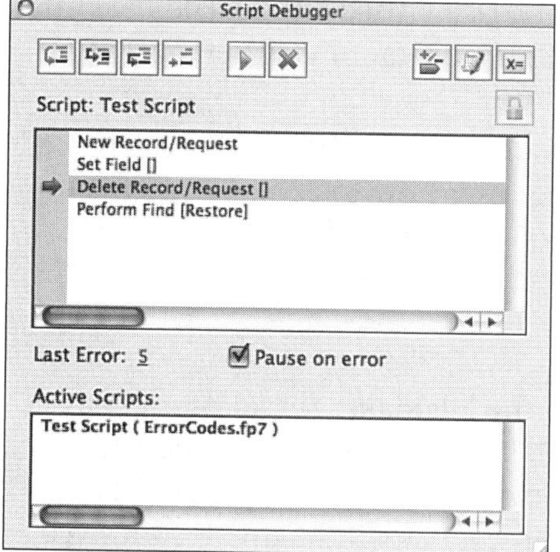

Figure 2.3

The Script Debugger in FileMaker Pro 9 Advanced has enhanced capabilities for identifying script errors.

And More...

In addition to the new features described already in this chapter, a number of other features and enhancements are introduced in FileMaker Pro 9. These are described briefly:

- Web Viewer objects can display a progress bar while loading pages. New check boxes in the Web Viewer Setup dialog provide control for displaying both the progress bar and status messages. The Web Viewer also now supports data URLs, which allow you to send data directly to the Web Viewer without writing it out as a file first.
- The default tab of a Tab Control object can be explicitly specified within the Tab Control Setup dialog. Another new choice in this dialog, Tab Width, provides better control over the appearance of tab labels.
- FileMaker Pro 9 has several new calculation functions: `Acos()`, `Asin()`, `Get ( TemporaryPath )`, `Get ( HostApplicationVersion )`, and `Self`. Details on syntax and usage for all of these can be found in Chapter 9, "Calculation Functions."
- The `Save As PDF` script step has a new option, Append to Existing PDF. As its name implies, this allows you to add pages to an existing PDF, facilitating the creation of much more complex outputs than was previously possible.
- Visual spell-checking, a feature added in FileMaker 8, can now be disabled at the field level via a check box in the Field Behavior dialog.
- Users can perform multiple levels of undo (and redo) when editing text fields and text objects.

- FileMaker Pro 9 is IPv6 compatible. Any place that URLs are used within FileMaker (for example, Web Viewer objects, the Open URL script step), you can use either an IPv6 address or a more common (today, at least) IPv4 address.
- A new menu item, File, Send Link, generates an email message with a URL to a hosted file. This makes it much easier to describe to another user how to access a specific shared database.

FileMaker Server 9

Many new and significant features have been added to the FileMaker Server product as well. Right off the bat, installing and configuring FileMaker Server 9 is faster and easier than in any previous version. During installation, you can choose to set up ODBC and web publishing options, as well as the number of machines that will be involved in web publishing.

The tool used to administer FileMaker Server has been completely redesigned. The new tool, called the FileMaker Server Admin Console, is a Java application that can be easily downloaded and run from any machine, and it provides much more information about hosted files and connected users than previous administration tools. There are also many new features, the most notable of which are described in the following sections.

Running ScriptMaker Scripts

FileMaker Server 9 has the capability to schedule the execution of ScriptMaker scripts in hosted files. For instance, you might want to execute a script at 3 a.m. each day that flags duplicate records, or one that stores the current date in each record so that aging calculations can be stored and indexed.

One restriction to be aware of is that FileMaker Server can perform only web-compatible script steps. This means, for example, that there's no printing, emailing, importing, or exporting. Nonetheless, the ability to schedule and automate many routine tasks makes this feature an indispensable part of a database administrator's toolkit.

File Upload

The Admin Console for FileMaker Server 9 has a tool for uploading files to the server for hosting. This is a significant workflow improvement over previous versions of FileMaker Server, which required an administrator to manually place files on the server. Using the File Upload feature all but eliminates the need to create shared directories on the server or to use remote administration software to manually move and manipulate files.

When a new version of an existing file is uploaded, FileMaker Server automatically moves the old file to an archive directory and time stamps it for future reference.

Email Notification

Email notification features make it easier than ever to monitor the health and activity of a FileMaker Server. FileMaker Server can, for instance, be configured to send out email about the success and/or failure of scheduled tasks. The administrator can also be notified via email of problems or crashes.

PHP Site Assistant

The PHP Site Assistant quickly generates basic PHP code for web-enabling a database, thereby simplifying and speeding up the custom web publishing process. The code can be inspected and modified as needed using any text editor.

CHAPTER 3

Overview of FileMaker 8.5 Features

Although this book focuses on the features and capabilities of FileMaker 9, the vast majority of features have been present in FileMaker Pro for some time now. In case you ever find yourself working with an older version, it can be useful to know which features were added in which version. Because the file format used for FileMaker Pro 9 files is the same as that used for FileMaker Pro 7, 8, and 8.5 files, there's also a chance that users will open a file with something other than the latest version of the application, in which case it's good to know what features are unavailable to that user.

FileMaker Pro 8.5

This chapter provides a list and brief description of the changes introduced in FileMaker Pro 8.5. Chapter 4, "Overview of FileMaker 8 Features," presents a similar list and description of changes introduced in FileMaker Pro 8.

Web Viewer

The most significant new feature introduced in FileMaker Pro 8.5 was a new layout object called the Web Viewer. Essentially, this provides a way to embed a web browser right into your FileMaker layout. When you add a Web Viewer object to a layout, you specify the URL that it will display. This could just be a hard-coded URL, but more often, the URL will either be set to the contents of a field (for example, a customer's web address, so that you'll see the customer's home page when you navigate to her record), or it will be the result of a calculation formula (for example, building a MapQuest link that includes a customer's address). The Web Viewer setup dialog includes syntax for assembling dynamic links to many useful and popular web tools, including Google, Wikipedia, MapQuest, and FedEx (see Figure 3.1).

In addition to the ability to set the initial URL for the Web Viewer when you set up the object on a layout, the `Set Web Viewer` script step provides a means for redirecting the Web Viewer any time you need.

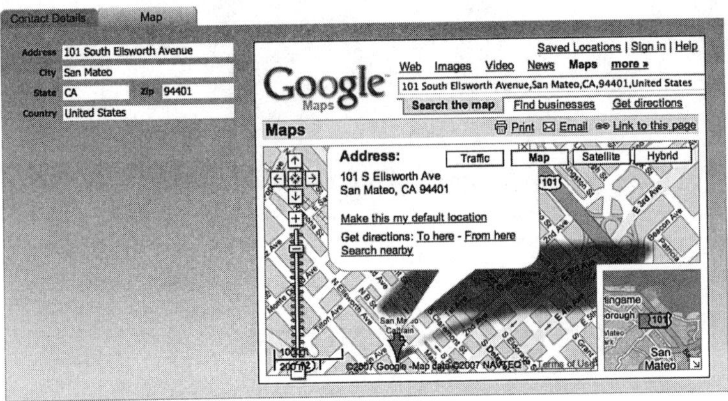

Figure 3.1

The Web Viewer object allows you to view the contents of a web page from within FileMaker Pro.

Object Names

Another enhancement introduced in FileMaker Pro 8.5 was the ability to name any object on a layout. Object names are shown (and set) in the Object Info palette, shown in Figure 3.2. In and of itself, naming objects isn't terribly useful; however, used in conjunction with a new calculation function and a new script step that were also added in FileMaker Pro 8.5, this feature begins to show its power.

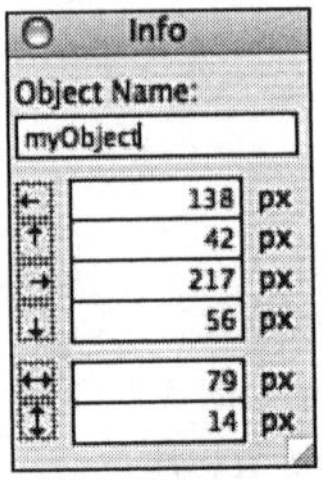

The new script step, Go to Object, lets you specify the name of an object the calling script should make its focus. For example, you might instruct a script to navigate to the third panel of a specific Tab Control object, or you might direct focus to a Web Viewer on a given layout to then refresh its web page. Importantly, the name can either be hard-coded or the result of a calculation function, which allows you to programmatically determine which object to go to. This has many interesting uses in advanced scripting situations.

Figure 3.2

Any layout object can be assigned a name using the Object Info palette.

The new calculation function, GetLayoutObjectAttrribute, which is covered more fully in Chapter 9, "Calculation Functions," can be used to investigate the attributes of a named object. For instance, for a named field object, the content attribute returns the contents of the field. And for a named Web Viewer object, the source attribute returns the current URL being displayed.

List Function

One other noteworthy calculation function was added to FileMaker Pro 8.5. The List function, described in more detail in Chapter 9, allows you to aggregate the text contained in a set of related records into a return-delimited list. It can thus be thought of as the textual equivalent of the Sum function. For example, if you had a Student record and a related set of Hobbies, you could assemble all the related hobbies for a student into a return-delimited text field in the Student table.

FileMaker Learning Center

The FileMaker Learning Center is a rich set of online tools and resources that can be accessed through the Help menu in the FileMaker Pro application. You'll find everything here from video tutorials to product documentation to community resources. There's also a link into the FileMaker Knowledge Base, which contains thousands of articles on current and past FileMaker products. Having all this information centrally, freely, and easily accessible is a valuable resource.

Support for Intel-Based Macs

Finally, the other significant feature of FileMaker Pro 8.5 is that it is a Universal application, which runs natively on Apple's Intel-based Mac OS X computers introduced in 2006. FileMaker Pro 8.5 boasts significant speed increases on an Intel-based Mac over PowerPC-based Macs. Similarly, FileMaker Pro 8.5 on an Intel-based Mac runs faster than FileMaker Pro 8 on an Intel-based Mac.

CHAPTER 4

Overview of FileMaker 8 Features

FileMaker Pro 8

Chapter 3, "Overview of FileMaker 8.5 Features," outlined the new features introduced in FileMaker Pro 8.5. In this chapter, we provide a similar overview of new features and enhancements first introduced in FileMaker Pro 8.

Script Variables

The ability to define script variables is one of the most powerful and far-reaching features added to FileMaker Pro 8. The Set Variable script step supplies the means for defining both *local* and *global* script variables. The values assigned to local variables persist only for the duration of a given script, whereas values assigned to global variables persist for the duration of a user's session (or until they are assigned a null value). You can tell the difference simply by the name of the variable: Variables that begin with a single $ are local script variables (such as, $foo and $myVariable); those prefixed by $$ are global script variables (such as, $$bar and $$fileName).

Script variables are useful as a temporary storage location for values needed during the course of a script, such as counters. In this respect, they fill a role served in prior versions of FileMaker by globally stored fields. Script variables thus obviate the need for many globally stored fields, saving time (because they don't need to be defined in advance), and reducing clutter (because they don't appear in your field lists). Variables also serve other needs uniquely. For instance, in any import or export dialog you can specify a script variable as the file path to use. This allows you to dynamically set the filename and path to use for such operations.

Tab Control

A layout tool called a Tab Control makes its debut in FileMaker Pro 8. This tool provides a quick and easy way to add the look and functionality of a tab-style interface to a FileMaker layout. You simply drag a rectangle describing the area for the Tab Control on the layout, give names to the various tabs you want to appear (called Tab Panels), and then place layout objects on various panels of the Tab Control simply by activating a tab and moving layout objects onto it.

As shown in Figure 4.1, a Tab Control is a great way to extend screen real estate and organize layouts that would otherwise be large and/or cluttered. You can place any layout object onto a Tab Panel, including another Tab Control itself, and a number of design options let you customize how the tabs will appear.

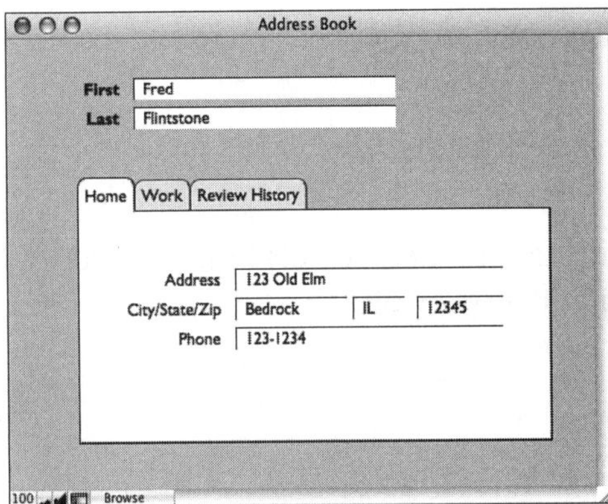

Figure 4.1

Use a Tab Control object to organize information on layouts and reduce clutter.

Buttons in the Tab Order

Layout objects that have been defined as buttons can be added to the tab order. When a user "tabs" to such a button, the button appears highlighted, at which point the script or action associated with the button can be triggered by either the spacebar or the Enter or Return key. The purpose of this feature is to give users the ability to perform scripted actions without having to manually move the mouse to the button object and click. For repetitive and/or high-speed data entry tasks, this can greatly increase a user's performance.

New Field Control Options

In addition to some slight changes in the way the Field Control/Options dialog is organized, FileMaker Pro 8 supplies a few additional formatting options not available in previous versions.

The first additional formatting option is the ability to format a field to include a drop-down calendar. Users are presented with a small pop-up calendar when they enter a date field (or they may click a calendar icon, if you choose to display it) and can navigate to and select a date visually. A related enhancement is the ability to display an arrow to show and hide the value list associated with fields formatted as drop-down lists.

Finally, a new check box appears in the Field/Control Setup dialog, Auto-Complete Using Value List. With this option selected, as users begin typing into a field, FileMaker "guesses" how to finish their entry by comparing what the user has typed so far with the field's index. Often referred to as *type-ahead*, this feature not only saves time during data entry but also ensures better data accuracy.

Go to Related Record by Found Set

The Go to Related Record script step, shown in Figure 4.2, is enhanced in FileMaker Pro 8 to include the option Match All Records in Current Found Set. An example demonstrates how this feature makes the Go to Related Records step much more powerful.

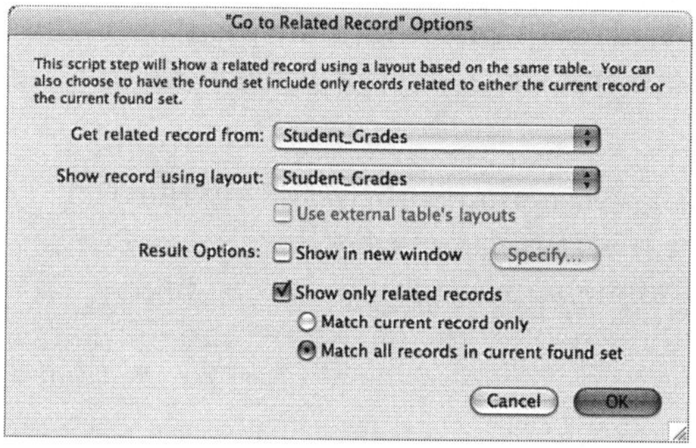

Figure 4.2

The option to match all records in the found set has many practical uses. In versions of FileMaker Pro prior to 8, this could be accomplished only by a cumbersome workaround.

Say, for example, that you had a system with a one-to-many relationship from an invoice table to a line item table. While looking at an invoice, a normal Go to Related Records script step—matching the current record only—would result in the set of line item records related to that one invoice. If, on the other hand, Match All Records in the Current Found Set is selected, all the line items that related to all the invoices in the active found set (as opposed to just the current invoice) are found.

This type of functionality has many uses in reporting routines. You can, for instance, manually find a set of invoices that you are interested in (for example, this month's invoices, all overdue invoices, all invoices for a certain customer), and then by doing the extended Go to Related Record script step, you would have the entire set of line items for that set of invoices, ready to print, export, or whatever.

Save as PDF

Users can quickly and easily generate PDF documents with the Save as PDF capability in FileMaker Pro 8. This feature doesn't require the installation or use of any third-party tools, and it works on both the Mac OS X and Windows platforms. The feature is found under the File, Save/Send Records As, PDF menu, but it can also be scripted using the Save Records as PDF script step.

Many options are available with this feature, including the abilities to specify a password for the PDF, set the initial view, and specify metadata for the file. When scripting a Save Records as PDF, the filename and path can be hard-coded in the script, determined by the user, or dynamically determined by using a script variable as the file path.

Save as Excel

The ability to send records to Excel has many of the same options and uses as the PDF Maker. The Save as Excel capability, found both as a script step and under the File, Save/Send Records As, Excel menu, allows a user to quickly export the set of data she's currently working with out to Microsoft Excel. Only data from the currently active layout and the current found set are included in the export, freeing the user from having to navigate through the typical export dialogs.

Options available within this feature include setting metadata for the resulting file and using the field names as column names in the first row. Similar to Save Records as PDF, when using the Save Records as Excel script step the filename and path can be hard-coded, determined by the user, or dynamically determined by using a script variable as the file path.

Fast Mail

Although FileMaker Pro has had a Send Mail script for quite a while, FileMaker Pro 8 introduces a new menu item, File, Send Mail. This new menu item allows users to generate email messages without scripting. All the parameters of the email message, including To, CC, BCC, Subject, and Message, can be hard-coded by the user, or—more powerfully—can be specified as the contents of a field or calculation formula. In addition, users have the option of sending one email to the entire found set, or multiple emails, one for each record in the found set.

Date and Time Range Shorthand Searching

FileMaker Pro 8 introduces several new and easier ways for finding records based on the contents of date, time, and timestamp fields. For instance, prior to FileMaker Pro 8, if a user wanted to find all invoices with an invoice date in 2007, he would have needed to enter "1/1/2007...12/31/2007" as the find criteria. Starting with FileMaker Pro 8, a user can simply enter "2007" as the find criteria. Table 4.1 shows examples that demonstrate the new search syntax.

Table 4.1 New Search Syntax for FileMaker 8

Field Type	Search String	Result
Date	7	All dates in July of the current year
Date	2/2007	All dates in February 2007
Date	1/2007. . .3/2007	All dates from January 1, 2007, through March 31, 2007
Date	{1. . .3}/2007	Same as above
Date	{1. . .3}/{2006. . .2007}	All dates in January through March of 2006 and 2007
Date	=Mon	All dates that are Monday
Date	8/{3. . .7}/2007	All dates from August 3, 2007, through August 7, 2007
Time	8am	All times from 8:00:00 a.m. through 8:59:59 a.m.
Time	8am. . .11am	All times from 8:00:00 a.m. through 11:59:59 a.m.
Time	Am	All times from 12:00:00 a.m. through 11:59:59 a.m.
Time	5:{15. . .30} pm	All times from 5:15:00 p.m. through 5:30:59 p.m.
Time	*:30	All times that are 30 minutes after any hour
Timestamp	// 7pm	All time stamps in the 7 o'clock hour today
Timestamp	6/2007 2pm	All time stamps in June, 2007, in the 2 o'clock hour
Timestamp	=Sun 2007	All time stamps that occur on a Sunday in 2007

Fast Match

Another way that FileMaker Pro 8 makes it easier to find records is via the new Fast Match feature. When a user right-clicks on a field (Control-clicks on a Mac), he is presented with a contextual menu that includes the three new Fast Match options: Find Matching Records, Constrain Found Set, and Extend Found Set.

All these options make it easy to find records similar to the record that the user is currently viewing. For instance, if you were looking at a student record and one of the fields on the layout showed a status of "Active," performing a Find Matching Records find on this field would yield the found set of all active students, just as if you had manually performed a find based on the criteria from the selected field. Constraining and extending the found set work similarly, except constraining only finds similar records within the existing found set, while extending expands the current found set to include all of the matching records as well.

Import as New Table

A new import feature in FileMaker Pro 8 allows you to create a new table and pull imported data into that table in one step. Rather than having to first set up the new table and fields and then import the data, you can simply import the data and instruct FileMaker to set up a new table for the data, as shown in Figure 4.3.

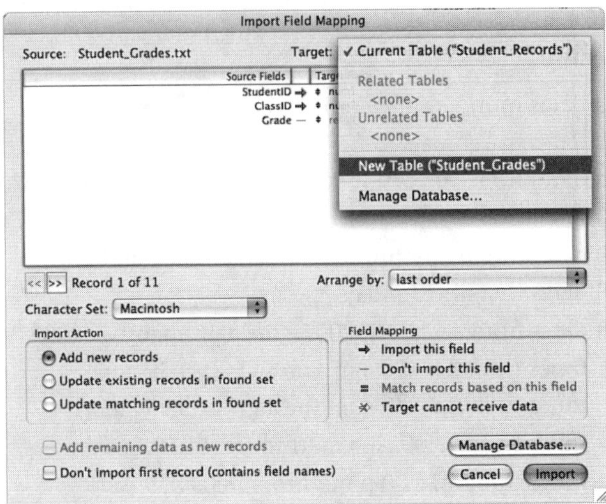

Figure 4.3

Data can be imported into a new table by specifying New Table as the Target in the Import Field Mapping dialog.

If the data source is a table in another FileMaker file, the new table will inherit all the field properties from the source table, including field names, auto-entry options, validation, storage options, and calculation formulas. For other types of files, the fields in the new table will be named simply f1, f2, f3, and so on, unless you select the Don't Import First Record (Contains Field Names) option, in which case the names will be taken from data found in the first record of the imported file.

Relationships Graph Enhancements

Several features and enhancements have been made to the Relationships Graph in FileMaker Pro 8. The most significant is arguably the ability to add notes to the graph. The notes look like standard "sticky notes," and they always lie behind table occurrences, making them useful for organizing and describing collections of table occurrences. Another useful enhancement is the ability to duplicate a table occurrence. Finally, starting in FileMaker Pro 8 it's easy to select sets of table occurrences based on certain characteristics. For instance, after selecting a table occurrence, you have options for selecting all other table occurrences based on the same source table, as well as the option to select all the tables that are one relationship away from the selected table.

New Calculation Functions

A number of new calculation functions have also been added to FileMaker Pro 8, including the following:

GetNthRecord()

Get (DesktopPath)

Get (DocumentsPath)

Get (FileMakerPath)

Get (SystemDrive)

TextColorRemove()

TextFontRemove()

TextSizeRemove()

TextFormatRemove()

For more information on the purpose and syntax of these functions, see Chapter 9, "Calculation Functions."

FileMaker Pro 8 Advanced

All the enhancements described for FileMaker Pro 8 can also be found in FileMaker Pro 8 Advanced. The Advanced product contains a few additional features, described in the sections that follow. In addition, most of the "advanced" features have been reorganized and consolidated under a new Tools menu, which is found only in FileMaker Pro 8 Advanced.

Custom Menus

The ability to control the menus available to users, and the behaviors of many existing menus, is one of the most significant new features of FileMaker Pro 8 Advanced. Developers can customize menu sets by rearranging, adding, deleting, or changing the function of menus and menu items. Such customized menu sets can then be installed as a file default, or individual layouts can be customized to use a particular menu set, overriding the file default. Additionally, a new Install Menu Set script step provides the ability to alter the menu set based on whatever actions and conditions you require.

Note that the ability to customize menus is available only to developers using FileMaker Pro 8 Advanced, but after a file's menus have been customized, users with the FileMaker Pro 8 product can see the result of that customization.

ToolTips

Starting with FileMaker Pro 8, any object on a layout can have a ToolTip assigned to it that is displayed to users as they hover their mouse over the object for a few seconds. You can use ToolTips to provide "help" to users who might need more information about what a particular object is or does, or you might use ToolTips to provide additional data about the referenced object. ToolTips are specified by right-clicking (Control-clicking on a Mac) on an object and selecting the Set ToolTip option. The contents of the ToolTip either can be hard-coded, as often is the case with simple help messages, or they can be the result of a calculation formula.

Note that the ability to attach ToolTips to layout objects requires FileMaker Pro 8 Advanced, but after ToolTips have been added, users with FileMaker Pro 8 can see the ToolTips.

Data Viewer

FileMaker Pro 8 Advanced added a powerful new developer tool called the Data Viewer. This tool allows you to monitor the values returned by any number of fields, variables, or expressions. Typically, it's used in conjunction with the Script Debugger so that a developer can watch what's happening to particular fields or variables as the script progresses.

Copying and Pasting Schema Objects

The last new feature available within the FileMaker Pro 8 Advanced product is the ability to copy and paste most schema objects. This includes tables, field definitions, scripts, and script steps. Having this capability can greatly speed up the development process and allows you to reuse your existing code more easily. Know, however, that FileMaker "comments out" any calculation formulas that can't be evaluated properly within the context that you're pasting into. You may need to manually check and adjust such formulas.

CHAPTER 5

Specifications and Storage Limits

Knowing Your Limits

Whenever you work with a piece of software, it's a good idea to be aware of the software's limits, both practical and theoretical. Important design considerations can hinge on a correct appraisal of the capabilities of your tools. For example, if you need to build a system that can correctly work with dates prior to those in the AD era (Anno Domini: from the year 1 forward), it's a good idea to be aware of the storage capabilities of the date field type in FileMaker Pro.

Some of these limits are more theoretical than practical, and you're better off observing the practical limits. We don't recommend you build systems with a million tables, for example, or write calculations containing 30K of text. If you feel you need to push these upper limits, you may want to recheck your assumptions and, if necessary, rethink your approach.

Table 5.1 provides the limits of some of the most important measurable capacities of the FileMaker product line.

Table 5.1 FileMaker Specs

Characteristic	Capacity
Maximum file size	8 terabytes
Maximum tables per file	1,000,000
Maximum fields per table	256 million over the life of the file
Maximum number of fields in a handheld database (FileMaker Mobile)	50
Maximum records per file	64 quadrillion over the life of the file
Maximum records in a handheld database (FileMaker Mobile)	5000

continues

Table 5.1 Continued

Characteristic	Capacity
Maximum field name length	100 characters
Maximum table name length	100 characters
Maximum field comment length	30,000 characters
Maximum calculation text length	30,000 characters
Maximum custom function text length	30,000 characters
Maximum amount of data in a text field	2 gigabytes (about a billion Unicode characters)
Maximum amount of data in a text field in FileMaker Mobile	2000 characters
Range of a number field	-10^{400} to -10^{-400} and 10^{-400} to 10^{400} (and 0 as well)
Precision of a number field	Up to 400 significant digits
Maximum amount of data in a number field in FileMaker Mobile	255 characters
Range of a date field	1/1/0001 – 12/31/4000
Range of a time field	1 – 2,147,483,647
Range of a time stamp field	1/1/0001 12:00:00 a.m. – 12/31/4000 11:59:59.999999 p.m.
Size of data in a container field	4 gigabytes
Maximum size of data used for indexing	Up to 100 characters of data per word
Maximum files open in FileMaker Pro client	Limited only by memory on the client computer
Maximum number of databases on a handheld device (FileMaker Mobile)	50
Maximum database files hosted by FileMaker Pro client, peer-to-peer	10
Maximum connected FileMaker Pro, Instant Web, or ODBC/JDBC clients, peer-to-peer	5
Maximum files hosted by FileMaker Server	125
Maximum connected FileMaker Pro clients, using FileMaker Server	250
Maximum Instant Web Publishing clients, using FileMaker Server Advanced	100
Maximum ODBC/JDBC clients, using FileMaker Server Advanced	50
Maximum RAM addressable by FileMaker Server	4 gigabytes
Maximum cache setting for FileMaker Server	800 megabytes
Maximum number of records in IWP table view	50
Maximum number of records in IWP list view	25
Maximum dimensions of a FileMaker Pro layout	121 inches × 121 inches

Notes to Table 5.1:

- Unicode characters take up a variable number of bits, dependent on the character, so it's not possible to define a precise upper limit to the size of a text field.
- FileMaker Pro clients and ODBC/JDBC clients draw from the same pool of available connections on FileMaker Server/Server Advanced, so the upper limit is a *total* of 250 connected users of both types together. Of these, no more than 50 may be ODBC/JDBC users.

External SQL Sources (ESS) Specifications

The FileMaker 9 product line has the capability to integrate data tables from external SQL sources (ESS). At present, FileMaker can integrate data tables from the following external SQL sources:

- Oracle 9g or 10g
- Microsoft SQL Server 2000 or 2005
- MySQL Community Edition 5.0

Each of these data sources has its own set of field sizes and limitations. If you're integrating one or more of these external sources into a FileMaker solution, you'll also need to be aware of the different limits and features of the data types in the other data sources you use. Date and number fields in external sources may have different ranges from their FileMaker counterparts, for example.

→ *For more discussion of the differences between FileMaker and SQL field types, and some links to reference material on the supported SQL data types,* ***see*** *Chapter 6, "Field Types and Import/Export Formats,"* ***p. 37****.*

CHAPTER 6

Field Types and Import/Export Formats

Knowing Your Data

Besides just knowing the raw statistics and capacities of your software tools ("speeds and feeds," as the machinists like to say), it's wise to understand the basic data formats with which your database software can work. In this chapter we give a brief overview of each of the underlying FileMaker field data types, and we also discuss the various data formats available for import and export.

First, a word about data types in FileMaker. Unlike certain other database engines, FileMaker is somewhat forgiving about data types. You can add text characters to a number field, for example, without being stopped by FileMaker. The price you pay for this flexibility is the possibility that you'll make a mistake or permit something undesirable to happen. So it's necessary to have a firm grasp of FileMaker's data types and how each of them works and relates to the others.

With the addition, in FileMaker 9, of the capability to integrate tables from external SQL data sources (ESS), you may also need to come to grips with the vagaries of field types in various SQL systems as well. You'll need to understand two things if you're working with SQL data:

- How SQL field types map to FileMaker field types. (FileMaker treats an Oracle `nvarchar2` field as a text field, for example.)
- How SQL field types may behave differently from their FileMaker counterparts. (For example, `date` fields in MySQL 5.0 can handle dates between 1/1/1000 and 12/31/9999, whereas FileMaker can handle dates between 1/1/0001 and 12/31/4000.)

We cover each of those topics as we discuss the individual FileMaker field types in the "ESS Notes" sections within each of the "FileMaker Field Types" sections. A complete discussion of the behaviors of SQL field types is beyond the scope of this book, but at the end of this chapter we offer links to detailed reference material on field types in each of the supported SQL sources.

FileMaker Field Types

In the Chapter 5, "Specifications and Storage Limits," we called out a number of the raw capacities of FileMaker's field types, in the briefest possible format. Here we dwell on each data type and its characteristics in a bit more detail.

Caution

Since FileMaker 9 can interact directly with certain SQL data sources, you'll need to take special care if you're building a solution that integrates with an SQL source. SQL data types are similar to, but not identical to, those found in FileMaker. Data that "fits" in a FileMaker field may get changed, truncated, or misinterpreted when inserted into an SQL field, and vice versa. If you're working with SQL sources, please take special note of the sections labeled "ESS Notes" within each of the sections that follow.

Text

FileMaker's text field type holds up to 2 gigabytes of character data per text field. FileMaker stores text internally as Unicode, which requires about 2 bytes per character (the exact number varies by the specific character and encoding). So a single FileMaker text field can hold about one billion characters of data (nearly half a million regular pages of text).

There's no need to specify the "size" of the text field in advance; FileMaker automatically accommodates any text you enter, up to the field size maximum.

FileMaker's text field can be indexed on a word-by-word basis, so it's possible to search quickly for one or more words anywhere within a text field.

ESS Notes

The following ESS data types are represented in FileMaker as text fields:

- **Oracle**—char, clob, long, nchar, nclob, nvarchar2, varchar2
- **Microsoft SQL Server**—char, nchar, ntext, nvarchar, text, varchar
- **MySQL**—char, enum, longtext, mediumtext, set, text, tinytext, varchar, year

Many of the ESS text types listed cannot hold as much text data as a FileMaker text field. If you need to move data from a FileMaker text field into an ESS text field, be aware of potential sizing conflicts. In such cases, you may need to consider imposing validation limits on the amount of text the FileMaker field can store.

Number

The number field type is FileMaker's only numeric data type. Unlike many SQL sources, FileMaker does not have separate data types for integers and floating point numbers. All numbers are capable of being treated as floating point.

FileMaker's numeric data type can store numbers in the range 10^{-400} through 10^{400}, and -10^{400} through -10^{-400}, as well as the value 0. The data type can account for 400 digits of precision. By default, though, functions involving numbers only account for 16 digits of precision. To achieve higher precision, you need to use the SetPrecision() function.

Numeric fields can accept character data entry, though the character data will be ignored. If the field's validation is also set to Strict Data Type: Numeric Only, the entry of character data will be disallowed.

ESS Notes

In other database systems, such as those based on SQL, integers and floating point numbers are generally treated as two different data types, and it's often necessary to choose in advance between lower-precision and higher-precision floating point numbers, though SQL does also offer arbitrary precision numbers as well.

The following ESS data types are represented in FileMaker as number fields:

- **Oracle**—float, number, raw
- **Microsoft SQL Server**—bigint, decimal, float, int, money, numeric, real, smallint, smallmoney, tinyint
- **MySQL**—decimal, double, float, int, integer, mediumint, numeric, real, smallint, tinyint

If you're working with ESS data, be aware of the distinction between integer and floating point types. If you try to move data from a FileMaker field containing floating point data into an ESS field that supports only integer data, you may get a validation error or suffer some data loss.

Date

FileMaker's date type can store dates from 1/1/0001 to 12/31/4000. Internally, these dates are stored as integer values between 1 and 1460970, indicating the number of days elapsed between 1/1/0001 and the date in question. This is significant in that it means that integer math can be performed on dates: 12/31/2001 + 1 = 1/1/2002, and 12/21/2001 – 365 = 12/21/2000.

FileMaker correctly interprets oddly formed dates, as long as they're within its overall date range. For example, 4/31/2005 is interpreted as 5/1/2005, whereas 12/32/2005 is interpreted as 1/1/2006. But 12/31/5000 is rejected outright.

FileMaker's date type is stricter than the text and number types and rejects any date outside the range just mentioned, including those containing textual data. Field validation options can also be configured to force entry of a full four-digit year.

Though the date type is stored as an integer, it can be entered and displayed in a wide variety of well-known or local date display formats. By default, it uses settings it inherits from the current user's operating system, but the date display format can be overridden on a field-by-field basis on each individual layout.

ESS Notes

SQL sources vary widely in how they store and manage date and time information. Oracle and MySQL are similar to FileMaker in that they manage such data with three different field types, representing date information, time information, and timestamp information. Microsoft SQL Server differs in providing only timestamp-style fields.

The following ESS data types are represented in FileMaker as date fields:

- **Oracle**—date, interval_year.
- **Microsoft SQL Server**—SQL Server has no direct equivalent to a date-only field. SQL Server's datetime and smalldatetime fields map to FileMaker timestamp fields, whereas SQL Server's timestamp field type is currently not supported.
- **MySQL**—date.

Be especially aware of the limits of ESS date, time, and timestamp fields: Their supported ranges may be different from the ranges supported in corresponding FileMaker field types.

Time

Like the date type, FileMaker's time data type stores its information in an underlying integer representation. In the case of the time field type, what's being stored is the number of seconds since midnight of the previous day, yielding a range of possible values from 1 to 86400. As with the date type, it's possible to perform integer math with time values: So Get(CurrentTime) + 3600 returns a time an hour ahead of the current time. And 15:30:00 – 11:00:00 returns 4:30:00 or 16200, depending on whether the calculation is set to have a time or number result, so "time math" can be used to compute time intervals correctly as well.

Also like the date data type, the time data type can accept entry and display of time data in a variety of formats. "Overlapping" times work in the same way as overlapping dates: FileMaker interprets the value 25:15:00 as representing 1:15 a.m. on the following day. (This is exactly what happens when you store a value greater than 86,400 in a time field, which FileMaker certainly allows.)

ESS Notes

SQL sources vary widely in how they store and manage date and time information. Oracle and MySQL are similar to FileMaker in that they manage such data with three different field types, representing date information, time information, and timestamp information. Microsoft SQL Server differs in providing only timestamp-style fields.

The following ESS data types are represented in FileMaker as time fields:

- **Oracle**—interval_day.
- **Microsoft SQL Server**—SQL Server has no direct equivalent to a time-only field. SQL Server's datetime and smalldatetime fields map to FileMaker timestamp fields, whereas SQL Server's timestamp field type is currently not supported.
- **MySQL**—time.

Be especially aware of the limits of ESS date, time, and timestamp fields: Their supported ranges may be different from the ranges supported in corresponding FileMaker field types.

Timestamp

FileMaker's timestamp data type is like a combination of the date and time types. A timestamp is displayed as something like 11/20/2005 12:30:00. Internally, like both dates and times, it is stored as an integer. In this case the internally stored number represents the number of seconds since midnight on 1/1/0001. The timestamp can represent date/time combinations ranging from 1/1/0001 00:00:00 to 12/31/4000 11:59:59.999999 (a range of more than a hundred billion seconds).

As with the related date and time field types, timestamps can be displayed and entered in a variety of formats. It's also possible to perform math with timestamps as with dates and times, but the math can get a bit unwieldy since most timestamps are numbers in the billions.

ESS Notes

SQL sources vary widely in how they store and manage date and time information. Oracle and MySQL are similar to FileMaker in that they manage such data with three different field types, representing date information, time information, and timestamp information. Microsoft SQL Server differs in providing only timestamp-style fields.

The following ESS data types are represented in FileMaker as timestamp fields:

- **Oracle**—timestamp.
- **Microsoft SQL Server**—datetime, smalldatetime. SQL Server's timestamp field type is a binary data type and so is not currently supported.
- **MySQL**—timestamp, datetime.

Be especially aware of the limits of ESS date, time, and timestamp fields: Their supported ranges may be different from the ranges supported in corresponding FileMaker field types.

Container

The container data type is FileMaker's field type for binary data (meaning data that, unlike text and numbers, does not have an accepted plain-text representation). Binary data generally represents an electronic file of some sort, such as a picture, movie, sound file, or file produced by some other software application, such as a word processor or page layout program.

A single container field can store a single binary object up to 4 gigabytes in size. Though any type of electronic file can be stored in a container field (one file per field), FileMaker has specialized knowledge of a few types of binary data and can play or display such objects directly, by calling on operating system services. Specifically, FileMaker can play or display pictures, sounds, and movies (and in fact any "movie-like" file supported by QuickTime, if QuickTime is installed). Additionally, on Windows, a container field can store and display Object Linking and Embedding (OLE) objects.

When working with container fields it's important to understand the distinction between storing the data directly (embedding the entire file in the FileMaker database and increasing its file size by tens or hundreds of K or indeed by megabytes) and storing it by reference (storing just the path to the specified file). The former leads to larger database files; the latter relies on the binary files being stored in a fixed location and not moving relative to the database.

ESS Notes

All of FileMaker's supported external SQL sources support a field type similar to FileMaker's container fields. In most SQL sources these are often referred to as *BLOB* (*Binary Large Object*) types.

Unfortunately, the present implementation of ESS in FileMaker does not support any of the various BLOB types offered in supported SQL sources. The BLOB types are not supported, and database columns based on those types will not be available when the table is accessed via FileMaker.

Calculation

From the point of view of data types, calculations are not a data type at all. They are instead a *field* type and can be constructed to return their results as any of the six fundamental data types: text, number, date, time, timestamp, or container.

ESS Notes

SQL sources vary in how they represent this field concept. From a strict point of view, calculation is not a data type (unlike, for example, text or date). Some SQL sources do have means for creating additional columns that automatically calculate based on values in other columns.

But in any case, no field from an SQL source will ever be represented in FileMaker as a Calculation field.

Summary

Summary fields are another example of a field type rather than a data type. Summary fields perform summary operations on sets of grouped records and always return a numeric result.

ESS Notes

SQL sources have no concept, at the level of field/column definitions, that maps to the FileMaker concept of a summary field.

No field from an SQL source will ever be represented in FileMaker as a summary field.

Additional ESS References

It's well worth your while to become aware of the differences and distinctions among the various data types used by the supported external SQL sources. Though a full discussion is beyond the scope of this book, the following links should provide a starting point for delving more deeply into the specifics of data typing in each supported data source:

- **Oracle**—http://download-east.oracle.com/docs/cd/B19306_01/server.102/b14220/datatype.htm
- **Microsoft SQL Server**—http://msdn2.microsoft.com/en-us/library/ms187752.aspx
- **MySQL**—http://dev.mysql.com/doc/refman/5.0/en/data-types.html

Importing Data

FileMaker Pro can import data from one or more files on the hard drive of a FileMaker client machine or on a shared network volume. FileMaker can also import data from remote data sources. The following sections outline the various sources for importing data and the specific requirements and limitations of each.

File-Based Data Sources

FileMaker can import data from individual files, available on a local hard drive or networked volume, in any of the following formats:

- Tab-separated text
- Comma-separated text
- SYLK
- DIF
- WKS
- BASIC
- Merge files
- DBase files

In addition to importing from these common text file formats, FileMaker can also perform more specialized imports from files created in Excel, or in FileMaker itself, as well as from ODBC-based and XML-based data sources.

Importing from Excel

When importing data from an Excel file, FileMaker can detect multiple worksheets within the source Excel file. FileMaker can also detect the existence of any *named ranges* in the source document. When importing, if named ranges or multiple worksheets are detected, FileMaker gives you a choice as to whether to import from a worksheet or named range and allows you to select the specific worksheet or range from which to import.

When importing from Excel, as with all imports, FileMaker brings in only the raw data it finds in the source file. Formulas, macros, and other programming logic are not imported.

FileMaker Pro assigns an appropriate field type (text, number, date, or time) if all rows in the column hold the same Excel data type. Otherwise, a column becomes a text field when imported into FileMaker.

Importing from FileMaker

You can also import data from other FileMaker Pro files, or even between tables in the same file. The only restriction on this is that you can only import data from versions of FileMaker that share the same file format as the file you're importing into. You can import data from FileMaker Pro 7, 8.x, or 9 into a FileMaker Pro 9 solution. These may be files present on the local client machine, or files hosted on another machine.

Much as an Excel file can contain multiple worksheets, a FileMaker database can contain multiple tables. It's necessary to choose a single table as your data source when importing from a FileMaker file.

Importing from FileMaker can be particularly convenient if the source file has a structure that matches that of the target file. In this case, rather than manually configuring the import mapping on a field-by-field basis, it's possible to choose the Arrange By Matching Field Names option. When you do so, fields of the same name in the source and target tables are paired in the import mapping.

Importing Multiple Files at Once

It's also possible to import data from multiple files at a time by selecting File, Input Records, Folder. You can import data in this fashion from either text or image files. You can import both the raw data in the file and also extra data about each source file's name and location.

In each case, the files being imported must all be grouped in or underneath a single folder. You can specify whether to look simply inside the one folder, or whether to search all the way down through any subfolders.

Importing from Multiple Text Files

When importing from a batch of text files, you may import up to three pieces of data from each text file:

- Filename
- Full path to file
- Text contents

You may choose to import any or all of these.

Unlike a regular import from a text file, the internal structure of the text file is disregarded. The entire contents, whether containing tabs, carriage returns, commas, or other potential delimiters, are imported into a single target field.

Importing from Multiple Image Files

Importing from multiple image files is similar to importing from multiple text files. When importing a batch of images, you may import any or all of the following data fields:

- Filename
- Full path to file
- Image
- Image thumbnail

In addition to filename, file path, and file contents (an image, in this case), FileMaker allows you to import an image thumbnail, either in addition to or instead of the full image. You may want to do this to save file space or screen space. FileMaker creates these thumbnails via its own algorithms, so you have no control over the exact details of thumbnail size or quality.

When importing images, you have the choice (as you always do when working with data in container fields) of importing the full image into the database, or merely storing a reference. Importing full images takes up more space in the database (probably much more), whereas importing only the references means that you'll need to make the original files continuously available from a hard drive or network volume that all users of the database can access.

Importing Digital Photos (Mac OS)

On the Mac, FileMaker can also import images directly from a digital camera, or from any device capable of storing digital photos. This process is similar to a batch import of images from a single folder, with only a few differences.

FileMaker allows you to specify which images to import. You may choose them individually, or via a range such as "last 12 images." FileMaker also handles transferring the files from the storage device to a download location of your choice. And, as with other imports, you can choose whether to import the full image into FileMaker or simply store a reference.

Whereas the regular batch import of images brings in only four pieces of data about each image, a digital image import may have access to much more data about each image. If the selected images contain EXIF data (a standard for embedding extra data into an image file), FileMaker can also detect and import many additional pieces of data about the image such as shutter speed, ISO setting, and the like.

Importing from an ODBC Data Source

FileMaker can import data from a data source accessed via ODBC. Many types of data can be accessed via ODBC, but it's most commonly used to retrieve data from a remote database, often one running some flavor of the SQL language.

Working with OBDC data sources requires three things:

- **A data source capable of providing data via ODBC**—Again, this is most often a remote database server of some kind. The administrators of the data source may need to perform specific configuration of the data source before it can accept ODBC connections.
- **An ODBC driver, installed on the local computer that's running FileMaker Pro, that can talk to the specific ODBC data source in question**—ODBC drivers need to be installed on each computer that can access a data source. So, much like a FileMaker plug-in, ODBC drivers generally need to be installed on the computer of each FileMaker user who will be using ODBC access. ODBC drivers are specific to a particular data source (the PostgreSQL or Sybase databases, for example) and also specific to a particular platform (Mac or PC). To connect to an ODBC data source, you must have a driver specific to both your data source and platform (Sybase 12 driver for Mac OS, for example).
- **A DSN (Data Source Name) that specifies the details of how to connect to a specific data source**—DSNs are configured differently on each platform and generally contain information about a specific data source (server name, username, password, database name, and the like).

After you have successfully configured and connected to an ODBC data source, the process for selecting data to import is a bit different than for regular imports. Before proceeding to the field mapping dialog, you need to build an SQL query that selects the specific fields and specific records you want. (For example, your SQL query might read SELECT name_last, name_first, city, state, zip FROM customer). After you've done this, you can map the resulting fields to those in your FileMaker database.

ESS Notes

With the introduction, in FileMaker 9, of the capability to integrate tables from external SQL sources (ESS) directly into the structure of your FileMaker database, it's now possible to access data from certain SQL sources much more fluidly, without an explicit import step. Those data sources are Oracle 9g and 10g, Microsoft SQL Server 2000 and 2005, and MySQL Community Edition 5.0.

If you need to work with data from supported sources, using the new ESS feature may be a better choice. If you need to work with data from an SQL data source that's not currently supported by ESS, the ability to import from an ODBC data source is important to consider.

→ *For more information on configuring FileMaker to work with external SQL sources,* **see** *Chapter 16, "JDBC/ODBC and SQL Connectivity,"* **p. 489**.

Importing from an XML-based Data Source

FileMaker Pro has the convenient ability to import from an XML-based data source. This could be something as simple as an XML-based disk file, but can be something as complex as an XML-based web service. The capability of importing from remote XML-based data sources is potentially very powerful. Just keep in mind that, before XML can be imported into FileMaker, it must follow the rules of the FMPXMLRESULT grammar. If the XML you're working with isn't in that format, you'll need to apply an XSLT stylesheet to the incoming XML in order to transform into data that follows the FMPXMLRESULT grammar.

→ *For further discussion of FileMaker XML grammars,* **see** *Chapter 14, "FileMaker XML Reference,"* **p. 439**.

Creating New Tables on Import

When importing data, you can specify that the inbound data should be placed in a new table, rather than adding to or updating an existing table. The new table takes its field names from those present in the data source.

Exporting Data

FileMaker can export its data to a variety of data types, as follows:

- Tab-separated text
- Comma-separated text

- SYLK
- DIF
- WKS
- BASIC
- Merge
- HTML table
- FileMaker Pro
- Excel

Most of these are straightforward: The records in the found set are exported to a file of the specified format. You may export data only from a single FileMaker table at a time.

A few of these formats deserve special mention and are detailed in the sections that follow.

Exporting to HTML

When exporting to an HTML table, the resulting file is a complete HTML document consisting of an HTML table that displays the chosen data, somewhat like FileMaker's Table View.

Exporting to FileMaker Pro

The result of the FileMaker Pro export choice is a new FileMaker Pro file, with fields and field types that generally match those of exported fields. But note that the logic underlying calculation and summary fields is not preserved. Those fields will be re-created based on their underlying data type: A calculation field returning a text result will be inserted into a Text field, whereas summary field data, if exported, will be inserted into a number field. Only the raw data from the original file will be exported; none of the calculation or scripting logic will carry over.

Exporting to Excel

When exporting records to Excel, you have the option to create a header row where the database field names will appear as column names. You can also specify a worksheet name, document title, document subject, and document author.

Exporting records to Excel is similar to, but a bit more flexible than, the Save Records as Excel feature. Save Records as Excel exports fields only from the current layout and does not export fields on Tab Panels other than the active one.

Exporting to XML

FileMaker can create an export text file in XML format. Without any transformation, the resulting file will be organized according to the FMPXMLRESULT grammar. It's also possible to transform the XML as it is being exported by specifying an XSLT style sheet. The style sheet needs to be able to process data in the FMPXMLRESULT grammar. The output format can be any text format capable of being generated by an XSLT style sheet, including HTML, or more complex formats such as RTF or WordML.

→ *For further discussion of FileMaker XML grammars,* ***see*** *Chapter 14, "FileMaker XML Reference,"* ***p. 439.***

Automatically Opening or Emailing Exported Files

FileMaker Pro has the capability to automatically open and/or email an exported file. These choices are selected via two check boxes in the Export dialog.

Automatically opening a file is a convenience for the user: A newly created Excel file would open right away in Excel. Automatic email is an even more powerful tool. When this choice is selected, a new email message is created in the user's default email client with the exported file as an attachment. (The user still needs to specify the email recipients manually.)

PART II

Calculation Functions

CHAPTER 7

Calculation Primer

The Calculation dialog in FileMaker serves as a fundamental element in nearly all development activities. Beyond simply defining calculation fields, you also work with the dialog within scripts, for setting some auto-enter field options, for field validation, for ToolTips, for conditional field formatting, and even within a file's security settings. We encourage all developers to become deeply familiar with calculation functions and to that end have assembled here a concise reference of how the dialog works.

The Calculation Function Interface

The Specify Calculation dialog allows developers easy access to the data fields in their solutions and to a complete function list (see Figure 7.1).

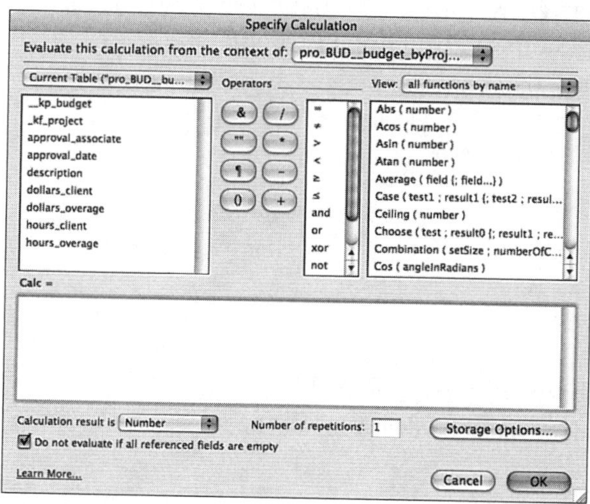

Figure 7.1

Both field names and calculation functions can be double-clicked to insert them into the expression editing area.

→ *If you'd like more detail on specific functions, including complete examples of how they work,* ***see*** *Chapter 9, "Calculation Functions,"* ***p. 69****.*

Calculations: Things to Remember

When working with calculation functions, there are some common issues to keep in mind:

- The four special operators in FileMaker are
  - & Concatenates the result of two expressions. "Joe" & "Smith" results in "JoeSmith"; 1 & 2 results in "12".
  - "" Designates literal text. You don't need quotation marks around numbers, field names, or functions.
  - ¶ Carriage return.
  - () Designates a function's parameter list and controls the order of operations for math expressions.
- Entering a less-than character followed by a greater-than character (<>) equates to the "not equal to" operator (≠) within an expression. The following expressions are functionally identical:

  ```
  1 <> 2
  1 ≠ 2
  ```

  This is also true for >= and <= for ≥ and ≤, respectively.
- Spaces, tabs, and carriage returns (¶ or "pilcrows") are ignored within the calculation syntax, except when within quotation marks (which designate them as literal text). This allows developers to use these characters to format calculation expressions for easy reading. So the following two expressions are functionally identical:

  ```
  If (fieldOne < 10;"less than 10";"not less than 10")

  If (
     fieldOne < 10 ;
     "less than 10" ;
     "not less than 10"
  )
  ```

- You may insert comments into calculation expressions in two forms:

  ```
  // this is a one-line comment, designated by two forward-slash characters

  /* this is a multi-line comment designated in a block
  by a beginning forward-slash-asterisk and
  closed by an ending asterisk-forward-slash.
  */
  ```

- To enter a tab character into an expression (either as literal text or simply to help with formatting), use Ctrl+Tab on Windows. Unfortunately the only way to insert a tab on the Mac is to have one on your Clipboard and to paste it into your expression.
- FileMaker allows for a shorthand approach to entering conditional Boolean tests for non-null, non-zero field contents. The following two expressions are functionally identical:

  ```
  Case ( fieldOne; "true"; "false" )
  Case ( IsEmpty (text) or text = 0; "false"; "true" )
  ```

  Please note that the authors do not recommend this shortcut as a best practice. We tend to believe one should write explicit (and, yes, at times more verbose) code, leaving no room for ambiguity.
- FileMaker allows for optional negative or default values in both the `Case( )` and `If( )` conditional functions. The following are all syntactically valid:

  ```
  Case ( fieldOne = 1; "true" )

  Case (
     fieldOne = 1; "one";
     fieldOne = 2; "two"
  )
  Case (
     fieldOne = 1; "one";
     fieldOne = 2; "two";
     "default"
  )
  ```

  We strongly recommend you always provide a default condition at the end of your `Case` statements, even if that condition should "never" occur. The next time your field shows a value of "never happens," you'll be glad you did. At the very least, use a null string ("") as the default so that you've explicitly defined how the function should resolve if none of the tests are true.
- The `Case( )` function features a *short circuiting* functionality whereby it evaluates conditional tests only until it reaches the first true test. In the following example, the third test will never be evaluated, thus improving system performance.

  ```
  Case (
     1 = 2; "one is false";
     1 = 1; "one is true";
     2 = 2; "two is true"
  )
  ```

- Similarly, logical functions involving "and" and "or" also have short circuiting behavior such that FileMaker will stop evaluating an expression after it can determine whether the condition will be satisfied. For example, consider the statement:

  ```
  If ( color = "blue" or color = "white", "something", "something else")
  ```

  If the color is indeed blue, FileMaker doesn't need to evaluate whether the color is white. In a series of "or" tests, after one test has been determined to be true, that is enough for FileMaker to evaluate the entire expression as true.
- Functions inserted from the function list in the upper right will use curly braces to denote either optional or repeating elements.
- Fields with repeating values can either be accessed using the GetRepetition( ) function or via a shorthand of placing an integer value between two brackets. The following are functionally identical:

  ```
  Quantity[2]
  GetRepetition ( Quantity; 2 )
  ```

- Although the default menu in the function list says All Functions by Name, it does not actually display all FileMaker functions (to the general bemusement of the community). The Get, Design, and External functions are excluded from those listed. To view these functions, you'll need to choose to view the desired function group specifically by choosing Get, Design, or External from the menu of function groups.
- When defining calculation fields, make careful note of the context option at the top of the Specify Calculation dialog. In cases where the calculation's source table is represented by more than one table occurrence on the Relationships Graph, this menu will become active. Calculation field and expression results can vary depending on the context from which a calculation is evaluated.
- Also when defining calculation fields, note the data type returned menu at the lower-left portion of the dialog. It is a common source of bugs for developers to forget to choose the correct data type for calculation results. (Returning a result as a number instead of a text type is a common and bewildering bug, at least the first time you see it.)
- Turning off the Do Not Evaluate If All Referenced Fields Are Empty option ensures that no matter the condition of referenced fields at least some value will be returned. This is useful for cases involving, for example, financial data where it's often desirable to see an explicit zero listed in a field, rather than for the field to be empty.
- Calculation fields that reference related data, summary fields, other unindexed calculation fields, or globally stored fields cannot be indexed; otherwise, even though by definition a calculation field returns different results based on different input values, a calculation field can be indexed.

- In a multiuser setting, calculation functions are typically evaluated on the FileMaker Pro client computer; however, certain unstored calculations are evaluated on the host or server computer. In cases where certain information relies on a client computer but is evaluated on the server, the server will essentially cache this information when an account logs in and can, at times, be out of sync with conditions on the client. The following functions may be subject to this:

  ```
  Get(ApplicationLanguage)
  Get(DesktopPath)
  Get(DocumentsPath)
  Get(FileMakerPath)
  Get(PreferencesPath)
  Get(PrinterName)
  Get(SystemDrive)
  Get(SystemIPAddress)
  Get(SystemLanguage)
  Get(SystemNICAddress)
  Get(UserName)
  ```

CHAPTER 8

Calculation Signatures

Aggregate Functions

Aggregate functions apply to a group of fields, a set of related records or repeating fields (see Table 8.1).

Table 8.1 Aggregate Functions

Syntax	Data Type Returned
Average (field {; field...})	number
Count (field {; field...})	number
List (field {; field...})	text
Max (field {; field...})	text, number, date, time, timestamp
Min (field {; field...})	text, number, date, time, timestamp
StDev (field {; field...})	number
StDevP (field {; field...})	number
Sum (field {; field...})	number
Variance (field {; field...})	number
VarianceP (field {; field...})	number

Date Functions

FileMaker Pro offers a range of date manipulation functions, including those for the Japanese calendar (see Table 8.2).

Table 8.2 Date Functions

Syntax	Data Type Returned
Date (month; day; year)	date
Day (date)	number
DayName (date)	text

continues

Table 8.2 Continued

Syntax	Data Type Returned
DayNameJ (date)	text (Japanese)
DayOfWeek (date)	number
DayOfYear (date)	number
Month (date)	number
MonthName (date)	text
MonthNameJ (date)	text (Japanese)
WeekOfYear (date)	number
WeekOfYearFiscal (date; startingDay)	number
Year (date)	number
YearName (date; format)	text (Japanese)

Design Functions

Design functions generally extract information about one's database and are helpful in debugging or for advanced scripting (see Table 8.3).

Table 8.3 Design Functions

Syntax	Data Type Returned
DatabaseNames	text
FieldBounds (fileName; layoutName; fieldName)	text
FieldComment (fileName; fieldName)	text
FieldIDs (fileName; layoutName)	text
FieldNames (fileName; layout/tableName)	text
FieldRepetitions (fileName; layoutName; fieldName)	text
FieldStyle (fileName; layoutName; fieldName)	text
FieldType (fileName; fieldName)	text
GetNextSerialValue (fileName; fieldName)	text
LayoutIDs (fileName)	text
LayoutNames (fileName)	text
LayoutObjectNames (filename ; layoutName)	text
RelationInfo (fileName; tableOccurrence)	text
ScriptIDs (fileName)	text
ScriptNames (fileName)	text
TableIDs (fileName)	text
TableNames (fileName)	text
ValueListIDs (fileName)	text
ValueListItems (fileName; valueListName)	text
ValueListNames (fileName)	text
WindowNames {(filename)}	text

External Functions

External functions originate from installed plug-ins and vary widely based on the plug-ins used (see Table 8.4).

Table 8.4 External Function

Syntax	Data Type Returned
External (nameOfFunction; parameter)	depends on the external function

Financial Functions

Financial functions assist with various specialized mortgage and interest calculations (see Table 8.5).

Table 8.5 Financial Functions

Syntax	Data Type Returned
FV (payment; interestRate; periods)	number
NPV (payment; interestRate)	number
PMT (principal; interestRate; term)	number
PV (payment; interestRate; periods)	number

Get Functions

Get functions generally provide information about a given user's current state, be it from within FileMaker Pro, from one's computer, or from a given network (see Table 8.6).

Table 8.6 Get Functions

Syntax	Data Type Returned
Get (AccountName)	text
Get (ActiveFieldContents)	text, number, date, time, timestamp, container
Get (ActiveFieldName)	text
Get (ActiveFieldTableName)	text
Get (ActiveLayoutObjectName)	text
Get (ActiveModifierKeys)	number
Get (ActiveRepetitionNumber)	number
Get (ActiveSelectionSize)	number
Get (ActiveSelectionStart)	number
Get (AllowAbortState)	number

continues

Table 8.6 Continued

Syntax	Data Type Returned
Get (AllowToolbarState)	number
Get (ApplicationLanguage)	text
Get (ApplicationVersion)	text
Get (CalculationRepetitionNumber)	number
Get (CurrentDate)	date
Get (CurrentHostTimestamp)	timestamp
Get (CurrentTime)	time
Get (CurrentTimestamp)	timestamp
Get (CustomMenuSetName)	text
Get (DesktopPath)	text
Get (DocumentsPath)	text
Get (ErrorCaptureState)	number
Get (ExtendedPrivileges)	text
Get (FileMakerPath)	text
Get (FileName)	text
Get (FilePath)	text
Get (FileSize)	number
Get (FoundCount)	number
Get (HighContrastColor)	text
Get (HighContrastState)	number
Get (HostApplicationVersion)	text
Get (HostIPAddress)	text
Get (HostName)	text
Get (LastError)	number
Get (LastMessageChoice)	number
Get (LastODBCError)	text
Get (LayoutAccess)	number
Get (LayoutCount)	number
Get (LayoutName)	text
Get (LayoutNumber)	number
Get (LayoutTableName)	text
Get (LayoutViewState)	number
Get (MultiUserState)	number
Get (NetworkProtocol)	text
Get (PageNumber)	number
Get (PortalRowNumber)	number
Get (PreferencesPath)	text
Get (PrinterName)	text
Get (PrivilegeSetName)	text

Syntax	Data Type Returned
Get (RecordAccess)	number
Get (RecordID)	number
Get (RecordModificationCount)	number
Get (RecordNumber)	number
Get (RecordOpenCount)	number
Get (RecordOpenState)	number
Get (RequestCount)	number
Get (RequestOmitState)	number
Get (ScreenDepth)	number
Get (ScreenHeight)	number
Get (ScreenWidth)	number
Get (ScriptName)	text
Get (ScriptParameter)	text
Get (ScriptResult)	text, number, date, time, timestamp, container
Get (SortState)	number
Get (StatusAreaState)	number
Get (SystemDrive)	text
Get (SystemIPAddress)	text
Get (SystemLanguage)	text
Get (SystemNICAddress)	text
Get (SystemPlatform)	number
Get (SystemVersion)	text
Get (TemporaryPath)	text
Get (TextRulerVisible)	number
Get (TotalRecordCount)	number
Get (UserCount)	number
Get (UserName)	text
Get (UseSystemFormatsState)	number
Get (WindowContentHeight)	number
Get (WindowContentWidth)	number
Get (WindowDesktopHeight)	number
Get (WindowDesktopWidth)	number
Get (WindowHeight)	number
Get (WindowLeft)	number
Get (WindowMode)	number
Get (WindowName)	text
Get (WindowTop)	number
Get (WindowVisible)	number
Get (WindowWidth)	number
Get (WindowZoomLevel)	text

Logical Functions

The logical functions are a disparate collection of tools for performing conditional tests and evaluating expressions (see Table 8.7).

Table 8.7 Logical Functions

Syntax	Data Type Returned
Case (test1; result1 {; test2; result2; defaultResult...})	text, number, date, time, timestamp, container
Choose (test; result0 {; result1; result2...})	text, number, date, time, timestamp, container
Evaluate (expression {; [field1; field2; ...]})	text, number, date, time, timestamp, container
EvaluationError (expression)	number
GetAsBoolean (data)	number
GetField (fieldName)	text, number, date, time, timestamp, container
GetLayoutObjectAttribute (objectName ; attributeName {; repetitionNumber ; portalRowNumber})	text
GetNthRecord (fieldName; recordNumber)	text, number, date, time, timestamp, container
If (test; result1; result2)	text, number, date, time, timestamp, container
IsEmpty (expression)	number
IsValid (expression)	number
IsValidExpression (expression)	number
Let ({[} var1=expression1 {; var2=expression2 ...] }; calculation)	text, number, date, time, timestamp, container
Lookup (sourceField {; failExpression })	text, number, date, time, timestamp, container
LookupNext (sourceField; lower/higher Flag)	text, number, date, time, timestamp, container
Self	text, number, date, time, timestamp, container

Number Functions

Number functions perform various mathematical operations within FileMaker Pro (see Table 8.8).

Table 8.8 Number Functions

Syntax	Data Type Returned
Abs (number)	number, time
Ceiling (number)	number
Combination (setSize; numberOfChoices)	number
Div (number; divisor)	number
Exp (number)	number
Factorial (number {; numberOfFactors })	number
Floor (number)	number

Syntax	Data Type Returned
Int (number)	number
Lg (number)	number
Ln (number)	number
Log (number)	number
Mod (number; divisor)	number
Random	number
Round (number; precision)	number
SetPrecision (expression; precision)	number
Sign (number)	number
Sqrt (number)	number
Truncate (number; precision)	number

Repeating Functions

Repeating functions facilitate working with repeating fields within other calculations (see Table 8.9).

Table 8.9 Repeating Functions

Syntax	Data Type Returned
Extend (non-repeatingField)	text, number, date, time, timestamp, container
GetRepetition (repeatingField; repetitionNumber)	text, number, date, time, timestamp, container
Last (repeatingField)	text, number, date, time, timestamp, container

Summary Function

Summary functions operate across multiple records based on a break field (sort criteria). The function in this category is the analogue of the subsummary part within reporting (see Table 8.10).

Table 8.10 Summary Function

Syntax	Data Type Returned
GetSummary (summaryField; breakField)	text, number, date, time, timestamp

Text Functions

Text functions provide a means for investigating and manipulating text strings within FileMaker Pro (see Table 8.11).

Table 8.11 Text Functions

Syntax	Data Type Returned
Exact (originalText; comparisonText)	number
Filter (textToFilter; filterText)	text
FilterValues (textToFilter; filterValues)	text
GetAsCSS (text)	text
GetAsDate (text)	date
GetAsNumber (text)	number
GetAsSVG (text)	text
GetAsText (data)	text
GetAsTime (text)	time
GetAsTimestamp (text)	timestamp
GetAsURLEncoded (text)	text
GetValue (listOfValues; valueNumber)	text
Hiragana (text)	text (Japanese)
KanaHankaku (text)	text (Japanese)
KanaZenkaku (text)	text (Japanese)
KanjiNumeral (text)	text (Japanese)
Katakana (text)	text (Japanese)
Left (text; numberOfCharacters)	text
LeftValues (text; numberOfValues)	text
LeftWords (text; numberOfWords)	text
Length (text)	number
Lower (text)	text
Middle (text; startCharacter; numberOfCharacters)	text
MiddleValues (text; startingValue; numberOfValues)	text
MiddleWords (text; startingWord; numberOfWords)	text
NumToJText (number; separator; characterType)	text (Japanese)
PatternCount (text; searchString)	number
Position (text; searchString; start; occurrence)	number
Proper (text)	text
Quote (text)	text
Replace (text; start; numberOfCharacters; replacementText)	text
Right (text; numberOfCharacters)	text
RightValues (text; numberOfValues)	text
RightWords (text; numberOfWords)	text
RomanHankaku (text)	text (Japanese)
RomanZenkaku (text)	text (Japanese)
SerialIncrement (text; incrementBy)	text

Syntax	Data Type Returned
Substitute (text; searchString; replaceString)	text
Trim (text)	text
TrimAll (text; trimSpaces; trimType)	text
Upper (text)	text
ValueCount (text)	number
WordCount (text)	number

Text Formatting Functions

Text formatting functions provide a means to manipulate the actual formatting of data within text and number fields in FileMaker Pro (see Table 8.12).

Table 8.12 Text Formatting Functions

Syntax	Data Type Returned
RGB (red; green; blue)	number
TextColor (text; RGB (red; green; blue))	text, number
TextColorRemove (text {; RGB (red; green; blue)})	text, number
TextFont (text; fontName {; fontScript })	text, number
TextFontRemove (text {; fontName; fontScript })	text, number
TextFormatRemove (text)	text, number
TextSize (text; fontSize)	text, number
TextSizeRemove (text {; sizeToRemove })	text, number
TextStyleAdd (text; styles)	text, number
TextStyleRemove (text; styles)	text, number

Time Functions

Time functions provide a means of manipulating time data within FileMaker Pro (see Table 8.13).

Table 8.13 Time Functions

Syntax	Data Type Returned
Hour (time)	number
Minute (time)	number
Seconds (time)	number
Time (hours; minutes; seconds)	time

Timestamp Function

The Timestamp function generates a timestamp from a date and a time (see Table 8.14).

Table 8.14 Timestamp Function

Syntax	Data Type Returned
Timestamp (date; time)	timestamp

Trigonometric Functions

Trigonometric functions extend math and number functions within FileMaker Pro to trigonometry (see Table 8.15).

Table 8.15 Trigonometric Functions

Syntax	Data Type Returned
Acos (number)	number
Asin (number)	number
Atan (number)	number
Cos (number)	number
Degrees (number)	number
Pi	number
Radians (angleInDegrees)	number
Sin (angleInRadians)	number
Tan (angleInRadians)	number

CHAPTER 9

Calculation Functions

Abs()

Syntax:

Abs (number)

Data type returned: **Number, Time** *Category:* **Number**

Parameters:

- **number**—Any expression that resolves to a numeric value.

Description:

Returns the absolute value of number; absolute value is always a positive number.

Examples:

Function	Results
Abs (-92)	Returns 92.
Abs (Get (CurrentPlatform))	Returns 1 for Mac OS and 2 for Windows.
Abs (RetailPrice - WholeSalePrice)	Returns the difference between the two prices, regardless of which one is larger.
Abs (2:15:00 – 3:30:00)	Returns 1:15:00.

Acos()

Syntax:

Acos (number)

Data type returned: **Number** *Category:* **Trigonometric**

Parameters:

- **number**—Any expression that resolves to a numeric value from -1 to 1.

Description:

The arc cosine of a number is the angle (measured in radians) whose cosine is the specified number. The range of values returned by the Acos function is 0 to Pi.

If Acos (x) = y, then Cos (y) = x.

Examples:

Acos (1) = 0
Acos (-1) = 3.1415926535897931, which is Pi radians, or 180 degrees.
Acos (0) = 1.5707963267948966, which is Pi/2 radians, or 90 degrees.

Asin()

Syntax:

Asin (number)

Data type returned: **Number** *Category:* **Trigonometric**

Parameters:

- **number**—Any expression that resolves to a numeric value from -1 to 1.

Description:

The arc sine of a number is the angle (measured in radians) whose sine is the specified number. The range of values returned by the Asin function is -(Pi/2) to Pi/2.

If Asin (x) = y, then Sin (y) = x.

Asin (x) = Asin (-x).

Examples:

Asin (0) = 0
Asin (1) = 1.5707963267948966, which is Pi/2 radians, or 90 degrees.
Asin (Sqrt (2) / 2) = .7853981633974484, which is Pi/4 radians, or 45 degrees.

Atan()

Syntax:

Atan (number)

Data type returned: **Number** *Category:* **Trigonometric**

Parameters:

- **number**—Any expression that resolves to a numeric value.

Description:

The arc tangent of a number is the angle (measured in radians) whose tangent is the specified number. The range of values returned by the Atan function is -(Pi/2) to Pi/2.

If Atan (x) = y, then Tan (y) = x.

Atan (x) = Atan (-x).

Examples:

Atan (0) = 0

Atan (1) = .785398163, which is Pi/4 radians, or 45 degrees.

Average()

Syntax:

Average (field {; field...})

Data type returned: **Number** *Category:* **Aggregate**

Parameters:

- **field**—Any related field, repeating field, or set of nonrepeating fields that represent a collection of numbers. Parameters in curly braces { } are optional and may be repeated as needed, separated by a semicolon.

Description:

Returns a numeric value that is the arithmetic mean of all nonblank values in the set designated by the parameter list. The arithmetic mean of a set of numbers is the sum of the numbers divided by the size of the set. Blank values are not considered as part of the set.

When the parameter list consists of two or more repeating fields, Average() generates a repeating field in which the corresponding repetitions from the specified fields are averaged separately. So, if a field Repeater1 has two values, 16 and 20, and another field, Repeater2, has two values, 14 and 25, Average (Repeater1; Repeater2) would return a repeating field with values 15 and 22.5.

Examples:

Function	Results
Average (field1; field2; field3)	Returns 2 when field1 = 1, field2 = 2, and field3 = 3.
Average (repeatingField)	Returns 2 when repetition1 = 1, repetition2 = 2, and repetition3 = 3.
Average (repeatingField[1]; repeatingField[2]; repeatingField[3])	Returns 2 when repetition1 = 1, repetition2 = 2, and repetition3 = 3.
Average (Customer::InvoiceTotal)	Returns 450 when a customer has three related invoice records with invoice totals of 300, 500, and 550.

Case()

Syntax:

Case (test1; result1 {; test2; result2; defaultResult...})

Data type returned: **Text, Number, Date, Time, Timestamp, Container**

Category: **Logical**

Parameters:

- **test(n)**—An expression that yields a Boolean result.
- **result(n)**—The value to return if corresponding test is true.
- **defaultResult**—The value to return if all tests are false. Parameters in curly braces { } are optional and may be repeated as needed, separated by a semicolon.

Description:

The Case function returns one of several possible results based on a series of tests.

Each test expression is evaluated in order, and when the first true expression (one that resolves to a Boolean 1) is found, the value specified in the result for that expression is returned. The function stops evaluating as soon as it finds a true test.

The default result at the end of the parameter list is optional. If none of the tests evaluate as true, the function returns the value specified for defaultResult. If no default result is specified, the Case function returns an "empty" result. If you believe that one of the tests in the Case should always be true, we recommend using an explicit default case, possibly with a value of "default" or "error" to assist in error trapping.

Consider using hard returns in long Case() statements to make them more readable, and indent lines with tabs, as shown in the following examples. (Note that the second example that follows makes repeated calls to Get(SystemLanguage); in practice it would be better to use Let() to make a single call to Get(SystemLanguage) so that it needs to be evaluated only once.)

Examples:

Function	Results
Case (IsEmpty (Contact_Name); 1)	Returns 1 if the Contact_Name field is empty.

Note that a default value is not required, making the usage of Case() shorter than If().

```
Case (
  Get(SystemLanguage) = "English"; "Welcome";
  Get(SystemLanguage) = "French"; "Bienvenue";
  Get(SystemLanguage) = "Italian"; "Benvenuto";
  Get(SystemLanguage) = "German"; "Willkommen";
  Get(SystemLanguage) = "Swedish"; "Välkommen";
  Get(SystemLanguage) = "Spanish "; "Bienvenido";
```

```
  Get(SystemLanguage) = "Dutch"; "Welkom";
  Get(SystemLanguage) = "Japanese"; "Irashaimasu" ;
  "Sorry... not sure of your language."    // default value
)
```

Returns a welcoming message in the language determined by the Get (SystemLanguage) function.

```
Case (
  SalesTotal < 10; .1;
  SalesTotal < 50; .2;
  SalesTotal < 100; .3;
  .35
)
```

Returns .1 when the value in the SalesTotal field is 5, and returns .2 when the value in the SalesTotal field is 12. Case() stops evaluating after it finds the first true test, so even if multiple tests are true (as when SalesTotal is 5), the result is unambiguous. This "short-circuiting" capability can help with performance tuning; put the tests that are most likely to return true near the beginning of a Case() function so that fewer expressions need to be evaluated.

Ceiling()

Syntax:

Ceiling (number)

Data type returned: **Number** *Category:* **Number**

Parameters:

- **number**—Any expression that resolves to a numeric value.

Description:

Returns number rounded up to the next integer.

One common use for the Ceiling function is finding out how many pages will be required to print *x* items if *y* items fit on a page. The formula for this is Ceiling (x / y). For instance, if you have 16 items, and 5 can print per page, you would need Ceiling (16 / 5) = Ceiling (3.2) = 4 pages. Analogously, if you needed to pack *x* Widgets into boxes, and you could pack *y* Widgets per box, the result of the formula Ceiling (x / y) would tell you how many boxes you'd need.

Examples:

Ceiling (1.05) = 2
Ceiling (-4.6) = -4
Ceiling (3) = 3

Choose()

Syntax:

Choose (test; result0 {; result1; result2...})

Data type returned: **Text, Number, Date, Time, Timestamp, Container**

Category: **Logical**

Parameters:

- **test**—An expression that returns a number greater than or equal to zero.
- **result(n)**—The value returned or the expression that is evaluated based on the result of the test. Parameters in curly braces { } are optional and may be repeated as needed, separated by a semicolon.

Description:

Returns one of the result values according to the integer value of test. FileMaker evaluates test to obtain an index number, which is used to then select the corresponding ordinal result.

The Choose function is a 0-based list. Choose (1; "a"; "b"; "c") returns "b".

Any fractional value of test is ignored (as opposed to rounded) when obtaining the index number. Choose (1.9; "a"; "b"; "c") returns "b".

If the index value returned by test exceeds the number of results available, the Choose function will not return any result; the field will be blank as opposed to having a "?" in it. There is no way to define a default value to use when the index value exceeds the number of results available.

Examples:

Function	Results
Choose (DayOfWeek (Get (CurrentDate)); ""; "Sun"; "Mon"; "Tue"; "Wed"; "Thu"; "Fri"; "Sat")	Returns a three-letter day name abbreviation for today's date.
Choose ((Month (myDate)/ 3.1); "Q1"; "Q2"; "Q3"; "Q4")	Returns Q1 for the instance where myDate contains 2/1/2008.

The following formula converts decimal values to fractional notation, rounded to the nearest eighth. Assume an input from a field (or parameter), myNumber.

```
Let ([
  n = myNumber;
  int = Int ( n );
  decimal = Mod ( n; 1 );
  numberOfEighths = Round ( decimal / .125; 0 );
  intDisplay = Case ( Abs ( int ) > 0; int & Case ( Abs ( decimal ) > 0; " - "; "" ); "" );
  fraction = Choose( numberOfEighths;
    Floor ( n );
    intDisplay & "1/8";
    intDisplay & "1/4";
    intDisplay & "3/8";
    intDisplay & "1/2";
    intDisplay & "5/8";
    intDisplay & "3/4";
    intDisplay & "7/8";
    Ceiling ( n )
    )
  ];
  fraction
)
```

If myNumber contained 3.45, this function would return 3 - 1/2.

Combination()

Syntax:

Combination (setSize; numberOfChoices)

Data type returned: **Number** *Category:* **Number**

Parameters:

- **setSize**—Non-negative numeric value (or an expression that results in one).
- **numberOfChoices**—Non-negative numeric value (or an expression that results in one).

Description:

Returns the number of ways to uniquely choose numberOfChoices items from a set of size setSize.

The formula used to determine the Combination value is n! / (n-x)! * x!, where n = set size, x = number of choices.

The numbers returned by the Combination function are the coefficients of the binomial expansion series. Useful in statistics, combinatorics, and polynomial expansions, the values returned by this function are referred to as *combination coefficients*. They form Pascal's triangle.

$(x + y)^4 = 1x^4 + 4x^3y + 6x^2y^2 + 4xy^3 + 1y^4$

```
Combination ( 4; 0 ) = 1
Combination ( 4; 1 ) = 4
Combination ( 4; 2 ) = 6
Combination ( 4; 3 ) = 4
Combination ( 4; 4 ) = 1
```

Examples:

Function	Results
Combination (4; 2)	Returns 6, reflecting that there are six ways of selecting two items from a set of four items. Given set {A, B, C, D}, these subsets would be {AB, AC, AD, BC, BD, CD}.
Combination (x; 0)	Returns 1 for any x, representing the empty set.
Combination (x; x)	Returns 1 for any x.
(13 * 12 * Combination (4; 2) * Combination (4; 3)) / Combination (52; 5)	Returns 0.00144057..., which is the probability of being dealt a full house in five-card poker (less than a 1% chance!).

Cos()

Syntax:

Cos (number)

Data type returned: **Number**

Category: **Trigonometric**

Parameters:

- **number**—Any expression that resolves to a numeric value that represents an angle measured in radians.

Description:

Returns the cosine of the angle represented by the value of the parameter measured in radians. Cos is a periodic function with a range from -1 to 1.

In any right triangle, the cosine of the two nonright angles can be obtained by dividing the length of the side adjacent to the angle by the length of the hypotenuse.

You can convert an angle measured in degrees into radians by using the Radians() function, or by multiplying the value by Pi/180. One radian is slightly more than 57 degrees.

Examples:

```
Cos ( 0 ) = 0
Cos ( Pi / 4) = .707106781 (which is 1 / Sqrt (2))
Cos ( Radians (60) ) = .5
```

Count()

Syntax:

Count (field {; field...})

Data type returned: **Number** *Category:* **Aggregate**

Parameters:

- **field**—Any related field, repeating field, or set of non-epeating fields; or an expression that returns a field, repeating field, or set of nonrepeating fields. Parameters in curly braces { } are optional and may be repeated as needed, separated by a semicolon.

Description:

Returns a count of the fields (or repetitions, in the case of repeating fields) in the parameter list that contain nonblank values.

When the parameter list consists of two or more repeating fields, Count() returns a repeating field in which the corresponding repetitions from the specified fields are counted separately. So if a field Repeater1 has three values, 16, 20, and 24, and another field, Repeater2, has two values, 14 and 25, Count (Repeater1; Repeater2) would return a repeating field with values 2, 2, and 1.

Examples:

Function	Results
Count (field1; field2; field3)	Returns 2 when field1 and field2 contain valid values, and field3 is empty.
Count (repeatingField)	Returns 2 when repetitions 1 and 2 contain valid values, and repetition 3 is empty.
Count (InvoiceItem::InvoiceID)	Returns 2 when the current record is related to two InvoiceItem records. When using the Count() function to count the number of related records, be sure to count a field that is guaranteed not to be blank, such as the table's primary key.

Beginning with FileMaker Pro 8, the Count() function also takes portal and field context into account. For example, in a scenario where a Customer table occurrence is related one-to-many with an Invoice table occurrence that is then related one-to-many to a LineItem table occurrence, evaluating a Count() function from Customer to LineItem will yield *all* LineItem records for the current Customer record if the user's context is on the Customer TO. But if the user's context is on the Invoice TO (if a user clicks in an Invoice portal row, say, or a script navigates into the portal using a Go To Field script step), Count(LineItem::field) will return a count of just those line items related to the currently selected invoice. Given that calculation fields explicitly specify their evaluation context, this issue is most likely to arise in scripting.

DatabaseNames

Syntax:

DatabaseNames

Data type returned: **Text** *Category:* **Design**

Parameters:

None

Description:

Returns a carriage return-delimited list of currently open databases (filenames), whether open as a client of another machine or open locally.

Note that on Windows, the .fp7 extension is not returned. This means that the function is consistent across both platforms.

Use caution when checking for hard-coded strings in calculations. If someone renames a file, any calculation containing the old value will no longer behave as before. Get (FileName) can be used in conjunction with a startup script to see whether a filename has been changed, and developers may want to consider establishing a centrally controlled custom function or variable for such checks.

Examples:

In a circumstance where three files are open, Customers, Invoices, and Invoice Line Items, DatabaseNames will return

```
Customers
Invoices
Invoice Line Items
```

```
PatternCount ( DatabaseNames; "Customers" )
```

Returns 1 if the Customers database is open.

Date()

Syntax:

Date (month; day; year)

Data type returned: **Date** *Category:* **Date**

Parameters:

- **month**—The month of the year (a number from 1 to 12).
- **day**—The day of the month (a number from 1 to 31).
- **year**—The year (four digits between 0001 and 4000). The year parameter should be passed as a four-digit number; if not, FileMaker will not infer or prepend a century (1/10/05 = January 10, 0005).

Note that regardless of your system settings, this function requires that its parameters be listed strictly in order: month, day, year. Localizations settings will not apply.

Description:

Returns a valid date of data type date represented by the three parameters.

Values for month and day outside normal ranges will be interpreted correctly. For instance, a month value of 13 returns a date in January of the following year. A day value of 0 returns the last day of the preceding month.

Parameters can be calculation expressions or fields; as long as the final result is valid, the date function will work correctly. Dates are stored internally as numbers (a unit of "1" represents one day); whole number math can be done on dates.

Be sure when returning dates as the result of calculation fields that you specify a calculation result of Date. If you were to define a field as Date (1; 1; 2000) and were to set the calculation result as Number, you would see 730120 as the calculation value. Internally, FileMaker stores dates as the number of days since January 1, 0001, and that internal representation is returned if you incorrectly specify the return data type.

Examples:

Function	Results
Date (1; 1; 2000)	Returns January 1, 2000 (formatting is determined on the layout and by system preferences).

Math can be performed on dates:

```
Date ( 1; 1; 2000 ) - 1
```

Returns December 31, 1999.

The parameters in a Date function can be calculated:

```
Date ( Month ( Get ( CurrentDate )); 1; Year ( Get ( CurrentDate )))
```

Returns the date of the first of the current month; if today were August 12, 1965, then August 1, 1965 would be returned.

The parameters in a Date function can be fields:

```
Date ( pickMonth; 1; Year ( Get ( CurrentDate )))
```

Returns the date of the first of a month specified by the value in the field pickMonth.

Day()

Syntax:

Day (date)

Data type returned: **Number** *Category:* **Date**

Parameters:

- **date**—Any valid date (1/1/0001–12/31/4000), expression that returns a date, or field that contains a date.

Description:

Returns the day of month (1–31) for any valid date.

Examples:

```
Day ( "1/15/2000" ) = 15
```

Other functions can be referenced in Day():

```
Day ( Get ( CurrentDate ))
```

returns the day of month for today.

Parameters in Day() can be calculated:

```
Day ( Get ( CurrentDate ) - 90 )
```

Returns the day number for the date 90 days before today, which may not be the same as today's day number.

DayName()

Syntax:

DayName (date)

Data type returned: **Text** *Category:* **Date**

Parameters:

- **date**—Any valid date (1/1/0001–12/31/4000), expression that returns a date, or field that contains a date. The parameter can also be the numeric representation of a date (1–1460970).

Description:

Returns a text string containing the name of a weekday for any valid date (1/1/0001–12/31/4000).

Note that the year is optional. DayName ("12/1") returns the day name for December 1st in the current year.

Examples:

Function	Results
DayName ("11/24/2003")	Returns Monday.
DayName (dateField)	Returns the day of week for the date stored in the field dateField.
DayName (Get (CurrentDate) - 30)	Returns the day name for the date 30 days prior to today.

DayNameJ()

Syntax:

DayNameJ (date)

Data type returned: **Text (Japanese)** *Category:* **Date**

Parameters:

- **date**—Any calendar date.

Description:

Returns a text string in Japanese that is the full name of the weekday for date.

To avoid errors when using dates, always use four-digit years. FileMaker will not infer or prepend a century on two-digit dates (1/10/05 = January 10, 0005)

Examples:

Function	Results
DayNameJ (Date (11; 1; 2005))	Returns Kaiyobi in whatever font/display preference a user's system supports.

DayOfWeek()

Syntax:

DayOfWeek (date)

Data type returned: **Number** *Category:* **Date**

Parameters:

- **date**—Any valid date (1/1/0001–12/31/4000), expression that returns a date, or field that contains a date. The parameter can also be the numeric representation of a date (1–1460970).

Description:

Returns a number from 1 to 7, representing the day of week (Sunday = 1, Saturday = 7) for any valid date (1/1/0001–12/31/4000).

DayOfWeek() can be used to perform conditional tests on days of week without concern for localization issues. The number returned is always the same regardless of what language version of FileMaker Pro the user is using. The number value returned by DayOfWeek() can also be used in mathematical calculations.

Note that the year is optional. DayOfWeek ("12/1") returns the appropriate integer for December 1st in the current year.

Examples:

Function	Results
DayOfWeek ("11/24/2003")	Returns 2 (Monday).
DayOfWeek (dateField)	Returns the day of week for the date stored in the field dateField.
DayOfWeek (Date (12; 25; Year (Get (CurrentDate))))	Returns the day number on which Christmas falls this year.

DayOfYear()

Syntax:

DayOfYear (date)

Data type returned: **Number** *Category:* **Date**

Parameters:

- **date**—Any valid date (1/1/0001–12/31/4000), expression that returns a date, or field that contains a date. The parameter can also be the numeric representation of a date (1–1460970).

Description:

Returns a number representing the day of year (1–366) for any valid date (1/1/0001–12/31/4000).

You can use the DayOfYear function to check whether a particular year is a leap year. Given a field Year, the formula DayOfYear (Date (12; 31; Year)) would return 366 if Year was a leap year and 365 if it wasn't.

Note that the year is optional. DayOfYear ("12/1") returns the appropriate integer for December 1st in the current year.

Examples:

Function	Results
DayOfYear ("12/31/2000")	Returns 366 (leap year).
DayOfYear ("12/31/2001")	Returns 365 (non-leap year).
DayOfYear ("1/24/2004")	Returns 24.
DayOfYear (dateField)	Returns the day number for the date stored in dateField.
DayOfYear (Get (CurrentDate) + 30)	Returns the day of year for a date 30 days from now.

Degrees()

Syntax:

Degrees (number)

Data type returned: **Number** *Category:* **Trigonometric**

Parameters:

- **number**—A number representing an angle measured in radians.

Description:

Converts an angle measured in radians to its equivalent in degrees. There are 2*Pi radians in 360°, so 1 radian is just over 57°.

Another way to convert radians to degrees is to multiply by 180/Pi.

Examples:

Function	Results
Degrees (0)	Returns 0.
Degrees (Pi / 4)	Returns 45.
Degrees (2 * Pi)	Returns 360.
Degrees (4 * Pi)	Returns 720.
Degrees (-Pi / 2)	Returns -90.

Div()

Syntax:

Div (number; divisor)

Data type returned: **Number** *Category:* **Number**

Parameters:

- **number**—Any expression that resolves to a numeric value.
- **divisor**—Any expression that resolves to a numeric value.

Description:

Returns the whole number element of the result of dividing the numerator number by the denominator divisor.

The Div() function is equivalent to Floor (numerator / denominator).

To obtain the remainder when a numerator is divided by denominator, use the Mod() function.

Examples:

Function	Results
Div (30; 4)	Returns 7 because 30/4 is 7, remainder 2.
Div (51; 8)	Returns 6 because 51/8 is 6, remainder 3.

Evaluate()

Syntax:

Evaluate (expression {; [field1; field2; ...]})

Data type returned: **Text, Number, Date, Time, Timestamp, Container** *Category:* **Logical**

Parameters:

- **expression**—Any valid calculation formula, field containing a valid formula, or expression returning a valid formula.
- **field(n)**—A list of optional fields that can then serve to trigger a reevaluation; the expression reevaluates when any of the included fields are updated.

Parameters in curly braces { } are optional. The optional field list must be enclosed by square brackets when there are multiple parameters.

Description:

The Evaluate() function returns the results obtained by evaluating expression.

The optional second parameter is a list of fields on which the calculation becomes dependent. When any of those fields are modified, the Evaluate() function reevaluates the expression specified by the first parameter.

The Evaluate() function expects that the first parameter passed to it is a string that contains a formula of some sort. If you are passing a literal string, as in the fourth of the following examples, using the Quote() function ensures that any quotation marks in the formula itself are properly encoded. If the first parameter is a field name or an expression, that field or expression is expected to return a formula, which the Evaluate() function then evaluates. In a nutshell, if the first parameter is *not* surrounded by quotation marks, the *result* of whatever field or expression is provided is evaluated.

Note that the execution of the expression does occur—in other words, do not think of Evaluate() as a "testing function" making use of its own memory space. If your expression modifies a global or local variable (using the Let() function), any applicable changes will be applied. If you need a calculation "scratch pad," consider using the Evaluate Now function of the FileMaker Advanced Data Viewer—though there again, any "side-effect" modifications of variables will occur "for real," a good example of why modifying variables from within calculations can be a questionable practice.

Examples:

Function	Results
Evaluate (MyFormula)	Returns 8 if MyFormula contains the string 5+3.
Evaluate (MyFormula)	Returns 4 if MyFormula contains the string "Length (FirstName)" and FirstName contains "Fred".
Evaluate ("MyFormula")	Returns a text string, 5+3 if MyFormula contains the string 5+3.
Evaluate (Quote ("The comment field was last updated on " & Get (CurrentDate) & " by " & Get (AccountName)); CommentField)	Returns a string containing information about the date and user who last modified the CommentField.

EvaluationError()

Syntax:

EvaluationError (expression)

Data type returned: **Number** *Category:* **Logical**

Parameters:

- **expression**—Any FileMaker calculation formula.

Description:

Returns whatever error code an expression may generate if executed. If the expression executes properly, a zero (no error) will be returned.

Note that the expression is executed if it is syntactically correct. If your expression manipulates local or global variables, they will be affected by this EvaluationError() check. Note also that two kinds of errors are returned: syntax errors, where the expression cannot be executed (and will not be executed by EvalutionError()), and runtime errors, where the expression is valid, but, for example, a field or record may be missing.

Important: The EvaluationError() function must enclose the Evaluate() function to return any syntax errors.

Examples:

Function	Results
EvaluationError (Evaluate (Length (<missingfield>)))	Returns error 102 (field missing).
EvaluationError (Evaluate (Case (1 = 1))	Returns error 1201 (too few parameters).
EvaluationError (Case (1 = 1))	Returns error 0 because there were no runtime errors. If you want to ensure you always get error codes including this syntax error, be sure to use the nested Evaluate() function. Note that this error is impossible to get unless you're working with calculation formulas in fields: If you were to enter this example into a calculation dialog, FileMaker would not allow it to be saved and would prompt the developer to correct the syntax.

Exact()

Syntax:

Exact (originalText; comparisonText)

Data type returned: **Number** *Category:* **Text**

Parameters:

- **originalText**—Any text expression, text field, or container field.
- **comparisonText**—Any text expression, text field, or container field.

Description:

The Exact function compares the contents of any two text or container expressions. This function is case sensitive. If the values of the parameters are identical, the result is 1 (True); otherwise, the result is 0 (False). For container fields, not only must the data be the same, but they must also be stored in the same manner (either embedded or stored by file reference). Note that for container fields the text representations of the file references are being compared.

Remember that Exact() considers the case of the two strings, whereas the = operator does not. If you need to compare two values in a conditional test, consider using If (Exact (A; B); . . . instead of If (A = B; . . ..

Examples:

Function	Results
Exact ("Smith"; "smith")	Returns 0 (False).
Exact (Proper (Salutation); Salutation)	Returns 1 if the contents of the Salutation field begin with initial caps.
Exact (Zip_Lookup::City_Name; City_Name)	Returns 1 if the value of City_Name is exactly the same as the one stored in a related ZIP code table.

Exp()

Syntax:

Exp (number)

Data type returned: **Number** *Category:* **Number**

Parameters:

- **number**—Any expression that resolves to a numeric value.

Description:

Returns the value of the constant *e* raised to the power of number. The Exp() function is the inverse of the Ln() function.

To return the value of the constant *e* itself, use Exp (1), which returns 2.7182818284590452. You can use the SetPrecision() function to return *e* with up to 400 digits of precision.

Examples:

Function	Results
Round (Exp (5); 3)	Returns 148.413.
Exp (Ln (5))	Returns 5.

Extend()

Syntax:

Extend (non-repeatingField)

Data type returned: **Text, Number, Date, Time, Timestamp, Container**

Category: **Repeating**

Parameters:

- **non-repeatingField**—Any nonrepeating field (a field defined to contain only one value).

Description:

Allows a value in nonrepeatingField to be used in every repetition in a calculation defined to have a repeating result. Without using the Extend() function, only the first repetition of a repeating calculation field will properly reference the value in non-repeatingField.

Examples:

Given a number field RepCommission, defined to hold three repetitions, a nonrepeating number field (SalePrice), and repeating calculation field (SalesCommission), defined as follows:

```
Round ( RepCommision * Extend ( SalePrice ); 2 )
```

RepCommission	SalePrice	SalesCommission
.10	18.00	1.80
.12		2.16
.15		2.40

Without the Extend() function, only the first repetition of SalesCommission would have returned the correct value.

External()

Syntax:

External (nameOfFunction; parameter)

Data type returned: **Depends on the external function** *Category:* **External**

Parameters:

- **nameOfFunction**—The name of the external function being called.
- **parameter**—The parameter that is being passed to the external function.

Description:

The External() function is used to call a function defined within a plug-in created for versions of FileMaker Pro prior to 7. A plug-in must be installed (located in the Extensions folder) and enabled (under the Plug-Ins tab of Preferences) for you to have access to its functions.

The function name and parameter syntax for an external function is defined by the plug-in developer. When calling external plug-ins, be sure to use the exact syntax specified in the documentation for the plug-in. The external function parameter can generally be passed as a field, as long as the contents of the field conform to the requirements set forth by the plug-in developer. Because only a single parameter may be passed to a function, parameters often consist of delimited lists of data, which are then parsed and interpreted inside the plug-in.

The External function syntax is not used by plug-ins created for FileMaker Pro 7 and later. Rather, the plug-in's functions have the same syntax and appearance as any other FileMaker calculation function; the function name and parameters are defined by the plug-in developer.

Examples:

```
External ( "myPlugin"; "param1|param2|param3" )

External ( "myPlugin"; myParamField )
```

Factorial()

Syntax:

Factorial (number {; numberOfFactors })

Data type returned: **Number** *Category:* **Number**

Parameters:

- **number**—Any expression that resolves to a positive integer.
- **numberOfFactors**—Any expression that resolves to a positive integer, representing how many factors to include in the factorial multiplication.

Parameters in curly braces { } are optional.

Description:

Returns the factorial of number, stopping either at 1 or stopping after the optional numberOfFactors. The factorial of a number *n* is defined as *n* * (*n*–1) * (*n*–2) * (*n*–3)...*1. Factorials are useful in statistics and combinatorics. In mathematics, factorials are usually represented by an exclamation mark. 4! = Factorial (4) = 4 * 3 * 2 * 1 = 24.

One application of factorials is to determine how many unique ways a set of objects can be ordered. For instance, a set of three objects {A, B, C} can be ordered 3! = 6 ways: {ABC, ACB, BAC, BCA, CAB, CBA}.

Examples:

Function	Results
Factorial (3)	Returns 6, which = 3 * 2 * 1.
Factorial (10; 3)	Returns 720, which = 10 * 9 * 8.

FieldBounds()

Syntax:

FieldBounds (fileName; layoutName; fieldName)

Data type returned: **Text** *Category:* **Design**

Parameters:

- **fileName**—Name of the file where the field resides.
- **layoutName**—Name of the layout where the field resides.
- **fieldName**—Name of a field on the specified layout.

Description:

Returns the physical position and rotation of a field that is described by the parameters. Note that the parameters are text and must either be expressions or be enclosed in quotation marks. Results are returned as a space-delimited text string in the form of "Left Top Right Bottom Rotation." The first four of these values represent the distance in pixels from either the left margin of the layout (in the case of Left and Right) or the top margin (in the case of Top and Right). The Rotation value will be 0, 90, 180, or 270, depending on the field's orientation on the layout.

The values returned are delimited by spaces; the MiddleWords() function can easily be used to parse them.

Be aware that changing the name of a file, layout, or field may cause literal references to them to be broken in functions that use FieldBounds.

The field name that is passed to FieldBounds() must be the name from the Manage Database dialog (not the field label); if a field appears on the layout more than once, the one that is farthest in the rear in the layering order will be used.

Related fields must be referenced by TableOccurenceName::FieldName.

Examples:

Function	Results
FieldBounds (myFile; myLayout; myField)	Might return 444 84 697 98 0.
FieldBounds (Get (FileName); Get (LayoutName); InvoiceDate)	Might return 138 48 391 62 0.

FieldComment()

Syntax:

FieldComment (fileName; fieldName)

Data type returned: **Text** *Category:* **Design**

Parameters:

- **fileName**—The name of an open file where the field is located.
- **fieldName**—The name of the field for which to return comments.

Description:

Returns the contents of any comment that has been entered in the Manage Database dialog for the specified field. The syntax Table::fieldName is required to reference fields outside the current table context. (The safest approach is to use this method in all cases.)

FieldComment() is useful for documenting a database. Care must be taken, however, because literal references to fields can be broken when file, table, or field names are changed. FieldNames() and TableNames() can be used to dynamically investigate all field names and load the results from FieldComment() into tables for browsing.

A field comment may contain a maximum of 30,000 characters, though it's doubtful such a large comment would constitute a sound development practice.

Examples:

Function	Results
FieldComment ("myDatabase"; "Contacts::FirstName")	Returns the comment, if any, for the FirstName field as it appears in the table definition.

FieldIDs()

Syntax:

FieldIDs (fileName; layoutName)

Data type returned: **Text** *Category:* **Design**

Parameters:

- **fileName**—The name of an open FileMaker database from which to return IDs.
- **layoutName**—The name of the layout from which to return field IDs.

Description:

Returns a list of the internal FileMaker field IDs for all fields on layoutName in fileName, separated by carriage returns. Fields outside the current table context are returned as TableID::RelatedFieldID. If layoutName is empty, the field IDs of the first table created (the "default" table) are returned.

Calls to FieldIDs() can be broken when file and layout names are changed. Field IDs are assigned by FileMaker and cannot be changed. In our practice we do not recommend using Field IDs when other means may exist to accomplish your needs.

Examples:

Function	Results
FieldIDs ("Invoices"; "List View")	Returns IDs of all unique fields, including related fields, on the List View layout in the Invoices file. In this case the returned data might be: 3 4 8::12

The last entry represents a field with ID of 12, from a table with an ID of 8.

FieldNames()

Syntax:

FieldNames (fileName; layout/tableName)

Data type returned: **Text** *Category:* **Design**

Parameters:

- **fileName**—The name of an open FileMaker database from which to return field names.
- **layout/tableName**—The name of the layout or table to reference.

Description:

Returns a carriage return-delimited list of field names.

When a table name is given (and is not also serving as a layout name), all fields for that table are returned. If a layout has the same name as a table, FileMaker will turn first to the layout in question and return only those fields that have been placed on that layout.

FieldNames() can be used to dynamically generate database structure information about any open FileMaker database.

When information about fields in a table is returned, the results are ordered according to the creation order of the fields. When the names of the fields on a particular layout are returned, the results are ordered according to the stacking order of the fields, from back to front. If an object appears on a layout more than once, it appears multiple times in the result list. Related fields appear as TableOccurrenceName::FieldName.

Examples:

Function	Results
FieldNames (Get (FileName); "Customers")	Returns a list of fields found in the table named Customers in the current database (assuming there isn't a layout named "Customers").

FieldRepetitions()

Syntax:

FieldRepetitions (fileName; layoutName; fieldName)

Data type returned: **Text** *Category:* **Design**

Parameters:

- **fileName**—The name of an open file where the field to be referenced is located.
- **layoutName**—The name of the layout where the field to be referenced is located.
- **fieldName**—The name of the field for which to return repetition information.

Description:

Returns a space-delimited text string that indicates the number of repetitions and orientation of the field in question. Note that you must pass a layout name. (A table name does not work.) The data is returned in the format of "NumRepetitions Orientation." The orientation will be either "vertical" or "horizontal."

The MiddleWords() function can be used to extract either component of the result.

If literal names of objects are used, calls to the function may be broken when file or object names are changed. Functions such as Get (FileName), LayoutNames(), and FieldNames() can be used to dynamically return information about a database. Also remember that only the number of repetitions that appear on the layout are returned, not the number of repetitions defined in the Manage Database dialog. Use FieldType() to return the number of repetitions specified in Manage Database.

Examples:

Function	Results
FieldRepetitions (Get (FileName); "Invoice_Detail"; "Payment_History")	Might return a string like 10 vertical.

FieldStyle()

Syntax:

FieldStyle (fileName; layoutName; fieldName)

Data type returned: **Text** *Category:* **Design**

Parameters:

- **fileName**—The name of an open file where the field is located.
- **layoutName**—The name of the layout where the field is used.
- **fieldName**—The name of the field for which to return results.

Description:

Returns a space-delimited string indicating the field style and any associated value list. The data is returned in the format of "Style {ValueListName}." The field styles are

Standard

Scrolling

Popuplist

Popupmenu

Checkbox

RadioButton

Calendar

Calls to FieldStyle() that rely on literal object names may be broken if file, layout, or field names are changed.

Examples:

Function	Results
FieldStyle (Get (FileName); "Invoice_Detail"; "Notes")	Might return Scrolling for a notes field that has scrollbars turned on.
FieldStyle (Get (FileName); "Invoice_Detail"; "Paid")	Might return RadioButton Yes_No for a field formatted as a radio button that uses a value list called Yes_No.

FieldType()

Syntax:

FieldType (fileName; fieldName)

Data type returned: **Text** *Category:* **Design**

Parameters:

- **fileName**—The name of an open file where the field is located.
- **fieldName**—The name of the field for which to return results.

Description:

Returns a space-delimited string indicating the field type of the field specified by fieldName. There are four components to the string, each of which can contain several possible values. The possible values for each item are

Item 1: Standard, StoredCalc, Summary, UnstoredCalc, or Global

Item 2: Text, Number, Date, Time, Timestamp, or Container

Item 3: Indexed or Unindexed

Item 4: Number of repetitions (1 for a nonrepeating field)

fieldName must be specified as Table::Field when referencing fields in tables outside the current table context. Using the Table::Field method for referencing fields as a matter of course avoids broken references when the current table context changes.

Examples:

Function	Results
FieldType (Get (FileName); "Contacts::ContactID")	Might return a string that looks like this: Standard Number Indexed 1.
FieldType (Get (FileName); "Contacts::gTempName")	Might return a string that looks like this: Global Text Unindexed 1.

Filter()

Syntax:

Filter (textToFilter; filterText)

Data type returned: **Text** *Category:* **Text**

Parameters:

- **textToFilter**—Any expression that resolves to a text string.
- **filterText**—A set of characters to preserve within the specified textToFilter.

Description:

The Filter() function strips from textToFilter all the characters not explicitly listed in filterText. All remaining characters are returned in the order in which they exist in textToFilter, including duplicates. If filterText doesn't have any characters, an empty string is returned, as opposed to a question mark. The Filter() function is case sensitive.

The Filter() function is frequently used to ensure that users have entered valid data into a field. The textToFilter parameter should contain any valid characters; the order of the characters within textToFilter isn't important.

Examples:

Function	Results
Filter ("ab123"; "abc")	Returns ab.
Filter (PhoneNumber; "0123456789")	Would strip any non-numeric characters from the PhoneNumber field.

FilterValues()

Syntax:

FilterValues (textToFilter; filterValues)

Data type returned: **Text** *Category:* **Text**

Parameters:

- **textToFilter**—A return-delimited text string or expression that generates a return-delimited text string.
- **filterValues**—A return-delimited text string or expression that generates a return-delimited text string representing values that you want to preserve within the specified textToFilter.

Description:

FilterValues() produces a return-delimited list of items in textToFilter that are included among the specified filterValues. With the exception of case, to be included in the returned list an item in textToFilter must exactly match an item in filterValues.

Values are returned in the order they appear in textToFilter. If filterValues is an empty string, or if no items in textToFilter are contained in the filterValues list, an empty string is returned.

FilterValues() can be used to determine whether a particular item is part of a return-delimited array. For instance, the WindowNames() function produces a return-delimited list of windows. If you wanted to know whether a window named Contact Detail existed, you could use the following formula:

```
ValueCount ( FilterValues ( WindowNames; "Contact Detail" ))
```

If the value count is anything other than zero that means the window name was found. The benefit of using FilterValues() for this rather than PatternCount() is that it will correctly exclude a window named Contact Detail - 2 from the returned list. PatternCount (WindowNames; "Contact Detail") would match partial names of windows and not entire item names.

Examples:

Function	Results
FilterValues (Offices; "San Francisco¶Philadelphia¶Chicago")	Returns Chicago¶Philadelphia when Offices contains: Chicago¶Philadelphia¶San Mateo.

Floor()

Syntax:

Floor (number)

Data type returned: **Number** *Category:* **Number**

Parameters:

- **number**—Any expression that resolves to a numeric value.

Description:

Returns number rounded down to the next lower integer.

For positive numbers, Floor() and Int() return the same results; however, for negative numbers, Int() returns the next larger integer, whereas Floor() returns the next smaller integer.

One use of Floor() is for generating random whole numbers. For instance, if you wanted to generate a random whole number between 0 and 9, you could use the formula Floor (Random * 10).

Examples:

Function	Results
Floor (1.0005)	Returns 1.
Floor (-1.0005)	Returns –2.
Floor (3)	Returns 3.

FV()

Syntax:

FV (payment; interestRate; periods)

Data type returned: **Number** *Category:* **Financial**

Parameters:

- **payment**—The nominal amount of the payment.
- **interestRate**—The per-period interest rate.
- **periods**—The number of periods in the duration of the investment.

Description:

Returns the future value of a periodic investment based on the payments and interest rate for the number of periods specified.

The FV() function doesn't account for the present value of your investment, and it assumes that payments are made at the end of each period.

Examples:

Function	Results
FV (50; .10; 2)	Returns 105, indicating the amount of money you would have after making two periodic deposits of $50 into an investment that paid 10% per period.

If the investment compounds monthly, divide the annual interestRate by 12 to express the periods as a number of months.

To figure out the future value of monthly investments of $250, earning 8% interest, for 10 years, you would use the formula FV (250; .08/12; 10 * 12) which returns 45736.51.

Get(AccountName)

Syntax:

Get (AccountName)

Data type returned: **Text** *Category:* **Get**

Parameters: None

Description:

Returns the name of the authenticated account being used by the current user of the database file. If a user is logged in under the default Admin account, Admin is returned. If a user is using the FileMaker Pro guest account, [Guest] is returned.

For external server authentication, Get (AccountName) returns the name of the authenticated account being used by the current user of the database file, not the group to which the user belongs. (The group name appears in the Account list when you define accounts and privileges in FileMaker Pro.) If an individual belongs to more than one group (account), the first group name listed when you View By Authentication Order while defining accounts and privileges determines access for the user.

Get (AccountName) can be used to retrieve the account name of the current user for purposes of logging or auditing database access.

Examples:

Function	Results
Get (AccountName)	Returns klove when the current user is logged in with the klove account.

Get(ActiveFieldContents)

Syntax:

Get (ActiveFieldContents)

Data type returned: **Text, Number, Date, Time, Timestamp, Container**

Category: **Get**

Parameters: None

Description:

Returns the contents of the field in which the cursor is currently placed. The contents of the field need not be highlighted.

Get (ActiveFieldContents) can return the contents of fields of any data type, but the field in which you place those contents may need to be of the same data type for it to display properly.

Note that in the case where the cursor is not placed in a field, a blank value is returned, as opposed to a question mark.

Examples:

Function	Results
Get (ActiveFieldContents)	Returns Rowena when the current field contains the name Rowena.

Get(ActiveFieldName)

Syntax:

Get (ActiveFieldName)

Data type returned: **Text** *Category:* **Get**

Parameters: None

Description:

Returns the name of the field in which the cursor is currently placed.

Even when the active field is a related or unrelated field from another table, Get (ActiveFieldName) simply returns the field's name. It does *not* use the double-colon syntax "relationshipName::FieldName."

Note that in the case where the cursor is not placed in a field, a blank value is returned, as opposed to a question mark.

Examples:

Function	Results
Get (ActiveFieldName)	Returns Name_First when the cursor is in the Name_First field.

Get(ActiveFieldTableName)

Syntax:

Get (ActiveFieldTableName)

Data type returned: **Text** *Category:* **Get**

Parameters: None

Description:

Returns the name of the table occurrence for the field in which the cursor is currently placed.

Note that the table occurrence name (from the Relationships Graph) is returned, rather than the source table name.

Note that in the case where the cursor is not placed in a field, a blank value is returned, as opposed to a question mark.

Examples:

Function	Results
Get (ActiveFieldTableName)	Might return Contacts2.

Get(ActiveLayoutObjectName)

Syntax:

Get (ActiveLayoutObjectName)

Data type returned: **Text** *Category:* **Get**

Parameters: None

Description:

Returns the name of the currently active layout object. Any object on a layout can be assigned a name using the Object Info palette. If no object is active, or if the currently active object has not been assigned a name, this function returns an empty string.

Examples:

Function	Results
Get (ActiveLayoutObjectName)	Might return DetailTab.

Get(ActiveModifierKeys)

Syntax:

Get (ActiveModifierKeys)

Data type returned: **Number** *Category:* **Get**

Parameters: None

Description:

Returns the sum of the constants that represent the modifier keys that the user is pressing on the keyboard. The constants for modifier keys are as follows:

1—Shift

2—Caps lock

4—Control

8—Alt (Windows) or Option (Mac OS)

16—Command key (Mac OS only)

When using Get() functions within field definitions, in most cases you should set the storage option to be "unstored" so that the field always displays current data.

Examples:

Function	Results
Get (ActiveModifierKeys)	Returns 4 if the Control key is being held down
	Returns 7 (1+2+4) if the Shift, Caps Lock, and Control keys are being held down.

The following formula can be used to show text values for keys being held down; it can be used in a calculated field or a custom function:

```
Let ( keys = Get (ActiveModifierKeys);
   Case ( Mod ( keys; 2 ); "Shift ") &
   Case ( Int ( Mod ( keys; 4 ) / 2 ); "Caps Lock ") &
   Case ( Int ( Mod ( keys; 8 ) / 4 ); "Control ") &
   Choose ( 2 * ( Int ( Mod ( keys ; 16 ) / 8)) +
      (Abs ( Get ( SystemPlatform )) - 1);
      "";""; "Option "; "Alt ")&
   Case ( keys >= 16; "Command")
)
```

If the user is holding down the Shift, Caps Lock, and Control keys when this function is evaluated, the text values for those keys are returned in the form of Shift, Caps Lock, and Control.

Get(ActiveRepetitionNumber)

Syntax:

Get (ActiveRepetitionNumber)

Data type returned: **Number** *Category:* **Get**

Parameters: None

Description:

Returns the number of the active repetition (the repetition in which the cursor currently resides) for a repeating field. Repetition numbers start with 1.

If the cursor is not in a field, 0 is returned.

Examples:

Function	Results
Get (ActiveRepetitionNumber)	Would return 2 when a user was clicked into the second repetition of a field.

Get(ActiveSelectionSize)

Syntax:

Get (ActiveSelectionSize)

Data type returned: **Number** *Category:* **Get**

Parameters: None

Description:

Returns the number of characters highlighted in the current field. The function returns 0 if no characters are highlighted, and returns a blank value if no field is active. When multiple windows are open (which leads to the possibility of multiple highlighted selections), only the active window is considered.

Carriage returns, tabs, spaces, and other invisible characters are counted by Get (ActiveSelectionSize).

Examples:

Function	Results
Get (ActiveSelectionSize)	Would return 10 if a user had highlighted 10 characters in any field in the active window.

Get(ActiveSelectionStart)

Syntax:

Get (ActiveSelectionStart)

Data type returned: **Number** *Category:* **Get**

Parameters: None

Description:

Returns the position of the first character in the highlighted text of the current field. If no text is highlighted (that is, the user has simply clicked into a block of text), the current position of the cursor is returned. It returns a blank value if no field is active. When multiple windows are open, only the active window is considered.

Remember that carriage returns, tabs, spaces, and other invisible characters are taken into account when evaluating Get (ActiveSelectionStart).

Used in conjunction with Get (ActiveSelectionSize), you can determine the string that a user has highlighted in any field, using the formula

```
Middle ( Get (ActiveFieldContents); Get (ActiveSelectionStart) ; Get (ActiveSelectionSize))
```

Examples:

Function	Results
Get (ActiveSelectionStart)	Returns 1 if the user has selected an entire field, or if the insertion point is at the beginning of a field.

Get(AllowAbortState)

Syntax:

Get (AllowAbortState)

Data type returned: **Number** *Category:* **Get**

Parameters: None

Description:

Returns 1 if Allow User Abort is On; returns 0 if Allow User Abort is Off.

If the setting for User Abort hasn't been explicitly set, a script runs as if Allow User Abort is On. Get (AllowAbortState) returns 1 in such cases.

Examples:

In the following script

```
Allow User Abort [Off]
Show Custom Dialog [Get ( AllowAbortState ) ]
```

the custom dialog would display 0.

In the following script

```
Allow User Abort [On]
Show Custom Dialog [Get ( AllowAbortState ) ]
```

the custom dialog would display 1.

Get(AllowToolbarState)

Syntax:

Get (AllowToolbarState)

Data type returned: **Number** *Category:* **Get**

Parameters: None

Description:

Developers may control whether users can make toolbars visible via the Allow Toolbars script step. This companion function returns a Boolean value representing whether toolbars are allowed to be visible. It returns 1 if toolbars are allowed; 0 if they are not.

By default, toolbars are allowed.

Examples:

Function	Results
Get (AllowToolbarState)	Returns 1 if toolbars are allowed to be visible.

Get(ApplicationLanguage)

Syntax:

Get (ApplicationLanguage)

Data type returned: **Text** *Category:* **Get**

Parameters: None

Description:

Returns a text string representing the current application language. The possible results are as follows:

English

French

Italian

German

Swedish

Spanish

Dutch

Japanese

The string returned will always be in English, even in versions of the product based on other languages. That is, it returns German, not Deutsch, in the German language version of FileMaker.

Examples:

Function	Results
Get (ApplicationLanguage)	Would return English for users using an English-language version of FileMaker Pro.

Get(ApplicationVersion)

Syntax:

Get (ApplicationVersion)

Data type returned: **Text** *Category:* **Get**

Parameters: None

Description:

Returns a text string representing the application and version of FileMaker in use by the current user:

Pro (version)	For FileMaker Pro
ProAdvanced (version)	For FileMaker Advanced

Runtime (version)	For FileMaker Runtime
Web (version)	For FileMaker Web Client in cases where IWP is being hosted from FileMaker Pro or Pro Advanced
Web Publishing Engine (version)	For FileMaker Server Advanced Web hosting

If you have allowed web access to a database, you may want to add conditional tests within some of your scripts so that they will behave differently for web and FileMaker Pro clients. To identify web users, use either of the following formulas:

```
PatternCount ( Get ( ApplicationVersion ); "Web")

Position ( Get ( ApplicationVersion ); "Web"; 1; 1)
```

If either of these returns anything other than 0, the user is a web client.

Examples:

Function	Results
Get (ApplicationVersion)	Returns ProAdvanced 9.0v1 for FileMaker Pro Advanced 9.0v1.

If you were to create an unstored calculation field with the formula Get (ApplicationVersion), and then extracted the data as XML via Custom Web Publishing, you may get

```
<field name="AppVersion">
  <data>Web Publishing Engine 9.0v1</data>
</field>
```

Get(CalculationRepetitionNumber)

Syntax:

Get (CalculationRepetitionNumber)

Data type returned: **Number** *Category:* **Get**

Parameters: None

Description:

Returns the current repetition number of a calculation field. If the calculation is not set to allow more than one value, Get (CalculationRepetitionNumber) returns 1.

Get (CalculationRepetitionNumber) is nothing more than the repetition number and doesn't imply or require that a particular field is active.

You can use the repetition number in conditional tests involving repeating fields. For instance, the following formula:

```
If (Get ( CalculationRepetitionNumber ) < 4; "foo"; "boo")
```

returns a repeating calculation field with values foo, foo, foo, boo, boo, and so on.

Examples:

Function	Results
Get (CalculationRepetitionNumber)	Returns 1 in the first repetition of a repeating field, 2 in the second repetition, and so on, up to the maximum number of repetitions the field has been defined to hold.

A calculation field defined to hold five repetitions and which has the following formula:

```
Get ( CalculationRepetitionNumber ) ^ 2
```

returns the repetition values 1, 4, 9, 16, 25.

Get(CurrentDate)

Syntax:

Get (CurrentDate)

Data type returned: **Date** *Category:* **Get**

Parameters: None

Description:

Returns the current date according to the operating system calendar.

The format of the result varies based on the date format that was in use when the database file was created. In the United States, dates are generally in the format MM/DD/YYYY. You can change a computer's date format in the Clock, Language, and Region Control Panel (Windows Vista), the Regional Settings Control Panel (Windows 2000), the Date and Time Control Panel (Windows XP), or the Date & Time System Preference (Mac OS X).

If the result is displayed in a field, it is formatted according to the date format of the field in the current layout.

When using Get() functions within field definitions, in most cases you should set the storage option to be "unstored" so that the field always displays current data.

Examples:

Function	Results
DayName (Get (CurrentDate) - 30)	Returns the day name for the date 30 days prior to today.
Get (CurrentDate) - InvoiceDate	Returns the number of days outstanding for a given invoice.

Get(CurrentHostTimestamp)

Syntax:

Get (CurrentHostTimestamp)

Data type returned: **Timestamp** *Category:* **Get**

Parameters: None

Description:

Returns the current timestamp (date and time) according to the host's system clock, to the nearest second.

Get (CurrentHostTimestamp) returns the date and time from the host machine, regardless of the date and time settings on the client machine. Get (CurrentHostTimestamp) is therefore useful for storing information about when records are created or edited because it disregards differences in time zones or improper settings of the client machines.

Function calls that run on the server may impact a network user's performance, especially when they are used in unstored calculations.

Examples:

Function	Results
Get (CurrentHostTimestamp)	Returns 1/1/2004 11:30:01 AM when the system clock on the host machine shows January 1, 2004, 11:30:01 AM.

Get(CurrentTime)

Syntax:

Get (CurrentTime)

Data type returned: **Time** *Category:* **Get**

Parameters: None

Description:

Returns the current time from the local system clock (on the client machine).

Note that the Time data type is stored internally as the number of seconds since midnight. Math can be performed on all Time() functions using multiples of seconds (60 = 1 minute, 3600 = 1 hour).

Remember that the time returned by Get (CurrentTime) is the local time on the system clock of the client machine. In cases where clients are accessing a database from different time zones, or someone has his clock set incorrectly, this data may be less useful than time extracted from the host machine's system clock with the Get (CurrentHostTimestamp) function.

When using Get() functions within field definitions, in most cases you should set the storage option to be "unstored" so that the field always displays current data.

Examples:

Function	Results
Get (CurrentTime) + 3600	Returns the time one hour from now.
Get (CurrentTime)	Returns the current time from the local system clock.

Get(CurrentTimestamp)

Syntax:

Get (CurrentTimestamp)

Data type returned: **Timestamp** *Category:* **Get**

Parameters: None

Description:

Returns the current timestamp (date and time) according to the local system clock to the nearest second.

Note that a timestamp is stored internally as an integer that represents the number of seconds since midnight on 1/1/0001. Therefore, calculations that use seconds as the base unit can be performed on timestamp data types.

Get (CurrentTimestamp) uses the date and time settings of the local machine (client) and may be less useful or accurate than Get (CurrentHostTimeStamp) in a database that is accessed by clients from different time zones.

Examples:

Function	Results
Get (CurrentTimestamp)	Might return 1/25/2004 8:28:05 PM.
GetAsDate (Get (CurrentTimestamp))	Extracts the date from a timestamp.
GetAsTime (Get (CurrentTimestamp))	Extracts the time from a timestamp.

Get(CustomMenuSetName)

Syntax:

Get (CustomMenuSetName)

Data type returned: **Text** *Category:* **Get**

Parameters: None

Description:

Returns the name of the active custom menu set. If the active menu set is the Standard FileMaker Menus (which is the initial default for all files), a blank value is returned.

Examples:

Function	Results
Get (CustomMenuSetName)	Returns SalesMenuSet when a custom menu set called SalesMenuSet has been defined and is active. Returns an empty string when the [Standard FileMaker Menus] menu set is active.

Get(DesktopPath)

Syntax:

Get (DesktopPath)

Data type returned: **Text**

Category: **Get**

Parameters: None

Description:

Returns the path to the desktop folder for the current user's computer. In Windows, the path format is /Drive:/Documents and Settings/UserName/Desktop/. In the Mac OS, the path format is /DriveName/Users/UserName/Desktop/.

Note that the user in this case is the operating system user account and should not be confused with the account with which a user logged in to a given database.

Examples:

Function	Results
Get (DesktopPath)	Might return /C:/Documents and Settings/Kai/Desktop/ for a user named Kai in Windows. Might return /MacintoshHD/Users/Erlend/Desktop/ for a user named Erlend in the Mac OS.

Get(DocumentsPath)

Syntax:

Get (DocumentsPath)

Data type returned: **Text**

Category: **Get**

Parameters: None

Description:

Returns the path to the documents folder for the current user. In Windows, the path format is /Drive:/Documents and Settings/UserName/My Documents/. In the Mac OS, the path format is /DriveName/Users/UserName/Documents/.

Note that the user in this case is the operating system user account and should not be confused with the account with which a user logged in to a given database.

Examples:

Function	Results
Get (DocumentsPath)	Returns /C:/Documents and Settings/Kai/My Documents/ for a user named Kai in Windows. Returns /MacintoshHD/Users/Erlend/Documents/ for a user named Erlend in the Mac OS.

Get(ErrorCaptureState)

Syntax:

Get (ErrorCaptureState)

Data type returned: **Number** *Category:* **Get**

Parameters: None

Description:

Returns 1 if Set Error Capture has been set to On, and 0 if Set Error Capture was either not set or set to Off.

It is not possible to tell with the Get (ErrorCaptureState) function whether Error Capture was explicitly turned off or simply not set.

Examples:

In the following script

```
Set Error Capture [Off]
Show Custom Dialog [ Get ( ErrorCaptureState ) ]
```

the custom dialog displays 0.

In the following script

```
Set Error Capture [On]
Show Custom Dialog [ Get ( ErrorCaptureState ) ]
```

the custom dialog displays 1.

Get(ExtendedPrivileges)

Syntax:

Get (ExtendedPrivileges)

Data type returned: **Text** *Category:* **Get**

Parameters: None

Description:

Returns a delimited list of extended privileges, separated by carriage returns, currently assigned for use by the active account in a given database file. Extended privileges are additional access rights assigned to a privilege set; they control such things as access via the Web, via ODBC/JDBC, and via FileMaker Networking, but developers can add their own extended privileges as well.

If the user's privilege set doesn't have any extended privileges enabled, Get (ExtendedPrivileges) returns an empty list.

To test whether a user has a certain extended privilege, use the following formula:

```
ValueCount ( FilterValues (Get ( ExtendedPrivileges ); "salesNorthWestRegion" ))
```

If this formula returns 0, the user does not have the specified extended privilege.

Examples:

If the currently logged-in account uses a privilege set that includes the extended privileges of Access via Instant Web Publishing (keyword fmiwp) and Access via FileMaker Network (keyword fmapp), Get (ExtendedPrivileges) returns fmiwp¶fmapp.

Get(FileMakerPath)

Syntax:

Get (FileMakerPath)

Data type returned: **Text** *Category:* **Get**

Parameters: None

Description:

Returns the path to the folder of the currently running copy of FileMaker Pro. In Windows, the path format is /Drive:/Program Files/FileMaker/FileMaker Pro 9/. In the Mac OS, the path format is /DriveName/Applications/FileMaker Pro 9/. (The actual path may vary if FileMaker was installed in a nonstandard location.)

Examples:

Function	Results
Get (FileMakerPath)	Returns /C:/Program Files/FileMaker/FileMaker Pro 9/ in Windows. Returns /MacintoshHD/Applications/FileMaker Pro 9/ in the Mac OS.

Get(FileName)

Syntax:

Get (FileName)

Data type returned: **Text** *Category:* **Get**

Parameters: None

Description:

Returns the filename of the current database file without the file extension.

Get (FileName) is useful in function calls that require a filename, even if the current file is being referenced. This way, if the filename changes, you don't need to change any of your calculation formulas.

If a calculation field in file Alpha.fp7 contains the formula Get (FileName), and that field is displayed on a layout in another file, Beta.fp7, via an external table occurrence, the field value will still return Alpha.

Examples:

Function	Results
Get (FileName)	Returns the value Contacts when the current database file is named Contacts.fp7.
GetNextSerialValue (Get (FileName); "Contacts:: PrimaryContactID")	Returns the next PrimaryContactID from the Contacts table in the current file. This function call is far less fragile than hard-coding the filename into the preceding expression. If the filename changes at some point in the future, this expression will continue to work as expected.

Get(FilePath)

Syntax:

Get (FilePath)

Data type returned: **Text** *Category:* **Get**

Parameters: None

Description:

Returns the full path to the currently active database file, including the file extension.

Returns file:/driveletter:/databaseName for local files in Windows.

Returns file://volumename/myfoldername/databaseName for remote files in Windows.

Returns file:/path/databaseName for local and remote files in the Mac OS.

Returns fmnet:/networkaddress/databaseName for FileMaker Pro networked files.

Remember that Get (FilePath) includes the filename and extension. Text parsing functions can be used to extract just the file path from the results returned by Get (FilePath). This can be useful for building dynamic paths to objects that are in the same directory as the current file.

If a field in file Alpha.fp7 contains the formula Get (FilePath), and that field is displayed on a layout in another file, Beta.fp7, via an external table occurrence, the field value will still return the file path for file Alpha.

Examples:

Function	Results
Get (FilePath)	Returns the current file path.
Left (Get (FilePath); Position (Get (FilePath); Get (FileName); 1; 1) -1)	Returns just the path to the current file's directory. The Position() function truncates the path before the filename.

Get(FileSize)

Syntax:

Get (FileSize)

Data type returned: **Number** *Category:* **Get**

Parameters: None

Description:

Returns the size of the current file in bytes.

Examples:

If the current file size is 1,404,928 bytes, Get (FileSize) returns 1404928.

Function	Results
Round (Get (FileSize) / 1024; 0)	Returns 1372, the file size in KB.
Round (Get (FileSize) / 1048576; 2)	Returns 1.34, the file size in MB.

Get(FoundCount)

Syntax:

Get (FoundCount)

Data type returned: **Number** *Category:* **Get**

Parameters: None

Description:

Returns a number that represents the number of records in the current found set.

If multiple windows are open in the current database file, each window can have its own found set. If the Get (FoundCount) function is used in a script, it returns the found count of the active layout in the active window.

Get (FoundCount) is often used in scripts, following finds, to determine navigation paths. In the following script, if one record is found, the Detail layout is shown. If multiple records are found, the List layout is shown. Finally, if no records are found, the script notifies the user with a dialog box.

```
If [ Get ( FoundCount ) = 1 ]
  Go To Layout [ Detail ]
Else If [ Get ( FoundCount ) > 1 ]
  Go To Layout [ List ]
Else
  Show Custom Dialog ["Empty Set"; "No Records Found"]
End If
```

Examples:

If 240 records are in the current found set, Get (FoundCount) returns 240.

Get(HighContrastColor)

Syntax:

Get (HighContrastColor)

Data type returned: **Text** *Category:* **Get**

Parameters: None

Description:

Windows only: Returns the name of the current high-contrast default color scheme. Returns an empty value (null) if Use High Contrast is unavailable or inactive, or if the function is called on the Mac OS.

Use High Contrast is an option under Control Panel, Accessibility Options, Display tab (Windows XP), and under Control Panel, Appearance and Personalization, Ease of Access Center, Set up High Contrast (Windows Vista). The standard options increase default font sizes and heighten screen contrast to assist users with impaired vision.

Examples:

Function	Results
Get (HighContrastColor)	Returns High Contrast White (large) when the Use High Contrast option in Windows XP is active and Black on White (large) is selected. Returns High Contrast White on Windows Vista when Use High Contrast option is active and Black on White is selected. Notice that the size indicator is not returned on Windows Vista. Returns High Contrast Black (large) when the Use High Contrast option in Windows XP is active and White on Black (large) is selected. Returns the name of the custom color scheme when the Use High Contrast option in Windows XP is active and a custom color scheme is selected. Returns null if the Use High Contrast option is not selected or if the computer is a Macintosh.

Get(HighContrastState)

Syntax:

Get (HighContrastState)

Data type returned: **Number** *Category:* **Get**

Parameters: None

Description:

Windows only: Returns a number representing the state of the Use High Contrast option in the Accessibility Options control panel.

Returns:

0 if Use High Contrast is unavailable, inactive, or if the function is used on the Mac OS.

1 if Use High Contrast is available and active.

Examples:

If you have users with impaired vision, you might create alternate versions of your layouts that are easier for them to use. If so, you can test in your navigation scripts whether Use High Contrast is active and go to an appropriate layout or zoom the window.

```
If [ Get ( HighContrastState ) = 1 ]
   Go to Layout ["ContactDetail (HC)"]
Else
   Go to Layout ["ContactDetail"]
End If
```

Get(HostApplicationVersion)

Syntax:

Get (HostApplicationVersion)

Data type returned: **Text** *Category:* **Get**

Parameters: None

Description:

Returns a text string representing the version of FileMaker Server or FileMaker Pro that is hosting the database file currently in use. If the current database is open as a single-user, nonhosted file, an empty string is returned. Both the name of the product and the version number are included in the output of Get (HostApplicationVersion).

Pro (version)	For FileMaker Pro
ProAdvanced (version)	For FileMaker Advanced
Server (version)	For FileMaker Server

Examples:

Function	Results
Get (HostApplicationVersion)	Returns Server 9.0v1 when a file is hosted by FileMaker Server 9.0 v1.

Get(HostIPAddress)

Syntax:

Get (HostIPAddress)

Data type returned: **Text** *Category:* **Get**

Parameters: None

Description:

Returns the IP address of the host computer for the current database. If the current database is open as a single-user, nonhosted file, an empty string is returned.

Examples:

Function	Results
Get (HostIPAddress)	Returns 14.156.13.121 (as an example) when the current database is being hosted by FileMaker Server on a computer with this IP address.

Get(HostName)

Syntax:

Get (HostName)

Data type returned: **Text** *Category:* **Get**

Parameters: None

Description:

Returns the registered name of the computer hosting the database file.

To change the registered name on a computer:

On Windows XP, the computer name is found on the Network Identification tab of the System Properties control panel. The Full Computer Name option displays the current registered name.

On Windows Vista, the computer name is found within Control Panel, System and Maintenance, System.

On Mac OS, the computer name is found within System Preferences, under the Sharing settings.

If a client connects to a file hosted by FileMaker Server, Get (HostName) returns the name of the server. The host name can be configured with the FileMaker Server Admin Console.

By default, FileMaker Server uses the system's name, but a custom name can be supplied instead.

We find it helpful in our practice to place a field that returns Get (HostName) on a prominent layout within our solutions so that we can see during development whether we're working on a live version, a development version, or a scratch file on our local laptops.

Examples:

If the computer on which FileMaker Server is installed is named "Maturin"

```
Get ( HostName )
```

results in Maturin.

Get(LastError)

Syntax:

Get (LastError)

Data type returned: **Number** *Category:* **Get**

Parameters: None

Description:

Returns the number of the error generated by the most recent script step. If there was no error, Get (LastError) returns 0. Use this function in combination with Set Error Capture [On] to trap and handle errors raised in scripts.

A common source of bugs in scripts is not remembering that the Get (LastError) function returns the error code from only the most recently executed script step. For example, in this script

```
Perform Find []
If [Get ( ErrorCaptureState ) = 0]
   Show Custom Dialog [ Get ( LastError ) ]
End If
```

the Get (LastError) step returns the result of the execution of the If script step, not the error code generated by the Find step.

→ *For a complete listing of error codes, see Chapter 18,* "FileMaker Error Codes."

If a script is running on the Mac OS and calls an AppleScript routine, any errors generated will also be passed through to and presented via this function.

Similarly, if an error occurs in FileMaker while performing an ODBC import or an Execute SQL script step, Get (LastError) returns a string that shows the ODBC error state.

Examples:

Consider the following script:

```
Set Error Capture [ On ]
Print Setup [ Restore ]
Set Variable [ $error; value: Get ( LastError ) ]
```

If the user cancels out of the Print Setup dialog, Get (LastError) returns 1 (user canceled action). If the Print Setup step executes successfully, Get (LastError) returns 0.

Get(LastMessageChoice)

Syntax:

Get (LastMessageChoice)

Data type returned: **Number** *Category:* **Get**

Parameters: None

Description:

Returns a number corresponding to the button clicked as a result of the Show Custom Dialog script step.

Returns:

1 for the default button.

2 for the second button.

3 for the third button.

Though it has a value of 1, the default button on a dialog is always on the far right side. For example, if there are three buttons, they will appear in 3-2-1 (for example, Cancel, Maybe, OK) order.

Examples:

For the following script step, where the default button is labeled OK, the second button is labeled Maybe, and the third button is labeled Cancel:

```
Show Custom Dialog [ "Alert!" ; "Would you like to proceed?" ]
```

If the user chooses OK, Get (LastMessageChoice) returns 1.

If the user chooses Maybe, Get (LastMessageChoice) returns 2.

If the user chooses Cancel, Get (LastMessageChoice) returns 3.

You can then use an If() statement to handle each possibility appropriately. The value will persist and can be retrieved until the user interacts with another custom dialog.

Note that if a custom dialog has input fields, it is only when the user clicks the default rightmost button that the data will be inserted into the input field.

Get(LastODBCError)

Syntax:

Get (LastODBCError)

Data type returned: **Text** *Category:* **Get**

Parameters: None

Description:

Returns a string that shows the ODBC error state (SQLSTATE), as published by ODBC standards, based on ISO/IEF standards.

The ODBC error state is cleared at the time the next ODBC-related script step is performed. Anytime before that happens, you can check to see whether an ODBC error was generated.

By setting the Set Error Capture script step to On, you can suppress the error messages that a user sees during execution of a script that uses ODBC functions.

Examples:

When attempting to execute an SQL statement with an invalid field name, Get (LastODBCError) returns S0022.

If no error is encountered, Get (LastODBCError) returns 00000.

Get(LayoutAccess)

Syntax:

Get (LayoutAccess)

Data type returned: **Number** *Category:* **Get**

Parameters: None

Description:

Returns a number that represents the current user's record access privileges level for the current layout. Privileges are assigned in the Custom Layout Privileges dialog box.

The Get (LayoutAccess) function can be used to alert users of restricted privileges at the layout level. Note that Get (LayoutAccess) returns information about only the current layout. Record access privileges for any other layout are not represented.

Note also that Get (LayoutAccess) does not return information about whether the layout itself is accessible, but rather what access the user has to edit record data via the current layout.

The Get (RecordAccess) function evaluates record access privileges independent of the Get (LayoutAccess) function. To fully evaluate record access, evaluate the return values of both the Get (LayoutAccess) and Get (RecordAccess) functions.

Examples:

Function	Results
Get (LayoutAccess)	Returns 0 if the custom layout privileges of an account's privilege set allow "no access" to records via this layout. Returns 1 if the custom layout privileges of an account's privilege set allow "view only" access to records via this layout. Returns 2 if the custom layout privileges of an account's privilege set allow "modifiable" access to records via this layout.

Get(LayoutCount)

Syntax:

Get (LayoutCount)

Data type returned: **Number** *Category:* **Get**

Parameters: None

Description:

Returns the total number of layouts within a file, including hidden layouts and layouts the user doesn't have privileges to see.

Examples:

Function	Results
Get (LayoutCount)	Returns 3 when there are three layouts in a database file.

Get(LayoutName)

Syntax:

Get (LayoutName)

Data type returned: **Text** *Category:* **Get**

Parameters: None

Description:

Returns the name of the layout currently displayed in the active window.

To change the name of a layout, in Layout mode, go to the Layouts menu, select the Layout Setup menu item, and then click the General tab. Layouts do not need to be uniquely named.

Examples:

Function	Results
Get (LayoutName)	Returns Data Entry when the Data Entry layout is displayed. Returns Invoice List when the Invoice List layout is displayed.

Get(LayoutNumber)

Syntax:

Get (LayoutNumber)

Data type returned: **Number** *Category:* **Get**

Parameters: None

Description:

Returns the number of the layout currently displayed in the active window. The order of layouts can be set in Layout mode by going to the Layouts menu and selecting the Set Layout Order menu item.

Get (LayoutNumber) can be used to keep track of the last layout a user visited. The following script takes a user from one layout to another, allows the user to complete other tasks, and then returns the user to the original layout:

```
Set Variable [ $lastLayout; Get ( LayoutNumber ) ]
Go to Layout ["Other Layout"]
[perform script, process, etc]
Go to Layout [$lastLayout]
```

Examples:

Function	Results
Get (LayoutNumber)	Returns 6 when the sixth layout on the Set Layout Order list is active.

Get(LayoutTableName)

Syntax:

Get (LayoutTableName)

Data type returned: **Text** *Category:* **Get**

Parameters: None

Description:

Returns the name of the table occurrence (not the source table) from which the current layout shows records.

Because there is no way of retrieving the name of the source table with which a layout is associated, consider prefixing the names of table occurrences with an abbreviation that represents the source table. For instance, you might name a table occurrence INV_CustomerInvoices. You can then use text parsing functions to retrieve the source table name from the results returned by the Get (LayoutTableName) function.

Note that when no windows are active or visible, an empty string is returned.

Examples:

Function	Results
Get (LayoutTableName)	Returns INV_Invoices when the current layout is attached to the table occurrence named INV_Invoices. Returns EMP_Employees when the current layout is attached to the table occurrence named EMP_Employees.

Get(LayoutViewState)

Syntax:

Get (LayoutViewState)

Data type returned: **Number** *Category:* **Get**

Parameters: None

Description:

Returns a number that represents the view mode for the current layout in the active window.

Get (LayoutViewState) is useful in scripts to test the state of the current layout. Unless a layout has been restricted not to be viewable in another state, users can manually change the state of the current layout, provided they have access to menu commands. You can detect whether the layout is in the proper state, and if necessary, change it with the View As script step.

Examples:

Get (LayoutViewState) returns 0, 1, or 2, depending on the current layout's view state:

0 = View as Form

1 = View as List

2 = View as Table

Get(MultiUserState)

Syntax:

Get (MultiUserState)

Data type returned: **Number** *Category:* **Get**

Parameters: None

Description:

Returns a number that represents the FileMaker sharing/networking status for the current file.

Returns 0 when network sharing is off, or when network sharing is on but no privilege sets have the [fmapp] Extended Privilege enabled.

Returns 1 when network sharing is on, the database file is accessed from the host computer, and some or all users have the [fmapp] Extended Privilege enabled.

Returns 2 when network sharing is on, the database file is accessed from a client computer, and some or all users have the [fmapp] Extended Privilege enabled.

Examples:

Function	Results
Get (MultiUserState)	Returns 2 whenever a user opens a file using FileMaker Pro as a guest of FileMaker Server.

Get(NetworkProtocol)

Syntax:

Get (NetworkProtocol)

Data type returned: **Text** *Category:* **Get**

Parameters: None

Description:

Returns the name of the network protocol that FileMaker Pro is using on the current machine.

Unlike in previous versions of FileMaker, the only network protocol supported by FileMaker Pro 9 is TCP/IP. Get (NetworkProtocol) always returns TCP/IP, even if FileMaker Network sharing is off.

Examples:

Function	Results
Get (NetworkProtocol)	Returns TCP/IP.

Get(PageNumber)

Syntax:

Get (PageNumber)

Data type returned: **Number** *Category:* **Get**

Parameters: None

Description:

When printing or previewing a document, this function returns the current page number. If nothing is being printed or previewed, Get (PageNumber) returns 0.

If you are printing a report of unknown length and you want to determine the total number of pages, you can have a script go to the last page in Preview mode and capture the value returned by Get (PageNumber) in a global field. This would then allow you to have something like "Page 2 of 5" appear in the footer of your report.

Examples:

Imagine you have an unstored calculation with the formula:

```
"Page " & Get ( PageNumber )
```

When printing a multipage report, this field could be placed in the footer of the layout, and it would return the proper page number when the report was previewed or printed.

Get(PortalRowNumber)

Syntax:

Get (PortalRowNumber)

Data type returned: **Number** *Category:* **Get**

Parameters: None

Description:

Returns the number of the currently selected portal row—a case where either the row itself is selected (highlighted in black) or the cursor is actively sitting within a field in the portal.

When no portal row is selected, Get (PortalRowNumber) returns 0.

Get (PortalRowNumber) should be used to determine with which row a user is working.

→ *See also "GetNthRecord()" later in this chapter.*

Examples:

When the user clicks on the third row of a portal, Get (PortalRowNumber) returns 3.

When the user clicks out of the portal onto the layout itself, Get (PortalRowNumber) returns 0.

Get(PreferencesPath)

Syntax:

Get (PreferencesPath)

Data type returned: **Text** *Category:* **Get**

Parameters: None

Description:

Returns the operating system path to a user's preferences and default options folder. In Windows, the path format is /Drive:/Documents and Settings/UserName/Local Settings/Application Data/. In the Mac OS, the path format is /DriveName/Users/UserName/Library/Preferences/.

Note that the user in this case is the operating system user account and should not be confused with the account with which a user logged in to a given database.

Examples:

Returns /C:/Documents and Settings/Nate/Local Settings/Application Data/ for a user named Nate in Windows.

Returns /MacintoshHD/Users/Eleanor/Library/Preferences/ for a user named Eleanor in the Mac OS.

Get(PrinterName)

Syntax:

Get (PrinterName)

Data type returned: **Text** *Category:* **Get**

Parameters: None

Description:

Returns information about the currently selected printer.

In Windows, Get (PrinterName) returns a text string containing the printer name, driver name, and printer port, separated by commas.

In Mac OS, Get (PrinterName) returns a text string with the name or IP address of the printer, and the name of the print queue, as it appears in the Print Center.

If in either operating system the printer information is unavailable for whatever reason, <Unknown> is returned.

If certain print jobs require that a specific printer be selected, you can test for Get (PrinterName) within a script and ask the user to select a different printer if necessary.

Examples:

In Windows,

```
Get ( PrinterName )
```

might return \\server1\Lexmark Optra M412 PS3, winspool,Ne02:.

In Mac OS X,

```
Get ( PrinterName )
```

may return the IP address 255.5.5.255.

Or it may return the name of the current printer (if the printer is not networked). For example, hp Laserjet 4200.

Get(PrivilegeSetName)

Syntax:

Get (PrivilegeSetName)

Data type returned: **Text** *Category:* **Get**

Parameters: None

Description:

Returns the name of the privilege set assigned to the active user account. Every account must be assigned one, and only one, privilege set. The privilege set defines the data, interface, and functionality constraints that are placed on the user as the user interacts with the database system.

Examples:

Function	Results
Get (PrivilegeSetName)	Returns [Full Access] if you haven't modified the security settings of a new database. Returns Sales if the current user is logged in with an account assigned to the Sales privilege set.

Get(RecordAccess)

Syntax:

Get (RecordAccess)

Data type returned: **Number** *Category:* **Get**

Parameters: None

Description:

Returns a number that represents the current account's access privileges for the current record. Record privileges are assigned via privilege set.

Returns 0 if the user does not have View or Edit privileges for the current record.

Returns 1 if the user has view-only access to the current record. This could mean the View is set to Yes for the current table, or that View is set to Limited and that the calculation defined for Limited access returns a value of True.

Returns 2 if the user has edit access for the current record. This could mean that Edit is set to Yes for the current table, or that Edit is set to Limited and that the calculation defined for Limited access returns a value of True.

The Get (RecordAccess) function can be used to alert users of restricted privileges at the record level. Note that Get (RecordAccess) returns information only about table record privileges. Record access may be restricted through the layout access as well. To fully evaluate current record access, evaluate both the return values of Get (LayoutAccess) and the Get (RecordAccess) functions.

Examples:

Function	Results
Get (RecordAccess)	Returns 1 if a user can view, but not edit, a given record.

Get(RecordID)

Syntax:

Get (RecordID)

Data type returned: **Number** *Category:* **Get**

Parameters: None

Description:

Returns the unique, internal ID number of the current record. This number is generated automatically by FileMaker Pro and does not change. The record ID is assigned sequentially within each table, beginning at 1. Record IDs are not reused; if a record is deleted, its ID is not reassigned.

When files are converted from previous versions, record IDs from the original file are preserved.

The record ID is required for editing and deleting records via Custom Web Publishing, as this is how the record to be changed or deleted must be identified.

Examples:

Function	Results
Get (RecordID)	Returns 275 when the internal FileMaker Pro ID for the current record is 275.

Get(RecordModificationCount)

Syntax:

Get (RecordModificationCount)

Data type returned: **Number** *Category:* **Get**

Parameters: None

Description:

Returns the total number of times the current record has been modified. A record change must be committed before the modification count updates. Committing multiple field changes at once is considered a single record modification. Each time a change is committed, the modification count increases.

Get (RecordModificationCount) can be used by custom web applications to ensure that one user's changes do not overwrite another's. At the time the record is loaded into the web browser, the record modification count can be stored. When the record is saved, the current record modification count can be checked against the stored one to see whether another user has updated the record in the meantime.

Duplicated records retain the same record modification count as the record from which they were created; the count is not reset to zero. There's no way to alter or reset the modification count.

Examples:

Function	Results
Get (RecordModificationCount)	Returns 0 if a record has never been modified. Returns 17 if a record has been modified 17 times since it was originally created.

Get(RecordNumber)

Syntax:

Get (RecordNumber)

Data type returned: **Number** *Category:* **Get**

Parameters: None

Description:

Returns a number that represents the position of a record in the current found set. This value changes depending on the found set and the sort order.

Get (RecordNumber) tells you a record's position within the found set. This is useful if you want to create a calculation to display "X of Y records" on a given layout.

When using Get() functions within field definitions, in most cases you should set the storage option to be "unstored" so that the field always displays current data.

To determine FileMaker's unique internal record ID, use Get (RecordID).

Examples:

Function	Results
Get (RecordNumber)	Returns 1 for the first record in the found set.
	Returns 83 for the 83rd record in a found set of 322 records.

Get(RecordOpenCount)

Syntax:

Get (RecordOpenCount)

Data type returned: **Number** *Category:* **Get**

Parameters: None

Description:

Returns the total number of open, uncommitted records in the current found set. An open record is one in which changes have been made but not yet saved by the user or currently executing script. Note that this function returns information only about the user's own session. It does not allow you to detect whether other users on the network have open records.

The only scenario in which Get (RecordOpenCount) would return a value greater than 1 is if a user is modifying records through a portal. Records modified via a portal remain in an open, uncommitted state until the user submits the parent record, so it's possible to have as many open records as portal rows that have been edited. Editing any portal row also puts the parent record into an open, locked state, so even if no data in the parent record has been modified, Get (RecordOpenCount) will return 2 the moment a user starts editing data in a portal row.

Get (RecordOpenCount) returns information only about open records in the currently active window. It is possible to have open, uncommitted records in windows that are not the active window.

Examples:

Returns 3 if there are three open records in the current window. This would presumably mean that a user had edited data in two portal rows, thereby locking each of those related records as well as the parent record.

Get(RecordOpenState)

Syntax:

Get (RecordOpenState)

Data type returned: **Number** *Category:* **Get**

Parameters: None

Description:

Returns a number representing the open/committed status of the current record.

Returns 0 for a closed or committed record.

Returns 1 for a new record that hasn't been committed.

Returns 2 for a modified record that hasn't been committed.

Get (RecordOpenState) provides information only about the status of records in the given user's session. It does not provide information about the state of a record that is being modified by another user on the network. To determine whether another user is editing a record, use the Open Record/Request script step, then test whether that action was successful by looking at the value returned by Get (LastError).

Examples:

Returns 1 if the current record is a new record that hasn't been saved.

Get(RequestCount)

Syntax:

Get (RequestCount)

Data type returned: **Number** *Category:* **Get**

Parameters: None

Description:

Returns the total number of find requests defined in the current window.

Get (RequestCount) can be used in scripted find routines to see whether the user has added any find requests to the default request. It is also useful as a boundary condition if you ever need to loop through all the find requests and either capture or set search parameters.

Examples:

If the current find request asks for invoices with values greater than $200.00,

Get (RequestCount) returns 1.

If the current find request asks for invoices with values greater than $200 or invoices with dates after 1/1/2004,

Get (RequestCount) returns 2.

Get(RequestOmitState)

Syntax:

Get (RequestOmitState)

Data type returned: **Number** *Category:* **Get**

Parameters: None

Description:

Returns 1 if the Omit check box is selected in Find mode; otherwise, returns 0. One use of this function would be as part of a routine for capturing and logging user find requests. Get (RequestOmitState) lets you know whether the user had clicked the Omit check box for a given find request.

Examples:

Returns 1 when the Omit check box is selected in the current find request.

Get(ScreenDepth)

Syntax:

Get (ScreenDepth)

Data type returned: **Number** *Category:* **Get**

Parameters: None

Description:

Returns the number of bits needed to represent the color or shade of gray of a pixel on the user's monitor. A value of 8, for instance, represents 256 (equal to 2^8) colors or shades of gray.

Use Get (ScreenDepth) to alert users if their monitor color settings are set too low to view images correctly. For example,

```
If [ Get ( ScreenDepth ) < 32 ]
  Show Custom Dialog ["Color";"Your monitor should be set to "Millions
  of colors" to display images correctly"]
End If
```

Examples:

Function	Results
Get (ScreenDepth)	Returns 32 on a display showing millions (2^32) of colors. Returns 16 on a display showing thousands (2^16) of colors. Returns 4 on a VGA display. Returns 1 on a black-and-white display.

Get(ScreenHeight)

Syntax:

Get (ScreenHeight)

Data type returned: **Number** *Category:* **Get**

Parameters: None

Description:

Returns the number of pixels displayed vertically on the current screen. This corresponds to a user's operating system settings for display resolution.

Note when the active window spans more than one screen, this function calculates the value for the screen that contains the largest percentage of the window.

Use Get (ScreenHeight) and Get (ScreenWidth) to check minimum resolution settings on a user's computer.

```
If [ Get ( ScreenHeight ) < 1200 or Get ( ScreenWidth ) < 1600 ]
  Show Custom Dialog ["Resolution";"This application requires a minimum
  of 1600 x 1200 screen resolution."]
  Perform Script ["Close Solution Files"]
End If
```

Examples:

Function	Results
Get (ScreenHeight)	Returns 854 on a monitor set to display at 1280 × 854.

Get(ScreenWidth)

Syntax:

Get (ScreenWidth)

Data type returned: **Number** *Category:* **Get**

Parameters: None

Description:

Returns the number of pixels displayed horizontally on the active screen. This corresponds to a user's operating system settings for display resolution.

Note when the active window spans more than one screen, this function calculates the value for the screen that contains the largest percentage of the window.

See Get (ScreenHeight) for an example of how to check minimum resolution settings on a user's computer.

Examples:

Function	Results
Get (ScreenWidth)	Returns 1280 when the user's monitor is set to display at 1280 × 854 resolution.

Get(ScriptName)

Syntax:

Get (ScriptName)

Data type returned: **Text** *Category:* **Get**

Parameters: None

Description:

Returns the name of the current script even if paused. When no script is running, Get (ScriptName) returns an empty string.

One use of Get (ScriptName) is to capture errors. In this example, the Log Error script takes the script name as a parameter:

```
If [ Get ( LastError ) <> 0]
  Perform Script [ "Log Error"; Parameter: Get ( ScriptName ) ]
End If
```

Passing the current script's name as a script parameter can be useful anytime a subscript can be called by multiple scripts.

Examples:

Function	Results
Get (ScriptName)	Returns Calculate Invoice if the current script is Calculate Invoice.

Get(ScriptParameter)

Syntax:

Get (ScriptParameter)

Data type returned: **Text** *Category:* **Get**

Parameters: None

Description:

Retrieves the parameter that was passed to a currently running script.

The value of a script parameter can be retrieved anywhere within a script, regardless of subscript calls. Script parameters cannot be altered during execution of a script.

Subscripts do not inherit the script parameter of the calling script. Rather, they can be passed parameters of their own that exist only for the duration of the subscript. If you want a subscript to inherit a script parameter, pass Get (ScriptParameter) as the subscript's parameter.

Only one value can be passed as a script parameter, but that value can contain a delimited list, thus allowing multiple values to be passed.

Script parameters can be specified when scripts are performed via buttons and via subscripts, but not when scripts are called manually from the Scripts menu or via a startup or shutdown script.

Examples:

In this example, the Navigate script is called, with the parameter West:

```
Perform Script ["Navigate"; Parameter: "West"]
```

Within the Navigate script, the script parameter value (West) is assigned to a variable ($direction) through the use of the following script step:

```
Set Variable ["$direction"; Get ( ScriptParameter ) ]
```

$direction now equals West.

Get(ScriptResult)

Syntax:

Get (ScriptResult)

Data type returned: **Text, Number, Date, Time, Timestamp, Container** *Category:* **Get**

Parameters: None

Description:

This function allows subscripts to pass results to their calling ("parent") script. Get (ScriptResult) returns whatever value was set by the Exit Script script step.

Note that after all scripts complete execution, no value is stored and Get (ScriptResult) returns a null (or blank) value.

Examples:

Consider a subscript that checks for duplicate records within a found set and passes a count of duplicates as a script result. Any number of scripts within a given solution can then call that subscript and perform a check like so:

```
Case ( Get ( ScriptResult ) > 1; "duplicates exist"; "no duplicates" )
```

Get(SortState)

Syntax:

Get (SortState)

Data type returned: **Number** *Category:* **Get**

Parameters: None

Description:

Returns a number that represents the sort state of the active window.

Get (SortState) can be used in a customized interface where the status area is normally hidden from the user. Also, Get (SortState) can be used to correctly display sort icons in a customized interface.

A sorted found set becomes semisorted if new records are created. Omitting or deleting records does not cause the sort status to change, however. Subsummary reports may not show expected results when the found set is semisorted.

Examples:

Function	Results
Get (SortState)	Returns 0 if the found set in the active window is not sorted. Returns 1 if the found set in the active window is sorted. Returns 2 if the found set in the active window is partially sorted (semisorted).

Get(StatusAreaState)

Syntax:

Get (StatusAreaState)

Data type returned: **Number** *Category:* **Get**

Parameters: None

Description:

Returns a number that represents the state of the status area of the active window.

If you want a single test that will tell you whether the status area is hidden (regardless of whether it's locked), use Mod (Get (StatusAreaState); 3). When this returns 0, the status area is hidden; when it's anything else, the status area is visible.

Examples:

Function	Results
Get (StatusAreaState)	Returns 0 if the status area is hidden.
	Returns 1 if the status area is visible.
	Returns 2 if the status area is visible and locked.
	Returns 3 if the status area is hidden and locked.

Get(SystemDrive)

Syntax:

Get (SystemDrive)

Data type returned: **Text** *Category:* **Get**

Parameters: None

Description:

Returns the drive letter (Windows) or volume name (Mac OS) where the currently running operating system is located.

Examples:

Returns /C:/ in Windows when the operating system is on the C: drive.

Returns /MyDrive/ in the Mac OS when the operating system is on a volume named MyDrive.

Get(SystemIPAddress)

Syntax:

Get (SystemIPAddress)

Data type returned: **Text** *Category:* **Get**

Parameters: None

Description:

Produces a return-delimited list of the IP addresses of all active NIC (Network Interface Controller) cards connected to the computer.

Examples:

Returns 202.27.78.34, for example, when there is only one active network interface.

If a machine were connected to both an Ethernet network and a WiFi network, Get (SystemIPAddress) might return:

```
192.168.101.161
192.168.101.162
```

Get(SystemLanguage)

Syntax:

Get (SystemLanguage)

Data type returned: **Text** *Category:* **Get**

Parameters: None

Description:

Returns the language setting of the user's machine. The returned text is the English language name for a language, regardless of system settings.

Examples:

Function	Results
Get (SystemLanguage)	Returns English on a system set to use English, returns German (as opposed to Deutsch) for a system set to use German.

Get(SystemNICAddress)

Syntax:

Get (SystemNICAddress)

Data type returned: **Text** *Category:* **Get**

Parameters: None

Description:

Produces a return-delimited list containing the hardware addresses of all the NIC (Network Interface Controller) cards connected to the machine.

In Windows, you can find this address by typing **ipconfig /All** from a command prompt. On Mac OS X, you can find the NIC address by using the Apple System Profiler utility.

If the user's machine has multiple NIC cards, Get (SystemNICAddress) generates a return-delimited list of all their addresses. You might, for instance, have both a built-in Ethernet card and a wireless networking card installed in a laptop. Or, a server might have multiple built-in Ethernet ports. In both of these cases, Get (SystemNICAddress) returns the addresses of both devices.

Examples:

Function	Results
Get (SystemNICAddress)	Might return 00:30:65:cf:df:98.

Get(SystemPlatform)

Syntax:

Get (SystemPlatform)

Data type returned: **Number** *Category:* **Get**

Parameters: None

Description:

Returns a number that represents the current platform on a user's computer.

Because FileMaker tends to change or add to the values in the platform-checking function (as new versions of operating systems become supported), checks against this function should be performed in a single, central location for ease of future updates. The results of the function may be stored in a global variable during startup and then referred to for subsequent platform checks throughout the rest of the database. We recommend using a custom function for this purpose.

To test whether the user is on a Mac platform, you can use the formula Abs (Get (SystemPlatform)) = 1 rather than testing separately for a postive and a negative 1.

Examples:

Function	Results
Get (SystemPlatform)	Returns -1 if the current platform is a PowerPC-based Mac.
	Returns 1 if the current platform is an Intel-based Mac.
	Returns -2 if the platform is Windows XP or Windows Vista.

Get(SystemVersion)

Syntax:

Get (SystemVersion)

Data type returned: **Text** *Category:* **Get**

Parameters: None

Description:

Returns the current operating system version level.

The values returned by Get (SystemVersion) will change as new versions of operating systems become available. As with checks against Get (SystemPlatform), you should try to perform tests of the system version in a single, central location within your files so that it will be easy to update in the future. We recommend using a custom function for this purpose.

Examples:

Function	Results
Get (SystemVersion)	Returns 10.5 for Mac OS X version 10.5. Returns 6.0 for Windows Vista. Returns 5.1 for Windows XP (SP 2).

Get(TemporaryPath)

Syntax:

Get (TemporaryPath)

Data type returned: **Text** *Category:* **Get**

Parameters: None

Description:

Returns the path to the temporary folder that FileMaker Pro uses on the user's computer. If you have script routines that need to generate temporary files (for example, for export/import routines), consider placing them in this folder so as not to interfere with the user's workspace. In Windows, the path format is /Drive:/Documents and Settings/UserName/Local Settings/Temp. In the Mac OS, the path format is /DriveName/private/var/tmp/folders/501/TemporaryItems/FileMaker/.

Note that the user in this case is the operating system user account and should not be confused with the account with which a user logged in to a given database.

Examples:

Function	Results
Get (TemporaryPath)	Might return /C:/Documents and Settings/Nate/Local Settings/Temp for a user named Nate in Windows. Might return /MacintoshHD/private/var/tmp/folders/501/TemporaryItems/FileMaker/ for a user on the Mac OS.

Get(TextRulerVisible)

Syntax:

Get (TextRulerVisible)

Data type returned: **Number** *Category:* **Get**

Parameters: None

Description:

Returns a Boolean value by which to determine whether the text ruler is visible. Returns 1 if the text ruler is displayed; otherwise, returns 0.

Examples:

Returns 1 when the current user's text ruler is visible.

Get(TotalRecordCount)

Syntax:

Get (TotalRecordCount)

Data type returned: **Number** *Category:* **Get**

Parameters: None

Description:

Returns the total number of records in the current source table, regardless of the state of the found set.

The Get (TotalRecordCount) function is most often used in unstored calculations and scripts. In an unstored calculation, Get (TotalRecordCount) returns the same value regardless of which table occurrence context is specified for the calculation. When using Get (TotalRecordCount) in a script, be sure to navigate to a layout that establishes the correct table context before referencing the function.

The total record count includes records that have been created but not yet committed. If such records are reverted, the total record count is decreased.

Examples:

Function	Results
Get (TotalRecordCount)	Returns 283 when there are 283 records in the current table, regardless of the size of the current found set.

Get(UserCount)

Syntax:

Get (UserCount)

Data type returned: **Number** *Category:* **Get**

Parameters: None

Description:

Returns the number of clients currently accessing the file, including the current user.

Only FileMaker Pro client connections are counted by the Get (UserCount) function. Web, ODBC, and JDBC connections are not counted.

Examples:

Function	Results
Get (UserCount)	Returns 4 if a database file is hosted via peer-to-peer networking and there are 3 clients and the host connected to the file. Returns 28 if a file is hosted by FileMaker Server and there are 28 clients connected to the current file.

Get(UserName)

Syntax:

Get (UserName)

Data type returned: **Text** *Category:* **Get**

Parameters: None

Description:

Returns the username that has been established for the current user's copy of FileMaker Pro. This username is specified on the General tab of the Preferences dialog and can be set to return either the system name or a custom name.

The returned name is the same for anyone opening any database on the machine, regardless of what account name and password he has used. It's an application-level setting, not a document-level setting. The username can always be manually changed, regardless of whatever security you've set up. For these reasons we recommend against using it.

For greater security, use Get (AccountName) to track and manage user access; a user cannot change the account name used to log in to a database file.

Examples:

Function	Results
Get (UserName)	Returns Delilah Bean when the user-specified name is Delilah Bean.

Get(UseSystemFormatsState)

Syntax:

Get (UseSystemFormatsState)

Data type returned: **Number** *Category:* **Get**

Parameters: None

Description:

This function is used to determine whether the option to Use System Formats (in the File Menu, File Options dialog, Text tab) is explicitly turned on. It returns a Boolean value representing the state of the Use System Formats option: 1 if Use System Formats is on; otherwise, returns 0.

Note that developers can use the Set Use System Formats script step to control this setting as well.

Examples:

Returns 1 when the option to Always Use Current System Settings is selected.

Returns 0 when the option to Always Use File's Saved Settings is selected.

Returns 0 when the option to Ask Whenever Settings Are Different is selected.

Get(WindowContentHeight)

Syntax:

Get (WindowContentHeight)

Data type returned: **Number** *Category:* **Get**

Parameters: None

Description:

Returns the height, in pixels, of the content area of the current window. The content area is the area inside a window's frame and doesn't include the title bar, scrollbars, or the Status Area.

Keep in mind that the relationship of the content area dimensions to the overall window dimensions are different on each platform. Because the script steps that control window sizing specify the overall window dimensions, a similarly sized window will have a different content area size on the Mac OS than it does on Windows.

Use Get (WindowHeight) to determine the outside height dimension of the current window.

Examples:

Function	Results
Get (WindowContentHeight)	On the Mac OS, returns 563 when the current window height is 600. The title bar and bottom scrollbar make up the other 37 pixels.

Get(WindowContentWidth)

Syntax:

Get (WindowContentWidth)

Data type returned: **Number** *Category:* **Get**

Parameters: None

Description:

Returns the width, in pixels, of the content area of the current window. The content area is the area inside a window's frame and doesn't include the title bar, scrollbars, or the status area.

Keep in mind that the relationship of the content area dimensions to the overall window dimensions are different on each platform. Because the script steps that control window sizing specify the overall window dimensions, a similarly sized window will have a different content area size on the Mac OS than it does on Windows.

Use Get (WindowWidth) to determine the outside width dimension of the current window.

Examples:

Function	Results
Get (WindowContentWidth)	On the Mac OS, returns 785 when the current window width is 800 and the status area is not showing. In the same window, if the status area is visible, the function returns 716.

Get(WindowDesktopHeight)

Syntax:

Get (WindowDesktopHeight)

Data type returned: **Number** *Category:* **Get**

Parameters: None

Description:

Returns the height, in pixels, of the desktop space.

In Windows, the desktop space is the FileMaker Pro application window. Get (WindowDesktopHeight) measures the total vertical space used by the application window. If the application is maximized, the application window height is the screen height, minus the height of the Start menu (if it's placed on the bottom of the screen).

On Mac OS X, the desktop space includes everything on the screen except the top menu.

You cannot programmatically set the window desktop height or width, nor on Windows can you tell where the application window has been positioned on the user's monitor.

Examples:

Function	Results
Get (WindowDesktopHeight)	Returns 746 in the Mac OS when the current monitor's resolution is set to 1152 × 768. The menu bar accounts for the other 22 pixels of height.

Get(WindowDesktopWidth)

Syntax:

Get (WindowDesktopWidth)

Data type returned: **Number** *Category:* **Get**

Parameters: None

Description:

Returns the width, in pixels, of the desktop space.

In Windows, the desktop space is the FileMaker Pro application window. Get (WindowDesktopWindow) measures the total horizontal space used by the application window. If the application is maximized, the application window width is the screen width, minus the width of the Start menu (if it's placed on the side of the screen).

On Mac OS X, the desktop space includes everything on the screen except the top menu.

You cannot programmatically set the window desktop height or width, nor on Windows can you tell where the application window has been positioned on the user's monitor.

Examples:

Function	Results
Get (WindowDesktopWidth)	Returns 1152 in the Mac OS when the current monitor's resolution is set to 1152 × 768.

Get(WindowHeight)

Syntax:

Get (WindowHeight)

Data type returned: **Number** *Category:* **Get**

Parameters: None

Description:

Returns the total height, in pixels, of the current window. The current window is usually the foreground window, but it's also possible for a script to run in a window that isn't the active foreground window.

The window height and width return the outside dimensions of a window. So, if you make a new window and specify a height and width of 300, the Get (WindowHeight) and Get (WindowWidth) would both return 300.

Be aware that the window height and width are different from the window content height and width, which return the inside dimensions of a window.

Examples:

Function	Results
Get (WindowHeight)	Returns 541 when the window that is being acted upon is 541 pixels tall.

Get(WindowLeft)

Syntax:

Get (WindowLeft)

Data type returned: **Number** *Category:* **Get**

Parameters: None

Description:

Returns the horizontal distance, in pixels, from the outer left edge of a window to the left edge of the application window on Windows or screen on Mac OS.

See Get (WindowDesktopHeight) for a discussion of how the application window is defined for each platform.

If any docked toolbars are placed along the left edge of the application window, the position of the origin shifts inward. The Get (WindowLeft) function is relative to the inside edge of the application window, inclusive of docked toolbars.

Get (WindowLeft) can return negative numbers. This may indicate the window is located on a second monitor positioned to the left of the first, or it may mean that a portion of the left side of the window is hidden.

Examples:

Function	Results
Get (WindowLeft)	Returns 0 when the left edge of the window being acted upon is flush with the left edge of the application window.

Get(WindowMode)

Syntax:

Get (WindowMode)

Data type returned: **Number** *Category:* **Get**

Parameters: None

Description:

Returns a number that indicates the mode of the active window.

Returns 0 for Browse mode.

Returns 1 for Find mode.

Returns 2 for Preview mode.

Returns 3 if printing is in progress.

Returns 4 for Layout mode.

If a script ever attempts to operate within the context of a window that is in Layout mode, the window is automatically switched to Browse mode and the script continues as expected.

Examples:

Function	Results
Get (WindowMode)	Assuming a window is in Browse mode, returns 0.

Get(WindowName)

Syntax:

Get (WindowName)

Data type returned: **Text** *Category:* **Get**

Parameters: None

Description:

Returns the name of the current window. The current window is usually the foreground window, but it's also possible for a script to run in a window that isn't the active foreground window.

The name of a window is the text string that appears in the window's title bar. A window's name can be specified when it is created with the New Window script step. It can also be altered with the Set Window Title script step.

Window names do not need to be unique. If a user manually creates a new window, the name of the new window will be the same as the active window at the time the user selected New Window, but will have a - 2 (or higher number if necessary) appended to it.

Examples:

Function	Results
Get (WindowName)	Returns Contacts if the window being acted upon is named Contacts.

Get(WindowTop)

Syntax:

Get (WindowTop)

Data type returned: **Number** *Category:* **Get**

Parameters: None

Description:

Returns the vertical distance, in pixels, from the top edge of a window to the inside of the top of the application window.

See Get (WindowDesktopHeight) for a discussion of how the application window is defined for each platform.

If any docked toolbars are placed along the top of the application window, this shifts the location of the inside edge of the application window.

Get (WindowTop) can return negative numbers. This may indicate the window is located on a second monitor positioned above the first, or it may mean that a portion of the top of the window is hidden.

Examples:

Function	Results
Get (WindowTop)	Returns 0 when the top edge of a window is positioned flush to the top of the application window.

Get(WindowVisible)

Syntax:

Get (WindowVisible)

Data type returned: **Number** *Category:* **Get**

Parameters: None

Description:

Returns a number indicating whether the current window is visible or hidden.

Returns 1 if the window is visible.

Returns 0 if the window is hidden.

When you call a subscript in another file, it operates from the context of the frontmost window in that file, but that window does not need to become the active window. The current window can therefore be different from the active, foreground window, and it can either be hidden or visible.

Examples:

Function	Results
Get (WindowVisible)	Returns 1, assuming the current window is visible.

Get(WindowWidth)

Syntax:

Get (WindowWidth)

Data type returned: **Number** *Category:* **Get**

Parameters: None

Description:

Returns the total width, in pixels, of the current window. Note that a window retains all its properties, such as height and width, even if it is hidden.

The window height and width measure the outside dimensions of a window, whereas the window content height and window content width measure the inside dimensions of a window.

Window height and width can be assigned when creating and resizing windows using the New Window and Move/Resize Window script steps.

Examples:

Function	Results
Get (WindowWidth)	Returns 650 when the window that is being acted upon is 650 pixels wide.

Get(WindowZoomLevel)

Syntax:

Get (WindowZoomLevel)

Data type returned: **Text** *Category:* **Get**

Parameters: None

Description:

Returns the zoom state (percentage) for the current window.

In Windows, an asterisk appears next to the zoom percentage when the Enlarge Window Contents to Improve Readability option is selected in the General tab of the Preferences dialog box.

Examples:

Returns 400 when the current window's zoom percentage is set to 400.

Returns 200* in Windows when the current window's zoom percentage is set to 200 and the Enlarge Window Contents to Improve Readability option is selected.

GetAsBoolean()

Syntax:

GetAsBoolean (data)

Data type returned: **Number** *Category:* **Data**

Parameters:

- **data**—Any field or expression that returns a text string, number, date, time, timestamp, or container.

Description:

Returns 0 if the expression or data passed into the function has a numeric value of 0 or is empty. All other values return 1.

Examples:

Function	Results
GetAsBoolean (myField) where myField = "hello":	Returns 0.
GetAsBoolean (myField) where myField = -1000:	Returns 1.
GetAsBoolean (myField) where myField = 0:	Returns 0.
GetAsBoolean (myField) where myField is empty:	Returns 0.

GetAsCSS()

Syntax:

GetAsCSS (text)

Data type returned: **Text** *Category:* **Text**

Parameters:

- **text**—Any expression that resolves to a text string.

Description:

GetAsCSS() returns a representation of the specified text string, marked up with CSS (Cascading Style Sheet) tags. CSS can capture rich text formatting that has been applied to a text string.

Representing formatted text as CSS means that you can export stylized text and have it rendered properly by CSS-aware applications, such as web browsers.

GetAsCSS() is also useful within FileMaker Pro itself because you can determine what special formatting, if any, has been applied to a field.

Examples:

The field myField contains Go Team and has manually been formatted as follows:

Font = Helvetica, Font Size = 36 points, Font Color = red, Font Style = bold.

GetAsCSS (myField) returns

```
<SPAN STYLE= "font-size: 36px;color: #AA0000;font-weight: bold;">Go Team</SPAN>
```

GetAsDate()

Syntax:

GetAsDate (text)

Data type returned: **Date** *Category:* **Text**

Parameters:

- **text**—Any text expression or text field that returns a date, formatted the same as the date format on the system where the file was created.

Description:

GetAsDate () interprets a text string that contains a date as an actual date. Anytime you use a date constant within a calculation formula, you should use the GetAsDate() or Date() functions to ensure that the date is interpreted correctly.

Note: To avoid errors, we recommend always using four-digit years; however, GetAsDate ("1/1") will resolve to 1/1/2008 assuming the current year is 2008. GetAsDate ("1/1/05") will resolve to 1/1/0005.

Examples:

Function	Results
GetAsDate ("1/1/2004")	Returns 1/1/2004 stored internally as a date.
GetAsDate ("1/1/2004") + 8	Returns 1/9/2004. In this case, had the GetAsDate() function not been used, "1/1/2004" + 8 would have returned 112012.

GetAsNumber()

Syntax:

GetAsNumber (text)

Data type returned: **Number** *Category:* **Text**

Parameters:

- **text**—Any valid text expression that contains numbers.

Description:

GetAsNumber() returns only the numbers from a text string, as a data type number. All non-numeric characters are dropped from the string.

Use GetAsNumber() to strip all non-numeric characters out of a text string. For instance, you might have a phone number field to which you want to apply some formatting. GetAsNumber (PhoneNumber) returns just the numeric characters from the field, stripping all punctuation and spaces, so that you can then apply whatever new formatting you want.

GetAsNumber() can also be applied to date and time fields to coerce the data into its integer representation. For instance,

```
GetAsNumber ( Get ( CurrentDate ))
```

returns 731689 when the date is 4/18/2004.

Examples:

Function	Results
GetAsNumber ("abc123")	Returns 123.
GetAsNumber ("$100.10")	Returns 100.1.

GetAsSVG()

Syntax:

GetAsSVG (text)

Data type returned: **Text** *Category:* **Text**

Parameters:

- **text**—Any expression that resolves to a text string.

Description:

GetAsSVG() returns a representation of the text string, marked up in SVG (Scalable Vector Graphics) format. SVG can capture rich text formatting that has been applied to a text string.

SVG format can be used to transfer formatted text from FileMaker to other applications. You can also test an SVG-formatted version of a text string to determine what, if any, formatting has been applied to the string.

Examples:

The field myField contains two phrases, Go Team and Hello World!, each with some text formatting applied to it.

```
GetAsSVG ( myField )
```

might return:

```
<StyleList>
<Style#0>"font-size: 36px;color: #AA0000;font-weight: bold;text-align: left;",
 Begin: 1, End: 8</Style>
<Style#1>"color: #000000;font-weight: normal;font-style:normal;text-align:
 left;", Begin: 9, End: 20</Style>
</StyleList>
<Data>
<Span style="0">Go Team </Span>
<Span style="1">Hello World!</Span>
</Data>
```

GetAsText()

Syntax:

GetAsText (data)

Data type returned: **Text** *Category:* **Text**

Parameters:

- **data**—Any field or expression that returns a number, date, time, timestamp, or container.

Description:

GetAsText() returns the text equivalent of data in any other data type. You can then manipulate the data as you would any other text string.

When applied to a container field that stores a reference to an object, GetAsText() returns the path to the container data. If the container data is embedded in the database, GetAsText() returns a question mark.

One frequent use of GetAsText() is to get the path and filename information for container data stored as a reference. You can then parse the path information and build links to other objects in the same location.

In most cases, you do not need to explicitly coerce number, date, and time data into text before performing text operations on the data. Text functions operate on numbers, dates, and times as if they were text strings, even if you don't wrap the data with GetAsText().

Examples:

Function	Results
GetAsText (Get (CurrentDate))	Might return 3/8/2007.

GetAsTime()

Syntax:

GetAsTime (text)

Data type returned: **Time** *Category:* **Text**

Parameters:

- **text**—Any text expression or text field containing a time.

Description:

GetAsTime() returns the data specified in the text string as data-type time. The value can then be manipulated like any other time data.

Examples:

Function	Results
GetAsTime ("01:30:30")	Returns 1:30:30 AM when you specify Time as the calculation result.
GetAsTime ("01:30:30")	Returns 1/1/0001 1:30:30 AM when you specify Timestamp as the calculation result.

You can also use GetAsTime() when working with literal time strings in calculation formulas.

```
GetAsTime ("15:30:00") - FinishTime
```

would yield the elapsed time between 3:30 p.m. and the FinishTime.

GetAsTimestamp()

Syntax:

GetAsTimestamp (text)

Data type returned: **Timestamp** *Category:* **Text**

Parameters:

- **text**—Any text string or text, number, date, or time field.

Description:

GetAsTimestamp() converts a timestamp contained in a text string into a data-type timestamp. It can then be used in formulas as any other timestamp would be.

GetAsTimestamp() also converts numbers into timestamps. See the Timestamp() function for more information on how timestamps can be represented as numbers.

Use GetAsTimestamp() anytime you include a literal string containing a timestamp in a calculation formula. For instance, to find out the amount of time (in seconds) that has elapsed between a fixed time in the past and now, you would use the following formula:

```
Get ( CurrentTimestamp ) - GetAsTimestamp ( "6/29/1969 4:23:56 PM" )
```

Examples:

Function	Results
GetAsTimestamp ("1/1/2004 1:10:10")	Returns 1/1/2004 1:10:10.
GetAsTimeStamp (61997169000)	Returns 8/12/1965 7:50:00 PM.

GetField()

Syntax:

GetField (fieldName)

Data type returned: **Text, Number, Date, Time, Timestamp, Container**

Category: **Logical**

Parameters:

- **fieldName**—A text string, field, or expression that returns a text string, which contains the name of a field.

Description:

Returns the contents of the fieldName field.

Essentially, GetField() provides a level of abstraction when retrieving the contents of a field. Instead of saying “Give me the value of the FirstName field,” for instance, it’s like saying “Give me the value of the field whose name is in the gWhatField field.” By putting a different field name in the gWhatField field, you can retrieve the contents of a different field.

The Evaluate() function can always be used in place of the GetField(). For instance, Evaluate (gSelectColumn) and GetField (gSelectColumn) both return the same result. The opposite is not true, however. Evaluate() can perform complex evaluations and can have trigger conditions defined, whereas GetField() can retrieve only the contents of a field.

Examples:

Function	Results
GetField ("myField")	Returns the contents of myField.
GetField (myField)	Returns the contents of FirstName, when myField contains the string "FirstName".
GetField (GetValue (fieldList; counter))	Returns the contents of the LastName field, when fieldList is a return-delimited list of field names containing "FirstName¶LastName¶City¶State¶Zip" and counter is 2.

GetLayoutObjectAttribute()

Syntax:

GetLayoutObjectAttribute (objectName ; attributeName {; repetitionNumber ; portalRowNumber})

Data type returned: **Text** *Category:* **Logical**

Parameters:

- **objectName**—A string or text expression that represents the name of an object on the current layout.
- **attributeName**—A string or text expression that represents the name of a supported attribute.
- **repetitionNumber**—A number or expression that returns a number specifying which repetition number of a repeating field you want to retrieve information about. This is an optional parameter.
- **portalRowNumber**—A number or expression that returns a number specifying which portal row you want to retrieve information about. This is an optional parameter.

Description:

Returns various information about the specified object. Objects are named using the Object Info palette. Using GetLayoutObjectAttribute() you can retrieve information about such things as the location, content, and formatting of the object.

The attributes about which you can retrieve information are the following:

Attribute Name	Value Returned
objectType	The object's type, in English: field, text, graphic, line, rectangle, rounded rectangle, oval, group, button group, portal, tab panel, web viewer, and unknown.
hasFocus	1 (True) if the object is currently active; otherwise, returns 0 (False). Objects that can have the focus are fields, portals, tab panels, and groups. Also returns 1 for a portal when a portal row is selected.
containsFocus	1 (True) if the object is currently active or if it contains an active object; otherwise, it returns 0 (False). Objects that can contain the focus are fields, portals, tab panels, and groups.
isFrontTabPanel	1 (True) if the object is the active tab panel.
bounds	A space-delimited list with five values representing the position (in pixels) of the object and its rotation. Unlike the FieldBounds() function, which returns a field's position relative to the upper-left corner of the active window, the values are relative to the bottom-left corner of the FileMaker menu bar (including any docked toolbars). The five values returned by the bounds attribute can be retrieved independently using the left, right, top, bottom, and rotation attributes.
left	The distance (in pixels) of the left edge of the object from the left edge of the FileMaker menu bar.
right	The distance (in pixels) of the right edge of the object from the left edge of the application window.
top	The distance (in pixels) of the top edge of the object from the bottom of the FileMaker menu bar.
bottom	The distance (in pixels) of the bottom edge of the object from the bottom of the FileMaker menu bar.
width	The width (in pixels) of the object.
height	The height (in pixels) of the object.
rotation	The rotation (in degrees: 0, 90, 180, 270) of the object.
startPoint	The position (horizontal and vertical, in pixels, separated by a space) of the start point of a line object, relative to the bottom-left corner of the FileMaker menu bar. Other object types will return the position of the object's top-left corner.
endPoint	The position (horizontal and vertical, in pixels, separated by a space) of the end point of a line object, relative to the bottom-left corner of the FileMaker menu bar. Other object types will return the position of the object's bottom-right corner.
source	A description of the source of the specified object, which varies for different types of objects. Web viewers: The current URL. Fields: The fully qualified field name (tableOccurrenceName::fieldName). Text objects: The text of the object itself, not including merge fields. Portals: The related table occurrence name. Graphics: Image data, such as the image name, type, and/or file path.

Attribute Name	Value Returned
content	The content of the specified object, which varies for different types of objects. Web viewers: The source code of the page being displayed. Fields: The data contained in the field, formatted using the specified object's properties. Text objects: The text of the object itself, including merge fields. Graphics: Image data, such as the image name, type, and/or file path.
enclosingObject	The name of the layout object that encloses the specified object. Only groups, tab panels, and portals can contain other objects.
containedObjects	A list of the object names contained within the specified object. Only groups, tab panels, and portals can contain other objects.

Examples:

Function	Results
GetLayoutObjectAttribute ("FirstName field"; "hasFocus")	Returns 1 if the user is clicked into the object named FirstName field.
GetLayoutObjectAttribute ("FirstName field"; "content")	Returns Fred when the content of the object named FirstName field is Fred.
GetLayoutObjectAttribute ("myObject"; "bounds")	Might return 452 85 502 105 0.
GetLayoutObjectAttribute ("myObject"; "enclosingObject")	Returns InfoTab if myObject is contained on a tab panel object named InfoTab.

GetNextSerialValue()

Syntax:

GetNextSerialValue (fileName; fieldName)

Data type returned: **Text** *Category:* **Design**

Parameters:

- **fileName**—A string or text expression that represents the name of an open file.
- **fieldName**—A string or text expression that represents the name of the field for which to return results.

Description:

Returns the next value for a field defined to auto-enter a serialized value.

It is good practice to use the TableOccurrence::FieldName syntax to reference the field in this formula so that it can be evaluated in any context. Without explicitly naming a table occurrence, this function assumes the field can be found in the current context, which may not be the case. Because the auto-entered serial number is defined at the table level, it doesn't matter which of a table's occurrences you reference, as they will all return the same result.

Examples:

Function	Results
GetNextSerialValue ("Invoices"; "InvoiceID")	Might return 5435.
GetNextSerialValue (Get (FileName); "Contacts::ContactID")	Might return 84.

GetAsURLEncoded()

Syntax:

GetAsURLEncoded (text)

Data type returned: **Text** *Category:* **Text**

Parameters:

- **text**—A text string or expression that returns a text string.

Description:

Returns an encoded version of text, suitable for use in a URL query. All characters in the text string are converted to UTF-8 format, and all text formatting is removed from the string. All non-alphanumeric characters except underscore (_) are replaced with a percent (%) sign followed by the character's two-digit hexadecimal value.

Use GetAsURLEncoded() anytime you need to include field data in formulas that will be used in URL queries, such as with the Web Viewer and the Open URL script step.

Examples:

Function	Results
GetAsURLEncoded ("Hello World!")	Returns Hello%20World!.
GetAsURLEncoded ("</the end>")	Returns %3C%2Fthe%20end%3E.

GetNthRecord()

Syntax:

GetNthRecord (fieldName; recordNumber)

Data type returned: **Text, Number, Date, Time, Timestamp, Container**

Category: **Logical**

Parameters:

- **fieldName**—The name of a related field, or of a field in the current table.
- **recordNumber**—An integer representing the record number from which you want data.

Description:

Returns the contents of fieldName from the provided recordNumber.

When fieldName is a field in the current table, recordNumber refers to a record's position within the current found set. When fieldName is a related field, recordNumber refers to a record's position within the set of related records, regardless of the found set. The order of related records is determined by the Sort setting in the Edit Relationship dialog; if no sort order is specified, the records are ordered by their creation order.

Note that the rules governing storage and indexing for related calculation values apply to GetNthRecord() just as they do for other functions. The result of an expression containing GetNthRecord() will not update when a related value is referenced unless it is set to be an unstored calculation or unless the relationship is reset/refreshed somehow.

Examples:

Function	Results
GetNthRecord (First Name; 2)	Returns the contents of the First Name field for record 2 of the current found set in the current table.
GetNthRecord (LastName; Get (RecordNumber) + 1)	Returns the contents of the LastName field for the next record in the current found set. Using this formula, you might set a ToolTip to show the next and previous names in a found set.
GetNthRecord (Contacts::LastName; 4)	Returns the contents of the LastName field for the fourth related Contact record.

GetRepetition()

Syntax:

GetRepetition (repeatingField; repetitionNumber)

Data type returned: **Text, Number, Date, Time, Timestamp, Container** *Category:* **Repeating**

Parameters:

- **repeatingField**—Any repeating field, or an expression that returns a reference to a repeating field.
- **repetitionNumber**—A positive integer representing the repetition number to retrieve.

Description:

Returns the contents of the specified repetition of a repeating field.

A shorthand notation can be used in place of the GetRepetition() function. The repetition number can be placed in square brackets after the name of the repeating field. For instance, GetRepetition (myField; 6) is the same as myField [6].

Examples:

Function	Results
GetRepetition (RepPercentage; 2)	Returns the contents of the second repetition of the RepPercentage field.

If you had a repeating text field called QuoteOfTheDay that contained 20 repetitions, you could extract a random quote using the following formula:

```
Let ( repNumber = Ceiling ( Random * 20 ) ; GetRepetition ( QuoteOfTheDay; repNumber ))
```

GetSummary()

Syntax:

GetSummary (summaryField; breakField)

Data type returned: **Number, Date, Time, Timestamp** *Category:* **Summary**

Parameters:

- **summaryField**—A field of type summary, or an expression that returns a reference to one.
- **breakField**—A field, or an expression that returns a reference to one.

Description:

The GetSummary() function returns the value of summaryField when summarized by breakField. The found set must be sorted by breakField for GetSummary() to return the proper value.

GetSummary() returns the same values that you would see if you were to place the specified summary field in a subsummary report. GetSummary() is necessary when you need to use summarized values in calculation formulas or for display purposes while in Browse mode.

To calculate a grand summary value, use the same summary field for both the summary field and the break field parameters.

Examples:

Given the following record set, sorted by Country, and a summary field called Sum_Sales defined as the Total of Sales:

Country	Region	Sales
U.S.	North	55,000
U.S.	South	45,000
China	North	35,000
China	South	40,000

A field SalesByCountry defined as

```
GetSummary ( Sum_Sales; Country )
```

returns 100,000 for the two U.S. records and returns 75,000 for the two China records.

GetValue()

Syntax:

GetValue (listOfValues; valueNumber)

Data type returned: **Text** *Category:* **Text**

Parameters:

- **listOfValues**—A list of carriage return-delimited values.
- **valueNumber**—A number representing which value to return from the list.

Description:

Returns a single value from a list of carriage return-delimited values. This can be useful in scripting routines for looping through a set of items. Many objects in FileMaker generate return-delimited lists, including value lists, fields formatted as check boxes, and functions such as WindowNames() and Get (ExtendedPrivileges).

Examples:

Function	Results
GetValue ("Red¶Green¶Light Green"; 2)	Returns Green.
GetValue (WindowNames ; 1)	Returns the name of the frontmost window.

Hiragana()

Syntax:

Hiragana (text)

Data type returned: **Text (Japanese)** *Category:* **Text**

Parameters:

- **text**—Any text expression or text field.

Description:

Converts written Japanese Katakana (Hankaku and Zenkaku) text to Hiragana.

Japanese has four written alphabets where it is possible to represent a syllable in a number of different ways. The Hiragana() function, along with the KanaHankaku(), KanaZenkaku(), and Katakana() functions, all enable conversion from one set of alphabetic glyphs to another.

Examples:

Hiragana (アイウエオ) returns あいうえお

Hour()

Syntax:

Hour (time)

Data type returned: **Number** *Category:* **Time**

Parameters:

- **time**—Any valid time value or expression that returns a valid time value.

Description:

The Hour() function returns an integer representing the number of hours specified by the time parameter.

When its parameter represents a specific time of day, the Hour() function returns a value from 0 to 23. To map this into the more familiar 1 to 12 range, you can use the following formula:

```
Mod ( Hour ( time ) -1; 12 ) + 1
```

The Hour() function can return an integer value outside the 0 to 23 range when its parameter represents a duration rather than a specific time of day. For instance, Hour ("65:12:53") returns 65.

Examples:

Function	Results
Hour ("10:45:20")	Returns 10.
Hour ("12:15 am")	Returns 0.
Hour ("11:15 pm")	Returns 23.
Hour (Get (CurrentTime))	Will return a value from 0 to 23.

If()

Syntax:

If (test; result1; result2)

Data type returned: **Text, Number, Date, Time, Timestamp, Container**

Category: **Logical**

Parameters:

- **test**—A logical expression that returns True (1) or False (0).
- **result1**—The expression to evaluate if test is true.
- **result2**—The expression to evaluate if test is false.

Description:

The If() function returns one of two possible results depending on whether the test supplied as the first parameter is True or False. Result1 is returned if the test is true; Result2 is returned if the test is false.

The test parameter should be an expression that returns a numeric or Boolean result. For numeric results, zero and null are both considered false; all other values are considered true.

If the test contains multiple conditions separated by "and" or "or," FileMaker stops evaluating the conditions as soon as it can determine the overall truthfulness of the test. For instance, if the test parameter is IsEmpty(FieldA) and IsEmpty(FieldB), if Field A is not empty, there's no way that the entire expression could be true. FileMaker will not evaluate the other condition involving FieldB, and will return the false result.

You can nest If() statements within one another, but it is usually more efficient to use a Case() statement rather than an If() in such cases.

Examples:

```
If( DayOfWeek (Get ( CurrentDate ))) = 1 ;
  "It's Sunday, no work!"; // true result
  "Get back to work!" // false result
)


If ( myFlagField; graphicTrue; graphicFalse )
```

Looks for a true value (nonzero, nonblank) in myFlagField and displays the correct graphic container.

```
If ( not IsEmpty ( Taxable ) and TaxRate > 0;
  Price + (Price * TaxRate);
  Price
)
```

Int()

Syntax:

Int (number)

Data type returned: **Number** *Category:* **Number**

Parameters:

- **number**—Any expression that resolves to a numeric value.

Description:

Returns the whole number (integer) part of the number parameter without rounding. Digits to the right of the decimal point are dropped.

Note that for positive numbers, Floor() and Int() return the same results; however, for negative numbers, Int() returns the next larger integer, whereas Floor() returns the next smaller integer.

There are many practical uses for the Int() function. For instance, given any date, to find the date of the Sunday preceding it, use the formula GetAsDate (Int (myDate / 7) * 7). Similarly, to test whether an integer is odd or even, you can test whether Int (num / 2) = num / 2.

Examples:

Function	Results
Int (1.0005)	Returns 1.
Int (-1.0005)	Returns -1.

IsEmpty()

Syntax:

IsEmpty (expression)

Data type returned: **Number** *Category:* **Logical**

Parameters:

- **expression**—Typically a field name, but can be any valid FileMaker Pro calculation formula.

Description:

Returns 1 (True) if the referenced field is empty or if the expression returns an empty string. Returns 0 (False) if the field or expression is not empty.

Remember that zero is a valid entry for a number field. If a number field contains a 0, it is not considered to be empty. If you need to test for zero or null, use GetAsBoolean().

Examples:

Function	Results
IsEmpty (myField)	Returns 1 if myField is empty.
IsEmpty (Name_First & Name_Last)	Returns 1 if the result of concatenating the two fields together is an empty string.

IsValid()

Syntax:

IsValid (expression)

Data type returned: **Number** *Category:* **Logical**

Parameters:

- **expression**—Typically a field name, but can be any valid FileMaker Pro calculation formula.

Description:

Returns either a 1 (True) or a 0 (False), depending on whether the field or expression returns valid data.

IsValid returns a 0 if there is a data type mismatch (for example, text in a date field) or if FileMaker cannot locate the table or field that is referenced. Otherwise, it returns 1, indicating that the data is valid.

Examples:

Function	Results
IsValid (myField)	Returns 1 (True) when myField is present and contains data appropriate to its defined data type.
IsValid (Contacts::Name)	Returns 0 (False) if the current record has no related records in the Contacts table, or if the fields in the records in question all contain invalid data.

IsValidExpression()

Syntax:

IsValidExpression (expression)

Data type returned: **Number** *Category:* **Logical**

Parameters:

- **expression**—A text string containing a calculation expression, or a field or expression that returns a text string that contains a calculation expression.

Description:

Returns 1 (True) if the expression syntax is correct. Returns 0 (False) if the expression has a syntax error.

The IsValidExpression() function is often used in conjunction with the Evaluate() function to ensure that Evaluate() is passed a valid expression. For instance, if users are allowed to enter a formula into a field called myFormula, and you want to have another field express the results of that formula, you could use the following:

```
If ( IsValidExpression ( myFormula ); Evaluate ( myFormula ); "Invalid formula: "
& TextColor ( myFormula; RGB ( 255; 0; 0 )))
```

An expression is considered invalid if it contains syntax errors or if any of the referenced fields cannot be found. Errors that might occur only during execution of the expression, such as record access restrictions, are not detected by the IsValidExpression() formula.

Examples:

Function	Results
IsValidExpression ("Length (SideA)")	Returns 1 (True) as long as there is, in fact, a field named SideA.
IsValidExpression ("Middle (myField; 1)")	Returns 0 (False) because the Middle function requires three parameters to be considered valid syntax.
IsValidExpression (myFormula)	Returns 1 (True) if the contents of myFormula would be considered a valid calculation expression.

KanaHankaku()

Syntax:

KanaHankaku (text)

Data type returned: **Text (Japanese)** *Category:* **Text**

Parameters:

- **text**—Any text expression or text field.

Description:

Converts Zenkaku Katakana to Hankaku Katakana.

Japanese has four written alphabets where it is possible to represent a syllable in a number of different ways. The KanaHankaku() function, along with the KanaZenkaku(), Hiragana(), and Katakana() functions, all enable conversion from one set of alphabetic glyphs to another.

Examples:

KanaHankaku (ﾃﾞｰﾀﾍﾞｰｽ) returns **データベース**

KanaZenkaku()

Syntax:

KanaZenkaku (text)

Data type returned: **Text (Japanese)** *Category:* **Text**

Parameters:

- **text**—Any text expression or text field.

Description:

Converts Hankaku Katakana to Zenkaku Katakana.

Japanese has four written alphabets where it is possible to represent a syllable in a number of different ways. The KanaZenkaku() function, along with the KanaHankaku(), Hiragana(), and Katakana() functions, all enable conversion from one set of alphabetic glyphs to another.

Examples:

KanaZenkaku ("ﾃﾞｰﾀﾍﾞｰｽ") returns **データベース**

KanjiNumeral()

Syntax:

KanjiNumeral (text)

Data type returned: **Text (Japanese)** *Category:* **Text**

Parameters:

- **text**—Any text expression or text field.

Description:

Converts Arabic numerals to Kanji numerals.

In Japanese, numbers are represented by either the Arabic "123… etc." character glyphs or by their Kanji equivalents. KanjiNumeral enables converting from Arabic to Kanji.

Note to convert in the opposite direction from Kanji to Arabic, one can use the GetAsNumber() function.

Examples:

KanjiNumeral (富士見台２の３の２５) returns 富士見台二の三の二五

Katakana()

Syntax:

Katakana (text)

Data type returned: **Text (Japanese)** *Category:* **Text**

Parameters:

- **text**—Any text expression or text field.

Description:

Converts from Hiragana to Zenkaku Katakana.

Japanese has four written alphabets where it is possible to represent a syllable in a number of different ways. The Katakana() function, along with the Hiragana(), KanaHankaku(), and KanaZenkaku() functions, all enable conversion from one set of alphabetic glyphs to another.

Examples:

Katakana (あいうえお) returns アイウエオ

Last()

Syntax:

Last (field)

Data type returned: **Text, Number, Date, Time, Timestamp, Container**

Category: **Repeating**

Parameters:

- **field**—Any repeating field or related field.

Description:

If the specified field is a repeating field, Last() returns the value from the last valid, non-blank repetition. If the specified field is a related field, it returns the last nonblank value from the set of related records. The order of the set of related records is determined by the sort order of the relationship. If no sort order has been specified, the creation order is used.

Examples:

When RepPercentage is a repeating field with the values .04, .05, and .06, Last (RepPercentage) returns .06.

```
Last ( PhoneNumber::Number )
```

returns the most recent phone number entry, assuming no sort is specified for the relationship.

LayoutIDs()

Syntax:

LayoutIDs (fileName)

Data type returned: **Text**

Category: **Design**

Parameters:

- **fileName**—A string or text expression that represents the name of an open file. It can include a file extension but doesn't need one.

Description:

Returns a carriage return-delimited list of all the internal layout IDs for the specified file. The list is ordered according to the current layout order, not the creation order.

LayoutIDs are assigned in sequential order beginning at 1. The original file's LayoutIDs are retained when older databases are converted to FileMaker Pro 9.

Examples:

Function	Results
LayoutIDs (Get (FileName))	Might return a list of values that looks like this: 3 9 10 24 13 28

LayoutNames()

Syntax:

LayoutNames (fileName)

Data type returned: **Text** *Category:* **Design**

Parameters:

- **fileName**—A string or text expression that represents the name of an open file. It can include a file extension but doesn't need one.

Description:

Returns a carriage return-delimited list of layout names for the specified file.

As with the LayoutIDs() function, the order of the layout names is determined by the current order of the layouts, not their creation order.

If you wanted to find out a particular layout's ID (say, the Contact_Detail layout), you can use the LayoutNames() and LayoutIDs() functions together, as follows:

```
Let ([
  curFile = Get ( FileName );
  LNs = LayoutNames ( curFile );
  LIs = LayoutIDs ( curFile );
  pos = Position ( LNs; "Contact_Detail"; 1; 1 );
  num = ValueCount ( Left ( LNs; pos - 1 )) + 1 ] ;

  Case ( pos > 0; GetValue ( LIs; num ) ; "" )
)
```

Examples:

Function	Results
LayoutNames (Get (FileName))	Might return a list of values that looks like this: Contact_List Contact_Detail Invoice_List Invoice_Detail

LayoutObjectNames()

Syntax:

LayoutObjectNames (fileName ; layoutName)

Data type returned: **Text** *Category:* **Design**

Parameters:

- **fileName**—The name of an open FileMaker database.
- **layoutName**—The name of the layout from which to return object names.

Description:

Returns a carriage return-delimited list of the names of objects on the specified layout. Any object on a layout can be given a name using the Object Info palette.

Object names are listed according to their stacking order on the layout, from back to front. For named objects that can contain other objects (tab controls, grouped objects, and portals), the object name is followed by a list of the enclosed objects, set off using angle brackets (<>). The angle brackets are listed even if there are no enclosed objects.

Examples:

```
LayoutObjectNames ( Get ( FileName ) ; Get (LayoutName ))
```

Returns the names of all objects on the current layout of the current file. This list might look something like the following:

```
FirstName field
LastName field
A random line
InfoTab
<
>
AddressTab
<
Address
City
State
>
Picture
```

Left()

Syntax:

Left (text; numberOfCharacters)

Data type returned: **Text** *Category:* **Text**

Parameters:

- **text**—Any expression that resolves to a text string.
- **numberOfCharacters**—Any expression that resolves to a positive integer.

Description:

Returns a string containing the first *n* characters from the specified text string, where *n* is the number specified in the numberOfCharacters parameter. If the string is shorter than numberOfCharacters, the entire string is returned. If numberOfCharacters is less than 1, an empty string is returned.

The Left() function is commonly used in text parsing routines to extract portions of a text string. It is often used in conjunction with other text functions. For example, to extract the City portion of a field (called "CSZ") containing "City, State Zip" data, you could use the following formula:

```
Let ( commaPosition = Position ( CSZ; ","; 1; 1 );
    Left ( CSZ; commaPosition – 1 )
)
```

Examples:

Function	Results
Left ("Hello" ; 2)	Returns He.
Left (FirstName ; 1)	Returns the first character of the FirstName field.

LeftValues()

Syntax:

LeftValues (text; numberOfValues)

Data type returned: **Text** *Category:* **Text**

Parameters:

- **text**—A return-delimited text string or expression that returns a return-delimited text string.
- **numberOfValues**—Any positive number or expression that returns a positive number.

Description:

The LeftValues() function returns the first *n* items from a return-delimited list, where *n* is the number specified in the numberOfValues parameter. The items will themselves be a return-delimited array, and there will always be a trailing return at the end of the last item.

You can remove the trailing return in a number of ways. If you are extracting a single item from the beginning of a list, you can use the Substitute() function to remove any return characters—for instance, Substitute (LeftValues (text; 1); "¶"; ""). You would not use this method when returning multiple items because the internal delimiters would be lost as well. Instead, the following function returns everything except the last character of the extracted list:

```
Let ( x = LeftValues ( text; n ); Left ( x; Length ( x ) - 1 ))
```

Another option is the following:

```
LeftWords ( LeftValues ( text; n ); 999999 )
```

This function takes advantage of the fact that the LeftWords() function ignores any leading or trailing delimiters. Be aware that this function also ignores leading or trailing delimiters from the actual items in the array (including punctuation symbols), so in some cases this function will not return the desired result. The safest formula to use in all cases is the Let() function.

Examples:

Function	Results
LeftValues("A¶B¶C¶D¶E"; 3)	Returns the following list: A B C
LeftValues (WindowNames ; 1)	Returns the name of the active window (followed by a carriage return).

LeftWords()

Syntax:

LeftWords (text; numberOfWords)

Data type returned: **Text** *Category:* **Text**

Parameters:

- **text**—Any expression that resolves to a text field.
- **numberOfWords**—Any positive number or expression that returns a positive number.

Description:

Returns the first *n* number of words in a text expression, where *n* is the number specified in the numberOfWords parameter.

Be aware of what symbols are considered to be word breaks by FileMaker Pro. Spaces, return characters, and most punctuation symbols are considered to be word breaks. Multiple word breaks next to each other (for example, two spaces, a comma, and a space) are considered as a single word break.

Certain punctuation symbols are word breaks when separating alpha characters, but not when separating numeric characters. These include the colon (:), slash (/), period (.), comma (,), and dash (-). For instance, LeftWords ("54-6"; 1) returns 54-6, but LeftWords ("x-y"; 1) returns x. The reason for this behavior is that those symbols are valid date, time, and number separators.

Leading and trailing punctuation around a word may be ignored by the LeftWords() function. For example, LeftWords ("John Q. Public, Jr."; 2) returns John Q, but LeftWords ("John Q. Public, Jr."; 3) returns John Q. Public.

Examples:

Function	Results
LeftWords ("the quick brown fox jumps"; 3)	Returns the quick brown.
LeftWords (FullName ; 1)	Returns Davie when FullName contains "Davie Jacques".

Length()

Syntax:

Length (text)

Data type returned: **Number** *Category:* **Text**

Parameters:

- **text**—Any expression that resolves to a text string.

Description:

Returns the number of characters in the specified text string. Numbers, letters, punctuation, spaces, and carriage returns are all considered as characters.

Length() also serves a second function in that it returns the size in bytes of the object data found in a container field.

The Length() function is often used as part of data validation rules. For instance, if you want to make sure that users enter phone numbers with either 7 or 10 digits, you could set up a validation by calculation rule as follows:

```
Length ( GetAsNumber ( Phone )) = 7 or Length ( GetAsNumber ( Phone )) = 10
```

Examples:

Function	Results
Length ("Hello there!")	Returns 12.
Length (LastName)	Returns 8 when LastName contains "Humphrey".
Length (Get (CurrentDate))	Returns 9 when the date is 3/27/2007. Note that in versions of FileMaker prior to 7, this last example would have returned 6, because the serialized numeric value for the current date would have been used (as opposed to the "3/27/2007"). To achieve that same result, use the following formula: Length (GetAsNumber (Get (CurrentDate)))
Length (myContainer)	Returns 156862 when the myContainer field holds an image that is approximately 157KB in size. (Operating systems report file size slightly differently. It is not unlikely that this function will return a slightly different number than that of your operating system.)

Let()

Syntax:

Let ({[} var1=expression1 {; var2=expression2 ...] }; calculation)

Data type returned: **Text, Number, Date, Time, Timestamp, Container**

Category: **Logical**

Parameters:

- **var(n)**—Any valid variable name. The rules for naming variables are the same as for defining fields.
- **expression(n)**—Any calculation formula, the results of which are assigned to the var(n) variable.
- **calculation**—Any calculation formula.

Parameters in curly braces { } are optional and may be repeated as needed, separated by a semicolon.

Description:

The Let() function enables you to declare local variables within a calculation formula. The variables exist only within the boundaries of the Let() function itself.

The first parameter of the Let() function is a list of variable names and expressions. If multiple variables are declared, the list needs to be enclosed in square brackets and separated by semicolons. The variables are set in the order in which they appear. This means that you can use previously defined variables as part of the expression to define another variable.

The final parameter, calculation, is some expression that you want to evaluate. That formula can reference any of the variables declared in the first half of the function.

Duplicate variable names are allowed and variables can be named the same as existing fields. If this happens, the value assigned to the variable, not the field, will be used in future references to the variable within the Let() function. In general this situation should be avoided to prevent confusion.

Let() can be used to simplify complex, nested calculation formulas. We cannot advocate its use strongly enough.

In the case where a subexpression is used many times within a formula, the Let() function may also provide a performance benefit because the subexpression is evaluated only once when it is assigned to the variable.

You can also use the Let() function to set script variables like so:

```
Let ([
   $var = 100;
   $$var = 500
   ];
   expression
)
```

Keeping track of variables that overlap scope—in this case overlapping the scope of a calculation expression with that of script or global variables—can often lead to code that is extremely difficult to work with and maintain. Although the preceding is entirely possible, we generally do not recommend it as a practice.

Examples:

The following formula extracts the domain name from an email address:

```
Let( [
  start = Position ( eMail ; "@" ;1 ;1 );
  numberOfCharacters = Length ( eMail ) – start ];
  Right ( eMail; numberOfCharacters )
)
```

The following example produces a summary of a student's grades:

```
Let ([
  TotalGradePoints = Sum ( Grades::GradePoints );
  CreditPoints = Sum ( Classes::CreditPoints );
  GPA = Round ( TotalGradePoints / CreditPoints; 2 )
  ];

  "Total Grade Points: " & TotalGradePoints & "¶" &
  "Available Credit Points: " & CreditPoints & "¶" &
  "Your GPA is: " & GPA
)
```

The final example formula returns the volume of a pyramid:

```
Let(
  SideOfBase = 2 * Sqrt ( 2 * SlantHeight^2 - Height^2 );
  SideOfBase^2 * Height / 3
)
```

Lg()

Syntax:

Lg (number)

Data type returned: **Number** *Category:* **Number**

Parameters:

- **number**—Any expression that resolves to a positive numeric value or a field containing a numeric expression.

Description:

Returns the base-2 logarithm of number. Negative values for number return an error.

The base-2 logarithm (often called the *binary logarithm*) of a number is the power of 2 that you would need to generate the number. Thus, if 2^x = y, then Lg(y) = x. The value returned by the Lg() function is increased by 1 every time that *x* is doubled.

Examples:

```
Lg ( 1 ) = 0
Lg ( 2 ) = 1
Lg ( 32 ) = 5
```

List()

Syntax:

List (field {; field...})

Data type returned: **Text** *Category:* **Aggregate**

Parameters:

- **field**—Any related field, repeating field, or set of nonrepeating fields that represent a collection of data. Parameters in curly braces { } are optional.

Description:

Returns a carriage return-delimited list of the collection of data referenced by the field parameter.

If field is a repeating field, then List (field) is a list of the nonblank values from each repetition, ordered by repetition.

If field is a related field, then List (field) is a concatenated list of the values in each related record, ordered by the sort order defined for the relationship.

When referencing multiple related fields, List () generates a repeating result where the first repetition is a list of the values in the first repetition of the reference fields, and so on.

Examples:

Function	Results
List ("blue" ; "white" ; "red")	Returns blue¶white¶red.
List (repeatingField)	Returns Fred¶Flintstone (when repetition 1 = Fred, repetition 2 = Flintstone).
List (Contact::FullName)	Returns a list of the contents of the FullName field from the related set of Contact records.

Ln()

Syntax:

Ln (number)

Data type returned: **Number** *Category:* **Number**

Parameters:

- **number**—Any positive number or expression that returns a positive number.

Description:

Returns the natural logarithm of the specified number. The natural logarithm uses the transcendental number e as its base. The value of e is approximately 2.71828.

Exp() and Ln() are inverse functions of one another.

The Log() and Lg() functions produce base-10 and base-2 logarithms, respectively. The Ln() function produces base-*e* logarithms, but it can also be used to solve a logarithm of any base. Log (base-*x*) of y is equivalent to Ln (y) / Ln (x).

Examples:

Function	Results
Ln (2.7182818)	Returns .9999999895305023.
Ln (100)	Returns 4.6051701859880914.
Ln (Exp (5))	Returns 5.

Log()

Syntax:

Log (number)

Data type returned: **Number** *Category:* **Number**

Parameters:

- **number**—Any positive number or expression that returns a positive number.

Description:

Returns the base-10 logarithm of number.

Logarithms are used to determine the power to which a number must be raised to equal some other number. If $x^n = y$, then $n = Log_x(y)$. The Log() function assumes a base (the variable *x* in the preceding formula) of 10. The Lg() function uses a base of 2, whereas the Ln() function uses a base of *e*.

Examples:

Function	Results
Log (1)	Returns 0 because 10^0 = 1.
Log (100)	Returns 2 because 10^2 = 100.
Log (1000)	Returns 3 because 10^3 = 1000.

Lookup()

Syntax:

Lookup (sourceField {; failExpression })

Data type returned: **Text, Number, Date, Time, Timestamp, Container** *Category:* **Logical**

Parameters:

- **sourceField**—Any related field.
- **failExpression**—An expression to evaluate and return if the lookup fails. This is an optional parameter.

Description:

Returns the contents of sourceField, or if no related record is found, the result of the failExpression. The table containing the sourceField must be related to the table where the Lookup() is defined.

A calculation field that contains a Lookup() function can be stored or unstored. If it is unstored, anytime the sourceField changes, the calculation field updates. If the calculation is stored, which is typically why you want to use a Lookup in the first place, changes to the sourceField do not cascade automatically through to the calculation field. Lookup() is retriggered when any of the relationship's match fields (in the current table, not the table that contains the sourceField) are modified, or when a relookup is triggered on any of those.

Lookup() is useful for addressing performance issues caused by interacting with related (and hence unindexed) values.

Examples:

Imagine you have a stored calculation field in an Invoice table called CustomerNameLookup, defined as follows:

```
Lookup ( Customer::CustomerName; "<Missing Customer>" )
```

Assume that the Invoice and Customer tables are related on the CustomerID. Whenever the CustomerID field is modified in the Invoice table, this triggers the lookup, and the name of the customer is copied into CustomerNameLookup. If an invalid CustomerID is entered, <Missing Customer> is returned. Because CustomerNameLookup is stored, indexed searches can be performed on it.

Be aware, however, that if the CustomerName field is updated in the Customer table, the change does not cascade automatically through to the Invoice table.

LookupNext()

Syntax:

LookupNext (sourceField; lower/higher Flag)

Data type returned: **Text, Number, Date, Time, Timestamp, Container**

Category: **Logical**

Parameters:

- **sourceField**—Any related field.
- **lower/higher Flag**—Keyword that indicates whether to take the next lower or higher value if no direct match is found.

Description:

Returns the contents of sourceField, or if no related record is found, the next lower or higher match value. The table containing the sourceField must be related to the table where the LookupNext() function is defined.

The LookupNext() function is similar to the Lookup() function; they differ only in how they handle the case of no matching record. The Lookup() function returns a fail expression in such cases, whereas the LookupNext() returns the value associated with the next lower or higher match.

The Lower and Higher flags are keywords and should not be placed in quotation marks.

See the Lookup() function to learn about how a lookup is triggered and how the storage options determine when the LookupNext() function is refreshed.

Looking up a value from the next higher or lower matching record is desirable when mapping a continuous variable onto a categorical variable. Think, for instance, of how student grades typically map to letter grades. A grade of 90 to 100 is considered an A, 80 to 89 is a B, 70 to 79 is a C, and so on. The percentage value is a continuous variable, whereas the letter grades are categorical.

Using the Lookup() function, if you wanted to use the student's percentage score to retrieve the letter grade from a related table, you would need to have records for every possible combination of percentage and letter grade.

The LookupNext() function makes it possible to have records representing only the border conditions. For student grades, you would need to have five records in your related lookup table: 90 is an A, 80 is a B, 70 is a C, 60 is a D, and 0 is an F. You could then relate a student's percentage score to this table and define the following formula as the StudentLetterGrade:

```
LookupNext ( GradeLookup::LetterGrade; Lower )
```

Given a percentage score of 88, which has no exact match, the next lower match (80) would return a letter grade of B.

Examples:

Function	Results
LookupNext (ShipRates::ShippingCost; Higher)	Returns the contents of the ShippingCost field from the ShipRates table. If no exact match is found, the next highest match is returned.

Lower()

Syntax:

Lower (text)

Data type returned: **Text** *Category:* **Text**

Parameters:

- **text**—Any expression that resolves to a text string.

Description:

Returns an all-lowercase version of the specified text string.

The Lower() function is one of three functions FileMaker has for changing the case of a text string. The other two are Upper() and Proper().

The following formula can be used to test whether a given text string is already written with all lowercase characters:

```
Exact ( text; Lower ( text ))
```

Examples:

Function	Results
Lower ("This is a test")	Returns this is a test.
Lower (Name)	Returns mary smith when the Name field contains "MARY Smith".

Max()

Syntax:

Max (field {; field...})

Data type returned: **Text, Number, Date, Time, Timestamp** *Category:* **Aggregate**

Parameters:

- **field**—Any related field, repeating field, or set of nonrepeating fields that represent a set of numbers. Parameters in curly braces { } are optional and may be repeated as needed, separated by a semicolon.

Description:

Returns the largest valid, nonblank value from the set of values specified by the field parameter.

When the parameter list consists of two or more repeating fields, Max() returns a repeating field in which the corresponding repetitions from the specified fields are evaluated separately. So, if a field Repeater1 has three values, 16, 20, and 24, and another field,

Repeater2, has two values, 14 and 25, Max (Repeater1; Repeater2) would return a repeating field with values 16, 25, and 24.

Because dates, times, and timestamps are represented internally as numbers, the Max() function can be used to compare data of these data types. For instance, to return the later of two dates, you could use the following type of formula:

```
GetAsDate ( Max ( Date (4; 1; 2008); Get ( CurrentDate )))
```

This would return either 4/1/2008 or the current date, whichever is greater.

Examples:

Function	Results
Max (44; 129; 25)	Returns 129.
Max (repeatingField)	Returns 54 (when repetition 1 = 18, repetition 2 = 10, and repetition 3 = 54).
Max (Invoice::InvoiceAmount)	Returns the largest invoice amount found in the set of related Invoice records.

Middle()

Syntax:

Middle (text; startCharacter; numberOfCharacters)

Data type returned: **Text** *Category:* **Text**

Parameters:

- **text**—Any expression that resolves to a text string.
- **startCharacter**—Any expression that resolves to a numeric value.
- **numberOfCharacters**—Any expression that resolves to a numeric value.

Description:

Returns a substring from the middle of the specified text parameter. The substring begins at startCharacter and extracts the numberOfCharacters characters following it. If the end of the string is encountered before the specified number of characters has been extracted, the function returns everything from the start position though the end of the string.

The Middle() function is often used in conjunction with other text functions as part of text parsing routines. For instance, if you had a field named CSZ containing city, state, and zip data where the entries were consistently entered as "city, state zip," you could extract the state portion of the string with the following formula:

```
Let (
    commaPosition = Position ( CSZ; ","; 1; 1);
    Middle ( CSZ; commaPosition + 2; 2 )
)
```

Examples:

Function	Results
Middle ("hello world"; 3; 5)	Returns llo w.
Middle (FirstName; 2; 9999999)	Returns everything except the first character of the contents of the FirstName field.

MiddleValues()

Syntax:

MiddleValues (text; startingValue; numberOfValues)

Data type returned: **Text** *Category:* **Text**

Parameters:

- **text**—Any return-delimited string or expression that generates a return-delimited string.
- **startingValue**—Any positive integer or expression that returns a positive integer.
- **numberOfValues**—Any positive number or expression that returns a positive integer.

Description:

Returns the specified number of items from the middle of the text parameter, starting at the value specified in the startingValue parameter.

The MiddleValues() function returns a slice from the middle of a return-delimited array. The output itself will be a return-delimited array, and there will always be a trailing return at the end of the last item.

See the LeftValues() function for a discussion of methods to remove the trailing return from the output of the MiddleValues() function.

Examples:

Function	Results
MiddleValues ("A¶B¶C¶D¶E"; 2; 3)	Returns the following: B C D

MiddleValues (test; 3; 1)	Returns the following: C When test contains: A B C D

MiddleWords()

Syntax:

MiddleWords (text; startingWord; numberOfWords)

Data type returned: **Text** *Category:* **Text**

Parameters:

- **text**—Any expression that resolves to a text string.
- **startingWord**—Any positive number or expression that returns a positive number.
- **numberOfWords**—Any positive number or expression that returns a positive number.

Description:

The MiddleWords() function extracts a substring from the middle of a text string. The substring begins with the *nth* word of the text string (where *n* represents the startingWord parameter) and extends for the number of words specified by the third parameter.

MiddleWords (text; 1; 1) and LeftWords (text; 1) are equivalent functions.

Be aware of what symbols are considered to be word breaks by FileMaker Pro. Spaces, return characters, and most punctuation symbols are considered to be word breaks. Multiple word breaks next to each other (for example, two spaces, a comma, and a space) are considered as a single word break.

Certain punctuation symbols are word breaks when separating alpha characters but not when separating numeric characters. These include the colon (:), slash (/), period (.), comma (,), and dash (-). The reason for this behavior is that those symbols are valid date, time, and number separators.

Leading and trailing punctuation around a word may be ignored by the MiddleWords() function. For example, MiddleWords ("John Q. Public, Jr."; 2; 1) returns Q, but MiddleWords ("John Q. Public, Jr."; 2; 1) returns Q. Public.

Examples:

Function	Results
MiddleWords ("the quick brown fox jumps"; 3; 2)	Returns brown fox.
MiddleWords (FullName; 2; 1)	Returns Allan when FullName contains "Edgar Allan Poe."

Min()

Syntax:

Min (field {; field...})

Data type returned: **Text, Number, Date, Time, Timestamp**

Category: **Aggregate**

Parameters:

- **field**—Any related field, repeating field, or set of nonrepeating fields that represent a set of numbers. Parameters in curly braces { } are optional.

Description:

Returns the lowest valid, nonblank value from the set of values specified by the field parameter.

When the parameter list consists of two or more repeating fields, Min() returns a repeating field in which the corresponding repetitions from the specified fields are evaluated separately. So, if a field Repeater1 has three values, 16, 20, and 24, and another field, Repeater2, has two values, 14 and 25, Min (Repeater1; Repeater2) would return a repeating field with values 14, 20, and 24.

Because dates, times, and timestamps are represented internally as numbers, the Min() function can be used to compare data of these data types. For instance, to return the earlier of two dates, you could use the following type of formula:

```
GetAsDate ( Min ( Date ( 4; 1; 2008 ); Get ( CurrentDate )))
```

This example would return either 4/1/2008 or the current date, whichever is less.

Examples:

Function	Results
Min (44; 25; 129)	Returns 25.
Min (repeatingField)	Returns 10 (when repetition 1 = 18, repetition 2 = 10, and repetition 3 = 54).
Min (Invoice::InvoiceAmount)	Returns the lowest invoice amount found in the set of related Invoice records.

Minute()

Syntax:

Minute (time)

Data type returned: **Number** *Category:* **Time**

Parameters:

- **time**—Any valid time value or expression that returns a valid time value.

Description:

The Minute() function returns an integer representing the number of minutes from the given time value.

The Minute() function always returns an integer in the range from 0 to 59. If you want the output of this function to be expressed always as a two-character string (for example, 07 instead of 7 when the time is 4:07 p.m.), use the following formula:

```
Right ( "00" & Minute ( time ); 2 )
```

Examples:

Function	Results
Minute ("10:45:20")	Returns 45.
Minute ("12:07 am")	Returns 7.
Minute (Get (CurrentTime))	Returns a value from 0 to 59.

Mod()

Syntax:

Mod (number; divisor)

Data type returned: **Number** *Category:* **Number**

Parameters:

- **number**—Any expression that resolves to a numeric value.
- **divisor**—Any expression that resolves to a numeric value.

Description:

Returns the remainder after number is divided by divisor.

Mod() is related to the Div() function; Div() returns the whole number portion of x divided by y, whereas Mod() returns the remainder.

There are many practical uses for the Mod() function. For instance, when *x* is an integer, Mod (x; 2) returns 0 if *x* is even, and 1 if *x* is odd. Mod (x; 1) returns just the decimal portion of a number. And if you had *n* eggs to pack into egg cartons that held 12 eggs each, Mod (n; 12) would tell you how many eggs you'd have left over after packing as many full cartons as possible.

Examples:

Function	Results
Mod (7; 5)	Returns 2.
Mod (-7; 5)	Returns 3.
Mod (13; 3)	Returns 1.
Mod (1.43; 1)	Returns .43.

Month()

Syntax:

Month (date)

Data type returned: **Number** *Category:* **Date**

Parameters:

- **date**—Any valid date (1/1/0001–12/31/4000). The parameter should be a string containing a date (for example, "3/17/2004"), an expression with a date result (for example, Date (6; 29; 1969)), or an integer that represents a serialized date value (for example, 718977).

Description:

Returns the month number (1–12) for any valid date (1/1/0001–12/31/4000).

The numeric value returned by Month() can be used in mathematical calculations as well as within the Date() function to construct a new date.

One common use of the Month() function is to build a formula that returns the quarter of a given date:

```
Case (
  Month ( myDate ) < 4; "First Quarter";
  Month ( myDate ) < 7; "Second Quarter";
  Month ( myDate ) < 9; "Third Quarter";
  "Fourth Quarter"
)
```

Examples:

Function	Results
Month ("5/1/2000")	Returns 5.
Month (718977)	Returns 6.
Month (Get (CurrentDate))	Returns 3 (if the current date is in March).

MonthName()

Syntax:

MonthName (date)

Data type returned: **Text** *Category:* **Date**

Parameters:

- **date**—Any valid date (1/1/0001–12/31/4000). The parameter should be a string containing a date (for example, "3/17/2004"), an expression with a date result (for example, Date (6; 29; 1969)), or an integer that represents a serialized date value (for example, 718977).

Description:

Returns the month name of the specified date.

The MonthName() function is frequently used for display purposes in subsummary reports. Although you display the name of the month, be sure that you summarize based on the month number (obtained with the Month() function). If you don't, your report will be summarized alphabetically by month rather than chronologically by month.

Examples:

Function	Results
MonthName ("1/1/2000")	Returns January.
MonthName (Date (5; 20; 2003))	Returns May.
MonthName (Get (CurrentDate))	Might return March.

MonthNameJ()

Syntax:

MonthNameJ (date)

Data type returned: **Text (Japanese)** *Category:* **Date**

Parameters:

- **date**—Any calendar date.

Description:

Returns the name of the month in Japanese.

To avoid errors when using dates, always use four-digit years.

Examples:

Function	Results
MonthNameJ ("6/6/2003")	Returns Rokugatsu in whatever alphabet the field is formatted to display.

NPV()

Syntax:

NPV (payment; interestRate)

Data type returned: **Number** *Category:* **Financial**

Parameters:

- **payment**—A repeating field or related field that contains one or more values representing loan and payment amounts.
- **interestRate**—An interest rate, expressed as a decimal number.

Description:

Returns the Net Present Value (NPV) of a series of unequal payments made at regular intervals, assuming a fixed interestRate per interval. If the field specified in the first parameter is a repeating field, it should contain all loan and payment amounts. The first parameter can also reference a set of related records, each representing a payment amount.

Examples:

Imagine someone borrows $300 from you and repays you $100, $50, $100, and $125 at regular intervals.

Assuming an interest rate of 5%, the NPV() function can tell you the actual profit, in today's dollars, that will be realized from this transaction. To calculate this, you would place the following values in a repeating number field: -300, 100, 50, 100, and 125. Then, use the formula

```
Round ( NPV ( Payments; .05 ) ; 2)
```

which returns $28.39. Your actual profit on the transaction would be $75 (simply the sum of the payments minus the original loan). That $75, however, is collected over time, so the present value is discounted by the assumed interest rate. The higher the interest rate, the less the NPV of the $75.

NumToJText()

Syntax:

NumToJText (number; separator; characterType)

Data type returned: **Text (Japanese)** *Category:* **Text**

Parameters:

- **number**—Any numeric expression or field containing a number.
- **separator**—A number from 0–3 representing a separator.
- **characterType**—A number from 0–3 representing a type.

Description:

Converts Roman numbers in the number parameter to Japanese text. If the values for separator and characterType are blank or other than 0 to 3, then 0 (no separator) is used.

Separator:

0—No separator

1—Every 3 digits (thousands)

2—Ten thousands (万) and millions (億) unit

3—Tens (十), hundreds (百), thousands (千), ten thousands (万), and millions (億) unit

Type:

0—Half width (Hankaku) number

1—Full width (Zenkaku) number

2—Kanji character number (一二三)

3—Traditional-old-style Kanji character number (壱弐参)

Examples:

Function	Results
NumToJText (123456789; 2; 0)	Returns 1億2345万6789 .
NumToJText (123456789; 3; 2)	Returns 一億二千三百四十五万六千七百八十九

PatternCount()

Syntax:

PatternCount (text; searchString)

Data type returned: **Number** *Category:* **Text**

Parameters:

- **text**—Any expression that resolves to a text string.
- **searchString**—Any expression that resolves to a text string, representing the substring for which you want to search within the text string.

Description:

Returns the number of times that searchString appears in the text string. PatternCount() returns 0 if the searchString is not found.

Only nonoverlapping occurrences of searchString are counted by PatternCount(). PatternCount() is not case sensitive.

Even though PatternCount() is designed to answer the question "how many?" it is often used simply to determine whether one string is contained within another. If it returns any value other than zero, the search string is found.

Examples:

Function	Results
PatternCount ("This is a test"; "is")	Returns 2.
PatternCount (WindowNames; "¶") + 1	Returns the number of carriage returns in the list returned by the WindowNames() function. This could be used to determine the number of windows that are available. The ValueCount() function could also be used for this purpose.
PatternCount ("abababa"; "Aba")	Returns 2.

Pi

Syntax:

Pi

Data type returned: **Number** *Category:* **Trigonometric**

Parameters: None

Description:

Returns the value of the trigonometric constant Pi, which is approximately 3.1415926535897932. Pi is defined as the ratio of the circumference to the diameter of any circle.

Pi is most often used in conjunction with other trigonometric functions, such as Sin(), Cos(), and Tan(), which each require an angle measured in radians as a parameter. There are 2×Pi radians in 360 degrees.

Examples:

Function	Results
Sin (Pi / 2)	Returns 1.
SetPrecision (Pi; 25)	Returns 3.1415926535897932384626434.

PMT()

Syntax:

PMT (principal; interestRate; term)

Data type returned: **Number** *Category:* **Financial**

Parameters:

- **principal**—A number or expression that returns a number, representing the initial amount borrowed.
- **interestRate**—A decimal number or expression that returns a number, representing the monthly interest rate used to amortize the principal amount. Given an annual interest rate, you can divide by 12 to get the monthly interest rate.
- **term**—A number or expression that returns a number representing the period of the loan, expressed in months.

Description:

Returns the monthly payment that would be required to pay off the principal based on the interestRate and term specified.

The PMT calculation makes it easy to see the effect of interest rates on the monthly payment of an installment loan. For instance, buying a $20,000 car at 6.9% for 48 months would require a $478.00 monthly payment, but at 3.9%, the payment would be $450.68.

Examples:

Someone borrows $1,000 from you, and you want to set up a payment schedule whereby the loan is paid off in 2 years at an interest rate of 6%. To determine the monthly payment,

```
PMT ( 1000; .06/12; 24 )
```

returns $44.32.

Position()

Syntax:

Position (text ; searchString ; start ; occurrence)

Data type returned: **Number** *Category:* **Text**

Parameters:

- **text**—Any expression that resolves to a text string in which you want to search.
- **searchString**—Any expression that resolves to a text string for which to search.
- **start**—An integer representing the character number at which to begin searching.
- **occurrence**—An integer representing which occurrence of searchString to locate. A negative number causes the search to proceed backward from the start character.

Description:

Returns the character number where the searchString is found within the specified text string. If the searchString is not found, the Position() function returns a 0.

In most cases, the Position() function is used to find the first occurrence of some substring within a string. Both the start and occurrence parameters will simply be 1 in such instances.

To find the *last* occurrence of a substring within a string, set the start parameter to be the length of the string and the occurrence parameter to be -1, indicating that the function should search backward from the end of the string for the first occurrence of the substring.

The Position() function is not case sensitive.

Examples:

Function	Results
Position ("This is a test"; "is"; 1; 1)	Returns 3.
Position ("This is a test"; "is"; 1; 2)	Returns 6.
Let (myString = "This is a test"; Position (myString; " "; Length (myString) ; -1))	Returns 10, which is the position of the last space in myString.

Proper()

Syntax:

Proper (text)

Data type returned: **Text** *Category:* **Text**

Parameters:

- **text**—Any expression that resolves to a text string.

Description:

Returns the specified text string with the initial letter of each word capitalized and all other letters as lowercase.

The Proper() function is one of three case-changing functions in FileMaker. The other two are Lower() and Upper().

The Proper() function is often used as part of an auto-entered calculation formula to reformat a user's entry with the desired case. For instance, in a City field, where you would expect the first letter of each word to be capitalized, you could set up an auto-entry option to enter Proper (City) and uncheck the option to not replace existing value. Then, if a user were to type SAN FRANCISCO, upon exiting the field the entry would be reset to San Francisco.

Examples:

Function	Results
Proper ("this is a TEST")	Returns This Is A Test.
Proper (Address)	Returns 123 Main Street when Address contains "123 main street".

PV()

Syntax:

PV (payment; interestRate; periods)

Data type returned: **Number** *Category:* **Financial**

Parameters:

- **payment**—A number or expression that returns a number, representing a payment amount made per period.
- **interestRate**—A decimal number or expression that returns a decimal number, representing the interest rate per period.
- **periods**—The number of periods of the loan.

Description:

The Present Value (PV) formula tells you what money expected in the future is worth today. The PV() function returns the present value of a series of equal payments made at regular intervals and assumes a fixed interestRate per interval.

Examples:

Imagine you have won $1,000,000 in a lottery. You have been offered either $50,000 per year for the next 20 years, or a one-time lump sum payment now of $700,000. Which option should you choose?

Assuming an inflation rate of 3% per year, the present value of the future payments is determined by

```
PV ( 50000; .03; 20 )
```

which returns 743873.74.

If you assume a 4% inflation rate, the present value of the future payments decreases to 679516.31. So, depending on your assumptions about inflation rates, you may or not be better off taking the lump sum payment.

As another example, consider the question of whether it would be better for someone to give you $10 today or $1 per year for the next 10 years. You can use the PV() function to tell you the present value of receiving $1 for 10 years. Assuming an inflation rate of 3%, the formula PV (1, .03, 10) shows that the present value of the future income is only $8.53. You're better off taking the $10 today.

Quote()

Syntax:

Quote (text)

Data type returned: **Text** *Category:* **Text**

Parameters:

- **text**—Any expression that resolves to a text string.

Description:

The Quote() function returns the specified text string enclosed in quotation marks. To escape any special characters within the text string, such as quotation marks and double backslashes, place a backslash before them in the text string.

The Quote() function is used primarily in conjunction with the Evaluate() function, which can evaluate a dynamically generated formula. If the formula you are assembling contains a literal text string enclosed by quotation marks, or if it includes field contents that may potentially have quotation marks in it, use the Quote() function to ensure that all internal quotation marks are escaped properly.

Examples:

If the FullName field contains the name Billy "Joe" Smith, then Quote (FullName) would return "Billy \"Joe\" Smith". The absence and presence of quotation marks here is deliberate; the quotation marks are part of the returned string.

Radians()

Syntax:

Radians (angleInDegrees)

Data type returned: **Number** *Category:* **Trigonometric**

Parameters:

- **angleInDegrees**—A number representing an angle measured in degrees.

Description:

The Radians() function converts an angle measured in degrees into an angle measured in radians.

The trigonometric functions Sin(), Cos(), and Tan() all take an angle measured in radians as their parameter. To find, say, the cosine of a 180° angle, you could use the formula Cos (Radians (180)). There are 2×Pi radians in 360°.

Examples:

Function	Results
Radians (60)	Returns 1.0471975511965977 (= Pi/3).
Radians (180)	Returns 3.1415926535897932 (= Pi).

Random

Syntax:

Random

Data type returned: **Number** *Category:* **Number**

Parameters: None

Description:

Returns a random decimal between zero and one (but will not return 1 nor 0). When used in a field definition, a new value is generated when the formula is updated. It is also updated anytime the formula reevaluates, such as when other field values referenced in the formula change. In an unstored calculation, the Random function reevaluates each time the field is displayed.

If you want to generate a random integer in a certain range, multiply the result returned by the random function by the range you want to produce; then use the Int(), Floor(), Ceiling(), Round(), or Truncate() functions to remove the decimals.

For instance, to return a random number from 1 to 6 (as in the roll of a die), use the formula:

```
Ceiling ( Random * 6 )
```

If you need to specify a lower bound for the random number, just add the bound to the results of the random number. For instance, to return a random number between 10 and 100, inclusive, use the following formula:

```
Int ( Random * 91 ) + 10
```

Examples:

Function	Results
Round (Random; 5)	Might return .07156.

RelationInfo()

Syntax:

RelationInfo (fileName; tableOccurrence)

Data type returned: **Text** *Category:* **Design**

Parameters:

- **fileName**—A string or text expression representing the name of an open file.
- **tableOccurrence**—A string or text expression representing the name of a particular table occurrence in fileName.

Description:

Returns a list of information about all the table occurrences related to the specified tableOccurrence.

The results are formatted as

```
Source: [Data Source Name of the related table occurrence]
Table: [related table occurrence name]
Options: ["Delete", "Create", and/or "Sorted"]
[match fields]
```

This information is repeated for each table occurrence that is directly related to the specified table occurrence.

Examples:

RelationInfo (Get (FileName); "Contacts 2") might return values that look like this:

```
Source:ContactDatabase
Table:Company
Options:
Company::CompanyID = Contacts 2::CompanyID
Company::ActiveFlag = Contacts 2::Status

Source:ContactDatabase
Table:Invoice
Options:Create Sorted
Invoice::ContactID = Contacts 2::ContactID
```

Replace()

Syntax:

Replace (text; start; numberOfCharacters; replacementText)

Data type returned: **Text** *Category:* **Text**

Parameters:

- **text**—Any expression that resolves to a text string.
- **start**—Any positive number or expression that returns a positive number.
- **numberOfCharacters**—Any positive number or expression that returns a positive number.
- **replacementText**—Any expression that resolves to a text string.

Description:

The Replace() function extracts a segment of a text string and replaces it with some other string. The segment to extract begins with the start character number and extends for numberOfCharacters. The replacement string is specified by the replacementText parameter.

The extracted segment and the replacement text do not need to be the same length.

The Replace() and Substitute() functions are often confused with one another. Substitute() replaces all occurrences of a particular substring with another string, whereas Replace() replaces a specified range of characters with another string.

Replace() is often used for manipulation of delimited text arrays. There is no function that will directly replace the contents of a particular item in an array with another. The Replace() function can do this by finding the appropriate delimiters and inserting the replacement item. For instance, if you have a pipe-delimited list of numbers (for example, 34|888|150|43) and you want to increase the third item in the list by 18, you could use the following formula:

```
Let ([
  item = 3;
  increase = 18;
  start = Position ( myArray; "|"; 1; ( item – 1 ) ) + 1;
  end = Position ( myArray; "|"; 1; item );
  itemValue = Middle ( myArray; start; end - start );
  newValue = itemValue + increase ];

  Replace ( myArray; start; end-start; newValue )
)
```

Given the example string as myArray, this would produce the string 34|888|168|43. Typically, the item and increase values would be supplied by other fields and not hard-coded into the formula.

Another great use of the Replace() function is to use it as an "Insert" function: Pass a zero as the numberOfCharacters parameter, and you will simply insert some amount of text in front of the start character without having to use a combination of Left(), Middle(), and Right() functions.

Examples:

Function	Results
Replace ("abcdef"; 4; 2; "TEST")	Returns abcTESTf.
Replace ("Fred Smith"; 1; 4; "Joe")	Returns Joe Smith.
Replace ("leftright"; 5; 0; "middle")	Returns leftmiddleright.

RGB()

Syntax:

RGB (red; green; blue)

Data type returned: **Number** *Category:* **Text Formatting**

Parameters:

- **red**—Any number or numeric expression containing a value ranging from 0 to 255.
- **green**—Any number or numeric expression containing a value ranging from 0 to 255.
- **blue**—Any number or numeric expression containing a value ranging from 0 to 255.

Description:

Returns a number that represents a color.

To calculate this integer, the red, green, and blue values are combined using the following formula:

(red * 256^2) + (green * 256) + blue

Use the RGB() function in conjunction with the TextColor() function to format text.

If a number above 255 is supplied as the parameter, the formula in the example still computes a result. If the result of the formula returns a value above the expected 0 to 16777215 range, the Mod (result; 16777216) is used to map the result into the expected range. So RGB (255; 255; 256), which returns a value one higher than white, returns the color black, just as 0 does.

Examples:

Table 9.1 lists the RGB values of some common colors.

Table 9.1 RGB Values

Function	Integer Result	Color
RGB (255; 0; 0)	16711680	Red
RGB (0; 255; 0)	65280	Green
RGB (0; 0; 255)	255	Blue
RGB (255; 255; 255)	16777215	White
RGB (0; 0; 0)	0	Black
RGB (24; 162; 75)	1614411	Dark Green
RGB (7; 13; 78)	462158	Dark Purple
RGB (23; 100; 148)	1533076	Bright Blue

Right()

Syntax:

Right (text; numberOfCharacters)

Data type returned: **Text** *Category:* **Text**

Parameters:

- **text**—Any expression that resolves to a text string.
- **numberOfCharacters**—Any expression that resolves to a numeric value.

Description:

Returns a string containing the last *n* characters from the specified text string. If the string is shorter than numberOfCharacters, the entire string is returned. If numberOfCharacters is less than 1, an empty string is returned.

The Right() function is commonly used in text parsing routines to extract everything after a certain character in a string. For example, if you were parsing email addresses and wanted to return everything after the "@" in the string as the domain, you could use the following formula:

```
Let ([
  len = Length ( email ) ;
  pos = Position ( email ; "@" ; 1 ; 1 ) ];
  Right ( email ; len – pos )
)
```

Examples:

Function	Results
Right ("Hello"; 2)	Returns lo.
Right (FirstName; 1)	Returns the last character of the FirstName field.

RightValues()

Syntax:

RightValues (text; numberOfValues)

Data type returned: **Text** *Category:* **Text**

Parameters:

- **text**—Any return-delimited text string or expression that generates a return-delimited string.
- **numberOfValues**—Any positive number or expression that returns a positive number.

Description:

The RightValues() function returns the last *n* items from a return-delimited array. The items themselves will be a return-delimited array, and there will always be a trailing return at the end of the last item.

See the LeftValues() function for a discussion of methods to remove the trailing return from the output of the RightValues() function.

Examples:

Function	Results
RightValues ("A¶B¶C¶D¶E"; 3)	Returns the following: C D E
RightValues (test; 1)	Returns C when test contains A B C

RightWords()

Syntax:

RightWords (text; numberOfWords)

Data type returned: **Text** *Category:* **Text**

Parameters:

- **text**—Any expression that resolves to a text string.
- **numberOfWords**—Any positive number or expression that returns a positive number.

Description:

Returns the last *n* number of words in a text expression, where *n* is the number specified in the numberOfWords parameter.

Be aware of what characters are considered to be word breaks by FileMaker Pro. Spaces, return characters, and most punctuation symbols are considered to be word breaks. Multiple word breaks next to each other (for example, two spaces, a comma, and a space) are considered a single word break.

Certain punctuation symbols are word breaks when separating alpha characters, but not when separating numeric characters. These include the colon (:), slash (/), period (.), comma (,), and dash (-). For instance, RightWords ("54-6"; 1) returns 54-6, but RightWords ("x-y"; 1) returns y. The reason for this behavior is that those symbols are valid date, time, and number separators.

Leading and trailing punctuation around a word will be ignored by the RightWords() function. For example, RightWords ("John Q. Public, Jr."; 2) returns Public, Jr, and RightWords ("John Q. Public, Jr."; 3) returns Q. Public, Jr.

Examples:

Function	Results
RightWords ("the quick brown fox jumps"; 3)	Returns brown fox jumps.
RightWords (FullName; 1)	Returns Smith when the FullName field contains Joe Smith.

RomanHankaku()

Syntax:

RomanHankaku (text)

Data type returned: **Text (Japanese)** *Category:* **Text**

Parameters:

- **text**—Any text expression or text field.

Description:

Converts from Zenkaku alphanumeric and symbols to Hankaku alphanumeric and symbols. Zenkaku alphanumeric and symbols represent Roman alphanumeric and symbols using Japanese Unicode characters.

Examples:

Function	Results
RomanHankaku ("Ｍａｃｉｎｔｏｓｈ")	Returns Macintosh.

RomanZenkaku()

Syntax:

RomanZenkaku (text)

Data type returned: **Text (Japanese)** *Category:* **Text**

Parameters:

- **text**—Any text expression or text field.

Description:

Converts from Hankaku alphanumeric and symbols to Zenkaku alphanumeric and symbols. Zenkaku alphanumeric and symbols represent Roman alphanumeric and symbols using Japanese Unicode characters.

Examples:

Function	Results
RomanZenkaku("Macintosh")	Returns Ｍａｃｉｎｔｏｓｈ.

Round()

Syntax:

Round (number; precision)

Data type returned: **Number** *Category:* **Number**

Parameters:

- **number**—Any expression that resolves to a numeric value.
- **precision**—A number or numeric expression representing the number of decimal points to which to round the number.

Description:

Returns the specified number rounded off to the number of decimal points specified by the precision parameter. The Round() function rounds numbers from 5 to 9 upward, and from 0 to 4 downward.

A precision of 0 rounds to the nearest integer. A negative number for the precision causes the number to be rounded to the nearest ten, hundred, thousand, and so on.

Examples:

Function	Results
Round (62.566; 2)	Returns 62.57.
Round (62.563; 2)	Returns 62.56.
Round (92.4; 0)	Returns 92.
Round (32343.98; -3)	Returns 32000.
Round (505.999; -1)	Returns 510.

ScriptIDs()

Syntax:

ScriptIDs (fileName)

Data type returned: **Text** *Category:* **Design**

Parameters:

- **fileName**—A string or text expression that represents the name of an open file.

Description:

Returns a carriage return-delimited list of script IDs from the specified file.

ScriptIDs are assigned sequentially by FileMaker, starting at 1 for each new file. The results returned by the ScriptIDs function are ordered according to the current order within ScriptMaker, not the creation order of the scripts.

When you convert a solution developed in an earlier version of FileMaker, the ScriptIDs of the original file are retained after conversion.

Any scripts that are set to "no access" for the current user's privilege set are not included in the list.

Examples:

Function	Results
ScriptIDs ("myFile")	Returns a list of script IDs for the current file that might look like this: 21 24 22 25

ScriptNames()

Syntax:

ScriptNames (fileName)

Data type returned: **Text** *Category:* **Design**

Parameters:

- **fileName**—A string or text expression that represents the name of an open file.

Description:

Returns a carriage return-delimited list of script names from the specified file.

As with the ScriptIDs() function, the order of the list returned by ScriptNames() is the current order of the scripts within ScriptMaker. The names of script groups are NOT included in the result produced by ScriptNames().

Any scripts that are set to "no access" for the current user's privilege set are not included in the list.

Examples:

Function	Results
ScriptNames (Get (FileName))	Returns a list of script names for the current file that might look like this: Contact_Nav Invoice_Nav - Contact_New Invoice_New - Contact_Delete Invoice_Delete

Seconds()

Syntax:

Seconds (time)

Data type returned: **Number** *Category:* **Time**

Parameters:

- **time**—Any valid time value or expression that returns a valid time value.

Description:

The Seconds() function returns an integer representing the number of seconds specified by the time parameter. It always returns a value from 0 to 59.

If you want to express the output of this function as a two-character string rather than as an integer (for example, 03 rather than 3), use the following formula:

```
Right ( "00" & Seconds ( Time ); 2 )
```

If the time parameter has a seconds value greater than 59, the Seconds() function returns the Mod-60 result of that value. For instance, Seconds ("12:42:87") returns 27. Note that the "overflow" of the seconds value is applied to the minutes value: Minute ("12:42:87") returns 43.

Examples:

Function	Results
Seconds ("10:45:20")	Returns 20.
Seconds ("12:15 am")	Returns 0.

Self

Syntax:

Self

Data type returned: **Text, Number, Date, Time, Timestamp** *Category:* **Logical**

Parameters: None

Description:

The Self function returns the contents of the object in which it is defined, thus avoiding the need to explicitly reference the object name. This allows you to reuse formulas for such things as ToolTips, auto-entered calculation formulas, and conditional formatting without having to edit the formula to refer to the new object.

For instance, if there were several fields in which you wanted to set up an auto-entry calculation to remove any text formatting from the user's entry (such as might be present when data is copied and pasted from another application), rather than use TextFormatRemove (FirstName) for the FirstName field and TextFormatRemove (LastName) for the LastName field, you could define both simply as TextFormatRemove (Self). This can be a big time saver because you can duplicate fields and not worry that references to the original object need to be edited.

The Self function is also useful when setting up conditional formatting of layout objects. For instance, if you want empty fields on a form to appear with a gray background, set a conditional formatting formula of IsEmpty (Self) on all those fields. Again, referencing Self rather than explicitly referencing a field will save a lot of time, and it will also ensure that when the layout object is duplicated, the new object's conditional formatting will reference itself and not some other field.

Examples:

Function	Results
TextFormatRemove (Self)	Returns the contents of the current object without any text formatting.
Trim (Self)	Returns the contents of the current object with leading and trailing spaces removed.
Self > Product::ReorderAmount	Returns 1 (True) if the value of the current object is greater than the value in the ReorderAmount field.

SerialIncrement()

Syntax:

SerialIncrement (text; incrementBy)

Data type returned: **Text** *Category:* **Text**

Parameters:

- **text**—Any text or text expression that contains an alphanumeric string.
- **incrementBy**—A number or numeric expression with which to increment the text value.

Description:

Returns the combined text and number from the text value, where the numeric portion of the text has been incremented by the value specified in the incrementBy parameter.

The incrementBy value is truncated to an integer when incrementing. Positive and negative numbers are accepted.

Examples:

Function	Results
SerialIncrement ("test1"; 2)	Returns test3.
SerialIncrement ("project_plan_v12.3"; -1)	Returns project_plan_v12.2.
SerialIncrement ("23"; 3)	Returns 26.

SetPrecision()

Syntax:

SetPrecision (expression; precision)

Data type returned: **Number** *Category:* **Number**

Parameters:

- **expression**—Any number or expression that returns a number.
- **precision**—An integer from 1 to 400.

Description:

FileMaker normally computes fractions with 16 digits of precision. The SetPrecision() function allows you to specify up to 400 digits of precision.

The expression specified in the first parameter is rounded at the digit specified by the second parameter.

The trigonometric functions do not support extended precision.

You can specify a number below 17 as the precision, but FileMaker still returns 16 digits of precision regardless. Use the Round() function instead to specify a precision up to 16.

Examples:

Function	Results
SetPrecision (Pi; 28)	Returns 3.1415926535897932384626433833.
SetPrecision (1 / 3; 30)	Returns .333333333333333333333333333333.

Sign()

Syntax:

Sign (number)

Data type returned: **Text** *Category:* **Number**

Parameters:

- **number**—Any expression that resolves to a numeric value.

Description:

Returns a value that represents the sign of number:

-1 when number is negative

0 when number is zero

1 when number is positive

For any *x* other than 0, multiplying *x* by Sign(x) yields the Abs(x).

Examples:

Function	Results
Sign (0)	Returns 0.
Sign (100)	Returns 1.
Sign (-100)	Returns -1.

Sin()

Syntax:

Sin (angleInRadians)

Data type returned: **Number** *Category:* **Trigonometric**

Parameters:

- **angleInRadians**—Any numeric expression or field containing a numeric expression, in radians.

Description:

Returns the sine of angleInRadians expressed in radians.

In any right triangle, the sine of the two nonright angles can be obtained by dividing the length of the side opposite the angle by the length of the hypotenuse.

Examples:

Function	Results
Sin (Radians (60))	Returns .8660254037844387.
Sin (Pi / 4)	Returns .7071067811865475.

Sqrt()

Syntax:

Sqrt (number)

Data type returned: **Number** *Category:* **Number**

Parameters:

- **number**—Any expression that resolves to a positive number.

Description:

Returns the square root of number.

Examples:

Function	Results
Sqrt (64)	Returns 8.
Sqrt (2)	Returns 1.414213562373095.

StDev()

Syntax:

StDev (field {; field...})

Data type returned: **Number** *Category:* **Aggregate**

Parameters:

- **field**—Any related field, repeating field, or set of nonrepeating fields that represent a collection of numbers. Parameters in curly braces { } are optional.

Description:

Returns the standard deviation of the nonblank values represented in the parameter list. Standard deviation is a statistical measurement of how spread out a collection of values is. In a normal distribution, about 68% of the values are within one standard deviation of the mean, and about 95% are within two standard deviations of the mean.

The difference between the StDevP() and StDev() functions is that StDev() divides the sum of the squares by *n*-1 instead of by *n*.

StDev() can also be calculated as the square root of the Variance() of a set of numbers.

Examples:

You can manually calculate the standard deviation of a set of numbers in several ways. One way is to take the square root of the sum of the squares of each value's distance from the mean, divided by *n*-1, where *n* is the number of values in the set.

For instance, given the set of numbers 8, 10, and 12, the mean of this set is 10. The distances of each value from the mean are therefore -2, 0, and 2. The squares of these are 4, 0, and 4. The sum of the squares is 8. The standard deviation is Sqrt (8 / (3 - 1)), which is 2.

```
StDev ( 8; 10; 12 )
```

returns 2.

Given a portal that contains a field called Scores with the following values (64, 72, 75, 59, 67),

```
StDev ( People::Scores )
```

returns 6.35.

StDevP()

Syntax:

StDevP (field {; field...})

Data type returned: **Number** *Category:* **Aggregate**

Parameters:

- **field**—Any related field, repeating field, or set of nonrepeating fields that represent a collection of numbers. Parameters in curly braces { } are optional.

Description:

Returns the standard deviation of a population represented by the nonblank values in the parameter list. Standard deviation is a statistical measurement of how spread out a collection of values is. In a normal distribution, about 68% of the values are within one standard deviation of the mean, and about 95% are within two standard deviations of the mean.

The difference between the StDevP() and StDev() functions is that StDev() divides the sum of the squares by n-1 instead of by n.

StDevP() can also be calculated as the square root of the VarianceP() of a set of numbers.

Examples:

You can manually calculate the standard deviation of a population in several ways. One way is to take the square root of the sum of the squares of each value's distance from the mean, divided by the number of values.

For instance, given the set of numbers 8, 10, and 12, the mean of this set is 10. The distances of each value from the mean are therefore -2, 0, and 2. The squares of these are 4, 0, and 4. The sum of the squares is 8. The standard deviation of the population is Sqrt (8 / 3), which is 1.633.

```
StDevP ( 8; 10; 12 )
```

returns 1.633.

Given a portal that displays the heights of a set of people (64, 72, 75, 59, 67),

```
StDevP ( People::Heights )
```

returns 5.68.

Substitute()

Syntax:

Substitute (text; searchString; replaceString)

Data type returned: **Text** *Category:* **Text**

Parameters:

- **text**—Any text string or expression that returns a text string.
- **searchString**—Any text string or expression that returns a text string.
- **replaceString**—Any text string or expression that returns a text string.

Description:

Returns a text string in which all instances of searchString in the text parameter are replaced with the replaceString.

Multiple substitutions may occur in the same Substitute() function by placing pairs of search and replacement strings in square brackets, separated by semicolons:

```
Substitute ( "This is a test"; ["i"; "q"]; ["s"; "$"] )
```

returns Thq$ q$ a te$t.

One common use of the Substitute() function is to remove all instances of a specified character from a string. To do this, use "" (a null string) as the replaceString, as in the third example that follows.

The Substitute() function is case sensitive.

Examples:

Function	Results
Substitute ("Happy Anniversary!"; "Anniversary"; "Birthday")	Returns Happy Birthday!.
Substitute ("This is a test"; "i"; "q")	Returns Thqs qs a test.
Substitute ("This is a test"; " "; "")	Returns Thisisatest.

Sum()

Syntax:

Sum (field {; field...})

Data type returned: **Number** *Category:* **Aggregate**

Parameters:

- **field**—Any related field, repeating field, or set of nonrepeating fields that represent a collection of numbers. Parameters in curly braces { } are optional.

Description:

Returns the sum of all valid values represented by the fields in the parameter list.

The Sum() function is most often used to add up a column of numbers in a related table.

Examples:

Function	Results
Sum (field1; field2; field3)	Returns 6 (when field1 = 1, field2 = 2, and field3 = 3).
Sum (repeatingField)	Returns 6 (when repetition 1 = 1, repetition 2 = 2, and repetition 3 = 3).
Sum (repeatingField1; repeatingField2)	Returns a repeating calculation field where the first value equals the sum of the values in repeatingField1, and the second repetition contains the sum of the values in repeatingField2.
Sum (Customer::InvoiceTotal)	Returns 420 (when the sum of InvoiceTotal in the related set of data is 420).

TableIDs()

Syntax:

TableIDs (fileName)

Data type returned: **Text** *Category:* **Design**

Parameters:

- **fileName**—A string or text expression that represents the name of an open file.

Description:

Returns a carriage return-delimited list of table occurrence IDs from the specified file.

Note that TableIDs() returns the IDs of table occurrences from the Relationships Graph, not the actual data tables. A database table may appear in the Relationships Graph more than once.

A unique TableID is assigned by FileMaker whenever a table occurrence is added to the Relationships Graph. The order of the IDs in the list is based on the alphabetic ordering of the table occurrence names themselves.

Examples:

Function	Results
TableIDs (Get (FileName))	Returns a list of table occurrence IDs for the current file that might look like this: 100021 100049 100002

TableNames()

Syntax:

TableNames (fileName)

Data type returned: **Text** *Category:* **Design**

Parameters:

- **fileName**—A string or text expression that represents the name of an open file.

Description:

Returns a carriage return-delimited list of table occurrence names from the specified file.

Note that TableNames() returns the names of table occurrences from the Relationships Graph, not the actual data tables. A database table may appear in the Relationships Graph more than once.

The list returned by the TableNames() function is ordered alphabetically.

Examples:

Function	Results
TableNames (Get (FileName))	Would return a list of table occurrence names for the current file that might look like this: Contacts Contact2 Invoice Lines Invoices

Tan()

Syntax:

Tan (angleInRadians)

Data type returned: **Number** *Category:* **Trigonometric**

Parameters:

- **number**—Any number representing the size of an angle measured in radians.

Description:

Returns the tangent of the specified angle.

The tangent of an angle can also be obtained by dividing the sine of the angle by its cosine. In any right triangle, the tangent of the two nonright angles can be obtained by dividing the length of the side opposite the angle by the length of the adjacent side.

Examples:

Function	Results
Tan (0)	Returns 0.
Tan (Pi / 6)	Returns .5773502691896257.
Tan (Radians (45))	Returns 1.

TextColor()

Syntax:

TextColor (text; RGB (red; green; blue))

Data type returned: **Text** *Category:* **Text Formatting**

Parameters:

- **text**—Any text string or expression that returns a text string.
- **RGB (red; green; blue)**—A function that accepts three parameters from 0 to 255 and returns a number from 0 to 16777215 representing a color. See the RGB() function for more information.

Description:

Returns the text string in the color specified by the RGB parameter. Use the TextColor() function within text expressions to emphasize words:

```
"We will have " & TextColor ( NumberItems; RGB ( 255; 0; 0 )) & " errors per cycle.
Unacceptable!"
```

TextColor() can also be used for conditional text formatting. The following calculation highlights losses in red:

```
Let ( Profit = GetAsText ( Earnings – Expenditures );
  Case (
    Profit > 0; TextColor ( Profit; RGB( 0; 0; 0 ));
    Profit < 0; TextColor ( Profit; RGB( 255; 0; 0 ));
    "")
)
```

If a field is formatted in the Number Format dialog, some options override the TextColor() function. For example, conditional color for negative numbers overrides TextColor(), unless the user has clicked into the field being formatted.

Examples:

Function	Results
TextColor ("this text will be blue"; RGB (0; 0; 255))	Returns this text will be blue, formatted in blue.
TextColor ("this text will be red"; 16711680)	Returns this text will be red, formatted in red.

TextColorRemove()

Syntax:

TextColorRemove (text {; RGB (red; green; blue)})

Data type returned: **Text** *Category:* **Text Formatting**

Parameters:

- **text**—Any text expression or text field.
- **RGB (red; green; blue)**— A function that accepts three parameters from 0 to 255 and returns a number from 0 to 16777215 representing a color. See the RGB() function for more information. Parameters in curly braces { } are optional.

Description:

Removes all font colors in text, or removes instances of a specific font color as an optional parameter, leaving others unchanged. After removing font color from a data string, it is rendered in whatever default text color is set for the layout object in which it is displayed.

Examples:

Function	Results
TextColorRemove ("This should be boring monochromatic stuff")	Returns This should be boring monochromatic stuff without a color "specified".
TextColorRemove ("No More Red Eye"; RGB (255; 0; 0))	Returns No More Red Eye without the specific red indicated by RGB (255;0;0), should there be any applied within the text. Any other colors that have been specified within the string will be unaltered.

TextFont()

Syntax:

TextFont (text; fontName {; fontScript})

Data type returned: **Text**

Category: **Text Formatting**

Parameters:

- **text**—Any text string or expression that returns a text string.
- **fontName**—Any font name available on the system. Must be enclosed in quotation marks.
- **fontScript**—The name of a character set (for example, Cyrillic, Greek, Roman). This is an optional parameter; quotation marks should not be used around the script name as they are keywords. Parameters in curly braces { } are optional.

Description:

Changes the text font to the specified fontName and optional fontScript.

If no matches for the specified font and script exist, FileMaker first looks for the font script and associated font in the Fonts tab of the Preferences dialog box. If the script is not specified in the Fonts tab, the TextFont() function uses the default font for the system. This font script might not be the same as the specified script.

The list of possible font scripts is as follows:

Roman

Greek

Cyrillic

CentralEurope

ShiftJIS

TraditionalChinese

SimplifiedChinese

OEM

Symbol

Other

Examples:

Function	Results
TextFont ("testing 123"; "Courier")	Returns the string testing 123 in Courier font.

TextFontRemove()

Syntax:

TextFontRemove (text {; fontName; fontScript})

Data type returned: **Text** *Category:* **Text Formatting**

Parameters:

- **text**—Any text string or expression that returns a text string.
- **fontName**—Any font name expressed in text.
- **fontScript**—The name of a character set that contains characters required for writing in the specified language. Parameters in curly braces { } are optional. Note that the fontScript parameter is not enclosed in quotation marks (" ") and requires specific keywords. These are listed in the description of the TextFont() function.

Description:

Removes all fonts applied to text, or removes only fonts and font scripts as specified by the two optional parameters, fontName and fontScript. After fonts have been removed, the data is displayed and treated as text entered into any FileMaker Pro field by adopting whatever font attributes have been applied to the layout objects in question.

Examples:

Function	Results
TextFontRemove ("Nuke all fonts")	Returns Nuke all fonts displayed in a layout object's default font.
TextFontRemove ("Two fonts enter, one font leaves"; "Comic Sans MS")	Returns Two fonts enter, one font leaves with the Comic Sans MS font removed (assuming the original text string made use of it).
TextFontRemove ("How's your Russian?"; "Arial"; Cyrillic)	Returns How's your Russian? with the Arial font removed from any Cyrillic character sets.

TextFormatRemove()

Syntax:

TextFormatRemove (text)

Data type returned: **Text** *Category:* **Text Formatting**

Parameters:

- **text**—Any text string or expression that returns a text string.

Description:

Removes all formatting from text including all fonts, styles, font sizes, and font colors. The resulting string is rendered using the default attributes from the layout object in which it appears.

This function can be particularly useful as part of an auto-entered calculation formula applied to fields into which users habitually paste formatted text from other applications (that is, email messages).

Examples:

Function	Results
TextFormatRemove ("Enough is enough")	Returns the text Enough is enough without any text formatting applied.
TextFormatRemove (Self)	Returns as unformatted text the data contained in the current object in which the calculation is defined.

TextSize()

Syntax:

TextSize (text; fontSize)

Data type returned: **Text, Number** *Category:* **Text Formatting**

Parameters:

- **text**—Any text string or expression that returns a text string.
- **fontSize**—Any font size expressed in pixels as an integer.

Description:

Returns the text string at the specified font size. When TextSize() is used as part of the definition of a calculation field, the calculation should be set to return a text or number result. Text formatting options are lost if the data type returned is anything other than text or number.

Examples:

Function	Results
TextSize ("Hello, world!"; 8)	Returns Hello, world! in 8-point font.
TextSize ("Large print book"; 18)	Returns Large print book in 18-point font.

TextSizeRemove()

Syntax:

TextSizeRemove (text {; sizeToRemove})

Data type returned: **Text, Number** *Category:* **Text Formatting**

Parameters:

- **text**—Any text string or expression that returns a text string.
- **sizeToRemove**—Any font size expressed as an integer.

Parameters in curly braces { } are optional.

Description:

Removes all font size applications in text, or removes just the font size specified by sizeToRemove. The text in question then adopts whatever font size has been specified for the layout object in which it displays.

Note that text formatting functions work only for data returned as text or number.

Examples:

Function	Results
TextSizeRemove ("It should be 8pt anyway")	Returns It should be 8pt anyway without font sizes specified.
TextSizeRemove ("It's too small!!"; 6)	Returns It's too small!! with the 6-point font size removed.

TextStyleAdd()

Syntax:

TextStyleAdd (text; style(s))

Data type returned: **Text** *Category:* **Text Formatting**

Parameters:

- **text**—Any text string or expression that returns a text string.
- **style**—Any named style, a list of styles separated by a plus (+) sign, or an integer that represents a combination of styles. Named styles, listed in Table 9.2, should not be placed in quotation marks and cannot be passed as field contents or variables.

Description:

Returns a text string that has the specified style(s) applied to it.

The style names are reserved keywords in FileMaker Pro and should not be placed within quotes. You also cannot place a keyword in a field and use the field as the style parameter within TextStyleAdd(). Styles can be specified as local variables within Let functions.

All the style names have numeric equivalents that you can use instead of the names. To combine multiple styles, simply add the numeric equivalents together. The numeric equivalent can be stored in a field, so use this method if you need to dynamically specify a text style.

Table 9.2 lists the styles and their numeric equivalents.

Table 9.2 Style Names and Numeric Equivalent

Style Name	Numeric Equivalent
Plain	0
Strikethrough	1
Smallcaps	2
Superscript	4
Subscript	8
Uppercase	16
Lowercase	32
Titlecase	48
Wordunderline	64
Doubleunderline	128
Bold	256
Italic	512
Underline	1024
Condense	8192
Extend	16384
Allstyles	32767

Examples:

Function	Results
TextStyleAdd ("word underline."; WordUnderline)	Returns word underline.
TextStyleAdd ("bold italic!"; Bold+Italic)	Returns ***bold italic!***.
TextStyleAdd ("bold italic!"; 768)	Returns ***bold italic!***.
TextStyleAdd ("Plain text"; Plain)	Removes all styles from the text. If the "Plain" style is combined with any other styles, "Plain" is ignored.

TextStyleRemove()

Syntax:

TextStyleRemove (text; style(s))

Data type returned: **Text** *Category:* **Text Formatting**

Parameters:

- **text**—Any text string or expression that returns a text string.
- **style**—Any named style, a list of styles separated by a plus (+) sign, or an integer that represents a combination of styles. Named styles should not be placed in quotation marks and cannot be passed as field contents.

Description:

Removes the specified styles from formatted text.

Removing AllStyles with TextStyleRemove() accomplishes the same thing as adding Plain with TextStyleAdd().

See TextStyleAdd() for a complete list of styles and a discussion of their numeric equivalents.

Examples:

Function	Results
TextStyleRemove ("word underline"; WordUnderline)	Removes the word underline formatting from the phrase "word underline".
TextStyleRemove ("bold italic!"; Bold+Italic)	Removes the bold and italic formatting from the phrase "bold italic!".
TextStyleRemove (sampleText; AllStyles)	Removes all formatting styles from the contents of the sampleText field.

Time()

Syntax:

Time (hours; minutes; seconds)

Data type returned: **Time** *Category:* **Time**

Parameters:

- **hours**—A number or numeric expression representing the hours portion of the desired time value.
- **minutes**—A number or numeric expression representing the minutes portion of the desired time value.
- **seconds**—A number or numeric expression representing the seconds portion of the desired time value.

Description:

Returns a time value built from the specified hours, minutes, and seconds parameters. The resulting value accurately calculates the effect of fractional parameters. Similarly, although the typical range for the minutes and seconds parameters is from 0 to 59, any values above or below are compensated for in the resulting time value.

The Time() function is often used in conjunction with the Hour(), Minute(), and Seconds() functions. For instance, the following formula takes the current time and returns the time of the next lowest hour:

```
Time ( Hour ( Get ( CurrentTime )); 0; 0 ))
```

Examples:

Function	Results
Time (8; 34; 15)	Returns 8:34:15.
Time (15.25; 0; 0)	Returns 15:15:00.
Time (22; 70; 70)	Returns 23:11:10.
Time (12; -30; 0)	Returns 11:30:00.

Timestamp()

Syntax:

Timestamp (date; time)

Data type returned: **Timestamp** *Category:* **Timestamp**

Parameters:

- **date**—Any calendar date or expression that returns a date. The date parameter can also be an integer from 1 to 1460970, representing the number of days since January 1, 0001.
- **time**—Any time value or expression that returns a time value. The time parameter can also be an integer representing the number of seconds since midnight.

Description:

Returns a timestamp from the two parameters in the format "12/12/2005 10:45:00 AM".

You can use text parsing functions or mathematical operations to extract the pieces of a timestamp. You can also use the GetAsDate() and GetAsTime() functions to retrieve just the date or time portion of a timestamp.

Internally, FileMaker Pro stores timestamp data as the number of seconds since 1/1/0001 12:00 a.m. You can use the GetAsNumber() function to see the numeric representation. For instance, GetAsNumber (Timestamp ("4/18/2004"; 12:00pm)) returns 63217886400.

You can manually calculate the integer value of a timestamp by using the following formula:

```
( GetAsNumber ( myDate ) -1 ) * 86400 + GetAsNumber ( myTime )
```

Examples:

Function	Results
Timestamp ("10/11/2005"; "10:20 AM")	Returns 10/11/2005 10:20 AM.
Timestamp ("10/11/2005"; "20:20:20")	Returns 10/11/2005 8:20:20 PM.
Timestamp (Date (10; 11; 2005); Time (10; 20; 0))	Returns 10/11/2005 10:20 AM.
Timestamp (laborDay ; 0)	Returns 9/5/2005 12:00:00 AM when laborDay is equal to 9/5/2005.
Timestamp (1; 0)	Returns 1/1/0001 12:00 AM.

Trim()

Syntax:

Trim (text)

Data type returned: Text *Category:* Text

Parameters:

- **text**—Any text string or expression that resolves to a text string.

Description:

Returns the specified text string with any leading or trailing spaces removed.

The Trim() function removes only leading and trailing spaces and not any other characters (such as carriage returns). See the custom functions fnTrimCharacters() and fnTrimReturns() for examples of how to trim characters other than spaces.

Trim() can be used to reformat data where users have inadvertently typed spaces at the end of an entry. This happens frequently with fields containing first names. To automatically have the entry reformatted when the user exits the field, have the field auto-enter Trim (Self) and uncheck the option not to replace any existing value in the field. Thus, if a user enters "Fred" into the FirstName field, it is replaced with "Fred" when the user exits the field.

Trim() is also used frequently to clean up fixed-width data that has been imported from some other data source. In such cases, fields have been padded with leading or trailing spaces to be a certain length. Remove them after importing by doing calculated replaces in the appropriate fields.

Examples:

Function	Results
Trim (" This is a test ")	Returns This is a test.

TrimAll()

Syntax:

TrimAll (text; trimSpaces; trimType)

Data type returned: **Text** *Category:* **Text**

Parameters:

- **text**—Any text expression or text field.
- **trimSpaces**—0 (False), 1 (True).
- **trimType**—0 through 3 depending on the trim style (listed in the Description section).

Description:

Returns text with all leading and trailing spaces removed and takes into account different Unicode representations of spaces.

Set trimSpaces to 1 if you want to include the removal of full-width spaces between non-Roman and Roman characters. Set trimSpaces to 0 if you do not.

Characters are considered Roman if their Unicode values are less than U+2F00. Characters with values greater than or equal to U+2F00 are considered non-Roman.

Characters within the Roman range belong to the following character blocks: Latin, Latin-1 Supplement, Latin Extended-A & B, IPA Extensions, Spacing Modifier Letters, Combining Diacritical Marks, Greek, Cyrillic, Armenian, Hebrew, Arabic, Devanagari, Bengali, Gurmukhi, Gujarati, Oriya, Tamil, Telugu, Kannada, Malayalam, Thai, Lao, Tibetan, Georgian, Hangul Jamo, and additional Latin and Greek extended blocks.

Symbols within the Roman range include punctuation characters, superscripts, subscripts, currency symbols, combining marks for symbols, letterlike symbols, number forms, arrows, math operators, control pictures, geometric shapes, dingbats, and so on.

Characters within the non-Roman range are those belonging to the CJK symbols/punctuations area, Hiragana, Katakana, Bopomofo, Hangul compatibility Jamo, Kanbun, CJK unified ideographs, and so on.

The trimType parameter controls how the function returns text in the following ways:

0 Removes spaces between non-Roman and Roman characters and always leaves one space between Roman words.

1 Always includes a half-width space between non-Roman and Roman characters and always leaves one space between Roman words.

2 Removes spaces between non-Roman characters (reducing multiple spaces between non-Roman and Roman words to 1 space) and leaves one space between Roman words.

3 Removes all spaces everywhere.

In all cases, spaces between non-Roman characters are removed.

Examples:

Function	Results
TrimAll (Full_Name; 1; 0)	Returns James Aloysius Kinsella when the value of Full_Name is "James Aloysius Kinsella ". It is useful for stripping extra spaces out of lengthy text fields.
TrimAll("名前,1,0")	Returns 山田太郎 when the value of 名前,1,0 is 山田　太.

Truncate()

Syntax:

Truncate (number; precision)

Data type returned: **Number** *Category:* **Number**

Parameters:

- **number**—Any expression that resolves to a numeric value.
- **precision**—Any expression that resolves to a numeric value.

Description:

Returns the specified number truncated to the specified number of decimal places (precision). Unlike the Round() function, the Truncate() function simply discards further digits without performing any sort of rounding.

Truncating a number by using a precision parameter of 0 has the same effect as taking the Int() of that number. Truncate (x; 0) = Int (x).

Negative values can be used for the precision parameter in the Truncate() function to truncate to nearest ten, hundred, thousand, and so on. For instance, Truncate (1234.1234; -1) returns 1230. Truncate (1234.1234; -2) returns 1200.

Examples:

Function	Results
Truncate (Pi; 6)	Returns 3.141592.
Truncate (Amount; 2)	Returns 54.65 when Amount contains 54.651259.
Truncate (1234.1234; 0)	Returns 1234.
Truncate (-1234.1234; 0)	Returns –1234.

Upper()

Syntax:

Upper (text)

Data type returned: **Text** *Category:* **Text**

Parameters:

- **text**—A string or text expression.

Description:

Returns a completely uppercase version of the specified text string.

The Upper() function is one of three functions FileMaker Pro has for changing the case of a text string. The other two are Lower() and Proper().

The Upper() function is often used to reformat user-entered data to ensure consistent data entry. Sometimes when exporting data that is to be used by external applications, you need to format the data entirely as uppercase characters to be consistent with data in the other system.

The following formula checks whether a given text string is already written in all uppercase characters:

```
Exact ( text; Upper ( text ))
```

Examples:

Function	Results
Upper ("This is a test")	Returns THIS IS A TEST.
Upper (AccessCode)	Returns 1ABC-2XYZ when AccessCode contains "1abc-2XYz".

ValueCount()

Syntax:

ValueCount (text)

Data type returned: **Number** *Category:* **Text**

Parameters:

- **text**—Any return-delimited string or expression that generates a return-delimited list.

Description:

Returns a count of the number of values in the text provided.

The presence or absence of a trailing return after the last item in the return-delimited list does not affect the result returned by ValueCount. For instance, ValueCount ("Blue¶Green") and ValueCount ("Blue¶Green¶") both return 2.

If there are multiple returns at any point in the list, the ValueCount() function recognizes the empty items as valid items. For instance, ValueCount ("¶¶Blue¶¶Green¶¶") returns 6. Note that this behavior is different from how the WordCount() function treats multiple delimiters. There, multiple delimiters in a row are considered to be a single delimiter.

Examples:

Function	Results
ValueCount ("A¶B¶C¶D¶E")	Returns 5.
ValueCount (officeList)	Returns 3 when officeList is equal to Chicago Philadelphia San Francisco

ValueListIDs()

Syntax:

ValueListIDs (fileName)

Data type returned: **Text** *Category:* **Design**

Parameters:

- **fileName**—A string or text expression that represents the name of an open file.

Description:

Returns a carriage return-delimited list of value list IDs from the specified file.

FileMaker Pro assigns a serial number to each value list created in a file. The order of the list returned by the ValueListIDs() function is the same as that in which the value lists are ordered in the Manage Value Lists dialog when the order is set to Custom Order. Changing the Custom Order changes the way the results are ordered, but selecting one of the other choices (Creation Order, Source, Value List Name) does not.

Examples:

Function	Results
ValueListIDs (Get (FileName))	Returns a list of value list IDs for the current file that might look like this: 21 92 90 108 15

ValueListItems()

Syntax:

ValueListItems (fileName; valueListName)

Data type returned: **Text** *Category:* **Design**

Parameters:

- **fileName**—A string or text expression that represents the name of an open file.
- **valueListName**—The name of a value list in fileName.

Description:

Returns a carriage return-delimited list of the items in the specified value list.

The ValueListItems() function can be used to return a list of all the items in a field's index. To do this, the value list should be set to "Use values from field" and to "Include all values" in the subsequent dialog. Although this practice works with value lists that show only related sets of data, the List() function is more suited for this purpose in most cases.

As with many design functions, we recommend against hard-coding specific text strings into calculations, but in this case it cannot be avoided. One practice we follow in our work is to name value lists that are referenced elsewhere by name with a suffix "DNR" for "do not rename." Another approach is to create a custom function that returns value list names and thus provides a single place to control edits.

Examples:

Function	Results
ValueListItems (Get (FileName); "Phone_Label")	Returns a list of values from the value list Phone_Label in the current file that mightlook like this: Home Work Cell Fax

ValueListNames()

Syntax:

ValueListNames (fileName)

Data type returned: **Text** *Category:* **Design**

Parameters:

- **fileName**—A string or text expression that represents the name of an open file.

Description:

Returns a carriage return-delimited list of value list names from the specified file.

The order of the list returned by the ValueListNames() function is the same as that in which the value lists are ordered in the Manage Value Lists dialog when the order is set to Custom Order. Changing the Custom Order changes the way the results are ordered, but selecting one of the other choices (Creation Order, Source, Value List Name) does not.

Examples:

Function	Results
ValueListNames (Get (FileName))	Returns a list of value list names from the current file that might look like this: Phone_Label Location Type Category

Variance()

Syntax:

Variance (field {; field...})

Data type returned: **Number** *Category:* **Aggregate**

Parameters:

- **field**—Any related field, repeating field, or set of nonrepeating fields that represent a collection of numbers.

Description:

Returns the variance of the nonblank values represented in the parameter list. Variance is a statistical measure of how spread out a set of values is.

The StDev() of a set of numbers is the square root of the Variance() of the set.

The difference between the Variance() and VarianceP() functions is that the Variance divides the sum of the squares by n-1 instead of by n.

Examples:

The Variance of a set of numbers can be calculated by summing the squares of the distance of each value from the mean, then dividing by n-1, where n is the number of values.

For instance, given the set of numbers 8, 10, and 12, the mean of the set is 10. The distance of each value from the mean is -2, 0, and 2. The squares of these distances are 4, 0, and 4, and the sum of the squares is 8. The Variance is 8 divided by (3–1), which is 4.

```
Variance (8; 10; 12)
```

returns 4.

```
Variance (7; 11; 13)
```

returns 9.33.

VarianceP()

Syntax:

VarianceP (field {; field...})

Data type returned: **Number** *Category:* **Aggregate**

Parameters:

- **field**—Any related field, repeating field, or set of nonrepeating fields that represent a collection of numbers.

Description:

Returns the variance of a population represented by the nonblank values in the parameter list. Variance of population is a statistical measure of how spread out a set of values is.

The StDevP() of a set of numbers is the square root of the VarianceP() of the set.

Examples:

The variance of a population represented by a set of numbers can be calculated by summing the squares of the distance of each value from the mean, then dividing by n, where n is the number of values.

For instance, given the set of numbers 8, 10, and 12, the mean of the set is 10. The distance of each value from the mean is -2, 0, and 2. The squares of these distances are 4, 0, and 4, and the sum of the squares is 8. The VarianceP is 8 divided by 3, which is 2.67.

```
VarianceP (8; 10; 12)
```

returns 2.67.

```
VarianceP (7; 11; 13)
```

returns 6.22.

WeekOfYear()

Syntax:

WeekOfYear (date)

Data type returned: **Number** *Category:* **Date**

Parameters:

- **date**—Any valid date (1/1/0001–12/31/4000). The parameter should be a string containing a date (for example, "3/17/2004"), an expression with a date result (for example, Date (6, 29, 1969)), or an integer that represents a serialized date value (for example, 718977).

Description:

Returns the week number of the specified date. Weeks are defined as starting on Sunday and ending on Saturday. A partial week at the beginning of the year is considered as week 1, so the WeekOfYear() function can return values from 1 to 54.

WeekOfYear() can be used to return the approximate number of weeks between two dates in the same year. For instance, WeekOfYear("6/1/2001") - WeekOfYear("5/1/2001") returns 4. It's also useful for reports where you need to subsummarize data by week.

January 1st of any given year is always part of week 1, no matter on what day of the week it falls.

Examples:

Function	Results
WeekOfYear ("3/12/2004")	Returns 11.
WeekOfYear ("12/31/2001")	Returns 53.

WeekOfYearFiscal()

Syntax:

WeekOfYearFiscal (date; startingDay)

Data type returned: **Number** *Category:* **Date**

Parameters:

- **date**—Any valid date (1/1/0001–12/31/4000). The parameter should be a string containing a date (for example, "3/17/2004"), an expression with a date result (for example, Date (6, 29, 1969)), or an integer that represents a serialized date value (for example, 718977).
- **startingDay**—A numeric value between 1 (Sunday) and 7 (Saturday).

Description:

The WeekOfYearFiscal() function returns an integer from 1 to 53 that represents the week number of the year of the specified date. Weeks are defined as starting on the day of week specified by the startingDay parameter.

The first week of a year is defined as the first week that contains four or more days of that year. For instance, January 1, 2004, was a Thursday. Using a startingDay of 5 (representing Thursday), the first fiscal week of the year would be considered as 1/1/2004 through 1/7/2004. The second fiscal week would begin on Thursday, 1/8/2004. However, if you used a startingDay of 1 (Sunday), then the first day of the fiscal year would be 1/4/2004. In the previous week (12/28/2003–1/3/2004), only three days are in 2004, so that would be considered as the 53rd fiscal week of 2003.

WeekOfYearFiscal() and WeekOfYear() often yield different results. WeekOfYear() is always based on a week defined as Sunday through Saturday, whereas WeekOfYearFiscal() can begin on whatever day you specify. Even when it begins on Sunday, however, you might have discrepancies because of the rule that the first week must have four or more days in the current year. Whereas WeekOfYearFiscal("1/1/2004" ; 1) returns 53, WeekOfYear("1/1/2004") returns 1.

Examples:

Function	Results
WeekOfYearFiscal ("3/21/2004", 4)	Returns 12.
WeekOfYearFiscal ("1/1/2004", 1)	Returns 53.
WeekOfYearFiscal ("1/1/2004", 2)	Returns 1.

WindowNames

Syntax:

WindowNames {(fileName)}

Data type returned: **Text** *Category:* **Design**

Parameters:

- **fileName**—A string or text expression that represents the name of an open file. This parameter is optional.

Description:

Returns a carriage return-delimited list of open window names.

WindowNames can return window names from all open FileMaker Pro files or just the file specified by the optional parameter. Window names do not need to be unique. The order of the list is determined by the stacking order of the windows, with the topmost window (the active window) listed first. Hidden windows are listed, but not any window that appears in the window list surrounded by parentheses. This indicates a file that is open but that doesn't have any windows, hidden or visible. Visible windows are listed first, then minimized windows, then hidden windows.

Examples:

Function	Results
WindowNames	Returns a list of values that might look like this: Customers Invoices myDatabase Invoices – 2
WindowNames (Get (FileName))	Returns a list of values that might look like this: Invoices Invoices - 2

WordCount()

Syntax:

WordCount (text)

Data type returned: **Number** *Category:* **Text**

Parameters:

- **text**—Any text string or expression that resolves to a text string.

Description:

Returns a count of the number of words in text.

Spaces, return characters, and most punctuation symbols are considered to be word breaks by FileMaker Pro. Multiple word breaks next to each other (for example, two spaces, a comma, and a space) are considered a single word break.

Certain punctuation symbols are word breaks when separating alpha characters, but not when separating numeric characters. These include the colon (:), slash (/), period (.), comma (,), and dash (-). For instance, WordCount ("54-6") returns 1, but WordCount ("x-y") returns 2. The reason for this behavior is that those symbols are valid date, time, and number separators.

Examples:

Function	Results
WordCount ("The quick brown fox jumps over the lazy dog.")	Returns 9.
WordCount (FullName)	Returns 4 when FullName contains "John Q. Public, Jr."

Year()

Syntax:

Year (date)

Data type returned: **Number** *Category:* **Date**

Parameters:

- **date**—Any valid date (1/1/0001–12/31/4000). The parameter should be a string containing a date (for example, "3/17/2008"), an expression with a date result (for example, Date (6, 29, 1969)), or an integer that represents a serialized date value (for example, 718977).

Description:

Returns the year portion of the date parameter.

The Year() function is often used in conjunction with the Date() function to assemble new date values. For instance, if you have a field called DateOfBirth that contains someone's birthdate, you can calculate the date of that person's birthday in the current year as follows:

```
Date ( Month ( DateOfBirth ), Day ( DateOfBirth ), Year ( Get ( CurrentDate )))
```

Examples:

Function	Results
Year ("1/1/2008")	Returns 2008.
Year (Get (CurrentDate))	Returns the current year.
Year (myBirthdate)	Returns the year portion of the field myBirthdate.

YearName()

Syntax:

YearName (date; format)

Data type returned: **Text (Japanese)** *Category:* **Date**

Parameters:

- **date**—Any calendar date.
- **format**—A number (0, 1, or 2) that controls the display format.

Description:

Returns the Japanese year name for the date specified.

The formats control how the name of Emperor is displayed: 0 = Long, 1 = Abbreviated, 2 = 2-byte Roman. "Seireki" is returned when date falls before Emperial names have been applied.

0 - Meiji (明治) 8, Taisho (大正) 8, Showa (昭和) 8, Heisei (平成) 8 (before 1868.9.8, Seireki (西暦xxxx)

1 - Mei (明) 8, Tai (大) 8, Sho (昭) 8, Hei (平) 8 (before 1868.9.8, Sei (西暦xxxx)

2 - M8, T8, S8, H8 (before 1868.9.8, A.D.xxxx)

Examples:

Function	Results
YearName (DateField; 0)	Returns 平成 14 when DateField contains 7/17/2002

PART III

Custom Functions

CHAPTER 10

Custom Function Primer

Custom functions are without a doubt one of the most powerful features in FileMaker; we cannot advocate their use strongly enough.

When added to a file by a developer, custom functions become available in various calculation dialogs as additional functions for use within expressions. They are snippets of code that, just as FileMaker's preestablished functions do, accept parameters and produce output. One example might be

```
fnCommission ( unitPrice; quantity; discount )
```

This function would presumably return a dollar amount based on some formula that multiplied unitPrice and quantity, subtracted a discount from the total, and then applied a percentage or some internal factoring to arrive at a sales commission.

Note that as a developer using a given custom function, you do not even need to know what that formula might be. All you require is that the function return a meaningful and consistent result when fed the necessary parameters.

Custom functions allow developers to abstract portions of code, independent from database schema or scripts, where it's then possible to reference a particular piece of logic throughout one's database. For example, if an organization's commission rates needed to change, the system's developer could edit a single custom function containing those rates, and all the calculations based on that function would immediately (depending on their storage settings) reflect and use the change.

Custom functions also facilitate code reuse: It's reasonably easy to copy code and insert a function into a different file. After being written and debugged, functions can be reused as necessary.

Custom functions can also serve as permanent "system variables" that are not subject to session issues as global fields and global variables are. The values within a custom function do not expire at the end of a user's session, they are consistent across all users of a database, and a developer can change them centrally as needed.

Note finally that FileMaker Pro 9 Advanced is required for authoring or editing custom functions. After a function is added to a file, however, it becomes available to any user or developer who has access to a calculation dialog, be it in the service of tasks such as defining fields, writing scripts, or even performing calculated replaces.

The Custom Function Interface

The Edit Custom Function dialog (see Figure 10.1) allows developers to define parameters that then serve as input for an expression written to reference those parameters.

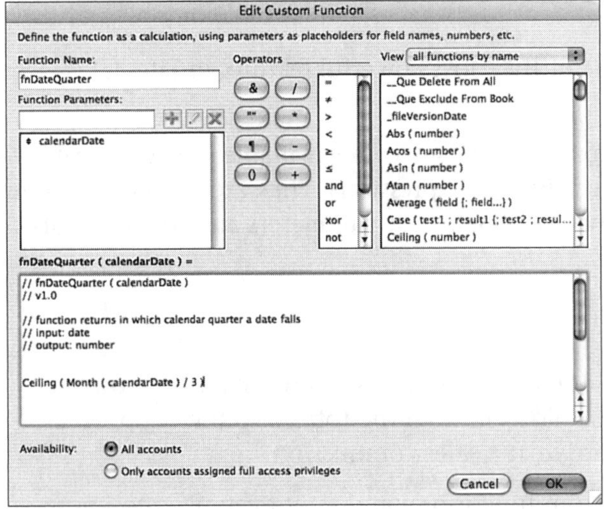

Figure 10.1

The Edit Custom Function dialog.

Custom Functions: Things to Remember

Custom functions work much like calculation functions, but it's important to understand the following aspects of custom functions:

- Custom functions follow the same rules for syntax that calculation functions follow.

→ *For a review of calculation syntax,* ***see*** *Chapter 7, "Calculation Primer,"* ***p. 53.***

- Instead of referencing schema information (data fields), custom functions use parameters. Values for these parameters are passed into the custom function from elsewhere in one's database via the Specify Calculation dialog.
- Custom functions return a single result.
- Custom functions cannot directly use or access container data.

- Custom functions can use all the functions built into FileMaker, including other custom functions and external functions.
- It is possible to make use of schema data fields by using the Evaluate() function. The following example illustrates a scenario where a sales commission is referenced:

```
fnSalesCommission ( unitPrice; quantity; discount )
// function to calculate the sales commission for various transaction totals.
// expected input:
//   unitPrice = dollar amount to two decimal places;
//   quantity = integer;
//   discount = any number (positive = discount)
// expected result: a dollar amount.

Let ([
   salePrice = unitPrice * quantity;
   total = salePrice - discount;
   discountPenalty = Case ( discount > 0;  .01; 0 );
   commissionPercent = Evaluate ( "ProductRate::Commission" ) - discountPenalty
   ]; // end variable declaration
   total * ( commissionPercent - discountPenalty )
)
```

- Just as custom functions can reference other functions, they can reference themselves as well. This allows you to write recursive functions in FileMaker. Keep in mind that recursive functions require an exit condition, or you end up with endless recursion and no result returned.

  The following is an example of a simple recursive function that reorders a carriage return-delimited list from bottom to top:

```
fnListBackwards ( valueList )
// function to reverse the order of a ¶-delimited list
// expected input:
//   valuelist = text values delimited by ¶
// expected result: a valuelist of text values delimited by ¶ in reverse order

Let ([
   numOfValues = ValueCount ( valuelist "");
   firstValue = LeftValues ( valuelist; 1 )
   remainingList = RightValues ( valuelist; numOfValues - 1 );
   resultList = Case ( numOfValues = 1; ""; fnListBackwards ( remainingList ) );
   ];
   resultList & firstValue
)
```

- If no exit condition in a recursive custom function exists or an error in logic occurs, the maximum number of recursions a function can make is 10,000. This assumes that it is a nested call that requires FileMaker to maintain a stack in memory of each recursion's result. FileMaker stops the recursive nest and returns a "?" as the result of any calculation using that function.

  If, on the other hand, you write a custom function so that the results of one recursion are passed into the subsequent recursive call as a parameter (and thus not requiring FileMaker to maintain a stack of results, but rather only calculating results in a series), the maximum limit is 50,000. This technique is referred to as *tail recursion*; here are some simple examples to demonstrate:

  ```
  fnSummation ( number; iterations; startValue )
  ```

  This function adds *number* to itself for as many times as *iterations* dictates. For example, fnSummation (5; 3; 0) adds 5 + 5 + 5 to return 15. fnSummation (5; 3; 4) adds 5 + 5 + 5 beginning at 4 to return 19.

  Nested technique, requiring that FileMaker "stack" the results in memory:

  ```
  Case ( iterations > 1;
              // iterate and then add the new number on the way down
     fnSummation ( number; iterations - 1 ; startValue ) + number ;
              // return the result
     startValue + number
  )
  ```

  Tail Recursion technique where the results from one iteration are passed entirely into the next iteration, requiring no saved stack:

  ```
  Case ( iterations > 1 ;
              // add the new number and then iterate
     fnSummation ( number; iterations - 1 ; startValue + number ) ;
              // return the result
     startValue + number
  )
  ```

Recursive Techniques

In the first example, FileMaker has to preserve each nested result (in a stack) to derive its final result. In the second, the function passes in everything required through the parameters of the function and does not require evaluation of the entire stack. The first example will only work up to 10,000 iterations. The second can be evaluated in serial, up to 50,000 iterations.

To understand tail recursion, consider an analogy. Assume that you want to measure how many cups a body of water contains. One method would be to use a single 1-cup measuring cup, scoop out the water, and keep a count of how many times you do so. This method, akin to stack recursion or nested recursion, requires that you keep track of how many times you've been through the process. Now imagine a second scenario where each time you measure out a new cup of water, you increase the size of your measuring cup. It starts as one cup, then holds two cups, and finally ends at the same number of cups the original body of water contained. You would not need to keep track of any count in the process: The result derived from your last iteration is the result you're looking for.

If you refer to the previous examples, notice that the first example combines a recursive call with an operator. In the third line of the function, *number* is being added to the recursive result of fnSummation again. This approach requires that FileMaker "keep track of" each result from each iteration of your recursive call to calculate the final result. It needs to create a stack of results and pass down the chain to the end point and back up again to calculate the final result. FileMaker literally processes each step of your recursion twice.

If you compare that to the second example, the recursive call in line three is not paired with an operator. It is simply called again with different parameters. It's a subtle but important difference. At the end of the recursive process, the results of the final recursive call are simply the result you're looking for. FileMaker can process each instance of the recursion loop and "forget" what the prior instance returned without processing the stack a second time.

The operator combined with your recursive call is a sign that you're not using tail recursion. Look to create recursive calls without operators, where you're simply passing new parameters into your recursive function, and your system will perform better and be capable of deeper processing limits.

- Custom functions can interact with global and local variables. In the case of local variables ($myVar), FileMaker stores values specific to a currently running script. In the case of a global variable ($$myVar), the value in the variable is updated and maintained throughout the file in a single user's individual session.

  If you want to create or set variables within a custom function, use the Let() function:

  ```
  Let ([
     myInternalVariable = $$globalVariable + 1;
     $$newVariable = 1 + 1;
     result = $$newVariable + myInternalVariable
     ];
     Result
  )
  ```

Custom functions are powerful tools for building abstract units of logic that can then be reused throughout a solution. After a custom function has been created (and tested!) it's easy enough to re-create it in other files for use throughout all your solutions. We strongly recommend you create a library of tools to refine and reuse over time. To that end, see Chapter 11, "Useful Custom Functions," for a selection of some of our favorites.

CHAPTER 11

Useful Custom Functions

Sample Custom Function Library

This chapter presents a sampling of custom functions that we've found useful, or that we feel serve as good examples of functions we use in our day-to-day practice. They're broken into groups according to their purpose, much as the calculation functions in FileMaker Pro are.

Please note that these functions are meant only to serve as examples—we've not tested them exhaustively, nor is this collection meant to be comprehensive. We hope you'll find some of them helpful directly, or that reading and analyzing others might provide a springboard for your own ideas. We have tried to reasonably test the code here, but in our own practice would test significantly more prior to using them in a system meant for production.

Number Calculations

fnHypotenuse (leg1Length; leg2Length)

Although FileMaker includes many common mathematical operations and formulas, no list can be exhaustive. This function applies the Pythagorean Theorem ($a^2 + b^2 = c^2$) to generate the length of a hypotenuse (the leg of a right triangle opposite the right angle). We find this a good teaching example to demonstrate the concept of custom functions.

Code:

```
// returns the length of a hypotenuse based on the Pythagorean Theorem ( a^2 + b^2 = c^2 )
// input: two numbers
// output: number
Let ([
   a2 = leg1Length * leg1Length;
   b2 = leg2Length * leg2Length;
   c2 = a2 + b2
   ];
   Sqrt ( c2 )
)
```

Example:

fnHypotenuse (3; 4) returns 5.

fnNthRoot (number; root)

FileMaker provides a built-in function for calculating the square root of a number, but not the nth root.

Code:

```
// returns the nth root of number
// input: two numbers
// output: number

Exp ( Ln ( number ) / root )
```

Example:

fnNthRoot (8; 3) returns 2.

fnNthRoot (256; 4) returns 4.

fnPolyAreaFromRadius (numberOfSides; radius)

This function computes the area of a regular polygon, given the number of sides and the radius of the polygon. (A regular polygon is a polygon in which all sides are of equal length.) The radius is the distance from the center of the polygon to any vertex. In other words, the radius of the polygon is the radius of a circle that exactly circumscribes the polygon. Note that this function calls another custom function, fnPolyAreaFromSide.

Code:

```
// computes the area of a regular polygon
// input:
//   numberOfSides = the number of the polygon's sides
//   radius = distance from the center of the polygon to a vertex
// output: area of the polygon in square units
// requires fnPolyAreaFromSide

Let ([
   n = numberOfSides;
   r = radius;
   sideLength = 2 * r * Sin ( Pi / n );
   result = fnPolyAreaFromSide ( n ; sideLength )
   ];
   result
)
```

Examples:

A pentagon with a radius of three meters would be evaluated like so: fnPolyAreaBySide (5 ; 3), which returns 21.399 (rounded) square meters.

An equilateral triangle with a radius of 4 inches: fnPolyAreaByRadius (3 ; 4) returns 20.723 square inches (rounded).

fnPolyAreaFromSide (numberOfSides; sideLength)

This function computes the area of a regular polygon, given the number of sides and the length of each side.

Code:

```
// computes the area of a regular polygon
// input:
//   numberOfSides = the number of the polygon's sides
//   sideLength = the length of one side
// output: area of the polygon in units squared

Let ([
   n = numberOfSides;
   l = sideLength;
   result = ( n * l^2) / ( 4 * Tan( Pi / n ) )
   ];
   result
)
```

Examples:

A hexagon with sides of length 3: fnPolyAreaFromSide (6 ; 3) returns 23.382 (rounded) units squared.

An equilateral triangle with sides of length 4: fnPolyAreaFromSide (3 ; 4) returns 6.928 (rounded) units squared.

fnPolygonArea (xlist; ylist)

This is a more advanced, more versatile function for calculating the area of a polygon: It does not require that the polygon be regular. In other words, any enclosed shape, with serial points at whichever angle, can be computed. The two parameter lists expect a series of X/Y coordinates at their points, with each subsequent point following the line that describes the shape (either clockwise or counterclockwise). The returned data is a number of whatever unit of measure the developer used to establish his grid, squared.

Code:

```
// calculates area of polygon using Double Meridian Distance
// requires fnPolygonAreaHelper; return delimited numeric arrays
//   of equal length and minimum 3 values.
//    key: Lat is Latitude; Dep is Departure

If ( ValueCount ( xlist ) ≥ 3 and ValueCount ( xlist ) = ValueCount ( ylist ) ;

  Let ([
    Lat = MiddleValues ( ylist ; 2 ; 1 ) - MiddleValues ( ylist ; 1 ; 1 ) ;
    Dep = MiddleValues ( xlist ; 2 ; 1 ) - MiddleValues ( xlist ; 1 ; 1 ) ;
    DMD = Dep ;
    DArea = Lat * DMD ;
    TotalDArea = DArea +
       fnPolygonAreaHelper ( xlist ; ylist ; Dep ; DMD ; 2 ; ValueCount ( xlist ) )
    ]; // end variables

    Abs ( TotalDArea ) / 2
  ) ;  //endLet

  "Lists must contain same number of values, minimum 3."

) //endIf
```

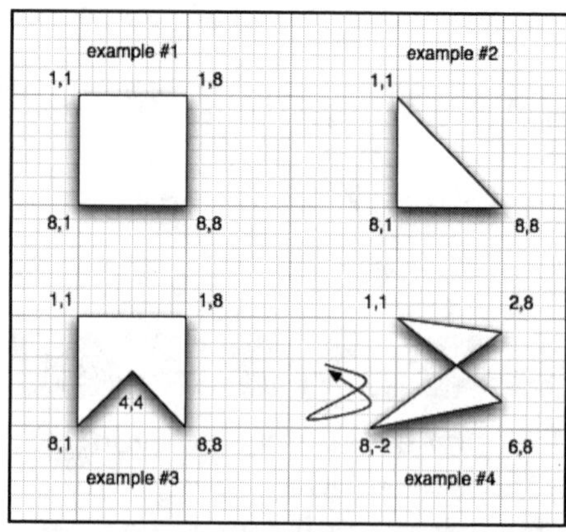

Figure 11.1

This function requires that you to describe shapes as a series of points on a grid.

Examples (refer to Figure 11.1):

Example 1: (square)

fnPolygonArea ("1¶1¶8¶8"; "1¶8¶8¶1") returns 49.

Example 2: (triangle)

fnPolygonArea ("1¶8¶8"; "1¶8¶1") returns 24.5.

Example 3: (enclosed shape)

fnPolygonArea ("1¶1¶8¶4¶8"; "1¶8¶8¶4¶1") returns 35.

Example 4: (crossed shape)

fnPolygonArea ("1¶2¶6¶8"; "1¶8¶8¶-2") returns 46.

fnPolygonAreaHelper (xlist ; ylist ; prevDep ; prevDMD ; i ; listLength)

This subfunction supports the main fnPolygonArea function.

Code:

```
//fnPolygonAreaHelper ( xlist ; ylist ; prevDep ; prevDMD ; i ; listLength )
//dependency: must be called from main function, fnPolygonArea

Let ([
   i = i+1 ;
   Lat = MiddleValues ( ylist ; i ; 1 ) - MiddleValues ( ylist ; i-1 ; 1 ) ;
   Dep = MiddleValues ( xlist ; i ; 1 ) - MiddleValues ( xlist ; i-1 ; 1 ) ;
   DMD = Dep + prevDep + prevDMD;
   DArea = Lat * DMD
   ]; // end variables

   DArea +

   If ( i < listLength ;
      fnPolygonAreaHelper ( xlist ; ylist ; Dep ; DMD ; i ; listLength ) ;

      Let ([ //innerLet
         Lat = MiddleValues ( ylist ; 1 ; 1 ) - MiddleValues ( ylist ; listLength ; 1 ) ;
         Dep = MiddleValues ( xlist ; 1 ; 1 ) - MiddleValues ( xlist ; listLength ; 1 ) ;
         DMD = Dep * -1 ;
         DArea = Lat * DMD
         ]; // end inner variables
```

```
        DArea
    ) //end InnerLet

  ) //end If
  ) //end OuterLet
```

fnRandomInRange (lowNumber; highNumber)

The Random function in FileMaker returns a value between 0 and 1, but developers almost always need a random integer within a range of numbers. For example, if you need a number between 10 and 50, the formula would be

```
Int ( Random * 41 ) + 10
```

This makes code somewhat difficult to read and requires that you think through the formula each time you need it. This function hides that required logic in an easy-to-use, specialized form.

Code:

```
// returns a random number from low to high range
// input: two numbers
// output: a random number within the range between the two

Int ( Random * ( highNumber - lowNumber + 1 )) + lowNumber
```

Example:

fnRandomInRange (3; 7) might return 4.

SphericalDistance (lat1; long1; lat2; long2; units)

This function computes the distance between two points on the surface of the earth, given in terms of decimal latitude and longitude. The coordinates must be decimal—in other words, 45.5, not 45 degrees 30 minutes—and must be given in degrees.

The function can return results in miles or kilometers. Any "units" value beginning with "m" yields miles; otherwise, the function returns kilometers.

The computation is based on the "haversine formula" and assumes a reasonable degree of mathematical precision in the software, which FileMaker possesses.

See http://en.wikipedia.org/wiki/Haversine_formula for further details.

Code:

```
// computes distance between two points on Earth's surface
// input:
//   lat1, long2, lat2, long2 = lat and long of two points, in DECIMAL DEGREES
```

```
//   units = "miles" or "km"
// output: distance between the two points in miles or kilometers

Let([
   D = Case ( Trim (Lower (Left (units;1))) = "m"; 3958.75; 6367.45 );
      // diameter of Earth in miles or km
   lat1R =   Radians(lat1);
   lat2R =   Radians(lat2);
   long1R =   Radians(long1);
   long2R =   Radians(long2);
   dlat =   lat2R - lat1R;
   dlong =   long2R - long1R;
   a = (Sin(dlat/2))^2 + Cos(lat1R) * Cos(lat2R) * (Sin(dlong/2))^2;
   c = 2 * Atan(Sqrt(a)/Sqrt(1-a));
   result = D * c
   ];
   result
)
```

Example:

The distance between San Francisco and Chicago in miles is fnSphericalDistance (37.799; 122.461; 41.886; 87.623; "miles"), which returns 1856.62.

Date Calculations

fnAgeInYears (dateOfBirth)

This function returns a person's age in years.

The GetAsDate() function is used to ensure that whatever is passed in—a date, an integer, or raw text—gets converted to a date and thus accounts for data type issues.

Code:

```
// calculates age in years
// input: date
// output: integer


Let ( [
    currentYear = Year(Get(CurrentDate));
    birthYear = Year( dateOfBirth );
    birthdayThisYear = Date ( Month(dateOfBirth) ; Day(dateOfBirth) ; currentYear )
```

```
    ];
    currentYear - birthYear - Case( Get(CurrentDate) < birthdayThisYear; 1; 0 )
)
```

Example:

fnAgeInYears ("6/6/1967") returns 39, when the date is 1/1/2007.

fnDateMonthEnd (calendarDate)

This particular function determines the last day of the month for a given date. Note that in FileMaker, subtracting one from the first day of a month results in the last day of the prior month.

Code:

```
// calculates the last day of the month for a given date
// input: date
// output: date
Date ( Month ( calendarDate ) + 1 ; 1; Year ( calendarDate )) - 1
```

Example:

fnDateMonthEnd ("1/1/2007") returns 1/31/2007.

fnDateQuarter (calendarDate)

This function returns a number from 1 to 4, representing the quarter of the year in which the calendarDate falls. If you wanted it to return text along the lines of "1st Quarter", "2nd Quarter", and so on, you'd need a formula that used a Case() or Choose() function, as shown in the alternate syntax presented in the following Code section.

You could also use this function to calculate fiscal quarters by adding a number at the end of the custom function's formula for whatever month begins the fiscal year for a given company.

Code:

```
// function returns in which calendar quarter a date falls
// input: date
// output: text

Ceiling ( Month ( calendarDate ) / 3 )
```

Here's a code section that returns text:

```
Choose ( Ceiling ( Month ( calendarDate ) / 3 ) - 1;
   "1st Quarter"; "2nd Quarter"; "3rd Quarter"; "4th Quarter" )
```

Example:

fnDateQuarter (12/1/2006) returns 4.

fnDateRepetitions (calendarDate; period; numberOfRepetitions)

Although we'd never recommend trying to replicate the full functionality of a calendaring program such as Outlook in FileMaker, we do often need to create date ranges in list form. This function generates a return-delimited list of dates. You can then extract individual dates using the GetValue() function.

Note that the function requires specific keyword inputs and returns an error message if it does not recognize the value passed for its period parameter.

Code:

```
// assembles a list of repeating dates based on a period keyword
// input:
//    calendarDate = date
//    period = "daily"; "weekly"; "monthly"; "quarterly"; "yearly"
//    numberOfRepetitions = integer
// output: return-delimited list of dates as a text string

Let ([
   startDate =  GetAsDate ( calendarDate );
   m = Month (startdate);
   d = Day (startdate);
   y = Year (startdate);
   nextDate = Case (
      period = "daily" ; startDate + 1 ;
      period = "weekly" ; startDate + 7 ;
      period = "monthly" ; Date ( m + 1 ; d ; y);
      period = "quarterly" ; Date ( m + 3 ; d ; y);
      period = "yearly" ; Date ( m  ; d ; y + 1)
      )

   ];
```

```
    Case ( numberOfRepetitions > 0 ;
      startDate & "¶" &
      fnDateRepetitions (nextDate ; period ; numberOfRepetitions - 1);
      ""

    )
  )
```

Example:

fnDateReptitions ("1/1/2007"; "quarterly"; 6) returns

1/1/2007

4/1/2007

7/1/2007

10/1/2007

1/1/2008

4/1/2008

fnNextDayOfWeek (calendarDate; numDayOfWeek)

This function returns a future next date based on a day of week provided. For example, from a starting date of 11/2/2005, which was a Wednesday, the next Friday is 11/4/2005. We often need this sort of function for reporting based on a "standard" week (week ending Friday, week starting Saturday, and the like).

The second parameter is an integer that corresponds to a day of the week. 1 = Sunday, 2 = Monday, and so on through to 7 = Saturday.

Code:

```
// returns the date of the next day of week requested
// input:
//   calendarDate = date
//   dayOfWeek = integer, 1 for Sunday ... 7 for Saturday

Let ([
  varDate = GetAsDate ( calendarDate )
  ];
  varDate + Mod ( numDayOfWeek - DayOfWeek ( varDate ); 7 )
)
```

Examples:

fnNextDayOfWeek ("4/25/2007"; 6) returns the Friday following 4/25/2007 = 4/29/2007.

fnNextDayOfWeek ("4/25/2007"; 4) returns the Wednesday following (or including) 4/25/2007: given that that date is itself a Wednesday, the function returns the original date of 4/25/2007.

Text and Data Conversions

fnConvertLengthUnits (number; unitFrom; unitTo)

Converting data between various unit types is a common need in database systems. This function serves as an example of converting length units between the various Metric and Imperial forms.

Note that it uses recursion to save dozens of lines of code. In its first pass, it converts its input into meters, and then in its second pass, converts meters to whichever unit the calling calculation has requested. This technique saves the function from having to create a massive matrix of 15 × 15 different options.

Code:

```
// converts common length units
// input:
//   number
//   unitFrom = specific text keyword
//   ( microinch | in | ft | yd | mile | league | league nautical |
//   µm | mm | cm | dm | m | dam | hm | km )
//   unitTo = same as above.
// output: number

Case (
  unitFrom = "microinch";
    fnConvertLengthUnits ( number * .0000000254; "m"; unitTo );
  unitFrom = "in";
    fnConvertLengthUnits ( number * .0254; "m"; unitTo );
  unitFrom = "ft";
    fnConvertLengthUnits ( number * .3048; "m"; unitTo );
  unitFrom = "yd";
    fnConvertLengthUnits ( number * .9144; "m"; unitTo );
  unitFrom = "mile";
    fnConvertLengthUnits ( number * 1609.3; "m"; unitTo );
  unitFrom = "league";
```

```
        fnConvertLengthUnits ( number * 4828.0417; "m"; unitTo );
    unitFrom = "league nautical";
        fnConvertLengthUnits ( number * 5556; "m"; unitTo );

    unitFrom = "µm"; fnConvertLengthUnits ( number * .000001; "m"; unitTo );
    unitFrom = "mm"; fnConvertLengthUnits ( number * .001; "m"; unitTo );
    unitFrom = "cm"; fnConvertLengthUnits ( number * .01; "m"; unitTo );
    unitFrom = "dm"; fnConvertLengthUnits ( number * .1; "m"; unitTo );
    unitFrom = "dam"; fnConvertLengthUnits ( number * 10; "m"; unitTo );
    unitFrom = "hm"; fnConvertLengthUnits ( number * 100; "m"; unitTo );
    unitFrom = "km"; fnConvertLengthUnits ( number * 1000; "m"; unitTo );

    unitFrom = "m";
        Case (
            unitTo = "µm"; number * 1000000;
            unitTo = "mm"; number * 1000;
            unitTo = "cm"; number * 100;
            unitTo = "dm"; number * 10;
            unitTo = "m"; number * 1;
            unitTo = "dam"; number * .1;
            unitTo = "hm"; number * .01;
            unitTo = "km"; number * .001;

            unitTo = "microinch"; number * 39370078.7401575;
            unitTo = "in"; number * 39.3700787;
            unitTo = "ft"; number * 3.2808399;
            unitTo = "yd"; number * 1.0936133;
            unitTo = "mile"; number * 0.0006214;
            unitTo = "league"; number * 0.0002071;
            unitTo = "league nautical"; number * 0.00018
                "unitTo parameter not recognized"
        );
    "unitFrom parameter not recognized"

)
```

Examples:

fnConvertLengthUnits (9; "in"; "m") returns .2286.

fnConvertLengthUnits (2.33; "ft"; "in") returns 27.9599999714808.

fnConvertLengthUnits (5; "km"; "cm") returns 500000.

fnConvertTemperature (number; inputUnit)

This function converts between Celsius to Fahrenheit.

Notice the fail condition for the Case() function. Given the specific values the inputUnit parameter requires, it's always best to test for errors.

Code:

```
// Converts Celsius to Fahrenheit and vice-versa
// input:
//   temperature = number
//   inputUnit = "C" | "F"
// output: temperature in opposite scale as inputUnit

Case (
   inputUnit = "F" ; Round ( ( temperature - 32 ) * 5/9 ; 0 );
   inputUnit = "C" ; Round ( ( temperature * 9/5 ) + 32 ; 0 );
   "error - inputUnit not recognized"
)
```

Examples:

fnConvertTemperature (65; "F") returns 18.

fnConvertTemperature (40; "C") returns 104.

fnConverttoUSAbrvState (text)

There's nothing particularly magical about this function; it converts long state names for the United States into their abbreviated form. It is useful only because once written it never has to be written again.

Note that to save space and avoid belaboring the obvious, we didn't include its partner, fnUSAStateConverttoLong(). That function can be found in the electronic files available on the book's web page at www.quepublishing.com or from www.soliantconsulting.com.

One could argue that this kind of lookup table is a good candidate for solving with a database structure. But it requires more work to reuse a database structure, and this list is closed-ended, meaning it is going to change slowly, if at all. If there were hundreds of data pairs and they changed frequently, a custom function would likely not be the ideal choice.

Code:

```
// Converts long US State names to 2-char abbreviations

Case (
   text = "Alabama"; "AL";
   text = "Alaska"; "AK";
   text = "Arizona"; "AZ";
   text = "Arkansas"; "AR";
   text = "California"; "CA";
   text = "Colorado"; "CO";
...
...
   text = "Wyoming"; "WY";
   text // default do nothing, return the value input
)
```

Note: List trimmed to save space. Please refer to the electronic file available for download for the complete code.

Examples:

fnConverttoUSAbrvState ("California") returns CA.

fnConverttoUSAbrvState ("Ican'tspell") returns Ican'tspell.

fnExplodeText (text)

Exploded text allows developers to create multiline keys within FileMaker and then to use those keys in relationships for filtering portal contents or other advanced techniques.

Code:

```
// returns a delimited list of all the possible values within a text string
// input: text
// output: delimited text
// note: if a field containing this data is indexed, it can result in very large storage blocks.
// note: 49999 iterations is the maximum

Let ([
   textLength = Length ( text )
   ];
   Case ( textLength > 1;
      fnExplodeText ( Left ( text; textLength - 1 ) ) & "¶" & text;
```

```
      text
    )
  )
```

An alternate function for limiting the size of the result follows:

```
// requires a second parameter: characterLimit
Let ([
  newText = Left ( text; characterLimit );
  textLength = Length ( newText )
  ];
  Case ( textLength > 1;
    fnExplodeText ( Left ( text; textLength - 1 ); characterLimit ) &
          "¶" & newText; newText
  )
)
```

Examples:

"fnExplodeText ('Zaphod')" returns:

Z

Za

Zap

Zaph

Zapho

Zaphod

Note that exploded text significantly increases the size of an index for a given field. If you are concerned about performance or file size, consider adding a limiter to this function: An integer that controls how many characters deep the function should extract text.

fnFormatDollars (number)

The following function uses the fnInsertRepeatingCharacters() function to format a number into U.S. currency. Note the isolation of logic: This function manages how to handle negative numbers and decimals, along with to what degree to round. The fnInsertRepeatingCharacters() function takes care only of comma placement. This preserves flexibility and reusability in both functions.

Code:

```
// converts number data into data with commas and $ symbol

// input: number
// output: text
// dependencies: fnInsertRepeatingString

Let ([

    positiveInteger = Abs ( Int ( number ));
    decimal = Abs ( number ) - positiveInteger ;
    decimalClean = Substitute ( decimal ; "." ;)
    ];

    Case ( number < 0; "-$"; "$" ) &
     fnInsertRepeatingString ( positiveInteger; ","; 3; "right") & "." &
     Left ( decimalClean & "00" ; 2 )
)
```

Examples:

fnFormatDollars (111) returns $111.00.

fnFormatDollars (33222111) returns $33,222,111.00.

fnFormatDollars (-4333.222) returns -$4,333.22.

fnFormatPhone (text)

Based on how much it consumes the attention of developers, one might assume phone number formatting to be a favorite pastime. This function represents an attempt to put the functionality to bed, once and for all.

This function is most often used in conjunction with the Auto-Enter by Calculation field option. If you turn off the Do Not Replace Existing Value check box associated with that option, the field in question automatically reformats itself whenever someone enters new data or edits its contents.

You can extend this function in a variety of ways: You could add recognition of an override character (say, for example, a "+" character) that would leave data entered exactly "as is" if users prefix the input with that override. Another modification could be to change the mask or style attributes of the function to refer to one or more preferences fields on a user record, if your system has a such a thing—allowing users to control phone formats dynamically.

This is where custom functions show their strengths: By abstracting the logic of this functionality into a central location, developers can efficiently modify and expand upon it.

Code:

```
// reformats phone numbers based on a mask style
// dependencies:
//   fnTextColor() & fnMaskReplace()
// input:
//   text = text string assumed to contain at least 10 numeral digits
//   style = specific keywords to allow for different
styles (international) within the same database
// output:
//   text string
// note: error returned in red if < 10 digits
// note: strings assume no more than 20 characters

Let ([
   minimumDigits = 10;
   digitsOnly = Filter ( text; "0123456789" );
   digitCount = Length ( digitsOnly );
   errorCheck = Case ( digitCount < minimumDigits;
         fnTextColor ( "error - too few numerals: " & text; "red" );
         0 );
   styleMask = Case (
      style = "usa_standard" ; "(***) ***-****";
      style = "usa_dot" "; "***.***.****";
      style = "japan_alternate" ; "* ** ***-****";
      style = "japan_standard" ; "** ****-****";
       "*** ***-****" );
    mask = styleMask & Case (digitCount > minimumDigits ; " x**********");
    formatText = fnMaskReplace ( mask; digitsOnly; "*" );
    finalBlackText = fnTextColor ( formatText; "black" )
   ];
   Case ( errorCheck <> 0; errorCheck; finalBlackText )
)
```

Examples:

fnFormatPhone ("1234567890111"; "usa_standard") returns (123) 456-7890 x111.

fnFormatPhone ("1234567890"; "usa_dot") returns 123.456.7890.

fnFormatPhone ("1122aabb"; "usa_dot") returns error - too few numerals: 1122aabb in red colored text.

fnInsertRepeatingCharacters (text; insertString; numberOfCharacters; startDirection)

Converting data into currency, or formatting a number with commas, requires some function that can insert characters at regular intervals. Rather than write a function that manages only a specific currency or situation, this function is more generic. It allows you to specify what character set you want to insert into some other body of text, the interval at which you need it inserted, and finally from which direction to begin counting. This function can then be used by other functions when setting up specific cases of, for example, a number formatted with commas or dealing with currency.

Note that FileMaker can display numbers with commas and with currency symbols, but these displays do not manipulate the actual data in question. This function operates at a data level, not a display level. It actually changes your data.

Code:

```
// inserts one string into another at regular intervals.  Useful for formatting numbers as currency.

// input:
//   text = source string
//   insertString = text to insert at intervals
//   numberOfCharacters = interval
//   startDirection = "right" or "left"
// output: text string

Let ([
   lengthText = Length ( text );
   remainder = Mod ( lengthText; numberOfCharacters );
    splitPosition = Case ( startDirection = "left" or remainder = 0 ;
                          numberOfCharacters ;
                          remainder
                  );
    outputCharacters  =  Left ( text ; splitPosition ) ;
    remainingText =  Right ( text ; lengthText - splitPosition )
  ];

     Case ( not ( startDirection = "right" or startDirection = "left" );
            "error - startDirection not recognized";
          numberOfCharacters < 0 ;
              "error - numberOfCharacters cannot be a negative number";
```

```
            lengthText > numberOfCharacters ;
                outputCharacters & insertString &
                fnInsertRepeatingCharacters ( remainingText ; insertString ; numberOfCharacters ; "left" );

            Right ( text ; lengthText )
    )
)
```

Examples:

fnInsertRepeatingCharacters ("Azeroth"; "*"; 2; "left") returns Az*er*ot*h.

fnInsertRepeatingCharacters ("Ironforge"; "*"; 3; "left") returns Iro*nfo*rge.

fnInsertRepeatingCharacters ("Darnassus"; "*"; 4; "right") returns D*arna*ssus.

fnInsertRepeatingCharacters ("1222333"; ","; 3; "right") returns 1,222,333.

fnInsertRepeatingCharacters ("1222333.444"; ","; 3; "right") returns 12,223,33.,444.

fnIsWhitespace (text)

This function looks for "filler" characters in a block of text and returns a 1 if that block of text is comprised only of filler characters, 0 otherwise. This example uses a tab, return carriage, and space for filler characters, but you could add whatever other characters to the Filter() function as you want.

Code:

```
// determines if a block of text contains nothing other than spaces,
 tabs and carriage return characters
// input: text
// output: 1 or 0
// dependencies: uses fnTab

Let ([
    filtered = Filter ( text; " ¶" & fnTab )
    ];
    If ( filtered = text; 1; 0 )
)
```

Examples:

fnIsWhitespace ("hello   ") returns 0.

fnIsWhitespace ("   ") returns 1.

fnMaskReplace (maskText; replacementText; wildcardCharacter)

This function is often called by other functions like fnFormatPhone() and fnFormatSSN(). It allows developers to create a character mask of some sort and insert characters into that mask.

Note that this function is recursive, replacing the first wildcard in the mask with the first character of the replacementText on each pass, like so:

```
fnMaskReplace ( "***hello***" ; "123456" ; "*" )
```

becomes

```
fnMaskReplace ( "1**hello***" ; "23456" ; "*" )
```

which becomes

```
fnMaskReplace" ( "12*hello***" ; "3456" ; "*" )
```

which becomes

```
fnMaskReplace ( "123hello***" ; "456" ; "*" )
```

and so on.

Code:

```
// replaces wildcard characters within a text string with the characters in a replacement string
// input:
//   maskText = text string with some number of wildcard characters
//   replacementText = text string meant to replace wildcard characters one for one
//   wildcardCharacter = the specific char used as a wildcard
// output:
//   text string
// note: if there are too many wildcard characters, they will be stripped out
// note: if there are too many replacement characters, the excess will be ignored
// note: limited to current nested recursion limits in FileMaker

Let ([
   charReplaceCount = Length ( replacementText );
   charWildcardCount = PatternCount ( maskText; wildcardCharacter );
   firstWildcardPosition = Position ( maskText; wildcardCharacter; 1; 1 );
   firstReplaceChar = Left ( replacementText; 1 );
   remainingReplaceChars =
      Right ( replacementText; charReplaceCount - 1 );
   oneCharReplaced =
      Replace ( maskText; firstWildcardPosition; 1; firstReplaceChar );
   returnText =
```

```
        Case ( charWildcardCount = 0;
         maskText;
              charReplaceCount > 1 and charWildcardCount > 1;
          fnMaskReplace ( oneCharReplaced; remainingReplaceChars;
          wildcardCharacter );
         oneCharReplaced
          );
    cleanText = Substitute ( returnText; wildcardCharacter; "" )
    ];
    cleanText
)
```

Examples:

Where a field, myPhone, contains 1234567890, fnMaskReplace ("(xxx) xxx-xxxx"; myPhone; "x") would return (123) 456-7890.

Another example might derive from a product name: AB12301Widget (pack of 10). In that case, fnMaskReplace ("**-**-*** ******************************"; productSKU; "*") might return AB-12-301 Widget (pack of 10).

fnPadCharacters (text; padLength; padCharacter; side)

We often face situations where a given text string needs to be a fixed number of characters in length. This function accommodates that need by providing means to pad a string of data with some sort of pad character.

It makes use of the fnRepeatText function. This simplifies the function significantly and is a good example of using a subfunction effectively.

Notice also that the side parameter requires specific values of "left" or "right."

Code

```
// function adds characters to either the right or left of a text string.
// dependencies: fnRepeatText()
// input:
//    text
//    padLength = total characters the string should reach
//    padCharacter = character to use in padding
//    side = "left" | "right"
// output: text
// note: in the case that text > padLength, function will truncate text
```

```
Let ([
   textLength = Length ( text );
   padString = fnRepeatText ( padCharacter; padLength - textLength )
   ];
   Case (
      textLength > padLength ; Left ( text ; padLength );
      side = "left" ; padString & text;
      side = "right" ; text & padString;
      "error: side not recognized."
   )
)
```

Example:

fnPadCharacters ("999"; 8; "0"; "left") returns 00000999.

fnPadCharacters ("Nate" ; 10 ; "+" ; "right") returns Nate++++++.

fnRecordMetaDisplay (createName; createTimestamp; modifyName; modifyTimestamp)

We recommend that for every table in a database, developers create what we've referred to as housekeeping fields: meta information stored about when a record was last created and/or modified and by whom. These four fields, fed by auto-enter field options, track this information for all records.

We find it useful to place this information somewhere innocuous on a layout. Often users benefit from knowing when something has been edited, and so on. To that end, this function creates a display that is easy for users to read.

Code:

```
// creates the record housekeeping field display
// input: creator name, created timestamp, modifier name, modified timestamp
// output: display text

// create portion
"Created " &
MonthName ( createTimestamp ) & " " &
Day ( createTimestamp ) & ", " &
Year ( createTimestamp ) & " (" &
```

```
// format time
Let ([
      h = Hour ( createTimestamp) ;
      m = Minute ( createTimestamp)
    ] ;
      Mod ( h - 1; 12 ) + 1 & ":" & Right ( "0" & m ; 2 ) &  Case ( h < 12 ; "am" ;  "pm" )
)

& ") by " & createName &

//modify portion
Case (
   not IsEmpty ( modifyTimestamp );
      "; modified " &
      MonthName ( modifyTimestamp )  & " " &
      Day ( modifyTimestamp ) & ", " &
      Year ( modifyTimestamp ) & " (" &

      // format time
       Let ([
           h = Hour ( modifyTimestamp) ;
           m = Minute ( modifyTimestamp)
         ] ;
           Mod ( h - 1; 12 ) + 1 & ":" & Right ( "0" & m ; 2 ) &  Case ( h < 12 ; "am" ;  "pm" )
       )
   & ") by " & modifyName ; ""
 )
& "."
```

Example:

fnRecordMetaDisplay ("UserA"; "11/10/2005 6:45:22 AM"; "UserB"; "11/10/2005 4:15:02 PM") returns Created November 10, 2005 (6:45am) by UserA; modified November 10, 2005 (4:15pm) by UserB.

fnRepeatText (text; numberOfRepetitions)

This is a great function to tinker with if you're new to recursive functions. Notice that it simply stacks its own results on top of each other, decreasing the numberOfRepetitions parameter until it reaches a numberOfRepetitions of 1.

Code:

```
// duplicates a text string n times
// input:
//   text
//   integer
// output: text
// note: function is limited to current nested recursion limits in FileMaker.

Case ( numberOfRepetitions > 1;
          text & fnRepeatText ( text; numberOfRepetitions - 1 ) ;
       numberOfRepetitions = 1 ;
         text ;
       ""
)
```

Examples:

fnRepeatText ("|"; 5) returns |||||.

fnRepeatText ("hello"; 3) returns hellohellohello.

fnTrimCharacters (text; trimCharacter; side)

FileMaker has a Trim() function that strips leading and trailing spaces from a block of text, but there are times when it would be helpful to have a function that recognized other characters as well. This custom function allows a developer to define which character she needs stripped away, and whether to strip from the start, end, or both sides of a text string.

Note that this function is not case sensitive. To make it so, use the Exact() function when comparing leftChar or rightChar to trimCharacter.

Code:

```
// removes leading and/or trailing characters from a string
// input:
//   text
//   trimCharacter = character to be trimmed away
//   side: "left"|"right"|"both"
// output: text
// note: this function is NOT case sensitive

Let ([
   leftChar = Left ( text; 1 );
```

```
    rightChar = Right ( text; 1 );
    remainderLength = Length ( text ) - 1
    ];
    Case (
      ( side = "left" or side = "both" ) and leftChar = trimCharacter;
        fnTrimCharacters ( Right ( text; remainderLength );
          trimCharacter; side );
      ( side = "right" or side = "both" ) and rightChar = trimCharacter;
        fnTrimCharacters( Left ( text; remainderLength );
          trimCharacter; side );
      text
    )
  )
```

Examples:

fnTrimCharacters ("xxxMarzenxxxxxx"; "x"; "both") returns Marzen.

fnTrimCharacters ("00001234"; "0"; "left") returns 1234.

fnTrimReturns (text)

This function is a common tool for doing data cleanup, especially when involving email. Text that has been hard-wrapped can sometimes end up formatted poorly. This function removes single line breaks but preserves double line breaks from the specified text string.

Note that this function does not insert or remove spaces. If a line ends with a carriage return but then does not include a space before the next word, the two words on either side of the line break will be concatenated.

Code:

```
// removes single line breaks but preserves double line breaks
// input: text
// output: text with ¶ line breaks removed

Substitute ( text ; ["¶¶"; "*#*#*#*#"];["¶";""];["*#*#*#*#";"¶¶"] )
```

Example:

Consider a field, originalText, with the following:

Hello. This is my
raw text. Notice that
it wraps poorly.

It also has two
paragraphs that
should be on two
lines.

fnTrimReturns (originalText) returns

Hello. This is my raw text. Notice that it wraps poorly.
It also has two paragraphs that should be on two lines.

fnDecimalToHex (decimal)

This function converts decimal numbers to hexadecimal numbers. This is useful when working with color encoding or other circumstances where an operation expects a base 16 number.

Code:

```
//Converts a decimal number to hexadecimal ( base 16 )
//You may alternately wrap it around the built in RGB function
//Example fnDecToHex ( RGB ( 255 ; 0 ; 0 ) )

Let ( [
   bit = Mod ( decimal ; 16 ) ;
   alpha = "0123456789ABCDEF" ;
   char = Middle ( alpha ; bit + 1 ; 1 ) ;
   next = Div ( Decimal ; 16 )
   ] ;   // end variables

   Case (
      next ;
      fnDecimalToHex ( next )
   )  // end Case
   & char
)  // end Let
```

Example:

fnDecimalToHex (11) returns B.

fnDecimalToHex (100) returns 64.

fnDecimalToHex (1234) returns 4D2.

fnFormatSSN (text)

This function uses the same mask function used by fnFormatPhone to format United States' Social Security numbers. It also uses the fnTextColor to return error information to the user.

Code:

```
// reformats social security numbers based on a mask style
// dependencies:
//    fnTextColor() & fnMaskReplace()
// input:
//    text = text string assumed to contain exactly 9 numeral digits
// output:
//    text string
// note: error returned in red if < 9 digits or >9 digits
// note: strings assume no more than 20 characters

Let ([
      minimumDigits = 9;
      digitsOnly = Filter ( text; "0123456789" );
      digitCount = Length ( digitsOnly );
      errorCheck = Case ( digitCount < minimumDigits; fnTextColor ( "error - too few numerals: " & text;
"red" ); digitCount > minimumDigits; fnTextColor ( "error - too many numerals: " & text; "red" ); 0 );
      formatText = fnMaskReplace ( "***-**-****"; digitsOnly; "*" );
      finalBlackText = fnTextColor ( formatText; "black" )
      ]; // end variables
      Case ( errorCheck ≠ 0; errorCheck; finalBlackText )
) // end let
```

Example:

fnFormatSSN (123456789) returns 123-45-6789 in black text.

fnFormatSSN (123) returns error - too few numerals: 123 in red text.

fnInitials (text)

This function returns the first letters, in caps, of words passed into it.

Code:

```
// returns in upper case the first letter of each word in text
// input: text
// output: text

Let ([
    numOfWords = WordCount ( text );
    firstInitial = Upper ( Left ( text; 1 ) )
    ];
    firstInitial & Case ( numOfWords > 1; fnInitials ( RightWords ( text; numOfWords - 1 ) ); "" )
)
```

Example:

fnInitials ("myname is fred") returns MIF.

Email Tools

fnEmailIsValid (text)

This function checks for a few common problems with email addresses and returns a 1 or 0 depending on whether a submitted block of text passes its tests.

Note that the function uses the fnEmailTLDs (top-level domains) function.

The function isn't meant to be exhaustive: It is still entirely possible to enter an invalid email address; we encourage you to add further conditions to the case function that handles testing.

Also note that the function as written returns a 1 or 0. Using the fnErrorHandler (discussed later in this chapter), you could derive more information from the function when an error condition existed. We wrote this as a Case() test rather than one long concatenated series of tests joined by and operators to explicitly test for each error and allow for the possibility of adding more error handling logic.

Code:

```
// tests for valid email address formatting and domain
// dependencies: fnEmailTLDs
// input: text (presumably an email address)
// output: 1 or 0
```

```
Let ([
   lengthText = Length ( text );
   positionAt = Position ( text; "@"; 1; 1 );
   positionLastDot = Position ( text; "."; lengthText; -1);
   validCharacters =
     ".0123456789abcdefghijklmnopqrstuvwxyzABCDEFGHIJKLMNOPQRSTUVWXYZ";
   userBlock = Left ( text; positionAt - 1 );
   domainBlock = Right ( text; lengthText - PositionAt );
   topLevelDomain = Right ( text; lengthText - positionLastDot );

   errorCondition = Case (
     lengthText < 1; 0;             // text parameter is empty
     positionAt = 0; 0;             // no @ symbol
     positionLastDot = 0; 0;          // no dot
     Filter ( userBlock; validCharacters ) <>  userBlock; 0;   // invalid chars in user block
     Filter ( domainBlock; validCharacters ) <>  domainBlock; 0;
       // invalid chars in domain block
     PatternCount ( " " & fnEmailTLDs & " "; " " & topLevelDomain & " " ) < 1; 0;
       // top level domain not recognized
     1                       // if no error condition is met, return 1.
     )
   ];
   errorCondition
)
```

Examples:

fnEmailIsValid ("kathiel@soliantconsulting.com") returns 1.

fnEmailIsValid ("kathielsoliantconsulting.com") returns 0.

fnEmailIsValid ("kathiel@soliant@consultingcom") returns 0.

fnEmailTLDs ()

This function serves as a system constant (we discuss that term later in the chapter) and simply holds a list of top-level domains. It is easy to keep the list up-to-date in this form and prevents developers from having to enter this rather unwieldy block of information in more than this one place (or within a larger, more complex function).

Notice that the fnEmailIsValid function requires that a space follow each domain.

Code:

```
// function contains a text block of space-delimited list of top level domains.
"ac ad ae aero ... zm zw"

// most values removed to save space. Please refer to the electronic files available for download from the book's web page at www.quepublishing.com or from www.soliantconsulting.com.
```

List Handlers

In FileMaker a list is defined as a return-delimited set of values. Most often developers encounter them in value lists, but they are also often used as simple one-dimensional arrays of data. FileMaker has a set of functions for manipulating list data (GetValue(), LeftValues(), RightValues(), MiddleValues()), and the following represent some useful additions.

fnBubbleSort (theList)

This function sorts a list of values using the "bubble sort" algorithm. It isn't an efficient sort (we've included an implementation of the "merge sort" algorithm, fnMergeSort(), which is generally much quicker), but it's a good example of some useful programming techniques.

This function is actually just a wrapper around a "helper" or "auxiliary" function that does the real work. The internal function is a recursive function that keeps track of some extra information, which it passes to itself as a parameter. In some cases FileMaker needs to pass information to itself in recursive functions that otherwise might confuse developers and need not be exposed to them. For that reason this master function was created so that the actual sort function, fnBubbleSort_iterations(), can be called with the proper parameters.

Code:

```
// calls fnBubbleSort_iterations
// necessary to avoid exposing the seed parameter

fnBubbleSort_iterations ( theList; ValueCount (theList) )
```

Example:

Consider a field, myList, with the following values:

```
fish
goat
bird
dog
```

fnBubbleSort (myList) results in

bird
dog
fish
goat

fnBubbleSort_iterations (theList; iterations)

This function is called by the master fnBubbleSort() function. This function performs the sort and results in a final sorted list. The purpose of the master function is to avoid having to pass the iterations parameter directly.

Code:

```
// sorts list items
// input:
//   theList = group of values to be shifted one iteration
//   iterations = starting number of values ( seed )
// output: modified list

Case ( iterations > 1; fnBubbleSort_iterations ( fnBubbleSort_shift (theList; 1 ); iterations - 1); theList)
```

fnBubbleSort_shift (theList; shift)

This function performs the inner comparison for a classic bubble sort. It should be called by fnBubbleSort_iterations().

Consider a list that contains:

fish
goat
bird
dog

fnBubbleSort_shift (myList; 1) results in

fish
bird
dog
goat

Code:

```
// performs an inner shift for fnBubbleSort
// input:
// theList = group of values to be shifted one iteration
//    shift = list item (integer) to be shifted
// output: modified list

Let ([
    numOfValues = ValueCount (theList)
    ];
    Case ( shift < numOfValues;
        fnBubbleSort_shift ( Case ( MiddleValues (theList; shift; 1 ) >
            MiddleValues (theList; shift + 1; 1 );
                LeftValues (theList; shift - 1) &
                MiddleValues (theList; shift + 1 ; 1 ) &
                MiddleValues (theList; shift; 1 ) &
                RightValues (theList; numOfValues - ( shift + 1 ));
            theList
            );
        shift + 1 );
    theList)
)
```

fnMergeSort (theList)

This function sorts a return-delimited list of values using the "merge sort" technique. The function is recursive. It operates by first splitting the list in two, sorting each sublist, and then merging the results back together into a single sorted list. It relies on the helper function fnMergeLists(), which is responsible for merging two sorted lists into one.

Code:

```
// sort a return-delimited list using the "mergesort" algorithm
// input: a return-delimited list of values
// output: the same list, sorted
// requires the fnMergeLists function
// http://en.wikipedia.org/wiki/Mergesort

Case(
    ValueCount ( theList ) <= 1; // if only one value left in the list ...
        LeftValues (theList; 1 );   // then just return that value
```

```
    Let ([                          // else ...
        length = ValueCount ( theList ) ;           // split the list in two ...
        leftLength = Floor ( length / 2 );
        rightLength = length - leftLength;
        leftList = LeftValues ( theList; leftLength);
        rightList = RightValues ( theList; rightLength);
        sortedLeft = fnMergeSort ( leftList );          // sort each sub-list ...
        sortedRight = fnMergeSort ( rightList );
        mergedList = fnMergeSortedValues ( sortedLeft; sortedright )
        // and merge the two sorted lists

    ];
    mergedList )
)
```

fnMergeSortedValues (list1; list2)

This function merges two sorted, return-delimited lists of values into a single sorted, return-delimited list. It's probably useful in its own right but is provided here as a necessary "helper" function for the fnMergeSort function.

Code:

```
// merges two sorted lists into a single sorted list
// input: two sorted, return-delimited lists
// output: a single sorted return-delimited list

Case (
    ValueCount ( list1 ) = 0 and ValueCount ( list2 ) = 0 ; "";
    ValueCount ( list1 ) = 0; list2;
    ValueCount ( list2 ) = 0; list1;

    Let ([
        first = LeftValues ( list1; 1 );
        second = LeftValues ( list2; 1 );
        lesser = Case ( first <= second; first; second );
        firstRemaining = Case ( first = lesser; RightValues ( list1; ValueCount ( list1 ) - 1 ); list1 );
        secondRemaining = Case ( second = lesser; RightValues ( list2; ValueCount ( list2 ) - 1 ); list2 );
        result = lesser & fnMergeSortedValues ( firstRemaining; secondRemaining )
        ];
        result
    )
)
```

fnValuesBackwards (theList)

List arrays can store simple data in cases where a database table would be overkill or inappropriate. They can be manipulated by a range of functions in FileMaker, and they're fairly easy to decipher. This function takes a list and flips the order of its values.

If the concept of recursion is a little opaque to you, this is a nice, "clean" recursion that would serve well for study purposes.

Code:

```
// function to reverse-order a ¶-delimited list
// expected input:
//   theList = text values delimited by ¶
// expected result:  a list of text values delimited by ¶ in reverse order

Let ([
   numOfValues = ValueCount ( theList );
   newList = RightValues ( theList; numOfValues - 1 );
   resultList = Case ( numOfValues <= 1; ""; fnValuesBackwards ( newList ) );
   firstValue = LeftValues ( theList; 1 )
   ];

   resultList & firstValue
)
```

Example:

fnValuesBackwards ("red¶green¶blue¶yellow¶") returns

yellow
blue
green
red

fnValuesCrossProduct (list1; list2)

This function creates the cross product of two lists. For example, if you had one list that contained (hello¶goodbye¶) and another with (1¶2¶3¶), the cross product of these lists would be (hello1¶hello2¶hello3¶goodbye1¶goodbye2¶goodbye3¶).

This function is a master function that calls a subfunction. The subfunction is a recursive function that requires a counter, and rather than require that a developer supply the initial value for the counter, this master function takes care of that for them.

Consider this the "public" version of the function. The other is a "private" subfunction and is meant to stay in the background to be called only by this controlling function.

Code:

```
// this function exists only to call fnValuesCrossProduct_sub.
// input: two lists
// output: output from fnValuesCrossProduct_sub

fnValuesCrossProduct_sub ( list1; list2; 1 )
```

fnValuesCrossProduct_sub (list1; list2; counter)

The cross product of two sets is a set containing all the two-element sets that can be created by taking one element of each set. For example, if Set1 contained {A, B} and Set2 contained {P, Q, R, S}, their cross product would consist of {AP, AQ, AR, AS, BP, BQ, BR, BS}. The number of elements in the cross product is the product of the number of elements in each of the two sets.

The fnValuesCrossProduct_sub() function "loops," incrementing a counter as it goes, until the counter is no longer less than the number of elements expected in the result set. With Set1 and Set2 from the previously mentioned scenario, the function would iterate 8 times. If it were on iteration 5, the function would work with the second item from the first list (because Ceiling (5/4) = 2), which is "B," and the first item from the second list (because Mod (4; 4) + 1 = 1), which is "P." "BP" becomes the fifth element of the result set.

Code:

```
// function combines two lists into concatenated cross-product lines
// input:
//   list1 = return delimited list of values
//   list2 = return delimited list of values
//   counter = should initially be set to 1; function then
calls itself and increments
// output: return delimited list of values

Let ([
   array1count = ValueCount ( list1 );
   array2count = ValueCount ( list2 );
   limit = array1count * array2count;

   pos1 = Ceiling ( counter / array2count) ;
   pos2 = Mod ( counter - 1; array2count ) + 1;
```

```
item1 = GetValue ( list1; pos1 ) ;
item2 = GetValue ( list2; pos2 )
];

Case (
    array1count = 0 ; list2;
    array2count = 0 ; list1;
    counter <= limit ;
      item1 & item2 & "¶" & fnValuesCrossProduct_sub ( list1; list2; counter + 1 )
  )
)
```

Examples:

fnValuesCrossProduct_sub ("A¶B¶C"; "1¶2¶3¶4"; 1) returns A1¶A2¶A3¶A4¶B1¶B2¶B3¶B4¶C1¶C2¶C3¶C4¶.

fnValuesCrossProduct_sub ("One¶Two¶Red¶Blue"; " fish" ; 1) returns

```
One fish
Two fish
Red fish
Blue fish
```

fnValuesRemove (theList; valuesToRemove)

This function provides a means to remove one or more items from a given list.

Code:

```
// removes from the first return-delimited list parameter a second return-delimited set of values
// input:
//   theList: return-delimited list of text
//   valuesToRemove: return-delimited set of text values to be removed from list
// output:
//   list of return-delimited text items
// note: This function is NOT case sensitive.

Let ([
  listCount = ValueCount ( theList );
  lastValue = GetValue ( theList; listCount );
  compare = PatternCount ( "¶" & valuesToRemove & "¶" ; "¶" & lastValue & "¶" );
```

```
    newList = LeftValues ( theList ; listCount -1 );
    includeValue = Case (compare = 0; lastValue & "¶" );

    resultList =
      Case ( listCount > 1;
        fnValuesRemove ( newList ; valuesToRemove ) & includeValue;
        includeValue
      )
    ];
    resultList
)
```

Example:

Consider a field, myList, holding the following list:

```
Black
Green
Yellow
Pink
Purple
Black
White
```

fnValuesRemove (myList; "Pink¶Black¶Yellow") will return

```
Green
Purple
White
```

fnMatchPrefix (theList; thePrefix)

This function looks within a list for an item that begins with the prefix (supplied via the second parameter) and returns the first value it finds. This is useful for, among other things, isolating instances of windows the user may have open.

Code:

```
Case ( not IsEmpty ( theList ) and not IsEmpty ( thePrefix ) ) ;

 If ( Left ( theList ; Length ( thePrefix ) ) = thePrefix) ;
  Substitute ( LeftValues ( theList ; 1 ) ; "¶" ; "" ) ;
  fnMatchPrefix ( MiddleValues ( theList ; 2 ; ValueCount ( theList ) - 1 ) ; thePrefix )
```

Examples:

fnMatchPrefix (myWindow 1¶myWindow 2¶myWindow 3¶anotherWindow 1; myWindow) returns myWindow 1.

fnMatchPrefixAll (theList; thePrefix)

This function looks within a list for items that begin with the prefix (supplied via the second parameter) and returns all the values it finds.

Code:

```
Case ( not IsEmpty ( theList ) and not IsEmpty ( thePrefix ) ;
Let ( newlist = fnMatchPrefixAll ( MiddleValues ( theList ; 2 ; ValueCount ( theList ) - 1 ) ; thePrefix ) ;
//do the recursion until theList is empty

 Case ( Left ( theList ; Length ( thePrefix ) ) = thePrefix ; //on the way back down the stack, return the
matches

   If ( ValueCount ( newlist ) > 0 ; //check to see if we're at the bottom of the stack yet...
    LeftValues ( theList ; 1 ) ; //... if not the bottom, return the matching value with it's ¶
    Substitute ( LeftValues ( theList ; 1 ) ; "¶" ; "" ) //... otherwise return the value and trim the ¶ off it
because it's last in the list (top of the stack)
   )//end If

 )//end Case
 & newlist //leave behind

)//end Let
)//end Case
```

Examples:

fnMatchPrefix (myWindow 1¶myWindow 2¶myWindow 3¶anotherWindow 1; myWindow) returns myWindow 1¶myWindow 2¶myWindow 3.

Developer Tools

The following functions tend not to do anything for users directly but represent some of our most-used behind-the-scenes tools.

fnErrorHandler (errorCode)

When adding error checking to functions—and we strongly recommend that you do—you will need to consider a few issues. First, is it necessary in every function to test for valid or non-empty parameters? FileMaker's standard functions don't, so in some cases we will opt to follow that approach and assume that the developer in question will test his code and be able to detect any error conditions in such cases.

However, for functions that veer off the beaten path—for example, by requiring specific keywords or employing complex logic—it's prudent to add some reasonable level of error checking.

You then need to decide how to manage the error results themselves. You might, if you want, return an error message as the result of your function. In all the examples we've provided in this book, that is the path we've chosen. It is straightforward to write error messages directly into the code of your functions, and it reduces the complexity of the material we're presenting; however, some software developers may argue that error results belong in a different memory space than function results.

In solutions that use more than a handful of custom functions, we add this fnErrorHandler() function to keep the error clutter in other functions to a minimum and to centralize the implementation of what a given system should do when it discovers an error.

Notice that this function contains no error checking logic (other than its own)—in other words, it does not test other functions. Instead it is meant to manage an error after another function encounters one.

Note also that this function sets a global variable to the error code passed into it, including zero (no error). This allows developers to check for errors after they've run routines that reference functions that in turn use this error handler.

For an example of how one might use this error handler from another function, refer to fnErrorHandlerExample().

Code:

```
// function does two separate things: returns a text explanation
of what error corresponds to which error code and secondly sets a
global variable with that code.
// input: integer that corresponds to an error code within FileMaker
or a custom error code established by another custom function.
// output: text description and also sets $$lastErrorCode

Let([
   $$lastErrorCode = errorCode
   ];
```

```
Case (
   errorCode = 0; "no error";

   // custom error codes
   errorCode = 90100; "fnMyCustomFunction encountered an error";
   errorCode = 90101;
      "input does not match the expected parameter keyword for fnErrorHandlerExample";
   // create as many error codes as you need here.
   // The two above are simply examples.

   // filemaker error codes
   errorCode = -1; "Unknown error";
   errorCode = 1; "User canceled action";
   errorCode = 2; "Memory error";
   errorCode = 401; "No records match Find request";
   // others omitted to save space...
   // refer to the electronic files for a complete listing

   // not recognized default value for case()
   "error not recognized by fnErrorHandler"
   )
)
```

fnErrorHandlerExample (text)

This function serves as an example of using a central error handler instead of passing error messages directly from your functions. Instead of intermingling error messages with all your functions (and being faced with maintaining consistency across possibly dozens of functions), this approach places the logic for presenting errors in a single place.

Notice in the case of an error, this function returns an error message derived from fnErrorHandler and also sets a $$lastErrorCodeglobal variable to a specific error code.

Note also that you need not return the results of fnErrorHandler(). This function does so, but the purpose of setting $$lastErrorCode is so that a developer can opt to not commingle error messages with function results if she wants.

Refer to fnErrorHandler() for more detail on error handling with custom functions.

Code:

```
// example of how to work with the fnErrorHandler() function.
// this function will always return an error, unless exactly
 the value "hello" is passed into it.

Case (
   Exact ( "hello"; text ) = 1;
      "All's well that ends well.";
      fnErrorHandler ( 90101 )
)

/* Here's another approach that does not return any error message
as a result of this function:

Let ([
   test = Exact ( "hello"; text );

   result = Case ( test = 1;
      "All's well that ends well.";
      ""
   );

   error = Case ( test = 0;
      fnErrorHandler ( 90101 );
      ""
   )];

   result
)
*/
```

fnModifierKeys ()

This function returns a return-delimited list of text descriptors for the modifier keys held down whenever it is evaluated. This is useful for those of us who can't remember which numbers correspond to which key combinations. For instance, developers can use this function in scripts or elsewhere by testing for the presence of "shift" in `fnModifierKeys` instead of having always to use `Get(ActiveModifierKeys) = 1`.

Code:

```
// identifies active modifier keys by text
// input: none
// output:
//    text value list corresponding to active modifier keys

Let ([
   keys = Get (ActiveModifierKeys)
   ];
   Case ( Mod ( keys; 2 ) = 1; "Shift¶"; "" ) &
   Case ( Int ( Mod ( keys; 4 ) / 2 ) = 1; "Caps Lock¶"; "" ) &
   Case ( Int ( Mod ( keys; 8 ) / 4 ) = 1; "Control¶"; "" ) &
   Choose ( 2 * ( Int ( Mod ( keys; 16 ) / 8 )) +
      ( Abs (Get (SystemPlatform) ) - 1 ); ""; ""; "Option¶"; "Alt¶" ) &
   Case ( keys >= 16; "Command¶"; "" )
)
```

Examples:

In the case where a user has the Shift key pressed, fnModifierKeys returns Shift.

In the case where a user has both the Shift and Ctrl keys pressed, fnModifierKeys returns

Shift

Control

System Constants

A *system constant* is a value that developers place in a custom function that then becomes permanent. It doesn't "evaporate" at the end of a session (as global field values and global variables do), nor does its value vary from user to user. Developers can count on them being persistent and can easily edit them as needed.

fnSolutionVersion ()

We find it valuable to track version numbers of our systems and at times need to use logical (script) routines that reference or use those version numbers. Rather than adding a field to the data schema of a solution, use a custom function.

We recommend also creating a similar fnSolutionNamespace() function.

Code:

```
// returns version of database solution and name
// input: none
```

```
// output: version number or text

1.003

/* version history
...etc...
```

Examples:

In all cases, fnSolutionVersion returns 1.003. Developers will want to update the hard-coded value as appropriate.

fnTab ()

FileMaker uses a pilcrow character ("¶") to represent carriage returns, but there's no analog for tab characters. This custom function is simple but vital if you need to format with tab characters. The alternative is seeing blank space within your formulas and being left to wonder what is in the space: Space characters? Tabs? Odd characters that can't display?

Note that Ctrl+tab inserts a tab character on Windows and Opt-tab on the Mac OS. The two are cross-platform compatible.

Code:

```
// tab character

"	"
```

fnTextColor (text; color)

With this function you can save yourself a bit of hassle by allowing the use of familiar terms for colors, rather than being forced to look up RGB numbers. But the real value here is in making use of the central nature of custom functions: If ever you need to change a color in your system you have one single place to do so. Tweak one of the RGB numbers in the function, and your database reflects that change throughout (however, some calculation results may be stored and therefore won't update until something they reference changes). This custom function also ensures consistency. By virtue of having only one instance of a color, you never get confused on which red you're using in a given system.

Code:

```
// returns colored text
// input:
//   text = text string
//   color = keywords defined below
```

```
// output:
//   text (w/color)

Let ([
   rgbValue = Case (
      color = "black"; RGB ( 0; 0; 0 );
      color = "white"; RGB ( 255; 255; 255 );
      color = "red"; RGB ( 255; 0; 0 );
      color = "green"; RGB ( 0; 255; 0 );
      color = "blue"; RGB ( 0; 0; 255 );
      color = "soliant"; RGB ( 231; 188; 19 );
      color = "ltgray"; RGB ( 170; 170; 170 );
      color = "dkgray"; RGB ( 120; 120; 120 );
      "color not recognized"
      )
   ];
   Case ( rgbValue = "color not recognized";
      rgbValue;
      TextColor ( text; rgbValue )
   )
)
```

Examples:

fnTextColor ("hello world"; "blue") returns hello world as blue text.

fnTextColor ("hello world"; "blurple") returns color not recognized.

Toolkit for Complex Data Structures

This next group of custom functions requires some explanation, and perhaps some evangelism as well. These functions are complex; our intent was to demonstrate, with a set of real examples from our own work, how it's possible to use custom functions and the power under the hood of this often underappreciated feature.

Data API Within FileMaker

This fnXML*** set of functions all exist to help manipulate a block of XML data, stored in a text field or variable. Together they represent a kind of small API (Application Programming Interface) and support some specific programming methodologies. In that way, this suite of functions is less general purpose than the earlier ones in this chapter.

The strength of these functions lies in their capability for manipulating complex data structures. You can add, delete, update, and extract data from a tree of nested data.

An API is a term borrowed (with a degree of liberty) from other programming environments such as C# and Java. It refers to a set of instructions that are largely independent and allow programmers to accomplish some set of functions without having to know how the API itself was constructed. Both Apple and Microsoft provide a large range of APIs with their operating systems, there's an Apache API for extending its capabilities as a web server, and there's even a FileMaker API for writing plug-ins. The idea here is that an API provides a framework and hooks into some set of functionality that you as a developer intend to leverage and reuse, without necessarily needing to understand all the details of how it works internally.

Data Tree

A *data tree* is a powerful programming concept also borrowed from other environments. Abstractly, it is essentially a data structure that can hold multiple values. These values can be referenced by their positions within the tree (or perhaps *array*, if you accept a loose interpretation of the term) and related in similar ways to a set of FileMaker tables. In crude terms, this data structure can be thought of as a database within a database.

Data trees and arrays are useful for a variety of things, including storing a simple list of values, efficiently moving multiple values as a single block from place to place in a system, and dealing with variable length data structures where it would be impractical or impossible to define fields or variables enough to hold them.

Perhaps an example would help; this is a simple one-dimensional array and represents a simple one-level hierarchy of tiered data:

```
[ red | green | blue | yellow ]
```

In this scenario, most FileMaker developers would choose—and rightly so—to work with either a repeating variable or a return-delimited list and the GetValue() function. (We've included list handlers in this book as well.)

But there are times when a one-dimensional array isn't enough for your needs. Consider a scenario where you need to store colors and, say, shirt sizes and quantities. Your pipe-delimited array needs some new delimiter characters:

```
[ red; large; 20 | green; large; 10 | blue; medium; 15 ... and so on ]
```

As you can see, even a two-dimensional array can start to feel complex.

This is where XML comes in. How does one describe an N-dimensional data structure in a way that can be interpreted by both humans and across multiple platforms?

Note that the issue is twofold: XML holds information about its data, as well as providing a structure in which to store it.

Using XML as a Data Structure

Entire books have been written on XML, and a complete discussion of it extends beyond the scope of this book; however, suffice it to say we chose XML for three reasons. First, it's self-documenting: Instead of identifying something by its position within an array, XML uses tags to clearly label data. <quantity>10</quantity> is a far more clear description than the preceding example using pipe and semicolon delimiters. Second, XML is an industry standard and has emerged as a leading means to transfer and express data between platforms and applications. Third, XML allows for "deep" data structures. Note that the following example represents a four-dimensional tree:

```
<inventory>
  <shirt>
    <shirtName>SiliconValleyT</shirtName>
    <shirtID>122</shirtID>
    <color>red</color>
    <sizes>
      <size>
        <sizeName>Extra Large</sizeName>
        <quantity>100</quantity>
      </size>
      <size>
        <sizeName>Large</sizeName>
        <quantity>200</quantity>
      </size>
    </sizes>
  </shirt>
</inventory>
<orders>
  <order>
    <orderNumber>1010</orderNumber>
    <shirtID>122</shirtID>
  </order>
  <order>
    <orderNumber>1011</orderNumber>
    <shirtID>142</shirtID>
  </order>
</orders>
```

Imagine trying to represent that data structure in a flat, delimited text list, and the mind boggles. Note too that even if you're unfamiliar with XML or with the data that this block is meant to express, you can infer a great deal by simply reading it.

Path-Based Selections

Having now decided on an API to manage a data tree, and having selected XML as a data format, this now brings us to FileMaker. We've worked with various sorts of arrays and trees for many years, but working with return-delimited lists or temporarily shoving things into makeshift data tables has never completely fit the need.

FileMaker 7 introduced script parameters and FileMaker 8 introduced script results. Neither of them supports anything other than one value; if you want to pass more than one piece of data by either of these two features of FileMaker, you'll need to use a block of text and delimit it somehow. Then the second part of the process is writing a parsing routine that extracts your multiple values from this data block.

This problem is a good candidate for one or more custom functions. Rather than writing a series of parsing routines throughout a database, we suggest building a set of array handlers that can abstract and centralize the entire set of functionality you need.

The approach we've developed here is admittedly complex. We wanted to get more than just a simple container of one or two dimensional data: We wanted to be able to name the values in our data and to hierarchically organize them to N layers deep. We have created a path syntax (inspired by XPath, for those of you familiar with it—http://en.wikipedia.org/wiki/Xpath) that can pull a variety of structured data from an XML source.

The six main functions do the following:

- **fnXMLselect**—Extracts a block of data from an XML source.
- **fnXMLupdate**—Replaces a block of data within an XML source with a new value.
- **fnXMLinsert**—Inserts a new block of XML into an XML source.
- **fnXMLdelete**—Deletes a block of XML from within an XML source.
- **fnXMLclean**—Strips an XML block of extraneous characters and formatting.
- **fnXMLformat**—Adds tab characters and return carriages to a block of XML for easy display/reading.

fnXMLselect() is the most powerful of the six functions and is used by three of the others. It takes two parameters, xmlSource and path, and returns a block of XML extracted from the value passed into xmlSource.

The path syntax is specific and is the key to understanding how to use all four functions. An example (referring to the preceding shirt inventory example) might be

```
inventory/shirt/color
```

This path would return the value for the first color element of the first shirt of the first inventory it finds. Think of this path exactly like a tree or a file directory structure. In the preceding case, this path would return

```
red
```

The path inventory/shirt/sizes would return from the XML on pages 240–241:

```
<size>
   <sizeName>Extra Large</sizeName>
   <quantity>100</quantity>
```

```
  </size>
  <size>
    <sizeName>Large</sizeName>
    <quantity>200</quantity>
  </size>
```

The path syntax here is specific and drives the logic of what data you manipulate within the block of XML. Valid syntax includes

node/subnode
(a tree of any depth comprised of simple path nodes)

node/subnode/
(function will strip trailing slashes)

node[2]/subnode
(specify an integer to take the Nth occurrence of a node; 1-based)

node[attribute="foo"]/subnode
(specify finding an occurrence of a node where a child attribute node contains specified data)

Note: This syntax does *not* support XML attributes.

Supported: <tag><name>foo</name></tag>

Not supported: <tag name ="foo">value</tag>

This syntax also does *not* support the empty/close shortcut style: <tag/>.

This syntax supports the use of carriage returns, tabs, and spaces within XML values. It will not strip them out and shouldn't produce bugs when encountered; however, using fnXMLinsert() and fnXMLdelete() in combination with XML formatted with such characters may end up looking fairly ugly. It should retain functionality, however.

Imagine a scenario where you want to create an audit trail. (Using auto-enter by calculation functions, you can trigger a second field to update itself when a given field is updated by the user.)

Rather than having to create double the amount of fields in your database, you'll likely want to store the audit information in one field. Likewise, you need to be able to store multiple values for a single field: who edited a field, what the old value was, what the new value is, and so on.

These functions would be perfectly suited for just such a scenario: Use fnXMLinsert to store information into the audit trail field, and then use fnXMLselect to extract it for a rollback if necessary. The data structure might look something like this:

```
<audittrail>
  <record>
    <id>12</id>
    <field>
      <name>CustomerID</name>
      <value>1001</value>
    </field>
    <field>
      <name>Address</name>
      <oldValue>123 Main Street</oldValue>
      <newValue>100 Center Drive</newValue>
      <editedBy>Molly Tully</editedBy>
      <editedTime>11/12/2005 11:10:14</editedTime>
    </field>
  </record>
</audittrail>
```

You can then extract the old value with a query like so:

```
fnXMLselect ( auditTrail; "audittrail/record[id=12]/field[name=Address]/oldValue" )
```

This function returns 123 Main Street.

The Functions

The following, finally, are the functions that comprise the suite of tools within this API.

fnXMLclean (xmlSource)

This function calls the fnXMLclean_sub() function and is used to supply default initial values to that function.

Code:

```
// strips extraneous characters between end tags and start tags
// input: text with proper <tag>value</tag> XML embedded
// output: cleaned XML
// dependencies: this is the calling function to fnXMLclean_sub that
needs a second parameter initialized

TextFormatRemove ( fnXMLclean_sub ( xmlSource; 1 ))
```

Example:

Assume a field exists, xmlSource, that includes XML data formatted with return characters and tabs or spaces:

```
<state>
   <name>California</name>
   <city>
      <name>San Mateo</name>
      <district>downtown</district>
   </city>
</state>
```

fnXMLclean (xmlSource) returns

fnXMLclean (xmlSource) returns

```
<state><name>California</name><city><name>San
Mateo</name><district>downtown</district></city></state>
```

Note that all text formatting (font, size, style, and color) will be removed as well.

fnXMLclean sub (xmlSource; afterStartTag)

This function takes a block of XML with some amount of extraneous characters sitting between end tags and start tags in the form of spaces, tabs, and carriage returns, and returns a block of XML stripped of all such detritus.

Note that it uses a subfunction to determine whitespace characters. If ever one's logic needed to be extended, this would easily allow for such.

Code:

```
// iterates through a block of XML and removes extraneous characters
// between close and open tags.
// input: text block of XML
//    afterStartTag = initial value should be 1. 1 if the prior tag
was a start tag (or at the start of the processing of the data), 0 if
the prior tag was an end tag.
// output: text - clean XML
// dependencies: uses fnIsWhitespace

Let ([
      nexttag = Position( xmlSource; "<"; 1; 1);
      ending = Position( xmlSource; ">"; nexttag + 1; 1);
```

```
      isStartTag = If ( Middle ( xmlSource; nexttag + 1; 1) = "/"; 0; 1)
   ];
 If ( nexttag = 0 or ending = 0; // Error case, or when source is empty
   If ( fnIsWhitespace ( xmlSource ); "" ; xmlSource );
   Let ([
      rest = fnXMLclean_sub (Right ( xmlSource; Length ( xmlSource ) - ending );
            isStartTag );
      start = Left ( xmlSource; nexttag - 1 );
      tag = Middle ( xmlSource; nexttag; ending - nexttag + 1 )
     ];
      Case ( isStartTag = 0 and afterStartTag = 1; start;
            fnIsWhitespace ( start ); "";
            start
       ) & tag & rest
    )
   )
 )
```

fnXMLdelete (xmlSource; path)

This function, along with its sibling functions fnXMLselect(), fnXMLupdate(), fnXMLinsert(), exists to help manipulate an XML data structure.

This particular function removes a block of data as controlled by the path parameter.

Code:

```
// Function removes a block of XML as controlled by a path.
// dependencies
//   makes use of two global vars => $$xmlSourceValueStart and
$$xmlSourceValueEnd. Needs to initialize them to ZERO.
//   uses fnXMLselect to find the proper position within xmlSource
// input:
//   xmlSource = a block of xml. Syntax is strict. Only use <tag></tag> pairs.
//   path = text string defining the hierarchical tree that should be used to
point to a specific branch or node within the block of XML.
//      see fnXMLselect comments for syntax options and examples.
// output:
//   xmlSource with data removed
```

```
Let ([
   $$xmlSourceValueStart = 0;
   $$xmlSourceValueEnd = 0;

   vValueLength = 0;
   vSourceLength = Length ( xmlSource );

   vBlock = fnXMLselect ( xmlSource ; path );

   vValuePosition =Position(xmlSource;"<"; $$xmlSourceValueStart;-1)-1;
   vBlockLength = $$xmlSourceValueEnd +
      ($$xmlSourceValueStart-vValuePosition)*2+1;
            end_position = vValuePosition + vBlockLength + 1;
            position_of_following_CR = Position(xmlSource;"¶";end_position;1);
            size_of_trailing_string = position_of_following_CR- end_position;
            trailing_string =
         Middle(xmlSource;end_position;size_of_trailing_string+1);
            vBlockLength =
If(Trim(trailing_string)="¶";vBlockLength+size_of_trailing_string+1;vBlockLength)

   ];

   Left ( xmlSource; vValuePosition ) &
      Middle ( xmlSource; vValuePosition + vBlockLength + 1;
         vSourceLength + vValueLength)
)
```

Examples:

```
fnXMLdelete ( xmlSource; "first_name" )
```

The result would be that within xmlSource, the <first_name> block would be removed, including the enclosing tags.

Consider the following source XML:

```
source XML =
   <root>
      <branch>
         <num>100</num>
         <text>foo</text>
```

```
      </branch>
   </root>
```

for fnXMLdelete (xmlSource; "root/branch") the result would be

```
   <root>
   </root>
```

fnXMLformat (xmlSource)

This function calls the fnXMLformat_sub() function and is used to populate default initial values.

Code:

```
Replace ( fnXMLformat_sub ( xmlSource; 1 ; "" ); 1; 1; "")
```

Example:

Assume a field exists, xmlSource, that holds

```
<state><name>California</name><city><name>San
Mateo</name><district>downtown</district></city></state>
```

fnXMLformat (xmlSource) returns

```
<state>
   <name>California</name>
   <city>
      <name>San Mateo</name>
      <district>downtown</district>
   </city>
</state>
```

fnXMLformat_sub (xmlSource; afterStartTag; indent)

This function is used to format a block of XML into an easy-to-read form. It inserts tab and carriage return characters, and colors the XML tags.

Notice that it uses subfunctions for the color choice, for the tab character, and for determining whether there is already some whitespace (spaces, tabs, and return characters) in the block of XML.

Further, this function uses two parameters for keeping track of its recursions. This is a subfunction that should never be called by anything other than its enclosing fnXMLformat() function.

Code:

```
// formats xmlSource with tab and return characters
// input:
//   xmlSource = text block of raw, unformatted xml
//   afterStartTag = initial value should be 1. 1 if the prior
tag was a start tag (or at the start of the processing of the data),
 0 if the prior tag was an end tag.
//   indent = initial value should be set to ""; used for recursion
to store iterative data
// output: formatted xmlSource
// dependencies: uses fnTab, fnIsWhitespace, fnTextColor

Let ([
        nexttag = Position(xmlSource;"<";1;1);
        ending = Position(xmlSource;">";1+nexttag;1);
        isStartTag = If(Middle(xmlSource;nexttag+1;1)="/"; 0; 1);
        indentStep = fnTab
     ];
   If(nexttag = 0 or ending=0;  // Error case, or when source is empty
     If(fnIsWhitespace(xmlSource); "" ; xmlSource);
     Let ([
         newIndent = If(isStartTag; indent & indentStep; Left(indent;Length(indent)-Length(indentStep)));
         rest = fnXMLformat_sub
          (Right(xmlSource;Length(xmlSource)-ending);isStartTag;newIndent);
         start = Left(xmlSource;nexttag-1);
         tag = Middle(xmlSource;nexttag+1; ending-nexttag-1)
       ] ;
         Case (isStartTag=0 and afterStartTag = 1; start;
                fnIsWhitespace(start); ¶ & If (isStartTag; indent; newIndent);
                start) // end Case
       & "<" & fnTextColor(tag;"blue") & ">" & rest
     ) // end Let
   ) // end If
) // end Let
```

fnXMLinsert (xmlSource; path; value)

This particular function creates a block of data as controlled by the path and value parameters.

Code:

```
// Function creates a block of XML with value as controlled by a path.
// dependencies
//   makes use of two global vars =>
//   $$xmlSourceValueStart and $$xmlSourceValueEnd. Needs to initialize them to ZERO.
//   uses fnXMLselect to find the proper position within xmlSource
// input:
//   xmlSource = a block of xml. Syntax is somewhat strict.
//   Only use <tag></tag> pairs.
//   path = text string defining the hierarchical tree
//   that should be used to point to a specific branch
//   or node within the block of XML.
//       see fnXMLselect comments for syntax options and examples.
//   value = a block of text or xml
// output:
//   xmlSource with new data

Let ([
   $$xmlSourceValueStart = 0;
   $$xmlSourceValueEnd = 0;

   vValueLength = Length ( value );
   vSourceLength = Length ( xmlSource );

   vBlock = fnXMLselect ( xmlSource ; path );

   vValuePosition = $$xmlSourceValueStart;
   vBlockLength = $$xmlSourceValueEnd
   ];

   Left ( xmlSource; vValuePosition ) & value &
   Middle ( xmlSource; vValuePosition + vBlockLength + 1; vSourceLength + vValueLength)
)
```

Examples:

```
fnXMLinsert ( xmlSource; "first_name"; "Alexander" )
```

The result would be that within xmlSource, a new <first_name> block would be created and given a value of "Alexander".

Consider the following source XML:

```
source XML =
  <root>
    <branch>
      <num>100</num>
      <text>foo</text>
    </branch>
  </root>
```

for fnXMLinsert (xmlSource; "root/branch"; "<data>999</data><date>11/20/2005</date>") the result would be

```
  <root>
    <branch>
      <num>100</num><text>foo</text><data>999</data><date>11/20/2005</date>
    </branch>
  </root>
```

fnXMLselect (xmlSource; path)

fnXMLselect() serves as both a subfunction for three of the other XML-parsing functions and as the means by which developers can extract data from an XML block.

Its primary mission is to take a path parameter (discussed in detail in the preceding pages) and return a block of XML extracted from a larger XML data source.

It also uses two global variables to keep track of where within the source XML a given block starts and ends.

Code:

```
// Function returns a block of XML as controlled by a path.
// It recursively iterates through a block of XML until it reaches
the end of the path parameter and returns a "child" block of XML.
// dependencies: makes use of two global vars =>
//   $$xmlSourceValueStart and $$xmlSourceValueEnd.
//   Expects them to start at ZERO
// input:
//   xmlSource = a block of xml. Syntax is somewhat strict. Only
```

```
use <tag></tag> pairs.
//   path = text string defining the hierarchical tree that should
be used to point to a specific branch or node within the block of XML.
//      see below for syntax options and examples.
// output:
//   text = a block of text as extracted from xmlSource

Let ([
      // Path Values
   vPathLength = Length ( path );
   vPath = Case ( Right ( path; 1) = """/";
      Left ( path; vPathLength - 1); path );
         // strips trailing slash if necessary
   vPathNodeCount = PatternCount ( vPath; "/") + 1;
      // counts the nodes in the path provided
   vPathSlashPosition = Position ( vPath; "/"; 1; 1);
   vPathNew = Middle ( vPath; vPathSlashPosition + 1;
      vPathLength - vPathSlashPosition );
         // crops the first root of the path out...
         // this will be passed recursively back into the function
   vPathFirstNode = Case ( vPathNodeCount > 1 ;
      Left ( vPath; vPathSlashPosition - 1 ); vPath );
         // the inverse of vPathNew, takes the first node and drops the rest

      // Isolate Expression Info
   vPathLBracketPosition = Position ( vPathFirstNode; "["; 1; 1 );
   vPathRBracketPosition = Position ( vPathFirstNode; "]"; 1; 1 );
   vPathExpression = Middle ( vPath; vPathLBracketPosition + 1;
      vPathRBracketPosition - vPathLBracketPosition - 1 );

      // Isolate First Tag within Path
   vPathRTagPosition = Case ( vPathLBracketPosition > 1;
      vPathLBracketPosition - 1; Length ( vPathFirstNode ) );
   vPathTag = Left ( vPath; vPathRTagPosition );

      // Expression Checks
      //  test to see if bracketValue is an INTEGER
      // or if it is a NAME-VALUE pair, by checking for an "=" char.
      //  in the case that it's a name-value pair, extract the
      // search tag in question.
```

```
vExpressionValue = Case ( PatternCount ( vPathExpression; "=" ) > 0;
   Let ([
      vExpressionTagEnd = Position ( vPathExpression; "="; 1; 1) - 1;
      vExpressionTag = Trim ( Left ( vPathExpression; vExpressionTagEnd ) );
      vExpressionLPosition = Position ( vPathExpression; "="; 1; 1) + 2;
      vExpressionValueLength = Length ( vPathExpression ) - vExpressionLPosition;
      vExpressionValue = Trim ( Middle ( vPathExpression; vExpressionLPosition;
         vExpressionValueLength ));
      vExpressionResult = "<" & vExpressionTag & ">" & vExpressionValue &
         "</" & vExpressionTag & ">"
      ]; // end variable declaration
      vExpressionResult
   ); // end let
   // else if there is no "=" within vPathExpression
   // return "IsInteger" as a control check for blockOccurence
   "IsInteger"
); // end case { vExpressionValue }

   // vParentCount will determine which parent node contains
   // the search string in question. should end up with an integer
   // to be used as an occurrence variable.
vExpressionTagPosition = Position ( xmlSource; vExpressionValue; 1; 1);
vCropSource = Left ( xmlSource; vExpressionTagPosition );
vParentCount = PatternCount ( vCropSource; "<" & vPathTag & ">" );

   // Set Occurrence
   // The following is used in the position functions below
   // for extracting blocks. This controls which of a given block
   // is taken, the first, second, third, etc.
   // If vPathExpression is an integer, use that for blockOccurrence.
   // If there's something in searchTagString, use the vParentCount as
   // blockOccurrence. Otherwise use 1.
vBlockOccurrence = Case (
   vExpressionValue <> "IsInteger"; vParentCount;
   vPathExpression > 1; vPathExpression;
   1   // default to 1
);  // end case { vBlockOccurrence }

   // Extract XML between vPath tags
vBlockStartChar = Position ( xmlSource; "<" & vPathTag & ">"; 1;
```

```
   vBlockOccurrence) + Length ( "<" & vPathTag & ">" );
vBlockEndChar = Position ( xmlSource; "</" & vPathTag & ">"; vBlockStartChar ; 1);
vBlockLength = vBlockEndChar - vBlockStartChar ;
vBlockRaw = Middle ( xmlSource ; vBlockStartChar ; vBlockLength );

   // Trim excess ¶ and space chars by excluding all but the block itself
vBlockPositionStart = Position ( vBlockRaw; "<"; 1; 1);
vBlockCountClose = PatternCount ( vBlockRaw; ">" );
vBlockPositionEnd = Case ( vPathNodeCount = 1;
   Length ( vBlockRaw ); Position ( vBlockRaw; ">"; 1; vBlockCountClose) );
vBlockTrimmed = Middle ( vBlockRaw; vBlockPositionStart;
   vBlockPositionEnd - vBlockPositionStart + 1 );

   // update global pointer to track beginning position
   // of block and value within xmlSource
   // ( allows for update, delete, insert )

$$xmlSourceValueStart = $$xmlSourceValueStart + vBlockStartChar - 1;
$$xmlSourceValueEnd = vBlockLength;

   // Error Checking
vErrorHasCloseTag = vBlockEndChar;
vErrorHasTag = PatternCount ( xmlSource; "<" & vPathTag & ">");
vErrorHasNameValueMatch = Case ( vExpressionValue = "IsInteger"";
   "Ignore"; Case ( PatternCount ( xmlSource; vExpressionValue ) > 0;
      "Ignore"; "No Match") );
vErrorOutOfBounds = Case ( vExpressionValue <> "IsInteger"";
   "Ignore"; Case ( PatternCount ( xmlSource; "<" & vPathTag & "">")
   < vBlockOccurrence; "Out Of Bounds"; "Ignore") );

   //Result
   //--> if you need to debug, just comment out the case below
   // and place one of your variables next to result.
vResult =

   Case (
            IsEmpty ( xmlSource ) and IsEmpty ( path );
         "Error: Missing Parameters ( xmlSource; path )";
     IsEmpty ( xmlSource ); "Error: Missing Parameter ( xmlSource )";
     IsEmpty ( path ); "Error: Missing Parameter ( path )";
```

```
        vErrorHasTag = 0; "Error: Invalid Tag (" & vPathTag & ")";
        vErrorHasCloseTag = 0; "Error: No Close Tag (" & vPathTag & ")";
        vErrorHasNameValueMatch <> "Ignore"; "Error: Invalid Name/Value "("
          & vExpressionValue & ")";
        vErrorOutOfBounds = "Out Of Bounds"";
          "Error: Invalid Index (" & vPathTag & "[" & vBlockOccurrence & "])";
          // now return valid xml block in the case that
          // no error is returned; recursive if additional nodes exist
        vPathNodeCount > 1; fnXMLselect ( vBlockRaw; vPathNew );
        vBlockTrimmed    // default to value
      ) // end case {result}

    ]; // end variable declaration

    vResult

  ) // end let
```

Examples:

fnXMLselect (xmlSource; "last_name")
which might return Smith.

Another call might look like this:
fnXMLselect (xmlSource; "new_record_request/invoice/fkey_customer")
and might return C_10012 as a customer ID.

Another approach can use filtering, using a square bracket construction similar to an XPath predicate:
fnXMLselect (xmlSource; "new_record_request/invoice[date="11/11/2005"]/fkey_customer")

This might return a different customer ID.

Consider the following source XML:

```
source XML =
  <root>
    <branch>
      <num>100</num>
      <text>foo</text>
    </branch>
    <branch>
```

```
        <num>200</num>
        <text>xyz</text>
      </branch>
    </root>
```

for path root/branch:

```
  result =
      <num>100</num>
      <text>foo</text>
```

for path root/branch/num:

```
  result =
      100
```

for path root/branch[2]:

```
  result =
      <num>200</num>
      <text>xyz</text>
```

for path root/branch[num="200"]:

```
  result =
      <num>200</num>
      <text>xyz</text>
```

for path root/branch[num="200"]/text:

```
  result =
      xyz
```

fnXMLupdate (xmlSource; path; value)

This particular function replaces a block of data within the source XML with the contents of the "value" parameter.

Code:

```
// Function replaces a block of XML with value as controlled by a path.
// dependencies
//    makes use of two global vars =>
//    $$xmlSourceValueStart and $$xmlSourceValueEnd.
//    Needs to initialize them to ZERO.
//    uses fnXMLselect to find the proper position within xmlSource
```

```
// input:
//   xmlSource = a block of xml. Syntax is somewhat strict.
//   Only use <tag></tag> pairs.
//   path = text string defining the hierarchical tree
//   that should be used to point to a specific branch or
//   node within the block of XML.
//      see  fnXMLselect comments for syntax options and examples.
//   value = a block of text or xml
// output:
//   xmlSource with new data

Let ([
   $$xmlSourceValueStart = 0;
   $$xmlSourceValueEnd = 0;

   vValueLength = Length ( value );
   vSourceLength = Length ( xmlSource );

   vBlock = fnXMLselect ( xmlSource ; path );

   vValuePosition = $$xmlSourceValueStart;
   vBlockLength = $$xmlSourceValueEnd
   ];

   Left ( xmlSource; vValuePosition ) & value &
   Middle ( xmlSource; vValuePosition + vBlockLength + 1; vSourceLength + vValueLength)
)
```

Examples:

```
fnXMLupdate ( xmlSource; "last_name"; "Smith" )
```

The result would be that within xmlSource, the first <last_name> block encountered would be given a value of "Smith".

Consider the following source XML:

```
source XML =
   <root>
      <branch>
         <num>100</num>
         <text>foo</text>
```

```
  </branch>
  <branch>
    <num>200</num>
    <text>xyz</text>
  </branch>
</root>
```

for fnXMLupdate (xmlSource; "root/branch/num"; 500) the result would be

```
<root>
  <branch>
    <num>500</num>
    <text>foo</text>
  </branch>
  <branch>
    <num>200</num>
    <text>xyz</text>
  </branch>
</root>
```

Storing (and Unstoring) Text Data as CSS

Like the XML examples given previously, this family of related custom functions is intended to serve as a real-world example of how custom functions can be grouped into suites to perform some fairly powerful processing tasks.

FileMaker has many powerful features for working with richly formatted text data. Within a FileMaker text field, you can change fonts, point sizes, styles, and colors with ease. These changes are all stored in the database and are visible the next time you, or anyone else, looks at the data. This styling can also carry over into other applications: Cut and paste styled text from FileMaker into a program such as Microsoft Word, and the styling comes right along with it.

This is all well and good, but suppose you want to store that styled text in a place or program that cannot retain the styling attributes? Suppose, for example, that you want to store the styled text in an Oracle database, using FileMaker's new External SQL Source integration feature. You could certainly move the text data into an Oracle field, but when you pulled it back out again, all the styling data would be lost.

Well, it might occur to you that FileMaker has some calculation functions that might help, called GetAsSVG() and GetAsCSS(). These calculations take a piece of data and transform it into a purely text-based representation, either HTML with CSS, or SVG. This data can then be viewed in a web browser or SVG viewer with the vast majority of its original styling intact. CSS and SVG are both purely text-based formats, and this data can be stored almost anywhere.

That still doesn't help you, though, if you want the styled data to be stored, say, in an Oracle field, yet still be available for styling and editing using FileMaker's rich text editing capabilities. For that, you'd really like a way to "reconstitute" the CSS or SVG data into a "real" FileMaker styled text block. That's where the following function family comes in.

These functions assume that a styled block of FileMaker text has been turned into CSS via the GetAsCSS() function. Given such a block of CSS, they will turn it back into a block of styled FileMaker text, making heavy use of FileMaker's text formatting functions.

Note the following:

- The translation is faithful but slightly imperfect. A few attributes of FileMaker text fields are not translated into the CSS and so can't be brought back out. At present, the only limits we're aware of are that the GetAsCSS() function will turn a double underline into a single underline, and that the CSS translation cannot preserve and reproduce tab stops within the styled text.
- These functions aren't meant to operate on CSS-styled HTML from sources other than FileMaker's GetAsCSS() function. They've been tested only with the output of GetAsCSS(). A custom function suite to translate a block of any styled HTML into FileMaker text would be quite an undertaking!
- These functions have not been tested on non-Latin character sets and may not work as well for such character sets.

How the Functions Work

As noted in the preceding section, the functions are designed to work with FileMaker styled text that has been through the GetAsCSS() function. GetAsCSS() transforms styled text into a series of HTML <SPAN> elements, each with an associated STYLE attribute.

For example:

```
<SPAN STYLE= "font-size: 24px;" >CUSTOM TEXT<BR></SPAN>

<SPAN STYLE= "" ><BR><BR></SPAN>

<SPAN STYLE= "color: #FF0000;" >COLORED TEXT</SPAN>
```

At their simplest, the functions simply pick over every SPAN in the output and then reapply the styles listed in the STYLE attribute. That's a mostly straightforward process. Exceptions and subtleties are noted in the descriptions of the individual functions.

Though there are 11 functions in this set, there is really only one main function, fnCssToText(). That function in turn draws on the other 10 functions as "helper" functions to perform various specific tasks.

So the basic usage of the library is simple: fnCssToText(cssText) results in styled FileMaker text.

The Functions

The following functions comprise the suite of tools within this API. We've opted not to include examples for most functions in this section, because the end result of most examples is a block of styled text, which won't reproduce particularly well in this book. As noted previously, you're mostly likely to only ever call one function, fnCssToText(), directly, and its usage is straightforward.

fnCssToText (cssText)

This function is the master function within the library

Code:

```
// fnCSStoText( cssText )
// v1.0
// converts the input parameter (text + inline css) into a FileMaker text object (text + formatting)
// input:
//     cssText = Text with inline CSS to be converted to a FileMaker text object
// output:
//     Text Object formatted according to the CSS
// notes:
//    -function is recursive
//    -unable to preserve layout properties (ie, align left/right/top/bottom)
➥as there are no documented FM Functions to re-create those properties for the text object.

Let ([

   firstSpanClose = Position ( cssText ; "</SPAN>" ; 1 ; 1 ) + 6;
   firstSpan = Left( cssText; firstSpanClose );

   remainder = Right(cssText; Length(cssText) - Length(firstSpan));


   remainderScrubbed = Right( remainder; Length( remainder ) - 2 ); // this is
➥to trim trailing space-CR after last </SPAN> if it's there;
   processedFirstSpan = Case( fnCssToText__isValidSpan( firstSpan); fnCssToText__processSpan(
➥firstSpan ); "(Invalid span)" );
   continue = Case( Left( remainderScrubbed; 5 ) = "<SPAN"; 1; 0 );
```

```
// process the next span until we hit the last result = processedFirstSpan &
➥Case( continue; fnCssToText( remainderScrubbed ); "" )

];

result )
```

fnCssToText__processSpan (spanText)

A simple function to process a single <SPAN>text</SPAN> element.

Code:

```
// fnCssToText__processSpan ( spanText )
//
// extracts style definition and content from a span and returns the text contents, processed with
➥formatting as a text object.
// the calling function will/must guarantee that we are passed a valid "CSS" span of the form
➥<SPAN STYLE="foo">text</SPAN>
// input:
//   spanText = text span to process
// output:
//   processed text span


Let ([

  //
  // Extract the styleDef
  // styleDef is the style parameter string contained inside the span tag.. ie:
  // <SPAN style="font-family: Arial">example string</SPAN>
 //

  firstSpanClose = Position ( spanText ; ">" ; 1 ; 1 );
  styleStart = Position ( spanText ; "=" ; 1 ; 1 ) +2 ;
  styleEnd = firstSpanClose - 2 ;
  styleDef = Middle ( spanText ; styleStart + 1; styleEnd - styleStart -1 );
```

```
//
// Extract the span content
// spanContent is the string contained between the <SPAN>..</SPAN> tags
//

spanContent = Middle ( spanText ; firstSpanClose + 1 ; Length( spanText ) - firstSpanClose - 7 ); // 7
➥chars for closing </SPAN>


// some initial processing
processedSpanContent = fnCssToText__processRawSpanText ( spanContent );



//
// Process the span
// If there is a style definition to this span, process it otherwise just return the span content
//

result = Case( IsEmpty(styleDef); processedSpanContent;
➥fnCssToText__processStyledSpan ( styleDef; processedSpanContent ))

];

result )
```

fnCssToText__isValidSpan (spanText)

A simple function to determine whether its input represents a valid <SPAN> …</SPAN> element.

Code:

```
// fnCssToText__isValidSpan ( spanText )
    //
    // returns true/false if span is valid
    // input:
    //    param_xxx = description
    // output:
    //    boolean - 1 if valid; 0 if invalid span

    Case( Left( spanText; 12) = "<SPAN STYLE=" and Right( spanText; 7 ) = "</SPAN>"; 1; 0 )
```

fnCssToText__processRawSpanText (spanText)

The text-only CSS form of the text may contain translations for many characters, the better to represent them in a pure-text format. For example, a section mark (§) within a block of styled FileMaker text will appear as "§" in the equivalent CSS. It's necessary to reverse-translate these entities (as they are known) back into their equivalent character codes. This is done by means of a large Substitute operation.

The function performs translations only for characters in the Latin (ISO-8859-1) character set. We designed the library for an application that can work within the Latin character set. FileMaker text fields can store Unicode data, which could include characters from many other character sets. These functions would have to be extended with additional translations to handle such additional character sets.

Code:

```
// fnCssToText__processRawSpanText ( spanText )
//
//
// this function is responsible for performing all necessary text substitutions on raw span text
// this includes <BR> -> ¶, and all Latin HTML entity substitutions
//
// input:
//   spanText = input text to process
// output:
//   spanText with conversions applied


//
// Make sure there are no duplicates when you add an entity.
// Makes sure &amp is translated last!
//
Substitute ( spanText ;


//
// Latin substitutions
//
["&iexcl;";"¡"]; //inverted exclamation mark
["&cent;";"¢"]; //cent sign
["&pound;";"£"]; //pound sign
["&curren;";" "]; //currency sign
["&yen;";"¥"]; //yen sign = yuan sign
["&brvbar;";"¦"]; //broken bar = broken vertical bar
```

```
["&sect;";"§"]; //section sign
["&uml;";"¨"]; //diaeresis = spacing diaeresis
["&copy;";"©"]; //copyright sign
["&ordf;";"ª"]; //feminine ordinal indicator
["&laquo;";"«"]; //left-pointing double angle quotation mark = left pointing guillemet
["&not;";"¬"]; //not sign
["&shy;";"–"]; //soft hyphen = discretionary hyphen
["&reg;";"®"]; //registered sign = registered trade mark sign
["&macr;";"¯"]; //macron = spacing macron = overline = APL overbar
["&deg;";"°"]; //degree sign
["&plusmn;";"±"]; //plus-minus sign = plus-or-minus sign
["&sup2;";"2"]; //superscript two = superscript digit two = squared
["&sup3;";"3"]; //superscript three = superscript digit three = cubed
["&acute;";"´"]; //acute accent = spacing acute
["&micro;";"µ"]; //micro sign
["&para;";"¶"]; //pilcrow sign = paragraph sign
["&middot;";"·"]; //middle dot = Georgian comma = Greek middle dot
["&cedil;";"¸"]; //cedilla = spacing cedilla
["&sup1;";"1"]; //superscript one = superscript digit one
["&ordm;";"º"]; //masculine ordinal indicator
["&raquo;";"»"]; //right-pointing double angle quotation mark = right pointing guillemet
["&frac14;";"1/4"]; //vulgar fraction one quarter = fraction one quarter
["&frac12;";"1/2"]; //vulgar fraction one half = fraction one half
["&frac34;";"3/4"]; //vulgar fraction three quarters = fraction three quarters
["&iquest;";"¿"]; //inverted question mark = turned question mark
["&Agrave;";"À"]; //Latin capital letter A with grave = Latin capital letter A grave
["&Aacute;";"Á"]; //Latin capital letter A with acute
["&Acirc;";"Â"]; //Latin capital letter A with circumflex
["&Atilde;";"Ã"]; //Latin capital letter A with tilde
["&Auml;";"Ä"]; //Latin capital letter A with diaeresis
["&Aring;";"Å"]; //Latin capital letter A with ring above = Latin capital letter A ring
["&AElig;";"Æ"]; //Latin capital letter AE = Latin capital ligature AE
["&Ccedil;";"Ç"]; //Latin capital letter C with cedilla
["&Egrave;";"È"]; //Latin capital letter E with grave
["&Eacute;";"É"]; //Latin capital letter E with acute
["&Ecirc;";"Ê"]; //Latin capital letter E with circumflex
["&Euml;";"Ë"]; //Latin capital letter E with diaeresis
["&Igrave;";"Ì"]; //Latin capital letter I with grave
["&Iacute;";"Í"]; //Latin capital letter I with acute
["&Icirc;";"Î"]; //Latin capital letter I with circumflex
```

```
["&Iuml;";"Ï"]; //Latin capital letter I with diaeresis
["&ETH;";"?"]; //Latin capital letter ETH
["&Ntilde;";"Ñ"]; //Latin capital letter N with tilde
["&Ograve;";"Ò"]; //Latin capital letter O with grave
["&Oacute;";"Ó"]; //Latin capital letter O with acute
["&Ocirc;";"Ô"]; //Latin capital letter O with circumflex
["&Otilde;";"Õ"]; //Latin capital letter O with tilde
["&Ouml;";"Ö"]; //Latin capital letter O with diaeresis
["&times;";"×"]; //multiplication sign
["&Oslash;";"Ø"]; //Latin capital letter O with stroke = Latin capital letter O slash
["&Ugrave;";"Ù"]; //Latin capital letter U with grave
["&Uacute;";"Ú"]; //Latin capital letter U with acute
["&Ucirc;";"Û"]; //Latin capital letter U with circumflex
["&Uuml;";"Ü"]; //Latin capital letter U with diaeresis
["&Yacute;";"Ý"]; //Latin capital letter Y with acute
["&THORN;";"Þ"]; //Latin capital letter THORN
["&szlig;";"ß"]; //Latin small letter sharp s = ess-zed
["&agrave;";"à"]; //Latin small letter a with grave = Latin small letter a grave
["&aacute;";"á"]; //Latin small letter a with acute
["&acirc;";"â"]; //Latin small letter a with circumflex
["&atilde;";"ã"]; //Latin small letter a with tilde
["&auml;";"ä"]; //Latin small letter a with diaeresis
["&aring;";"å"]; //Latin small letter a with ring above = Latin small letter a ring
["&aelig;";"æ"]; //Latin small letter ae = Latin small ligature ae
["&ccedil;";"ç"]; //Latin small letter c with cedilla
["&egrave;";"è"]; //Latin small letter e with grave
["&eacute;";"é"]; //Latin small letter e with acute
["&ecirc;";"ê"]; //Latin small letter e with circumflex
["&euml;";"ë"]; //Latin small letter e with diaeresis
["&igrave;";"ì"]; //Latin small letter i with grave
["&iacute;";"í"]; //Latin small letter i with acute
["&icirc;";"î"]; //Latin small letter i with circumflex
["&iuml;";"ï"]; //Latin small letter i with diaeresis
["&eth;";"∂"]; //Latin small letter eth
["&ntilde;";"ñ"]; //Latin small letter n with tilde
["&ograve;";"ò"]; //Latin small letter o with grave
["&oacute;";"ó"]; //Latin small letter o with acute
["&ocirc;";"ô"]; //Latin small letter o with circumflex
["&otilde;";"õ"]; //Latin small letter o with tilde
["&ouml;";"ö"]; //Latin small letter o with diaeresis
["&divide;";"÷"]; //division sign
```

```
["&oslash;";"ø"]; //Latin small letter o with stroke = Latin small letter o slash
["&ugrave;";"ù"]; //Latin small letter u with grave
["&uacute;";"ú"]; //Latin small letter u with acute
["&ucirc;";"û"]; //Latin small letter u with circumflex
["&uuml;";"ü"]; //Latin small letter u with diaeresis
["&yacute;";"ý"]; //Latin small letter y with acute
["&thorn;";"þ"]; //Latin small letter thorn
["&yuml;";"ÿ"]; //Latin small letter y with diaeresis

//
// Other substitutions
//
["&OElig;";"Œ"]; //Latin capital ligature OE
["&oelig;";"œ"]; //Latin small ligature oe
["&Scaron;";"Š"]; //Latin capital letter S with caron
["&scaron;";"š"]; //Latin small letter s with caron
["&Yuml;";"Ÿ"]; //Latin capital letter Y with diaeresis
["&circ;";"ˆ"]; //modifier letter circumflex accent
["&tilde;";"˜"]; //small tilde
[" ";"–"]; //en space
[" ";"  "]; //em space
[" ";" "]; //thin space
["&zwnj;";" "]; //zero width non-joiner
["&zwj;";" "]; //zero width joiner
["&lrm;";""]; //left-to-right mark
["&rlm;";""]; //right-to-left mark
["&ndash;";"–"]; //en dash
["&mdash;";"—"]; //em dash
["&lsquo;";"'"]; //left single quotation mark
["&sbquo;";","]; //single low-9 quotation mark
["&ldquo;";"\""]; //left double quotation mark
["&bdquo;";"\„"]; //double low-9 quotation mark
["&dagger;";"†"]; //dagger
["&Dagger;";"‡"]; //double dagger
["&permil;";"‰"]; //per mille sign
["&lsaquo;";"‹"]; //single left-pointing angle quotation mark
["&rsaquo;";"›"]; //single right-pointing angle quotation mark
["&euro;";"€"]; //euro sign


//
```

```
// Basic HTML entities
//
["<BR>"; "¶" ];
["&#9;"; "	" ]; // TAB character


["&quot;"; "\"" ];
["&apos;"; "'" ];

["&lt;"; "<" ];
["&gt;"; ">" ];

["&rsquo;"; "'" ];
["&rdquo;"; "\"" ];

//
// The conversion for &amp; must be done last otherwise it will cause unexpected results
//
["&amp;"; "&" ]

)
```

fnCssToText_processStyledSpan (styleDef, content)

After a span has been broken apart into a style definition and some content, this function hands those elements off to other functions for specific processing. The four types of formatting added through further processing are styling (bold, italic, and so on), font size, color, and font family.

Code:

```
// fnCssToText_processStyledSpan ( styleDef, content )
//
// returns a span with styles and formatting applied
// input:
//   styleDef = style paramter string extracted from a css span
//   content = content string
// output:
//   returns the span with styles applied
//
```

```
Let ([

    //
    // Accumulate style formattings and then return the end result.
    //
    withStyles = fnCssToText__applyStyles( styleDef; content);
    withFontSize = fnCssToText__applyFontSize ( styleDef; withStyles );
    withColor = fnCssToText__applyColor ( styleDef; withFontSize );
    withFontFamily = fnCssToText__applyFontFamily( styleDef; withColor);

    result = withFontFamily
    ];

    result
)
```

fnCssToText__applyFontSize (styleDef, text)

This function extracts any font sizing information from a style definition and applies it to a block of text.

Code:

```
// fnCssToText__applyFontSize ( styleDef, text)
  //
  // applies font-size formatting to text
  // input:
  //   styleDef =  style paramter string extracted from a css span
  //   text= text object to apply style to
  // output:
  //   returns text with formatting applied
  //

  Let ([

    sizeStyleStart = Position ( styleDef ; "font-size" ; 1 ; 1 );
    sizeStart= sizeStyleStart + 11; // length of "font-size ";
    sizeEnd = Position ( styleDef ; "px" ; sizeStart ; 1 ) - 1;
    fontSize = Middle ( styleDef ; sizeStart ; sizeEnd-  sizeStart + 1 );
```

```
        // superscripting and subscripting will cut the font size in half
        // if those attributes (expressed as vertical-align) are present,
        ➥we need to double the size going out

        // set a flag if we are using Super/Sub script by testing the presence
        ➥of the vertical-align strings
        // the flag will be used to determine if we double the font size
        verticalAlignTrue = Case( Position(styleDef;"vertical-align: text-top;";1;1) or
        ➥Position(styleDef;"vertical-align: text-bottom;";1;1) ; 1;0);
        finalFontSize = Case( verticalAlignTrue; 2* fontsize; fontsize );

    result = Case( sizeStyleStart < 1;  text; TextSize ( text ; finalFontSize ) )

    ];

      result
      )
```

fnCssToText__applyFontFamily (styleDef, text)

This function extracts any font family information from a style definition and applies it to a block of text.

Code:

```
    // fnCssToText__applyFontFamily ( styleDef, text)
    //
    // applies font family formatting to text
    // input:
    //    styleDef =  style paramter string extracted from a css span
    //    text= text object to apply style to
    // output:
    //    returns text with formatting applied

    Let ([

       fontFamilyStart = Position ( styleDef ; "font-family: " ; 1 ; 1 );
       fontNameStart= fontFamilyStart + 14; // length of "font-family '";
       // account for fact font families are in quotation marks
       fontNameEnd = Position ( styleDef ; ";" ; fontNameStart ; 1 ) – 2;
       fontName = Middle ( styleDef ; fontNameStart ; fontNameEnd-  fontNameStart + 1 );
```

```
      result = Case( fontFamilyStart < 1;  text; TextFont ( text ; fontName ) )

  ];

    result
    )
```

fnCssToText__applyColor (styleDef, text)

This function extracts any text coloring information from a style definition and applies it to a block of text.

Code:

```
// fnCssToText__applyColor ( styleDef, text)
  //
  // applies color formatting to text
  // input:
  //    styleDef =  style paramter string extracted from a css span
  //    text= text object to apply style to
  // output:
  //    returns text with formatting applied
  //
  // requires:
  //    custom function fnHexToRGB

  Let ([

    colorStyleStart = Position ( styleDef ; "color: #" ; 1 ; 1 );
    colorStart = colorStyleStart + 7;
    colorEnd = Position ( styleDef ; ";" ; colorStart ; 1 ) - 1;
    fontColor = Middle ( styleDef ; colorStart ; colorEnd-  colorStart + 1 );

    result = Case( colorStyleStart < 1;  text; TextColor ( text ; fnHexToRGB
    ➥( fontColor; "RGB" ) ) )


    ];

    result
  )
```

fnCssToText_applyOneStyle (styleDef, text, oneStyleString, styleValue)

This function checks for the presence of a single style attribute with styleDef. If the attribute is present, the function applies the corresponding FileMaker style to text.

Code:

```
// fnCssToText__applyOneStyle ( styleDef, text, oneStyleString, styleValue)
//
// applies styles to text
// input:
//   styleDef = style parameter string extracted from a css span
//   text = input text
//   oneStyleString = identifier of style to apply
//   styleValue = value of the style
// output:
//   text object with styles applied

Case( Position ( styleDef ; oneStyleString ; 1 ; 1 ) > 0; TextStyleAdd ( text ; styleValue ); text )
```

fnCssToText_applyOneStyle (styleDef; text; "font-weight:bold"; Bold) checks the styleDef for the existence of the "font-weight:bold" attribute. If the attribute is present, the function applies the command TextStyleAdd(text; Bold).

This is a helper function that's called repeatedly by the function fnCssToText_applyStyles().

fnCssToText_applyStyles (styleDef, text, oneStyleString, styleValue)

This function uses the fnCssToText_applyOneStyle function to check for and apply a variety of possible styles from the CSS to the FileMaker text block being output.

Code:

```
// fnCssToText__applyStyles ( styleDef, text)
//
// applies styles to text
// input:
//   styleDef =  style parameter string extracted from a css span
//   text= text object to apply style to
// output:
//   text object with styles applied
//
```

```
// NOTE: FM8.5 and above set styleDef to : font-weight: normal;font-style:normal;text-decoration:
➥ none;font-variant:normal;letter-spacing: normal;text-transform: none;
// when it is styled as "PLAIN"

Case ( // TEST FOR PLAIN STYLE
   Position(styleDef;"font-weight: normal;font-style:normal;text-decoration:none;font-
variant:normal;letter-spacing: normal;text-transform: none;";1;1);

   // We have a "PLAIN" styled text span -- this must be handled as an exception
   ➥to the others because
   // PLAIN styles must be defined by itself (any other style will cancel it out)
   TextStyleAdd(text;Plain);

   // We have "known" styles and will apply them below.
   // Styles are applied in an accumulated manner.

   Let ([

      result =    fnCssToText__applyOneStyle ( styleDef; text;
      ➥"line-through;"; Strikethrough );
      result1 =  fnCssToText__applyOneStyle ( styleDef; result;
      ➥"font-variant:small-caps"; SmallCaps );
      result2 =  fnCssToText__applyOneStyle ( styleDef; result1;
      ➥"vertical-align: text-top"; Superscript );
      result3 =  fnCssToText__applyOneStyle ( styleDef; result2;
      ➥"vertical-align: text-bottom"; Subscript );
      result4 =  fnCssToText__applyOneStyle ( styleDef; result3;
      ➥"text-transform: uppercase"; Uppercase );
      result5 =  fnCssToText__applyOneStyle ( styleDef; result4;
      ➥"text-transform: lowercase"; Lowercase );
      result6 =  fnCssToText__applyOneStyle ( styleDef; result5;
      ➥"text-transform: capitalize"; Titlecase );
      result7 =  fnCssToText__applyOneStyle ( styleDef; result6;
      ➥"underline;"; Underline );
      result8 =  fnCssToText__applyOneStyle ( styleDef; result7;
      ➥"font-weight: bold"; Bold );
      result9 =  fnCssToText__applyOneStyle ( styleDef; result8;
      ➥"font-style:italic"; Italic );
      result10 = fnCssToText__applyOneStyle ( styleDef; result9;
```

```
    ➥"letter-spacing: -2px"; Condense );
    result11 = fnCssToText__applyOneStyle ( styleDef; result10;
    ➥"letter-spacing: 2px"; Extend );

    finalResult = result11

  ];

  finalResult
  )
) // Close case which tests for plain style.
```

fnHexToRGB (Hex, RGorB)

This function takes a standard hexadecimal color string (common in HTML and CSS) and transforms it in the corresponding FileMaker RGB value.

Code:

```
/*

Returns a decimal integer that represents a color obtained by converting
standard 6 character hexadecimal input.
If you pass any value to the RGorB param other than "R" or "G" or "B"
the function will return the full spectrum decimal value.
The RGorB parameter is a switch modifies the calculation to return only
the red, green or blue decimal value of Hex.

Hex = Hexadecimal input. Handles inputs containing leading/trailing
spaces and/or # symbol.

RGorB = Switch that determines the spectrum of output ( "R" = red; "G" =
green; "B" = Blue; "RGB" or "0" or [not null] = RGB ).


--------------------------
*/

Let (
  Boolean = Case ( RGorB = "B" ; 1 ; RGorB = "G" ; 1 ; RGorB = "R" ; 1 ; 0 ) ;
  Spectrum = Case ( RGorB = "B" ; 5 ; RGorB = "G" ; 3 ; 1 ) ;
  CleanHex = Trim ( Substitute ( Hex ; "#" ; "" ) ) ;
```

```
  HexInput = If ( Boolean = 1 ; Middle ( CleanHex ; Spectrum ; 2 ) ; CleanHex );
  Character = Right ( HexInput ; 1 ) ;
  Length = Length ( HexInput ) ] ;

( Position ( "0123456789ABCDEF" ; Character ; 1 ; 1 ) - 1 ) + If (
Length > 1 ; 16 * fnHexToRGB ( Left ( HexInput ; Length - 1 ) ; 0 ) )

)
```

Example:

fnHexToRGB ("CCA1FF" ; "") yields the result 13410815 (a sort of a pale mauve).

PART IV

Script Steps

CHAPTER 12

Scripting Primer

About FileMaker Scripting

Scripts are the lifeblood of an interactive FileMaker solution: They are the means by which you can automate various processes and capture user actions. In this section we try to distill FileMaker scripting down to its essentials. Scripts in FileMaker Pro are written in a point-and-click interface where steps and their options are added to individual scripts. Most scripts are executed by the press of a button or a menu selection. When users run scripts in FileMaker, only one script can execute at a time; however, it is possible to nest scripts, running a script as a sub-script of another.

The ScriptMaker Interface

All script editing is done within FileMaker Pro's ScriptMaker, shown in Figures 12.1 and 12.2. ScriptMaker lives in the Scripts menu and is accessible from the keyboard via ⌘-Shift-S (Mac OS X) or Ctrl+Shift+S (Windows).

Many time-saving shortcuts are available in ScriptMaker. We list these in the section of this book devoted to shortcuts.

➔ *For more information on shortcuts available within ScriptMaker,* ***see*** *"Scripting" in Chapter 19, "FileMaker Keyboard Shortcuts,"* ***p. 521****.*

Where Scripts Live

Scripts are attached to an individual file (no matter how many tables the file has). Though one script may call a script in another file, a given script may act directly only on data and records contained or referenced in the same file as the script.

Scripts may be moved between files in several ways. From within ScriptMaker, it's possible to import scripts from another file. Simply click the Import button in ScriptMaker, navigate to the file containing the scripts you want to import, and then click a check box for each script you want to bring over and import. FileMaker moves the scripts and does its best to resolve any references they contain (references to fields, files, scripts, or value lists, for example), though you should still check over the scripts and fix any references that might not have translated as you intended.

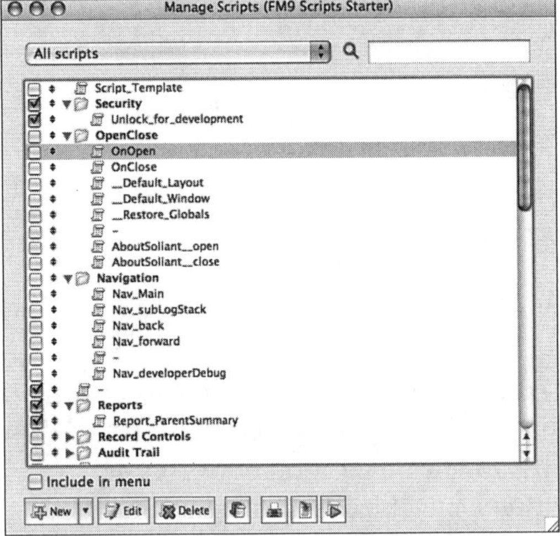

Figure 12.1

The main ScriptMaker dialog shows a list of scripts for a given file. Use this dialog to manage your list of scripts and any script you may want to use for organizational purposes.

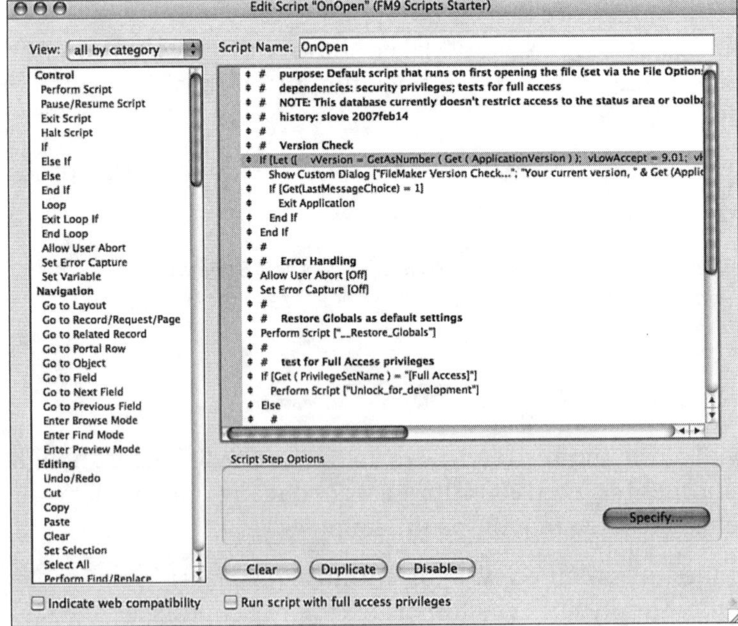

Figure 12.2

The ScriptMaker script editing dialog allows you to edit a single script.

Using FileMaker Pro 9 Advanced, you can also copy and paste scripts and script steps by using the standard commands from the Edit menu or their keyboard equivalents.

> *Note*
>
> FileMaker Pro 8 Advanced used to have buttons in ScriptMaker for these functions, but the buttons have been replaced with the Edit commands in FileMaker 9.

Note also that in both FileMaker Pro and Pro Advanced it is possible to open multiple scripts and edit them simultaneously. ScriptMaker is no longer modal, and any script that is not yet saved, and has been modified, will show an asterisk after its name in the Edit Script window. If you have a script open already you won't be able to open it a second time, and if you or a user happens to run the script, only the saved version will run.

Organizing Scripts

FileMaker 9 introduces the ability to collect scripts into groups. Using the menu at the lower left of the ScriptMaker window, you can create a group and then move scripts into a given group. Groups can then be moved as units within ScriptMaker (up or down, or inside another group), and you can delete, copy, and paste a group as a whole. You can also use Ctrl+Up/Down Arrow (Windows) or ⌘-Up/Down Arrow (Mac OS X) to move a script up and down in the list.

Another aspect to groups is that they become hierarchical menu choices within the Scripts menu if you opt to include a given set of scripts and groups in that menu.

Filtering Scripts

The upper-right corner of the ScriptMaker dialog now includes a search mechanism that dynamically filters your list of scripts by name. This tool is powerful: It searches for character fragments and allows developers to quickly find a script within a larger list. (For example, "help" will find a script named "Help Button" and also "Ineedhelp.")

The menu to the left of the filter mechanism allows developers to view scripts by group as well.

Script Privileges

Access to scripts is controlled via FileMaker's Accounts and Privileges setting. A given privilege set may be allowed to edit and execute scripts, or to execute only, or may not be permitted to use scripts at all. These settings can be customized on a per-privilege-set, per-script basis.

When a script is executed, it runs with the privileges of the current user. For example, if a script tries to delete a record, and the user running that script does not have sufficient privileges to delete that record, the script step will fail.

This hurdle can be overcome by checking the Run Script with Full Access Privileges check box within ScriptMaker for a specific script. When this option is selected, the script will run as though the current user has the [Full Access] privilege set. Note that if you use a function such as Get(PrivilegeSetName) while such a script is running, the function will return [Full Access]. It will *not* return the name of the privilege set normally associated with the current user's account.

Debugging Scripts

FileMaker Pro Advanced contains two powerful script debugging tools: the Script Debugger and the Data Viewer. The Script Debugger, shown in Figure 12.3, enables you to step through running scripts line by line, with fine-grained control over execution. The Data Viewer, shown in Figure 12.4, enables you to watch the values of both fields and variables within your script as well as other expressions you specify, and often is used along with the Script Debugger to monitor these values as a given script executes.

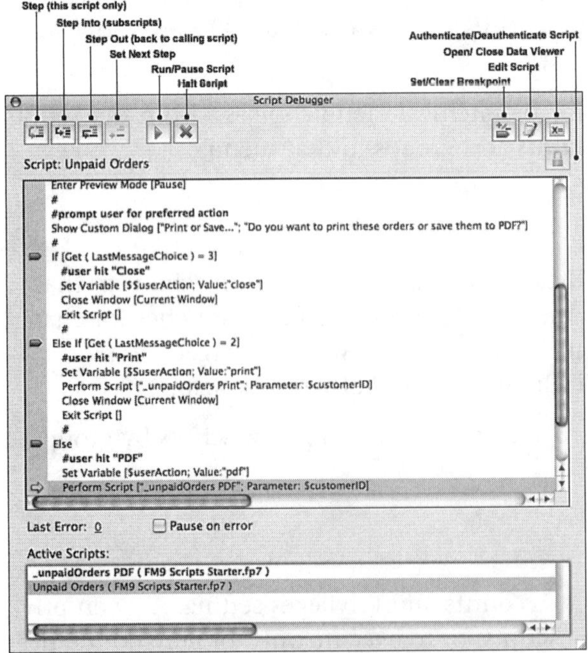

Figure 12.3

The Script Debugger allows you to step through scripts and watch the results as they execute.

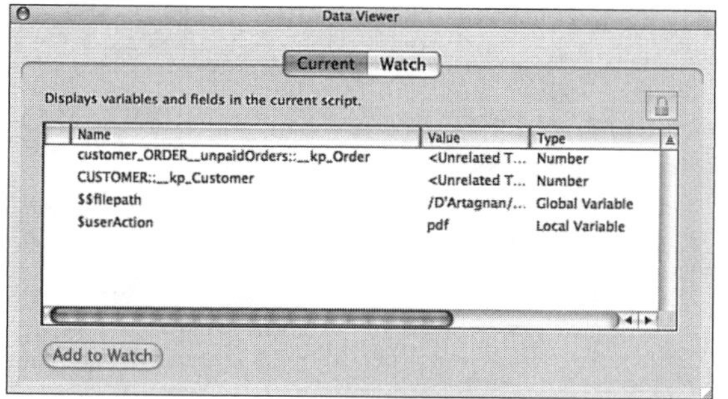

Figure 12.4

The Data Viewer allows you to view the results of expressions (either calculation fields, variables, or others you enter on the Watch tab) and in the new Current tab will automatically display those found in the current script.

FileMaker Pro 9 Advanced introduced the capability in the Script Debugger to see error values returned as a script executes. Also new is the Current tab in the Data Viewer, which automatically shows the values in fields and variables referenced in the currently running script.

It is possible to open the Script Debugger with various privilege sets within FileMaker. While logged in with an account with privileges other than [Full Access] or modify privileges for a given script, a developer can authorize viewing of a script by clicking the Authorize/Deauthorize button. This allows you to enter credentials and then proceed to view and potentially edit a script. The current privilege set changes to [Full Access] (or whichever privilege set is associated with the credentials provided) and remains changed for as long as the data viewer is open.

FileMaker Pro Advanced includes one other useful addition for script troubleshooting: the Disable Script Step feature. If you select one or more script steps and click the Disable button in ScriptMaker, those steps will be disabled and will not execute. This allows you to quickly "comment out" sections of a script as part of a troubleshooting effort.

Scripting for the Web

Scripts can be invoked from a web-published FileMaker database, both via Instant Web Publishing (IWP) and via Custom Web Publishing (CWP). But not all script steps can be run from the Web. The Indicate Web Compatibility check box provides a visual indication of which steps will and will not work on the Web. (In general, any script step that requires user interaction, such as a confirmation dialog, or a script step that opens some element of the FileMaker interface such as the Manage Database dialog is not web-compatible.)

If a script executed from the Web contains one or more non-web-compatible script steps, the noncompatible script steps will either be skipped, or the script will stop in its entirety. Which of these occurs depends on whether Allow User Abort is set to On or Off in the script. If Allow User Abort is set to Off, unsupported script steps will be skipped. If Allow User Abort is set to On, an unsupported script step will cause the script to stop completely.

CHAPTER 13

Script Step Reference

About the Script Step Reference

This chapter details all of the FileMaker Pro script steps. It is similar in some ways to FileMaker's online help system but adds more detailed examples and commentary where possible. The listing for each script step also indicates its platform compatibility, any menu equivalent, and whether the script step is web-compatible. A number of web-compatible steps are marked with an asterisk. This indicates that though the step as a whole is web-compatible, one or more specific options of the step are not.

Add Account 

Syntax:

Add Account [Account Name: <account name>; Password: <password>; Privilege Set: "<privilege set>"; Expire password]

Options:

- **Account Name** is the account name to be added to the file in question. Literal text can be entered or Specify can be clicked to create a new account name from a calculation.
- **Password** is the new password associated with this new account. Literal text can be entered or Specify can be clicked to create a new password from a calculation.
- **Privilege Set** allows you to assign a preexisting privilege set for the user or to create a new one. (Full Access cannot be assigned via this script step. Accounts with Full Access must be created manually.)
- **User Must Change Password on Next Login** forces users to change their password the next time they log in to the database.

Description:

This script step adds an account and password to a database file's security configuration and associates the new account with one of the privilege sets defined in the file. Account and password text may be defined in a calculation or typed into the script step itself. The account name must be unique, and full access to the file is required to execute this step.

Note that as with the rest of FileMaker security, accounts are specific to individual files: It is often with this script step that accounts are propagated throughout a multifile solution.

This script step allows developers to create administrative account functions within databases without having to grant full access to the security privileges within a solution.

Note that there are circumstances where you should not set an account to force the user to change her password at next login. If the user will not have a direct means to do this, the option should not be set. The best example is an account that will be used to access a FileMaker database via Instant Web Publishing: IWP provides no means for a user to change her password, so this setting locks the user out of the database. Similarly, if the account is externally authenticated, it may be risky to tie the account to a privilege set requiring that the password be changed at some point, or have a minimum length.

Examples:

```
Add Account [Account Name: "User_Account"; Password: "User_Password"; Privilege
Set: "[Data Entry Only]"; Expire password]
```

Adjust Window

Syntax:

Adjust Window [Resize to fit/Maximize/Minimize/Restore/Hide]

Options:

- **Resize to Fit** shrinks a window to the minimum possible size bounded on the right by the rightmost layout object and on the bottom by the bottommost layout part.
- **Maximize** expands the current window to the size of the user's screen, or on Windows to the size of the application window.
- **Minimize** minimizes the current window to an icon on the Mac OS X Dock or to a small window bar within the application window on Windows.
- **Restore** returns the current window to the size it was prior to the last resize.
- **Hide** hides the current database window.

Description:

This script step hides or otherwise controls the size of the current window. Given minor differences in how each operating system manages windows, the Resize to Fit option is commonly used to ensure that layouts are properly displayed regardless of platform.

Note that on Windows, FileMaker restores all windows when a new window is opened or an existing window is resized. Maximize on Windows should be used only for one-window databases.

Examples:

Go to Layout ["Detail"]
Adjust Window [Maximize]

Allow Toolbars 

Syntax:

Allow Toolbars [<On/Off>]

Options:

- **On** allows FileMaker's native toolbars to be utilized.
- **Off** hides and makes inaccessible FileMaker's toolbars as well as the toolbar submenu options in the View menu.

Description:

This script step hides or shows the FileMaker Pro toolbars and whether they may be accessed via the View menu. Turning them off is generally done when a developer wants to control screen real estate and access to the functions on the toolbars. Note that this script step applies only to the current file: In multifile solutions, each file's toolbar state needs to be managed (by interlinked scripts or opening routines, for example). This option has no effect in Kiosk mode because toolbars are always hidden in Kiosk mode.

Examples:

Allow Toolbars [Off]

Allow User Abort

Syntax:

Allow User Abort [<On/Off>]

Options:

- **On** allows users to halt the execution of a script by pressing the Esc key (or ⌘-period on Mac OS X).
- **Off** disables the halting of scripts by users.

Description:

Allow User Abort is used to control the user's ability to cancel scripts by using the Esc key (or the ⌘-period key combination on Mac OS X). This step is usually used in scripts whose operation should not be arbitrarily canceled by the user, such as login logic, data import/export, or any script that must process a set of records without interruption. Most of FileMaker's menu options are also unavailable while a script is running in the Allow User Abort [Off] state.

If a script involves any processes that could work with large record sets, such as sorting, looping, or running a Replace script step, the user sees a progress dialog for the duration of that operation. If Allow User Abort is on, as it is by default, users can cancel the script and disrupt those operations, leaving them partially incomplete. This can be an area of significant problems if a database's operations assume a process that has been cancelled by the user has concluded properly. If a script contains any process that must not be interrupted before completion, it should use Allow User Abort[Off] to ensure that these processes can finish without user interruption.

Examples:

```
Allow User Abort[Off]
```

Arrange All Windows 

Syntax:

Arrange All Windows [Tile Horizontally/Tile Vertically/Cascade Window/Bring All ➥to Front]

Options:

- **Tile Horizontally** positions open windows from left to right across the screen. They are resized to avoid any overlaps.
- **Tile Vertically** positions open windows from top to bottom down the screen. They are resized to avoid any overlaps.
- **Cascade Window** positions windows overlapping diagonally from upper left to lower right. The idea of this arrangement is, presumably, to allow the reading of the title bar of each window. The windows are resized to fit the available screen space.
- **Bring All to Front** (Mac OS only) brings all open windows to the front without resizing or otherwise moving or rearranging them. In the event that any open FileMaker windows have been hidden by (that is, are behind) any other application's windows, this step ensures that all FileMaker windows are above other application windows.

Description:

This script step resizes and/or repositions open windows but does not affect which window has focus. The active record also remains the same.

Examples:

```
New Window [Name: "Trees"; Height: 200; Width: 600; Top: 16; Left: 16]
Arrange All Windows [Tile Vertically]
```

Beep

Syntax:

Beep

Options:

None

Description:

This script step plays a beep sound at the default volume of the machine on which it is played.

You may want to use the beep as a means of drawing further attention to alert dialogs, or to confirm when long processes come to an end.

Examples:

```
Set Error Capture [On]
Perform Find [Restore]
If [Get (FoundCount) = 0]
  Beep
  Show Custom Dialog ["No records were found that match your find criteria."]
End
```

Change Password

Syntax:

Change Password [Old Password: <old password>; New Password: <new password>; No dialog]

Options:

- **Old Password** is the password for the currently active account. It can be specified by calculation or entered directly.
- **New Password** is the desired new password for the currently active account. It can be specified by calculation or entered directly.
- **Perform Without Dialog** suppresses the Change Password dialog for this action. Rather than prompting the user for old and new passwords, the script step uses whatever values have been specified and stored with the script step.

Description:

This script step changes the password for the current account. By default, a Change Password dialog is displayed unless the Perform Without Dialog option is selected. If error capture has been enabled (in the Set Error Capture script step) and Perform Without Dialog is not selected, the user is given five attempts at changing his password. If error capture has not been enabled and Perform Without Dialog is not selected, the user is given only one attempt at changing the password. Run Script With Full Access Privileges enables a user to change the password for the current account even if he lacks the explicit permission to do so.

A number of FileMaker script steps perform functions similar or identical to choices available in the FileMaker menus. For reasons of security or solution design, a developer might choose to limit user access to the FileMaker menus. If access to menus is limited, it may be necessary or desirable to reproduce some functionality available through menus by creating a scripted interface instead. A user without access to menus might instead then see a Change Password button or clickable link, which invokes the Change Password script step.

When programming for the Web, be sure to select Perform Without Dialog. Leaving the box unchecked is not web-compatible.

Examples:

The following script uses a custom Change Password dialog, rather than the standard dialog used by FileMaker. This allows a developer to pass values for the new password to other database files or to more fully control her user interface, if desired.

```
Change Password [Old Password: 'r@wfi5h!'; New Password: 'il0ve5u54i'; No Dialog]
// Change Password can be used in conjunction with "Show Custom Dialog" to
➥cascade password changes throughout several files:
Allow User Abort [ Off ]
Set Error Capture [ On ]
#
Show Custom Dialog [ Title: "Password Change"; Buttons: "OK", "Cancel";
➥Input #1: zgPassword_Old. t, "Old Password:";
➥Input #2: zgPassword_New. t, "New Password:" ]
#
If [ Get(LastMessageChoice)=1 ]
  Change Password [ Old Password: zgPassword_Old. t;
➥New Password: zgPassword_New. t ]
  # send password change to other files
  Perform Script [ "Change Password"; from file "Contacts" Parameter:
➥zgPassword_Old. t&"¶"&zgPassword_New. t ]
  Perform Script [ "Change Password"; from file "Invoices" Parameter:
➥zgPassword_Old. t&"¶"&zgPassword_New. t ]
End If
# be sure to clear the globals for security reasons
Set Field [zgPassword_Old. t; ""]
Set Field [zgPassword_New. t; ""]
Commit Record/Request [no dialog]
```

Check Found Set

Syntax:

Check Found Set

Options:

None

Description:

This script step uses the spell check features in FileMaker Pro to check the spelling of the contents of all fields in all the records currently being browsed that contain text content. The step checks spelling in all fields of type Text, all calculation fields with a calculation result type of Text, and in any other field where text is stored: for example, a number field that happens to contain text. It is an interactive script step that displays a spelling dialog for every questionable spelling that the system finds.

This option is normally available via the FileMaker menus. If one or more users have limited access to menu items, it may be necessary to write scripts that give them access to functionality normally available through menus, such as spell check functions.

Examples:

```
Perform Find [Restore]
Check Found Set
```

Check Record

Syntax:

Check Record

Options:

None

Description:

This script step uses FileMaker Pro's spelling checker to check the spelling of the contents of text fields in every record in every field of the current record. This step checks spelling in all fields of type Text, all calculation fields with a calculation result type of Text, and in any other field where text is stored: for example, a number field that happens to contain text. It is an interactive script step that displays a spelling dialog for every questionable spelling that the system finds. See also the `Check Found Set` script step for further discussion.

This option is normally available via the FileMaker menus. If one or more users have limited access to menu items, it may be necessary to write scripts that give them access to functionality normally available through menus, such as spell check functions.

Examples:

```
Go to Record/Request/Page [First]
Loop
  Check Record
  Go to Record/Request/Page [Next; Exit after last]
End Loop
```

Check Selection

Syntax:

Check Selection [Select; table::field]

Options:

- **Select Entire Contents** checks the spelling of the entire contents of the designated field. If this option is not chosen, only the text that has been selected (highlighted) is checked.
- **Go to Target Field** moves focus to a specified field on which to perform a spell check. Assumes the field in question is accessible on the current layout.

Description:

This script step uses the spell check features in FileMaker Pro to check the spelling of the contents of a single field. The step can check spelling in any field that contains text content. It is an interactive script step that displays a spelling dialog for every questionable spelling that the system finds.

This option is normally available via the FileMaker menus. If one or more users have limited access to menu items, it may be necessary to write scripts that give them access to functionality normally available through menus, such as spell check functions.

Examples:

```
Check Selection [Select; Product::Description]
```

Clear

Syntax:

Clear [Select; <table::field>]

Options:

- **Select Entire Contents** allows for the deletion of the entire contents of a field, regardless of what portion of its contents have been selected (highlighted) by the user.
- **Go to Target Field** specifies which field is to have its contents or selected contents deleted.

Description:

This script step removes either the entire contents of a field (if the Select Entire Contents option has been designated) or the selected portion of a field (if the Select Entire Contents option has not been designated). It is important to note that Clear is distinct from the Cut operation in that it does not place the deleted content on the Clipboard. In a web-published database, it is necessary to use a Commit Record/Request script step to update the record that had one (or more) of its fields cleared.

Clear is one of a number of script steps that depend on the presence of specific fields on the current layout. For these steps to take effect, the targeted field must be present on the current layout, the user must have access, and the current mode must be Browse mode. Note, however, that these script steps take effect even if the field has been marked as not enterable in Browse mode. Other script steps with the same limitations include Cut, Copy, Paste, and Set Selection.

These script steps are generally thought to be fragile: They replicate the actions of a user editing record data and depend on layout and field accessibility. It is recommended that the Set Field script step be used in lieu of the Clear script step.

Examples:

```
#The following example clears the values in a repeating field with three repetitions.
Clear [Select, table::field[3]]
Clear [Select, table::field[2]]
Clear [Select, table::field]
```

Close File

Syntax:

Close File [Current File/"<filename>"]

Options:

- **Specify** allows you to select a FileMaker Pro file to close from among the list of existing predefined file references.
- **Add FileMaker Data Source** allows the selection of a file to close while at the same time adding it to the list of defined file references.
- **Add ODBC Data Source** allows the selection of an OBDC connection. This assumes drivers and DSN are already established.
- **Manage Data Sources** allows for existing file references (both FileMaker and ODBC) to be modified or deleted.

Description:

This script step closes the specified file; if no file is specified, it halts any running scripts and closes the file from which it is called. If an ODBC data source is specified, it will disconnect from that source.

If you used File, File Options to specify a script that should run when a file is closed, that script is triggered when the Close File script step is run.

Choosing to close an ODBC connection allows you to subsequently log in again with potentially different permissions.

Examples:

```
Close File ["Line_Items"]
```

Close Window

Syntax:

Close Window [Current Window or Name: <name of window>]

Options:

- **Specify** allows you to either enter a name directly or to return a name based on a calculation.
- **Current file only** causes FileMaker to search only within windows opened by the current file.

Description:

This script step allows you to close a window by name, or, if no name is specified, the current window.

Closing the last open window in a database closes the database and halts execution of the currently running script. This also triggers any script that has been set to run when the file closes.

Current file only allows a developer to restrict the scope of window management script steps to consider only windows based on the current file. This prevents the script from inadvertently closing a window from another open file which may coincidentally share the same name as that which was intended.

Examples:

```
Close Window [Name: "Sales records"]
```

Comment

Syntax:

#<comment text>

Options:

- **Specify** allows for the entry of comment text in a dialog box.

Description:

This script step allows for the addition of comments to scripts. You can see these comments when a script is viewed in ScriptMaker, or when a script is printed.

Development best practices often advocate commenting to explain branches in logic, to record by whom and when a script was created, and to insert white space for legibility. The following example is representative of what may generally be considered best practice, but preference among developers does vary.

Examples:

```
# purpose: manages opening routine, establishes defaults
# starting/ending context: People table
# dependencies: none
# history: slove 2007apr01
#
# Version Check - dialog if not supported
If [ Let ([
      vVersion = GetAsNumber ( Get ( ApplicationVersion ) );
      vLowAccept = 9.01;
      vHighAccept = 9.09;
      vTest = Case ( vVersion < vLowAccept or vVersion > vHighAccept; 1; 0 )
      ];
      vTest
      ) ]
Show Custom Dialog [ Title: "FileMaker version check...";
➥Message: "Your current version, " & Get (ApplicationVersion) & ",
➥is not supported by this file.¶¶Open or Quit?"; Buttons: "Quit", "Open" ]
      If [ Get(LastMessageChoice) = 1 ]
         Exit Application
      End If
End If
#
# Restore Globals as default settings
Perform Script [ "__restore Globals" ]
#
# test for Full Access privileges
If [ Get ( PrivilegeSetName ) = "[Full Access]" ]
      Perform Script [ "__unlock for Development" ]
Else
      # NOTE: this system is currently OPEN
      # to lock it down, simply change the settings below
```

```
      Allow Toolbars [ On ]
      Show/Hide Status Area
      [ Show ]
   End If
   #
   Exit Script [ ]
```

Commit Records/Requests 

Syntax:

Commit Records/Requests [No dialog]

Options:

- **Skip Data Entry Validation** overrides any data entry validation options set for fields and commits the record regardless of any errors. This option skips validation only for fields set with the Only During Data Entry validation option in the Options for Field dialog box; fields set to Always Validate still validate, even if the Skip Data Entry Validation option is selected in this script step.

Examples:

```
Show Custom Dialog ["Commit record?";
"Click 'Commit' to save your changes."]
If [Get(LastMessageChoice) = 1]
  Commit Records/Requests
Else
  Revert Record/Request [No dialog]
End
```

Description:

This script step commits (saves) a record. In other words, it exits the current record or find request and updates the field data for the record. It has the effect of causing the user to exit the record, in the sense that no field will be active on the current layout after the record is committed. Exiting a record in this fashion also has the effect of saving any changes made to it. Exiting/committing a record can be accomplished in many non-scripted ways as well, including changing to another record or merely clicking on a layout outside any field so that no field is selected. See the Revert Record/Request script step for more discussion.

While a user is editing a record, any changes she makes to the record can't be seen by other users. Only when she commits the record are her changes saved to the database and broadcast to other users. This script step has wide applicability. Any time you change data in a record via a script, it's a good idea to commit the record explicitly. This is especially true if the changes result in significant screen updates. For example, if data changes in a record would lead to different data being displayed in a portal on the current layout, it's important to make sure the data changes are explicitly committed. As a best practice we recommend using this step in any script where record data is altered. It's also necessary to add this script step to scripts that are called from the Web, if those scripts change record data.

It's also critical to use this step liberally when the Set Field step is used in a script. Lack of an appropriate commit can leave a record in a locked (as though it were still being edited) state. For example, if the last step in a script is a Set Field step, you should finish the script with a Commit Records/Requests step. Otherwise, the affected record will remain "open" and will be locked until committed. Similarly, we recommend you perform Commit Records/Requests after any Set Field steps that may precede a Perform Script step, to ensure the changes take effect before the next script runs. Problems with record locking in these circumstances are common in complex, scripted systems converted from FileMaker Pro 6.

When programming for the Web, be sure to select Perform Without Dialog. Leaving the box unchecked is not web-compatible.

Constrain Found Set

Syntax:

Constrain Found Set [Restore]

Options:

- **Specify Find Requests** creates and stores a find request with the script step. See the Perform Find script step for more information.

Description:

This script step specifies a find request that will be used to narrow the current found set. This is equivalent to applying two find requests with a logical AND operator.

Constrain is useful when searching unindexed fields as part of a complex find. If a search includes criteria for both stored and unstored fields, a performance gain may be achieved by first performing a find on the indexed fields and then using Constrain to limit the search for the unindexed criteria to the smaller found set.

Examples:

```
# Find all employees older than 60 years of age.
Enter Find Mode [ ]
Set Field [Age; ">60" ]
Perform Find []
# Now find which of these want early retirement
Enter Find Mode [ ]
Set Field [Early_Retire; "Yes" ]
Constrain Found Set[]
```

Convert File

Syntax:

Convert File ["<filename>"]

Options:

- **Specify Data Source** allows for the designation of a data source to be converted into a .fp7 file.

  The possible data sources are File, XML, and ODBC

Description:

This script step converts a file from a variety of supported formats into a FileMaker Pro 9 file. This command works on only one file at a time. Supported data formats are BASIC format, Comma-Separated Text format, dBase III and IV DBF format, DIF format, FileMaker Pro format, HTML Table format, Lotus 1-2-3 WK1/WKS formats, Merge format, Microsoft Excel format, SYLK format, Tab-Separated Text format, and XML format. Designation of various data sources follows the same procedures as an import. See the Import Records script step for further discussion.

This step is analogous to the effects of using File, Open to open a non-FileMaker 7/8/9 file. A variety of formats can be opened/converted, each with its own set of options.

Examples:

```
Convert File ["datafile.fp5"]
```

Copy

Syntax:

Copy [Select; <table::field>]

Options:

- **Select Entire Contents** copies the entire contents of a field to the Clipboard rather than just the selected portion of the designated field's contents.
- **Go to Target Field** or **Specify** allow you to select the field from which you want to copy the contents to the Clipboard. If no field is specified and nothing is selected, FileMaker Pro copies the values from all fields of the current record.

Description:

This script step places the contents of the specified field onto the Clipboard. If no field is specified, all fields from the current record are copied, causing the step to function identically to the Copy Record step.

Copy is generally a poor way to move data within scripts. It requires that the current layout contain the field to be copied and that the user have access to that field. This is fragile because the script malfunctions if the field is removed. Additionally, the contents of the Clipboard are overwritten, without the consent of the user. This is handy if the user intentionally wants the information on the Clipboard, intrusive if not. Copy does have some interesting uses, however: When in Preview mode, Copy takes an image of the screen, and this image can then be pasted into a container field. Copy is one of a number of script steps that depend on the presence of specific fields on the current layout. Other script steps with the same limitations include Cut, Copy, Paste, and Set Selection.

Examples:

```
Go to Layout[ "Customer Entry" (Customer)]
Copy [Select; CustomerTable::Shipping_Address]
Show Custom Dialog [ Title: "Copy..."; Message: "Your customer's billing address is
➥now on your clipboard."; Buttons: "OK" ]
```

Copy All Records/Requests 

Syntax:

Copy All Records/Requests

Options:

None

Description:

This script step copies the values of all fields in all the records in the current found set to the Clipboard in a tab-delimited export format. Styles and formatting are not copied. The field values are exported in the order in which they appear on the current layout. Only those fields that appear in the current layout are included. Within a record, individual fields are separated by tabs, and records are delimited by carriage returns. Repeating field values are separated by a group separator character between each repetition. Carriage returns within a field are copied to the Clipboard as the "vertical tab" character (ASCII value 11), just as they are when being exported.

Copy All Records/Requests is one of a number of script steps that depend on the presence of specific fields on the current layout. Other script steps with the same limitations include Cut, Copy, Paste, and Set Selection.

This script step was used for a variety of reasons in prior versions of FileMaker, but the use of Export Records, Go to Related Record, and other current scripts steps have rendered this largely obsolete. It is useful for gathering table data onto the user's Clipboard.

Examples:

```
# Copy Current Record
Go to Layout ["Detail"]
Copy All Records/Requests
Show Custom Dialog [ Title: "Copy..."; Message: "Your Detail records are
➥now on your clipboard."; Buttons: "OK" ]
```

Copy Record/Request

Syntax:

Copy Record/Request

Options:

None

Description:

This script step copies the values of all fields in the current record to the Clipboard in a tab-delimited export format. Styles and formatting are not copied. The field values are exported in the order in which they appear on the current layout. Only those fields that appear in the current layout are included. Within a record, individual fields are separated by tabs, and records are delimited by carriage returns. Repeating field values are separated by a group separator character between each repetition. Carriage returns within a field are copied to the Clipboard as the "vertical tab" character (ASCII value 11), just as they are when being exported.

Copy Record/Request is one of a number of script steps that depend on the presence of specific fields on the current layout. Other script steps with the same limitations include Cut, Copy, Paste, and Set Selection.

Examples:

```
# Copy Current Record
Go to Layout ["Detail"]
Copy Record/Request
Show Custom Dialog [ Title: "Copy..."; Message: "Your current record is
➥now on your clipboard."; Buttons: "OK" ]
```

Correct Word

Syntax:

Correct Word

Options:

None

Description:

This script step opens the spelling dialog box to allow for the correction of the spelling of a word that has been identified as having been misspelled by the FileMaker Pro spell check operation. The option to Check Spelling as You Type must be selected. A word can be corrected only if FileMaker has identified it as being misspelled.

This option is normally available via the standard FileMaker menus. If one or more users have limited access to menu items, it may be necessary to write scripts that give them access to functionality normally available through menus, such as spell check functions.

Examples:

```
Check Selection [Select; Product::Description]
Correct Word
```

Cut

Syntax:

Cut [Select; <table::field>]

Options:

- **Select Entire Contents** copies the entire contents of a field to the Clipboard, rather than just the selected portion of the designated field's contents. The field is cleared of its contents.
- **Go to Target Field** or **Specify** allow you to select the field from which you want to cut the contents to the Clipboard. If no field is specified and nothing is selected, FileMaker Pro cuts the values from all fields of the current record.

Description:

This script step places the contents of the selected field (or of all fields on the current layout if no field is selected or designated within the script itself) onto the Clipboard and then clears the contents of that field.

Cut is generally a script step that bears avoiding. It requires that the current layout contain the field to be cut and for the user in question to have access. This is fragile because the script malfunctions if the field is removed. Additionally, the contents of the Clipboard are overwritten, without the consent of the user. If multiple fields are involved, it can be difficult to reinstate the information. Often the intended procedure can be accomplished in a layout-independent, less intrusive fashion by using Set Field or other script steps.

Examples:

```
Enter Browse Mode [ ]
Cut [Select, Table1::Recent Notes]
```

Delete Account

Syntax:

Delete Account [Account Name: <account name>]

Options:

- **Specify** allows for the selection or input of the account to be deleted.

Description:

This script step deletes the specified account in the current database. Full access is required to complete this operation, and an account with full access may not be deleted with this script step. It is possible to specify Run Script with Full Access Privileges to ensure that any user can execute this script; however, care must be taken to ensure that such usage does not create a security hole. After Run Script with Full Access Privileges has been checked, any user who can see the script can run it, including those who have external access from other FileMaker files and web access.

In cases where a class of users lack access to the security dialog, this step can be used to help build administrative tools for your database.

Examples:

```
Delete Account [Account Name: "Regional Sales"]
```

Delete All Records 

Syntax:

Delete All Records [No dialog]

Options:

- **Perform Without Dialog** allows for the deletion of all records in the current found set without user intervention.

Description:

This script step deletes all records in the current found set. It can be set to operate without user approval if you select the Perform Without Dialog option. Special care should be exercised in the use of this script step because it is not possible to undo the operation after it has been completed.

Note that any records that are "in use" (currently locked) by other users are not deleted by this step. Records are considered to be in use if other users are actively editing them and have not committed/saved their changes, or if they have been left open as a result of script actions. You may want to check explicitly whether this has occurred, either by examining the found set, or by using Get(LastError) to check for a script error. You should also decide how you want to handle cases where the step doesn't execute completely for reasons such as these. Note that this script step is context-dependent. The current layout determines which table is active, which determines from which table the records are deleted.

When programming for the Web, be sure to select Perform Without Dialog. Leaving the box unchecked is not web-compatible.

Examples:

```
// use a custom dialog to warn user before deleting all records
Allow User Abort [ Off ]
Set Error Capture [ On ]
Show Custom Dialog [ Title: "Delete All Records";
➥Message: "Are you really sure you want to delete all records?";
➥Buttons: "Cancel", "Delete" ]
If [Get(LastMessageChoice)=2 ]
# the user wants to delete
   Show Custom Dialog [ Title: "Delete All Records";
   ➥Message: "Do you have a current backup?"; Buttons: "No", "Yes" ]
If [ Get(LastMessageChoice)=2 ]
   # after they confirmed twice, go ahead with delete
   Show All Records
   Delete All Records[ No dialog ]
   End If
End If
```

Delete Portal Row 

Syntax:

Delete Portal Row [No dialog]

Options:

- **Perform Without Dialog** allows for the deletion of the current related record without user approval.

Description:

This script step deletes the currently selected portal row. In other words, it deletes a record that's related to the current record and is displayed in a portal on the current layout. It can be set to operate without user approval if you select the Perform Without Dialog option. Special care should be exercised in the use of this script step because it is not possible to undo the operation after record changes have been committed.

Performance of this step can be inhibited if the record represented by the specified portal row is in use by another user. See the Delete All Records script step for further discussion.

Note that this script step deletes a portal row even if the Allow Deletion of Portal Records check box in the Portal Setup dialog box is unchecked.

When programming for the Web, be sure to select Perform Without Dialog. Leaving the box unchecked is not web-compatible.

Examples:

```
Go to Portal Row [Last]
Delete Portal Row [No dialog]
Commit Record/Request [No dialog]
```

Delete Record/Request 

Syntax:

Delete Record/Request [No dialog]

Options:

- **Perform Without Dialog** allows for the deletion of the current record or find request without user approval.

Description:

This script step deletes the current record (when in Browse mode) or current find request (when in Find mode). It can be set to operate without user approval if you select the Perform Without Dialog option. Special care should be exercised in the use of this script step because it is not possible to undo the operation.

If the current layout has a portal and a portal row is selected, the user is prompted to specify whether the master record or the related record should be deleted. If the step is performed without a dialog, the action automatically applies to the master record. If a portal row is selected and the portal is not set to Allow Deletion of Portal Records, the option to delete a related record never appears. Note that this is in contrast to the Delete Portal Row step, which deletes an active portal row regardless of whether Allow Deletion of Portal Records is enabled. Performance of this step can be inhibited if the record is in use by another user. See the Delete All Records script step for further discussion. Note that this script step is context-dependent. The current layout determines which table is active, which determines from which table the record is deleted. Note too that the Revert Record menu item can undo the deletion of a child record up until a Commit Record/Request action is executed.

When programming for the Web, be sure to select Perform Without Dialog. Leaving the box unchecked is not web-compatible.

Examples:

```
Go to Record/Request [Last]
Delete Record/Request [No dialog]
```

Dial Phone

Syntax:

Dial Phone [No dialog; <phone number>]

Options:

- **Perform Without Dialog** prevents the Dial Phone dialog from displaying when this script step executes.
- **Specify** displays the Dial Phone options as follows:
  - **Phone Number** allows the entry of a telephone number.
  - **Specify** allows the creation of a calculation to generate the telephone number to be dialed.
  - **Use Dialing Preferences** applies the preestablished telephone dialing preferences to the number to be dialed, based on the designated location information.

Description:

This script step allows FileMaker Pro to dial a telephone number from within a script. The number to be dialed may be entered within the script itself, contained within a field, or generated by a specified calculation. Current telephone dialing preferences can be applied optionally based on location information. Letters within telephone numbers are translated into the appropriate numbers (q and z being, of course, omitted). Note: This script step does not work on Mac OS.

You might use this script step if you want to be able to dial the phone numbers of people or organizations whose contact information is stored in FileMaker. You might also use it to perform more low-level serial-line tasks, in conjunction with a plug-in that can communicate directly with a computer's serial port.

Examples:

```
Dial Phone [No Dialog, Contacts::Phone_Home]
```

Duplicate Record/Request 

Syntax:

Duplicate Record/Request

Options:

None

Description:

This script step duplicates the current record while in Browse mode and the current find request in Find mode. Values in fields with auto-entry options are not carried to the new duplicate record: new values are generated for these fields, according to the details of the specific auto-entry options. If this script step is used when a portal row is selected, and the portal relationship allows for the creation of related records, the related record is duplicated, resulting in a new related record displayed via the portal, rather than the master record.

If you want to make sure that certain fields are never duplicated, you can set them to auto-enter an empty string (""). On duplication, the auto-entry option takes effect and clears the field in the new record.

Examples:

```
Go to Record/Request/Page [Last]
Duplicate Record/Request
```

Edit User Dictionary 

Syntax:

Edit User Dictionary

Options:

None

Description:

This script step opens the User Dictionary dialog box. This is often used to display the User Dictionary dialog box when user privileges do not allow for the dialog to be chosen directly from the standard FileMaker menus.

Examples:

```
Edit User Dictionary
```

Else

Syntax:

Else

Options:

None

Description:

The Else script step is used to control logical branching within scripts. It can be placed after an If or Else If statement and immediately before an End If statement. The designated code block for the Else statement is executed only if all the previous If and Else If statements have evaluated as false. It is thus often used as a way to deal with values that do not fit within expected parameters or as a default action.

Examples:

```
If [gUsername = "Tom"]
  Show Custom Dialog ["Hello Tom"]
Else If [gUsername =  "Raul"]
  Show Custom Dialog ["Hola Raul"]
Else If [gUsername = "Guido"]
  Show Custom Dialog ["Ciao Guido"]
Else
  Show Custom Dialog ["I don't know who you are!"]
End If
```

Else If

Syntax:

Else If [<Boolean calculation>]

Options

- **Specify** allows for any available fields, functions, and operators to be used to enter the Boolean calculation into the Specify Calculation dialog box. Only a zero (0), false, or null (empty) result is construed as a Boolean false.

Description:

The Else If script step is used to control logical branching within scripts. It must follow the If script step or the Else If script step. It performs an action or actions based on the value of the Boolean calculation. The statements in the Else If block are executed only if none of the previous If or Else If statements are true.

An arbitrary number of Else If statements can be between an If statement and an End If statement. Their Boolean calculations are evaluated in the sequence in which they appear. If one should happen to evaluate to True, its code block is executed and all subsequent Else If and Else clauses that appear before the End If are ignored.

Examples:

```
If [gUsername = "Tom"]
  Show Custom Dialog ["Hello Tom"]
Else if [gUsername =  "Raul"]
  Show Custom Dialog ["Hola Raul"]
Else If [gUsername = "Guido"]
  Show Custom Dialog ["Ciao Guido"]
Else
  Show Custom Dialog ["I don't know who you are!"]
End If
```

Enable Account

Syntax:

Enable Account [Account Name: <account name>; Activate/Deactivate]

Options:

- **Specify** displays the Enable Account Options dialog box, as follows:
  - **Account Name** allows either the manual entry of or designation of a calculation to generate an account name.
  - **Activate Account** enables the specified account.
  - **Deactivate Account** disables the specified account.

Description:

This script step enables or disables a specific preexisting account. For this script step to be performed, the user must be assigned the Full Access privilege set or the Run Script with Full Access Privileges option must be selected. Accounts with Full Access may not be deactivated with this script step.

This script step allows developers to create administrative account functions within databases without having to grant full access to the security privileges within a solution.

Examples:

```
Enable Account [Account Name:"UserAccount"; Activate/Deactivate]
```

End If

Syntax:

End If

Options:

None

Description:

This script step designates the end of an [If][Else If][Else] structure. See Else and Else If for more information.

Examples:

```
If [gUsername = "Tom"]
   Show Custom Dialog ["Hello Tom"]
Else If [gUsername =  "Raul"]
   Show Custom Dialog ["Hola Raul"]
Else If [gUsername = "Guido"]
   Show Custom Dialog ["Ciao Guido"]
```

```
Else
   Show Custom Dialog ["I don't know who you are!"]
End If
```

End Loop

Syntax:

End Loop

Options:

None

Description:

This script step marks the end of a Loop structure. The steps between Loop and End Loop are executed until the loop is explicitly exited. This step passes control to the step immediately following the Loop command preceding it.

Note that this step doesn't cause a loop to stop executing, it simply defines the point at which FileMaker should return to the top of a loop and iterate steps. Without termination logic, a loop will run forever. Use the Exit Loop If script step to establish the conditions under which the loop will stop running and control will pass to the script step immediately following.

Examples:

```
Set Variable [$counter; Value: "0"]
Loop
   New Record/Request
   Set Variable [$counter; Value: $counter + 1]
   Exit Loop If [$counter > 10]
End Loop
```

Enter Browse Mode

Syntax:

Enter Browse Mode [Pause]

Options:

- **Pause** stops the script's execution to allow for user data entry and record navigation. The user may resume the script by clicking the Continue button in the Status Area, or by executing a Resume Script script step through a button or directly through the FileMaker Scripts menu.

Description:

This script step places the current window into Browse mode. This script step is generally used only when a routine has taken the user out of Browse mode and needs then to be returned to it.

Examples:

```
Allow User Abort [Off]
Set Error Capture [On]
Go to Layout ["Monthly Report']
Enter Preview Mode [Pause]
Go to Layout [Original Layout]
Enter Browse Mode []
```

Enter Find Mode 

Syntax:

Enter Find Mode [Restore; Pause]

Options:

- **Pause** stops the script's execution to allow for user data entry and record navigation. On resumption, the script performs the find request entered. The user may resume the script by clicking the Continue button in the Status Area, or by executing a Resume Script script step through a button or directly through the FileMaker Scripts menu.
- **Specify Find Requests** enables you to create and edit find requests for use with the script step.

Description:

This script step places the current layout into Find mode. In Find mode, find requests may be created, edited, deleted, and duplicated. In addition, find requests can be stored with the script step if you check the Restore check box and use the Specify dialog. String multiple find requests together to create complex find requests. A single find request may either omit records from or add them to the existing found set.

Enter Find Mode is one of several script steps capable of saving complex options along with the script step. Other such script steps are Perform Find, Sort Records, Import Records, Export Records, and Print Setup. Use the Pause option if you want the user to be able to enter his own search criteria, or modify a search that's saved with the script. If the status area is visible, the user sees a Continue button, as well as a Cancel button if Allow User Abort is set to "on" in the script. Be sure to set Allow User Abort to "off" if you don't want to offer an option to cancel the script at that point. If the status area is hidden, these buttons won't be accessible, and the user needs to either show the status area or use keyboard equivalents for Continue (Enter or Return) or Cancel (Escape or ⌘-period).

Examples:

```
#an example of a find that is executed from requests stored with the script
Go to Layout ["Detail View"]
Enter Find Mode [Restore]
Perform Find []
#this example waits for the user to enter find criteria and execute the find
Go to Layout ["Detail View"]
Enter Find Mode [Pause]
Perform Find[]
```

Enter Preview Mode 

Syntax:

Enter Preview Mode [Pause]

Options:

- **Pause** stops the script's execution to allow for a user to review the results of a preview—often subsummary data or a layout formatted for printing. The user may resume the script by clicking the Continue button in the status area or by pressing the Enter key.

Description:

This script step places the current layout into Preview mode, where an approximation of what a layout will look like when it is printed is displayed. Preview mode is helpful for viewing layouts that use special layout parts for reporting, such as title headers, leading grand summaries, subsummaries, trailing grand summaries, and title footers. Preview is the only FileMaker mode that displays all layout parts. Generally only the body part is useful in Browse mode, and all the report/summary parts do not appear. Header and footer parts appear but serve no function different from body; whereas, in Preview, they comprise consistent top and bottom areas of each page.

Use the Pause option if you want the user to be able to spend time in Preview mode reviewing the displayed data. If the status area is visible, the user sees a Continue button, as well as a Cancel button, if Allow User Abort is set to "on" in the script. Be sure to set Allow User Abort to "off" if you don't want to offer an option to cancel the script at that point. If the status area is hidden, these buttons aren't accessible, and the user needs to either show the status area or use keyboard equivalents for Continue (Enter or Return) or Cancel (Escape or ⌘-period).

Examples:

```
Enter Preview Mode [Pause]
```

Execute SQL

Syntax:

Execute SQL [No Dialog; ODBC: <datasource name>; <native SQL or calculated SQL>]

Options:

- **Perform Without Dialog** prevents the Specify SQL dialog box, the Select ODBC Data Source dialog box, and the Password dialog box from displaying when the script step executes.
- **Specify** displays the Specify SQL dialog box, where you can set the following options:
  - **Specify** displays the Select ODBC Data Source dialog box. This allows for the selection of an ODBC connection and allows for the entry of the appropriate username and password.
  - **Calculated SQL Text** allows for the creation of a calculation to generate the desired SQL query.
  - **SQL Text** allows for the direct entry of a text SQL query.

Description:

This script step executes a designated SQL query over a selected ODBC connection. This allows for manipulation of SQL data sources through standard queries. A script can contain multiple Execute SQL steps that act on different SQL data sources.

Examples:

```
Execute SQL [No Dialog; ODBC: SQL_Server; "UPDATE Customers SET Status = '" &
➥Customer::Status & "' where CustID = '" & Customer::CustomerID & "' ;"]
```

Exit Application

Syntax:

Exit Application

Options:

None

Description:

This script step closes all open files and exits the FileMaker Pro Application.

The Exit Application step triggers the closing scripts of any files that have a closing script established in the File Options dialog.

Examples:

```
Exit Application
```

Exit Loop If

Syntax:

Exit Loop If [<Boolean calculation>]

Options:

- **Specify** allows for the definition of the Boolean calculation that determines whether a loop is exited.

Description:

This script step terminates a loop if its specified Boolean calculation evaluates to true (nonzero and non-null). Upon termination, control is passed to the next script step after the End Loop script step that applies to the current script step. If the Boolean calculation evaluates to false (zero or null), control is passed to the next script step, or to the step at the beginning of the loop if no further steps are specified within the loop.

Developers often want to have at least one Exit Loop If script step inside any loop you write. Without at least one such statement, it's difficult to exit a loop, except by performing a subscript that performs a Halt Script or using a Go to Record/Request/Page [Next; Exit after last] script step.

Examples:

```
Set Field [Table1::gCounter; "0"]
Loop
  New Record/Request
  Set Field [Table1::gCounter; Table1::gCounter + 1]
  Exit Loop If [gCounter > 10]
End
```

Exit Script

Syntax:

Exit Script [Result]

Options:

- **Specify** is used to specify a value to be returned from the script as the *script result*. This result will be accessible elsewhere via the Get(ScriptResult) calculation function.

Description:

Exit Script forces the current script to stop executing; any remaining steps in the script are ignored. If the current script was called by another script, the remaining script steps in the calling script continue to execute.

It's important to distinguish this script step from the related script step Halt Script. Halt Script forces the termination of *all* currently running scripts, whereas Exit Script simply exits the current script. The use of Exit Script instead of Halt Script is generally considered significantly better practice.

Developers can optionally pass data from a script at its conclusion. A script result is accessed via the Get(ScriptResult) function in a calling script. Generally the use of Set Variable is preferred, however, because it is more explicit and easier to notice (as its own discrete script step) within ScriptMaker.

Examples:

```
Perform Find [Restore]
If [Get (CurrentFoundCount)=0]
   Show All Records
   Go to Layout ["Detail View"]
   Exit Script [ Result: Get (FoundCount) ]
Else
      Print []
      Exit Script [ Result: Get (FoundCount) ]
End If
```

Export Field Contents

Syntax:

Export Field Contents [<table::field>; "<filename>"]

Options:

- **Specify Target Field** allows for the specification of the field whose contents are to be exported.
- **Specify Output File** allows the desired filename and file path for the exported data to be specified.

Description:

Export Field Contents creates a named file on disk with the contents of the specified field.

Export Field Contents is a flexible command when used in conjunction with container fields. FileMaker Pro allows the user to store a file of any type in a container field (including FileMaker Pro files). Export Field Contents writes the file out to disk in its native format, where the file can then be opened with the appropriate application. Any type of file, including images can be saved in a FileMaker database and then written out to disk.

Using script variables, it is possible to set the name and path of the output file dynamically, rather than hard-coding a file reference within the script. The file path dialog accepts a variable ($var or $$var) designation in addition to a path reference. This allows developers to programmatically control where a document is saved/exported by FileMaker.

Examples:

Go to Layout [Pictures::Agent_Picture]
Export Field Contents [Pictures::Picture_Full; Pictures::filename]

Export Records

Syntax:

Export Records [No dialog; "<output filename>"]

Options:

- **Perform Without Dialog** prevents the display of dialog boxes that let the user set new export criteria when the script step executes.
- **Specify Output File** allows the desired filename and file path for the exported data to be specified as well as its file type. If XML Export is selected, the XML Export Options dialog is displayed and allows the selection of an appropriate XML grammar and stylesheet for the export.

  You can also export records directly to the Excel file format by choosing Excel from among the available file types.
- **Specify Export Order** displays the export order that was in effect when you added the script step. The last export order used in the file appears as the default and can be edited or deleted.

Description:

This script step exports records from the current found set to a specified file in a specified format. The current sort order of the found set is used for the export order of the records. Note that Group By works only for fields included in the current sort order. (Sorted fields appear in the Group By box; check off any fields by which you want to group.)

Using script variables, it is possible to set the name and path of the output file dynamically, rather than hard-coding a file reference within the script. The file path dialog accepts a variable ($var or $$var) designation in addition to a path reference.

Because it's possible to create FileMaker field names that are not valid names for XML elements, use caution when exporting in the FMPDSORESULT grammar: The resulting XML may be invalid. FMPDSORESULT is deprecated in this version of FileMaker Pro and should probably be avoided.

Examples:

Export Records [No dialog, "Contracts"]

Extend Found Set

Syntax:

Extend Found Set [Restore]

Options:

- **Specify Find Requests** allows for the creation and storage of find requests with the script step.

Description:

This script step allows the current found set to be extended if you append additional search criteria to the previous search, or, put differently, if you apply designated search criteria only to records *not* included in the current found set. (This is equivalent to a logical OR search combined with the results of the previously executed search.)

Similar to the Constrain Found Set script step, this step enables you to combine the results of more than one search. Whereas Constrain Found Set enables you to limit the results of one found set by the results of a second search (an operation known as an *intersection*), the Extend Found Set command enables you to add the results of one search to the results of another search (an operation known as a *union*).

Examples:

```
#This script finds records within a table of addresses
#that are designated "local" or have a specific zip code
Enter Find Mode [ ]
Set Field [Local; "Yes"]
Perform Find [ ]
Enter Find Mode [ ]
Set Field [Zip; "94965"]
Extend Found Set[]
```

Flush Cache to Disk

Syntax:

Flush Cache to Disk

Options:

None

Description:

This script step causes FileMaker Pro's internal disk cache to be written to disk. This operation is automatically performed by FileMaker Pro periodically or after structural changes such as defining fields or modifying calculation definitions occurs. This script step enables the developer to explicitly write out the contents of memory at whatever time she deems necessary. In the example given, this step may be useful to force screen redraw to occur.

Note that this script step flushes the contents of the cache for a local client copy of FileMaker Pro. It has no effect on the cache of any instance of FileMaker Server or of any other FileMaker Pro client.

Examples:

```
Replace Field Contents [Line_Items::ProductID; Line_Items::NewProductID]
Flush Cache to Disk
```

Freeze Window 

Syntax:

Freeze Window

Options:

None

Description:

This script step halts the updating of the active window as script steps are performed. For example, in the case of a loop that steps through records, the user would ordinarily see FileMaker navigating from one record to the next. This can slow performance or prove irritating for users, so developers often use Freeze Window to avoid forcing users to watch automated routines. The window resumes refreshing either at the end of the script where it was frozen or after a Refresh Window script step is executed within a script.

Freeze Window is useful in creating more professional-looking applications because it prevents the screen from flashing or redrawing while other script steps execute (for example, those that navigate to "utility" layouts, perform some work there, and then return to a main interface layout). It's also possible to realize some performance gains from freezing a window; scripts that would otherwise cause changes to the contents or appearance of the active window run more quickly if the active window doesn't need to be refreshed.

Examples:

```
Freeze Window
Replace Field Contents [Line_Items::ProductID; Line_Items::NewProductID]
Sort [Restore; No Dialog]
Refresh Window
```

Go to Field

Syntax:

Go to Field [Select/perform; <table::field>]

Options:

- **Select/Perform** directs FileMaker to select all contents of the designated field. If the field is a container field and an action is associated with that field (such as playing a movie or sound file), that action is performed.
- **Go to Target Field** allows for the specification of the field to go to, using the standard FileMaker Pro field selection dialog box.

Description:

This script step moves focus to a specified field in the current layout. If the Select/Perform option is selected, then if an action is associated with a field, that action is performed. (Actions are associated with container field types, such as sound files or movies—in these cases the associated action would be to play the sound or movie file.) In cases where there is no implied action, the entire contents of the field are selected.

Go to Field allows the developer to insert the cursor into a specific field after a record has been created from a script.

Like other script steps such as Cut, Copy, and Paste, this step depends on the specified field being present and accessible on the current layout.

Examples:

```
#New Record Routine
Go to Layout ["Contracts"]
New Record/Request
Go to Field [Contracts::Signatory]
```

Go to Layout 

Syntax:

Go to Layout ["<layout name or layout number>"]

Options:

- **Specify** allows the target layout to be selected. The following choices are available.
  - **Original Layout** refers to the layout that was active when the script was initiated.
  - **Layout Name by Calculation** enables you to enter a calculation that generates the name of the desired layout.

- **Layout Number by Calculation** enables you to enter a calculation that will generate the number of the desired layout. Layout numbers correspond to the order in which layouts are listed.

An existing layout may also be specified directly by name.

Description:

This script step makes the specified layout active in the current window. This step can navigate only to layouts in the currently active file. In the case where multiple layouts have the same name, the first match is selected for a calculated layout name. (It is not generally considered best practice to have two layouts share the same name.)

This script step is vital for establishing the proper context for any subsequent script steps that operate on record data. Any script steps that directly deal with FileMaker data or records do so in the context of the table occurrence of the currently active layout.

It's also possible to draw either the name or the number of a layout from a calculation.

Examples:

```
Set Variable [ $navDestination; Value:Get (ScriptParameter) ]
If [ $navDestination = "home" ]
      Go to Layout [ "resource_HOME" ]
Else If [ $navDestination = "list" ]
      Go to Layout [ "equipment_LIST" ]
Else If [ $navDestination = "detail" ]
      Go to Layout [ "equipment_DETAIL" ]
Else
      Show Custom Dialog [ Title: "Navigation Error..."; Message:
         "The navigation script did not recognize the parameter: "
         & $navDestination; Buttons: "OK" ]
End If
```

Go to Next Field

Syntax:

Go to Next Field

Options:

None

Description:

This script step moves to the next field in the established tab order for the current layout. If no field is selected, the first field in the established tab order for the current layout is selected. If the user regains control, either by pausing in Browse mode or by exiting the script, the cursor remains in the selected field. If there is no tab order on the layout, the fields are traversed in the order in which they were originally added to the layout.

Note that this script can override the effect of field behaviors that prevent entry into a field. This allows developers to write scripts to control entry into fields and to add other programmatic routines to the process.

Examples:

```
Go to Field [Table1::First Name]
Set Field [Table1::gCounter; "0"]
Loop
   Set Field [Table1::gCounter; Table1::gCounter + 1]
  Exit Loop If [gCounter > Table1::ActiveField]
  Go to Next Field
End Loop
```

Go to Portal Row

Syntax:

Go to Portal Row [<first/last/previous/next/by calculation>]

Options:

- **First** selects the first row of the currently active portal.
- **Last** selects the last row of the currently active portal.
- **Previous** selects the previous row of the currently active portal based on the currently targeted row. If the Exit After Last option is selected and the script is currently performing a loop, an Exit Loop action is performed when the first row in the designated portal is reached.
- **Next** selects the next row of the currently active portal based on the currently targeted row. If the Exit After Last option is selected and the script is currently performing a loop, an Exit Loop action is performed when the last row in the designated portal is reached.
- **By Calculation** selects the row number determined by the designated calculation.

Description:

This script step allows navigation among related records in the active portal on the current layout. If no portal is active, the first portal in the layout stacking order is assumed: FileMaker gives focus to the first row of the backmost portal. This step attempts to maintain the selected portal field when it changes rows. If no field is selected, the first enterable field is selected in the new row.

Examples:

```
Go to Portal Row [Select, First]
```

Go to Previous Field

Syntax:

Go to Previous Field

Options:

None

Description:

This script step moves focus to the previous field in the current layout's tab order. If no field is selected, the last field in the current layout's tab order is selected (consistent with the looping nature of tab order in FileMaker). If the user regains control, either by pausing in Browse mode or by exiting the script, the cursor remains in the selected field. If there is no tab order on the layout, the fields are traversed in the order in which they were originally added to the layout.

Note that this script can override the effect of field behaviors that prevent entry into a field.

Examples:

```
Go to Previous Field
```

Go to Record/Request/Page

Syntax:

Go to Record/Request/Page [<first/last/previous/next/by calculation>]

Options:

- **First** moves to the first record in the current found set, displays the first find request, or moves to the first page of the currently displayed report if in Preview mode.
- **Last** moves to the last record in the current found set, displays the last find request, or moves to the last page of the currently displayed report.
- **Previous** moves to the previous record in the current found set, displays the previous find request, or moves to the previous page of the currently displayed report. If the Exit After Last option is selected and the script is currently performing a loop, an Exit Loop action is performed when the first record is reached; otherwise, no action is taken. If the record pointer is already on the first page, FileMaker generates an error code of 101, which is not reported to the user.
- **Next** moves to the next record in the current found set, displays the next find request, or moves to the next page of the currently displayed report. If the Exit After Last option is selected and the script is currently performing a loop, an Exit Loop action is performed

when the last record is reached; otherwise, no action is taken. If the record pointer is already on the last page, FileMaker generates an error code of 101, which is not reported to the user.

- **By Calculation** selects the record, find request, or report page determined by the designated calculation. FileMaker expects an integer returned by the calculation and will take the user to the record in that relative position within the current found set. Note that this function always executes relative to the current found set and that a wide array of operations (both scripted and directly initiated by the user) change record positions within found sets.

Description:

This script step moves to a record in the found set if the file running the script is in Browse mode, to a find request if it is in Find mode, and to a report page if it is in Preview mode.

Using this script step in conjunction with loops is one of the most common areas in which it is used: The Exit After Last option allows developers to write routines that step through a set of records and exit a loop gracefully when an end point is reached.

Examples:

```
# Sample looping script: a very inefficient way of counting records
Go to Record/Request/Page [First]
Set Variable [$count; Value: "0"]
Loop
  Set Variable [$count; $count + 1]
  Go to Record/Request/Page [Next; Exit After Last]
End Loop
# $count now contains the number of records in the found set.
# This could have been more easily accomplished by:
# Set Variable [$count; Value: Get(FoundCount)]
```

Go to Related Record 

Syntax:

Go to Related Record [From table: "<table name>"; Using layout "<layout name>"]

Options:

- **Get Related Record From** allows the selection of a table that's related to the current table. If an appropriate table is not in the list or if you need to add or change a relationship, Manage Database displays the Manage Database dialog box, where you can create or edit relationships.

- **Use External Table's Layouts** opens the file containing the external table you specify and displays any related record(s), using the specified layout in that file.
- **Show Record Using Layout** displays related target record(s), using a specified layout in the current file. Layouts shown are those tied to the same source table as the table occurrence specified in the Get Related Record From setting.
- **Show Only Related Records** creates a found set in the related table containing only related records. For example, if you use this script step on a relationship that has four matching records in Table B for the current record in Table A, this option replaces any current found set in Table B with a new found set of just these four records. If the relationship has a sort order applied in the table occurrence to which you're navigating, this option causes the found set to be sorted by the relationship's sort criteria. If the Show Related Records Only option is not selected, the resulting found set is not sorted.
- **Match Current Record Only** finds only those records in the related table that are a match for the current record in the current table. This corresponds to the behavior of the Go to Related Records script step in previous versions of FileMaker.
- **Match All Records in the Current Found Set** finds records in the related table that are a match for *any* record in the current found set in the current table. This function allows developers to establish a found set and then display all related records to that found set in another table. This function is often referred to as "Extended Go to Related Record."

Description:

This script step goes to the table designated by the relationship selected in the script step, bringing its window to the foreground and selecting the first related record in the process. This step also works with portals. If a portal row is selected and the Go to Related Record step—specifying the portal's relationship—is executed, the related table is brought to the forefront and the row that was selected in the portal corresponds to the record that is selected in the related table. This step may also use relationships to external files so that when the step is executed, the selected external file is opened and brought to the forefront, with its found set consisting of related records only. Further, if a layout was selected, the records are displayed in that layout.

This script step goes to one or more records in a related table (that is, a table that is related to the currently active table by one or more relationships in the Relationships Graph). There are a number of options to this script step, and they relate in somewhat complex ways. If more than one record in the target table is related to the current record in the table where the script is being called, FileMaker selects the first related record in the target table. If the relationship has a sort order on the target table, that sort order is used to determine which is the first of several related records. For example, if you have a table of Customers and a table of Orders, and a relationship between the two that is sorted on the Order side by OrderDate ascending, the "first" related record when navigating from a specific customer to related orders is a given customer's earliest order. If the relationship has no sort order specified on the target table, the first record is determined based on the creation order of the related records.

As part of this script step, you need to determine the destination layout that should be used to display the related records. If the target table is part of an externally referenced file, you may choose to display the records on a layout in the external file. If you choose to do so, that file comes to the forefront. You may also choose to display the related record set in a new window. If you choose to do so, you can specify a set of new window options, such as the window name, height, width, and screen position.

One unfortunate limitation is that you can't direct the related records to appear in an existing window other than the currently active one. If you had to have that effect, you could select the desired target window, capture its name, dimensions, and positions into global fields, and then close that window and create a new window with exactly the same dimensions and use that as the target of this script step.

If the option to Show Related Records Only is checked, FileMaker creates a found set in the target table that contains only those records related to the current record or the current found set in the table in which the script is executing. For example, given a table of Salespeople and a table of Orders related to Salespeople by a SalespersonID field, if you issue a Go to Related Record[From table:"Orders"; Using layout "<Current Layout>"][Show only related records] while on a record in Salespeople, you end up with a found set of only those Orders related to the current Salesperson by the SalespersonID.

If the option to Show Only Related Records is unchecked, the behavior is more complex: If there's a found set on the target layout and the first related record is within that found set, the found set is unchanged. If there's a found set on the target layout and the first related record is outside that found set, all records in the target table are found (though only the first related record is selected). If there is no found set on the target layout (that is, all records are currently found), that remains the case. No matter whether Show Related Records Only is checked, and no matter what the state of any found set on the target layout is, the first related record is always selected.

If there are no related records, no navigation takes place, and a FileMaker error of 101 is generated. Note that this is a common source of bugs for FileMaker developers: They will write routines that use Go to Related Record that assume in all cases that the navigation was successful, and hence continue their script steps with a new context in mind. Best practices dictate that you test for no navigation due to an error of 101 (no related records).

Examples:

```
#The following example goes to a related record in the table "LineItems"
#   and shows a found set of related records only.
Go to Related Record [Show only related records;
From table: "LineItems"; Using layout: "List View"]


#This script demonstrates a simple error check when using
#   the Go to Related Records script step.
Go to Related Record [ From table: "child"; Using layout: "child" (child) ]
```

```
[ Show only related records; New window ]
If [ Get (LastError) = 101 ]
    Show Custom Dialog [ Title: "No Related Records";
    Message: "There are no related Child records for this Parent record.";
    Buttons: "OK" ]
Else
    #Run the rest of your script here, if you intend to
    operate further on your new context of related records.
End If
```

Halt Script

Syntax:

Halt Script

Options:

None

Description:

This script step causes all script activity to stop immediately. All scripts, subscripts, and external scripts are cancelled, and the system is left in whatever state it was in when the Halt step was executed. Halt Script is different from Exit Script in that the latter merely aborts the current script and allows any scripts that may have called the current script to continue running, whereas Halt Script stops all script activity, whether it is run from a script, a subscript, and so on.

Experienced developers generally avoid using this script step, especially when working in teams. It is common practice to call scripts from other scripts, and it can be difficult to predict what problems will occur if a given script stops not only its own execution but that of all other scripts as well. Best practice strongly recommends reworking the logic of a routine to use Exit Script instead.

Examples:

```
# Example of using 'Halt Script' to return control immediately back to the user.
Show Custom Dialog ["Print Report?"]
If [Get (LastMessageChoice) = 2]
  Halt Script
End If
Print[]
```

If 

Syntax:

If [<Boolean calculation>]

Options:

- **Specify** allows the definition of the Boolean calculation by which the If step determines its branching.

Description:

The If step introduces a block of conditional logic. It needs to be used with an End If statement, and, optionally, one or more Else and Else If statements. This script step contains a calculation, which should perform a logical true/false test. If the specified Boolean calculation results in a 1 (or any number greater than 1), the specified action(s) will be performed. If the specified Boolean calculation results in a 0 (or nothing or any non-number), the specified action(s) will be skipped and control passed to the next Else If or Else clause. If there are no more such clauses, control passes to the End If step and proceeds to any subsequent steps. Else If and Else clauses are optional. End If is required when If is used.

Comments:

If you don't provide a Boolean test in the If step, it defaults to a result of False.

Examples:

```
#Script presents one of various versions of a report,
#based on what date was passed into the script.
Set Variable [ $date; Value:Get (ScriptParameter) ]
If [ Ceiling ( Month ( $date ) / 3 ) = 1 ]
     Perform Script [ "salesReport Q1version" ]
Else If [ Ceiling ( Month ( $date ) / 3 ) = 2 ]
     Perform Script [ "salesReport Q2version" ]
Else If [ Ceiling ( Month ( $date ) / 3 ) = 3 ]
     Perform Script [ "salesReport Q3version" ]
Else If [ Ceiling ( Month ( $date ) / 3 ) = 4 ]
     Perform Script [ "salesReport Q4version" ]
Else
     Show Custom Dialog [ Title: "Missing Date Parameter";
     Message: "This function expects a date parameter.";
     Buttons: "OK" ]
End If
```

Import Records

Syntax:

Import Records [No dialog; "<source or filename>"; Add/Update existing/Update ➥matching; <platform and character set>]

Options:

- **Perform Without Dialog** prevents the display of FileMaker Pro's Import Records dialog box, which enables the user to select a file from which to import, to set new import criteria, to map fields from import to target fields, and to see a summary of facts about the import after it has been successfully completed.
- **Specify Data Source** allows for the selection of the source for the data to be imported. Data can be imported into FileMaker Pro from a file, a folder of files, a digital camera (Mac OS), an XML data source, or an ODBC data source.
- **Specify Import Order** allows the order in which FileMaker imports records to be set. The last import order used is used as the default for the subsequent import. This option allows control of how FileMaker is to handle repeating field data, either by splitting it among new records or keeping it together as a repeating field in the destination table. Also, the import can be made to add new records with the imported data, to replace the records in the found set with the imported data, or to attempt to reconcile data by matching keys (ID fields).

Description:

This script step imports records from another file or data source specified either dynamically through the Import Records dialog or within the script step configuration itself. Import order can be specified as either manually defined or based on matching field names. (It is important to note that when import source fields and target fields are mapped with matching names, field name matching is performed dynamically each time the script step is performed.)

FileMaker Pro has the capability to create a new table in the target database when importing data. When this option is selected, the imported data will be used to create a new table. The field names in the new table depend on the data source. If it's a data source, such as an XML file or an Excel file with headers, that contains field name information, FileMaker uses the provided field names. Otherwise, FileMaker names the fields f1, f2, f3, and so on.

Note that this capability is different from the capability, in FileMaker Pro Advanced, to import table definitions from another file. That technique imports only the table definition, not any data within the table, whereas specifying a new table as an import target always populates the new table with the imported data.

Examples:

Import Records [Restore; No dialog; "Contacts"; Mac Helvetica]

Insert Calculated Result 

Syntax:

Insert Calculated Result [Select; <table::field>; <formula>]

Options:

- **Select Entire Contents** replaces the contents of a field. If this option is not selected, Insert Calculated Result replaces only the selected portion of the current field, or inserts the result at the insertion point. The default insertion point is at the end of the field's data.
- **Go to Target Field** allows the selection of the field into which the result of the specified calculation is to be inserted. The specified field must be available and accessible with write privileges on the current layout for this script step to operate properly.
- **Calculated Result** allows the definition of a calculation whose result is inserted into the specified target field by this script step.

Description:

This script step pastes the result of a calculation into the current (or specified) field on the current layout.

In web-published systems, use a Commit Record/Request script step after an Insert Calculated Result script step to update the record in the browser window. This script step does not exit the field in question nor commit data. All the Insert... functions depend on the presence of fields on the current layout. If the correct field is not present, FileMaker generates an internal error of 102. Generally these steps are not recommended: They are overly layout dependent, and Set Field allows for a higher level of control without the same dependency.

Examples:

Insert Calculated Result [Books::Author; Get(AccountName)]

Insert Current Date 

Syntax:

Insert Current Date [Select; <table::field>]

Options:

- **Select Entire Contents** replaces the contents of the selected field with the current date. If this option is not selected, the current date is appended to the end of the current contents of the field.

- **Go to Target Field** allows for the selection of the field into which the current date will be inserted.

Description:

This script step pastes the current system date into the specified field on the current layout.

In a web-published database, use a Commit Record/Request script step after an Insert Current Date script step to update the record in the browser window. All the Insert... functions depend on the presence of fields on the current layout. If the correct field is not present, FileMaker generates an internal error of 102. Generally these steps are not recommended: They are overly layout dependent and Set Field allows for a higher level of control without the same dependency.

Examples:

```
New Record/Request
Go to Layout ["Invoice"]
Insert Current Date [Select; Invoices::Invoice Date]
```

Insert Current Time 

Syntax:

Insert Current Time [Select; <table::field>]

Options:

- **Select Entire Contents** replaces the contents of the selected field with the current time. If this option is not selected, the current time is appended to the end of the current contents of the field.
- **Go to Target Field** allows for the selection of the field into which the current time is to be inserted.

Description:

This script step pastes the current system time into the specified field on the current layout.

In a web-published database, use a Commit Record/Request script step after an Insert Current Time script step to update the record in the browser window. All the Insert... functions depend on the presence of fields on the current layout. If the correct field is not present, FileMaker generates an internal error of 102. Generally these steps are not recommended: They are overly layout dependent, and Set Field allows for a higher level of control without the same dependency.

Examples:

New Record/Request
Go to Layout ["Invoice"]
Insert Current Date [Select; Invoices::Invoice Date]
Insert Current Time [Select; Invoices::Invoice Time]

Insert Current User Name  

Syntax:

Insert Current User Name [Select; <table::field>]

Options:

- **Select Entire Contents** replaces the contents of the selected field with the current username (as established in each client computer's preferences dialog within FileMaker). If this option is not selected, the current username is appended to the end of the current contents of the field.
- **Go to Target Field** allows for the selection of the field into which the current username is to be inserted.

Description:

This script step pastes the current username into the specified field on the current layout.

In a web-published database, use a Commit Record/Request script step after an Insert Current User Name script step to update the record in the browser window. All the Insert... functions depend on the presence of fields on the current layout. If the correct field is not present, FileMaker generates an internal error of 102. Generally these steps are not recommended: They are overly layout dependent, and Set Field allows for a higher level of control without the same dependency.

Use of this script step is also not recommended because a user can enter any number of things into his preferences. Set Field with Get (AccountName) is the better practice.

Examples:

New Record/Request
Go to Layout ["Invoice"]
Insert Current Date [Select; Invoices::Invoice Date]
Insert Current Time [Select; Invoices::Invoice Time]
Insert Current User Name [Select; Invoices::Entered_By]

Insert File

Syntax:

Insert File [Reference; <table::field>; "<filename>"]

Options:

- **Store Only a Reference** instructs FileMaker Pro to store only a link to a file in the container field, rather than the entire file. This option may reduce the size of your FileMaker Pro file, but if you move or delete the file being referenced, FileMaker Pro can't display it.
- **Go to Target Field** or specify allows you to specify the container field into which to insert the selected file.
- **Specify Source File** or specify allows you to designate the file to be inserted.

Description:

This script step inserts a file into a selected container field on the current layout. Files may be stored in their entirety within FileMaker Pro, or you may choose to store only a file reference. File references certainly take up much less space within the database, but they remove an element of control over a database's behavior. Files stored by reference can be moved or deleted, whereas this is much more difficult to achieve within FileMaker itself.

All the Insert... functions depend on the presence of fields on the current layout. If the correct field is not present, FileMaker generates an internal error of 102.

Examples:

```
Set Variable [ $path; Value:Get (DesktopPath) & "/myNewFile.fp7" ]
Insert File [ myStuff::containerField; "$path" ]
```

Insert From Index

Syntax:

Insert From Index [Select; <table::field>]

Options:

- **Select Entire Contents** replaces the contents of the selected field. If this option is not selected, the selected index value is appended to the end of the current contents of the field if the field does not contain the cursor, or at the current cursor position if it does.
- **Go to Target Field** allows for the selection of the field into which the selected index value is to be inserted.

Description:

This script step displays the index (if one exists) of the designated field in a dialog box and allows one of its values to be inserted into the field. If the Select Entire Contents option is selected, the contents of the field are replaced with the selected value. If this option is not selected, the value is inserted either at the position of the cursor in the field or appended to the end of the field's contents, depending on whether the field has the cursor in it. Note: If the specified field does not exist on the layout where the script is being performed or indexing has been disabled for the selected field, Insert From Index returns an error code that can be captured with the Get(LastError) function.

All the Insert... functions depend on the presence of fields on the current layout. If the correct field is not present, FileMaker generates an internal error of 102.

This script step does not work with fields from External ODBC Data Sources.

Examples:

```
Enter Find Mode [ ]
Insert From Index [Users::User_Name]
Perform Find [ ]
```

Insert From Last Visited

Syntax:

Insert From Last Visited [Select; <table::field>]

Options:

- **Select Entire Contents** replaces the contents of the selected field. If this option is not selected, the value from the last visited field is appended to the end of the current contents of the field if the field does not contain the cursor or at the current cursor position if it does.
- **Go to Target Field** allows for the selection of the field into which the last visited field value is to be inserted.

Description:

This script step pastes the value of the specified field from the same field in the last active record. This step is compatible with both Find and Browse mode. A record is considered as having been active if it has been operated on by FileMaker Pro in some way.

In a web-published database, use a Commit Record/Request script step after an Insert From Last Visited script step to update the record in the browser window. All the Insert... functions depend on the presence of fields on the current layout. If the correct field is not present, FileMaker generates an internal error of 102.

Examples:

```
Go to Record/Request/Page [Next]
Go to Field [Vendor Name]
Insert From Last Visited []
#Will use vendor from previous record
```

Insert Object

Syntax:

Insert Object ["<object type>"]

Options:

- **Specify** displays the Insert Object dialog box.
- **Object Type** allows the selection of the type of object to embed or link from the list of available file and application types.
- **Create New** embeds a blank object of the specified object type.
- **Create from File** allows the specification of the name of an existing file as the object to be embedded or linked.
- **Link** can be selected, when **Create from File** has been selected, to indicate that the object should be a linked object. When Link is not selected, the object is embedded instead.
- **Display As Icon** tells FileMaker Pro not to display the embedded or linked object completely, but to display an icon that represents the object. The Change Icon button can be used to select a different icon for display. When Display As Icon is not selected, the complete object is displayed in the container field.

Description:

This Windows-specific script step allows the user, through the Insert Object dialog box, to select an OLE object and insert it into the current container field. If the specified object/file does not exist on the computer on which the script is being run, Insert Object returns an error code that can be captured with the Get(LastError) function.

All the Insert... functions depend on the presence of fields on the current layout. If the correct field is not present, FileMaker generates an internal error of 102. Insert Object works only on the Windows platform. Insert Object returns an error code if run on the Mac OS.

Note that OLE support on the Windows platform is inconsistent within various applications and that their interaction with FileMaker is difficult to predict. Using this feature is generally not recommended unless a database is deployed within an environment where the versions of various applications can be controlled and tested against.

Examples:

```
Go to Field [Profile::Greeting]
Insert Object ["Video Clip"]
```

Insert Picture

Syntax:

Insert Picture [Select; <table::field>]

Options:

- **Store Only a Reference to the File** allows graphics to be stored by file system reference, thereby alleviating the need to store the actual image in the database. However, if the file is moved from the designated file path, FileMaker Pro can no longer display the actual image and instead displays a file icon.
- **Specify Source File** or **Specify** allows the designation of the file path to the desired image file.

Description:

This script step imports an image file into the current container field. The desired field must be selected before this script is run. If the desired image file has not been specified, the user is given the Insert Picture dialog box.

All the Insert... functions depend on the presence of fields on the current layout. If the correct field is not present, FileMaker generates an internal error of 102.

Examples:

```
Set Variable [ $path; Value:Get (DesktopPath) & "/myKidPhoto.jpg" ]
Insert File [ myStuff::containerField; "$path" ]
```

Insert QuickTime

Syntax:

Insert QuickTime ["<filename>"]

Options:

- **Specify Source File** or **Specify** allows the designation of the file path to the desired QuickTime file.

Description:

This step imports a QuickTime movie or sound file into the current container field. A container field must be selected before this step can function. If an appropriate QuickTime file has not been designated, a dialog box is presented to the user, through which she may select and preview the file to be imported. This step requires that QuickTime be installed on the system being used to import the desired file.

All the Insert... functions depend on the presence of fields on the current layout. If the correct field is not present, FileMaker generates an internal error of 102.

Examples:

```
Set Variable [ $path; Value:Get (DesktopPath) & "/myMovie.m4v" ]
Insert File [ myStuff::containerField; "$path" ]
```

Insert Text

Syntax:

Insert Text [Select; <table::field>; "<text>"]

Options:

- **Select Entire Contents** replaces the contents of a field. If this option is not selected, Insert Text inserts the specified value at the end of the field's data.
- **Go to Target Field** or **Specify** allows you to specify the field to receive the pasted information. If no field is selected, the Insert Text command places the specified text after the insertion point. If no field is active at the time the command executes, it has no effect. If the selected field is not present on the current layout, the Insert Text command has no effect.
- **Specify** displays the Specify dialog box where you can enter the text to be pasted.

Description:

This script step inserts text into the selected text field in the current record. If the Select Entire Contents option has not been selected, the designated text is inserted at the cursor position or at the end of the field's contents, depending on whether there is a cursor in the field. The text to be inserted needs to be specified explicitly. If you want to insert variable text data, use the Insert Calculated Result script step or the Set Field script step.

In a web-published database, use a Commit Record/Request script step after an Insert Text script step to update the record in the browser window. All the Insert... functions depend on the presence of fields on the current layout. If the correct field is not present, FileMaker generates an internal error of 102.

Examples:

```
Insert Text [Select; Profile::Favorite_Color; "Red"]
```

Install Menu Set

Syntax:

Install Menu Set [specified menu set name]

Options:

- **Use as File Default** causes the specified menu set to be used as the default menu set for the current file, for the duration of the current user session. The default menu set is displayed in all circumstances where it is not overridden by a more specific menu set. Examples of "more specific" settings include menu sets that are specified at the individual layout level, and menu sets installed by later invocations of the Install Menu Set script step.

Description:

This script step installs a new menu set based on the specified menu set name. This may be a custom menu set (defined by a developer using FileMaker Pro Advanced), or it may be the default FileMaker menu set.

This script step affects only the current user. Others who may be using the file simultaneously will not see a change of menu sets, unless they too invoke a script containing this step. Likewise, when the current user closes the file, the effects of this step are terminated.

Examples:

```
# Install a user-specific menu set
If [$userRole = "Sales"]
  Install Menu Set["SalesMenus"]
Else
  Install Menu Set["RegularMenus"]
End If
```

Loop

Syntax:

Loop

Options:

None

Description:

This script step marks the beginning of a Loop structure. The end of the Loop structure is defined by a matching End Loop step. Script control passes from the Loop step through all intervening steps to the End Loop step and back again until an Exit Loop directive is encountered or until a Halt Script or Exit Script step is encountered. The Exit Loop directive is available as an option with the Exit Loop If step, the Go to Record/Request/Page step, and the

Go to Portal Row step. Loops are often used to perform an action over a group of records or portal rows.

Examples:

```
# Create 10 new blank records
Set Variable [$counter; Value: "0"]
Loop
  New Record/Request
  Set Variable [$counter; Value: $counter + 1]
  Exit Loop If [$counter > 10]
End
```

Modify Last Find

Syntax:

Modify Last Find

Options:

None

Description:

This script step activates Find mode and then recalls the last find request(s) used. The find request(s) may then be modified and executed with the Perform Find script step.

Examples:

```
Modify Last Find
Set Field [Contacts::Birthdate; "1/1/1974. . 1/1/1985"]
Perform Find[]
```

Move/Resize Window

Syntax:

Move/Resize Window [Current Window or Name: <name of window>; Height: <n>; ➥Width: <n>; Top: <n>; Left: <n>]

Options:

- **Specify** allows the setting of the move/resize options.
- **Current Window** causes the changes to be performed on the current window.
- **Window Name** causes the changes to be performed on an open window, specified by name. Literal text may be entered or Specify clicked to create a window name from a calculation.
- **Current File Only** causes FileMaker to search only within windows based on table occurrences from within the current file.

- **Height** is the height of the adjusted window in pixels. A number may be entered or Specify can be clicked to generate a number from a calculation.
- **Width** is the width of the adjusted window in pixels. A number may be entered or Specify can be clicked to generate a number from a calculation.
- **Distance from Top** is the adjusted window's distance in pixels from the top of the screen (Mac OS) or from the top of the FileMaker Pro window (Windows). A number may be entered or Specify clicked to generate a number from a calculation.
- **Distance from Left** is the adjusted window's distance in pixels from the left of the screen (Mac OS) or from the left of the FileMaker Pro window (Windows). A number may be entered or Specify clicked to generate a number from a calculation.

Description:

This script step adjusts the size and location of the selected window. Every other aspect of the window, including found set, current table, and current record, remains unchanged. Where an option is left without a value, the current value of that option is used. If position or size options exceed or fall below allowable minimums or maximums for a machine's particular operating system and configuration, the allowed minimums or maximums are used instead of the chosen values. In multiple-monitor environments, the use of negative position values makes it possible to position a window on monitors other than the main monitor.

Note for Windows: FileMaker Pro orients the moved window to the top-left corner of the visible part of the application window. Note that this may not be the (0, 0) point of the window, depending on how the current file window is positioned (for example, if half of the file window extends past the left border of the application window, you would need to scroll to the left to see the [0, 0] point of the application window).

Current file only allows the developer to restrict the scope of window management script steps to consider only windows based on the current file.

Examples:

```
Move/Resize Window [Name:Invoices ; Height: 400; Width: 600; Top: 16; Left: 16]
```

New File

Syntax:

New File

Options:

None

Description:

This script step enables the user to create a new database file in FileMaker Pro's usual Create New File dialog box. If the Show Templates in New Database Dialog Box preference is selected, the script step shows the New Database dialog box.

The user is taken to the Manage Database dialog. When he's finished defining the new database, and has closed the Manage Database dialog, the script that invoked the New File command continues. The new database stays open but is not activated.

Examples:

```
New File
```

New Record/Request

Syntax:

New Record/Request

Options:

None

Description:

This script step creates a new, blank record if the system is in Browse mode, and a new find request if the system is in Find mode.

Note that this script step is context-dependent. The current layout determines which table is active, which determines in which table the record is created.

Examples:

```
# Create 10 new blank records
Set Variable [$counter; Value: "0"]
Loop
  New Record/Request
  Set Variable [$counter; Value: $counter + 1]
  Exit Loop If [$counter > 10]
End
```

New Window

Syntax:

New Window [Name: <name of window>; Height: n; Width: n; Top: n; Left: n]

Options:

- **Specify** allows the setting of options for the new window.
- **Window Name** is the name specified for the new window. Literal text may be entered or Specify clicked to create a window name from a calculation.
- **Height** is the height of the new window in pixels. A number may be entered or Specify clicked to generate a number from a calculation.
- **Width** is the width of the new window in pixels. A number may be entered or Specify clicked to generate a number from a calculation.

- **Distance from Top** is the new window's distance in pixels from the top of the screen (Mac OS) or from the top of the FileMaker Pro window (Windows). A number may be entered or Specify clicked to generate a number from a calculation.
- **Distance from Left** is the new window's distance in pixels from the left of the screen (Mac OS) or from the left of the FileMaker Pro window (Windows). A number may be entered or Specify clicked to generate a number from a calculation.

Description:

This script step creates a new window based on the current window. The new window inherits the same context, layout, and attributes as the current window except in the specified options. In the case where an option is left without a value, the default value (as demonstrated by the Window menu, New Window command) for that option is used. If position or size options exceed or fall below allowable minimums or maximums for a machine's particular operating system and configuration, the allowed minimums or maximums are used instead of the chosen values. In multiple monitor environments, the use of negative position values makes it possible to position a window on alternate monitors.

Note for Windows: FileMaker Pro orients the moved window to the top-left corner of the visible part of the application window. Note that this may not be the (0, 0) point of the window, depending on how the current file window is positioned. (For example, if half of the file window extends past the left border of the application window, you would need to scroll to the left to see the [0, 0] point of the application window.)

Examples:

```
New Window [Name: "Profile"; Height: 500; Width: 700; Top: 25; Left: 25]
```

Omit Multiple Records 

Syntax:

Omit Multiple Records [No dialog; <number of records>]

Options:

- **Perform Without Dialog** prevents a dialog box from displaying when the script step executes. Without this option selected, the user sees a dialog that allows the user to enter the number of records to be omitted.
- When Perform Without Dialog is selected, if a number of records to omit is not specified, only the current record is omitted.
- **Specify Records** or **Specify** allows the entry of the exact number of records to omit. The Specify button may also be clicked in the Options dialog box to allow for the entry of a calculation. The calculation result must be a number.

Description:

This script step omits the specified number of records from the found set, leaving the next available record as the current record. Omitted records are not deleted; they are just excluded from the found set. They remain in the database, and can be easily verified if you re-execute the Find Request that generated the found set in the first place.

When programming for the Web, be sure to select Perform Without Dialog. Leaving the box unchecked is not web-compatible.

Examples:

```
Perform Find [Restore]
# Omit the first 10 records found
Omit Multiple Records [ 10 ]
[ No dialog ]
```

Omit Record 

Syntax:

Omit Record

Options:

None

Description:

This script step omits the current record from the current found set when executed in Browse mode. The next available record becomes the new current record, or the prior record in the case of omitting the last record in a found set. Omitted records are not deleted. They are merely removed from the current found set.

If this script step is executed while in Find mode, the current find request's Omit check box is toggled. (If it was checked, it will be unchecked, and if it is unchecked, it will be checked.) A find request that has the omit check box checked becomes an omit request that subtracts from rather than adds to the found set.

Examples:

```
# Omit records marked for omission without modifying the found set
Go to Record/Request/Page [First]
Loop
 If [Contacts::Omit]
  Omit Record
 End If
 Go to Record/Request/Page [Next; Exit After  Last]
End Loop
```

Open Manage Database

Syntax:

Open Manage Database

Options:

None

Description:

This script step opens the Manage Database dialog box, where the user can create or edit tables, fields, and relationships. This script step is not performed if the user's account does not have the Full Access privilege set. (The script may be set to Run Script With Full Access Privileges in the ScriptMaker menu.) When the user closes the dialog box, the remaining steps in the script, if any, are executed.

Examples:

```
If [Get (LastMessageChoice) = 1]
  #1=Yes, 2=No
  Open Manage Database
End If
```

Open Manage Data Sources 

Syntax:

Open Manage Data Sources

Options:

None

Description:

This script step opens the Manage Data Sources dialog box, where the user can create or edit references to files and data sources used throughout the database. This script step is not performed if the user's account does not have the Full Access privilege set. (The script may be set to Run Script With Full Access Privileges in the ScriptMaker menu.) When the user closes the dialog box, the remaining steps in the script, if any, are executed.

Examples:

```
Show Custom Dialog ["Do you want to create or edit a file
reference for a data source?"]
If [Get (LastMessageChoice) = 1]
  #1=Yes, 2=No
  Open Manage Data Sources
End If
```

Open Manage Value Lists

Syntax:

Open Manage Value Lists

Options:

None

Description:

This script step opens the Manage Value Lists dialog box, where the user can define new or edit existing value lists. This script step is not performed if the user's account does not have the Full Access privilege set. (The script may be set to Run Script With Full Access Privileges in the ScriptMaker menu.) When the user closes the dialog box, the remaining steps in the script, if any, are executed.

Examples:

```
Show Custom Dialog ["Do you want to create or edit a value list?"]
If [Get (LastMessageChoice) = 1]
  #1=Yes, 2=No
  Open Manage Value Lists
End If
```

Open File

Syntax:

Open File [Open hidden; "<filename>"]

Options:

- **Open Hidden** causes FileMaker Pro to open the specified database hidden (that is, with its window minimized).
- **Specify** allows the selection of a FileMaker Pro database to be opened. Within the Specify menu, Add File Reference provides a dialog box to assist in the location and selection of a filename. After a file is selected, it is added to the Specify list. In the same menu, Manage File References allows one to modify or delete a file reference already added to the list.

Description:

This script step opens the specified file or allows the user to select a file to open in the Open File dialog box. The Open File dialog box is invoked when no file is specified in the script step or if the specified file cannot be found. The active file before the Open File step is executed remains active after it has completed.

Examples:

```
Open File [Open Hidden; "Tempfile.fp7"]
```

Open File Options

Syntax:

Open File Options

Options:

None

Description:

This script step opens the File Options dialog box to the General preferences area. This script step is not performed if the user's account does not have the Full Access privilege set. (The script may be set to Run Script With Full Access Privileges in the ScriptMaker menu.)

Examples:

```
Show Custom Dialog ["Open File Options dialog box?"]
If [Get (LastMessageChoice) = 1]
  #1=Yes, 2=No
  Open File Options
End If
```

Open Find/Replace

Syntax:

Open Find/Replace

Options:

None

Description:

This script step opens the Find/Replace dialog box. The remaining steps in the script, if any, are executed after the user closes the dialog box or completes a search.

Examples:

```
Show Custom Dialog ["Open the Find/Replace dialog box?"]
If [Get (LastMessageChoice) = 1]
  #1=Yes, 2=No
  Open Find/Replace
End If
```

Open Help

Syntax:

Open Help

Options:

None

Description:

This script step opens the FileMaker Pro Help system. By default, the user is placed in the Help System Contents screen.

The Help dialog is nonmodal, so any additional script steps after the Open Help step execute right away, possibly pushing the help window into the background.

Examples:

```
Show Custom Dialog ["Do you need Help?"]
If [Get (LastMessageChoice) = 1]
  #1=Yes, 2=No
  Open Help
End If
```

Open Preferences

Syntax:

Open Preferences

Options:

None

Description:

This script step opens the Preferences dialog box. The General Preferences area is selected by default.

Comments:

When the user closes the dialog box, the remaining steps in the script, if any, are executed.

Examples:

```
Show Custom Dialog ["Open Preferences dialog box?"]
If [Get (LastMessageChoice) = 1]
  #1=Yes, 2=No
  Open Preferences
End If
```

Open Record/Request

Syntax:

Open Record/Request

Options:

None

Description:

This script step attempts to acquire exclusive access to the current record. Exclusive access prevents other users from editing the record. It has the same effect as a user selecting a data field on a layout (by clicking or tabbing) and then beginning to enter or edit field data. These actions either give exclusive access to that user, or, if another user has already acquired exclusive access (otherwise known as a *lock*), the user attempting to gain control of the record sees an error message with a warning that another user has control of the record. It can be useful to try to gain exclusive access to a record in the course of a script.

If you are looping over records and need to change each one, if a user is editing one of the records, your script may be prevented from changing it. Open Record/Request cannot override another user's access, but if the script step fails it generates an error that your script can inspect with the Get (LastError) statement.

Examples:

```
Perform Find [Restore]
Go to Record/Request/Page [First]
Open Record/Request
If [ Get(LastError) = 200 or Get(LastError) = 300]
  Show Custom Dialog ["An error has ocurred. This record is locked or you do
  ➥not have sufficient permission to access it."]
End If
```

Open Remote

Syntax:

Open Remote

Options:

None

Description:

This script step opens the Open Remote dialog box to allow the opening of a shared FileMaker Pro database over a network connection.

Comments:

When the user closes the dialog box, the remaining steps in the script, if any, are executed.

Examples:

```
Show Custom Dialog ["Do you want to look for a networked database?"]
If [Get (LastMessageChoice) = 1]
  #1=Yes, 2=No
  Open Remote
End If
```

Open ScriptMaker

Syntax:

Open ScriptMaker

Options:

None

Description:

This script step opens the ScriptMaker dialog box, which enables a user to create, edit, rename, and duplicate scripts. When this script step is performed, FileMaker halts the current script because if any currently executing scripts were to be edited, the resulting behavior could be unpredictable.

Examples:

```
Show Custom Dialog ["Open ScriptMaker?"]
If [Get (LastMessageChoice) = 1]
  #1=Yes, 2=No
  Open ScriptMaker
End If
```

Open Sharing

Syntax:

Open Sharing

Options:

None

Description:

This script step opens the FileMaker Network Settings dialog box where users can configure network database sharing.

Examples:

```
Show Custom Dialog ["Do you want to open the sharing dialog?"]
If [Get (LastMessageChoice) = 1]
  #1=Yes, 2=No
  Open Sharing
End If
```

Open URL

Syntax:

Open URL [No dialog; <URL>]

Options:

- **Perform Without Dialog** prevents the Open URL Options dialog box from displaying when the script step executes.
- **Specify** may be selected to display the Open URL Options dialog box, where the URL can be typed directly into the text entry area or created by a calculation.

Description:

This script step allows a URL to be opened in the appropriate application. Supported schemes include HTTP, FTP, file, mailto, HTTPS, and fmp7 for opening FileMaker files. FileMaker consults the operating system preferences to help decide which application to use to service a particular URL scheme.

When programming for the Web, be sure to select Perform Without Dialog. Leaving the box unchecked is not web-compatible.

Examples:

```
Open URL [No dialog; "http://www.apple.com/"]
Open URL [No dialog; "file://c:/addresses.txt"]
Open URL [No dialog; "mailto:no-one@name.net"]
Open URL [No dialog; "fmp7://system:password@192.168.10.46:591/WebDB"]
#Note about the last example: "system" is the FileMaker Pro account name,
➥ "password" is that account's password, and "WebDB" is the FileMaker Pro filename.
```

Paste

Syntax:

Paste [Select; No style; <table::field>]

Options:

- **Select Entire Contents** replaces the contents of a field with the contents of the Clipboard. If Select Entire Contents is not used, Paste copies the contents of the Clipboard to the currently selected portion of the field.

- **Paste Without Style** tells FileMaker Pro to ignore all text style and formatting associated with the Clipboard contents.
- **Go to Target Field** or click the **Specify** button to specify the field into which to paste.
- **Link If Available** (Windows only) tells FileMaker Pro to choose a link over other formats on the Clipboard. If both a link and an embedded object are present on the Clipboard, the link is selected. If a link is available, it is selected over other formats.

Description:

This script step pastes the contents of the Clipboard into the specified field in the current record. If the data type of the data being pasted does not match the type of the field being pasted into, FileMaker Pro displays the customary validation alert when the record is committed. (It's also possible that the script that calls the Paste step may leave the record in an uncommitted state, in which case the error dialog appears later, when the record is committed.) If the field is not on the current layout, FileMaker Pro returns an error code, which can be captured with the Get(LastError) function. In a web-published database, use a Commit Record/Request script step after a Paste script step to update the record in the browser window.

Paste is one of a number of script steps that depend on the presence of specific fields on the current layout. Other script steps with the same limitations include Cut, Copy, Paste, and Set Selection.

Examples:

```
#Assumes customer address is on clipboard
Paste [Select; No style; Customer::Address]
```

Pause/Resume Script 

Syntax:

Pause/Resume Script [Duration (seconds) <n>]

Options:

- **Specify** displays the Pause/Resume Options dialog box, where the following options can be set:
  - **Select Indefinitely** to pause the script until the user clicks the Continue button in the status area.
  - **Select for Duration** to enter the number of seconds to pause the script.
  - **Select for Duration** and click Specify to create a calculation that determines the number of seconds to pause.

Description:

This script step pauses a script for a specified period of time or indefinitely. This enables the user to perform data entry or other tasks before continuing the script. This step brings the active window of the file in which the script step is running to the foreground if it is not already there. The duration of a pause must be a number and represents the number of seconds that the pause will last before resuming execution for the script. Most FileMaker Pro menu options are not available to users while in a paused script. While paused, a script displays a Continue button in the status bar. The pause is terminated when a user clicks this button. There is also a Cancel button, which appears only if the Allow User Abort option is set to On. This button exits the currently running script. In the case where the status bar is hidden, the Enter key performs the same function as the Continue button. Buttons that run other scripts function while the current script is paused. A script run in this way is run as a subscript of the paused script.

Examples:

```
# Open pop-up window
Allow User Abort [off]
New Window [ Name: "About Soliant Consulting...";
    Height: 50; Width: 50; Top: 40; Left: 100 ]
Go to Layout [ "About" (zRESOURCES__anchor) ]
Show/Hide Status Area
    [ Lock; Hide ]
Adjust Window
[ Resize to Fit ]
#
Pause/Resume Script [ Indefinitely ]
# wait for user to hit ENTER key or CLOSE button
#
Close Window [ Current Window ]
```

Perform AppleScript

Syntax:

Perform AppleScript ["<applescript text>"]

Options:

- **Specify** displays the Perform AppleScript Options dialog box, where the following options can be set:
  - **Calculated AppleScript** lets you draw the AppleScript code from the result of a calculation.
  - **Native AppleScript** allows you to enter an AppleScript by hand (up to 30,000 characters long).

Description:

This script step sends AppleScript commands to an AppleScript-aware application. The AppleScript may be typed in manually or generated as the result of a specified calculation.

Calculated scripts are compiled every time the script is run, whereas typed-in scripts are compiled only when the script is edited. Obviously, the latter is a faster process, but creating AppleScript code via a calculation provides much greater flexibility.

Perform AppleScript is supported only on the Mac OS. The script step generates an error on Windows. For more information on AppleScript and AppleEvents, see the "Apple Events Reference" included with FileMaker Pro.

Examples:

```
#This example sets the primary monitor to its minimum bit depth.
Perform AppleScript ["tell application "Finder" to set bounds of window
➥"My Files" to {100, 100, 100, 100}"]
```

Perform Find

Syntax:

Perform Find [Restore]

Options:

- **Specify Find Requests** or **Specify** allows you to create or edit one or more find requests that will be stored with the script steps.
- **New** opens a dialog box that enables you to create and specify a new find request to be stored with the script step.
- **Edit** opens a selected find request from the existing list for editing.
- **Duplicate** duplicates one or more selected find requests from the list and adds them to the stored set.
- **Delete** deletes one or more selected find requests from the list.
- **Edit Find Request** dialog box works with find request criteria.
- **Find Records** or **Omit Records** specifies the behavior of the request. Selecting `Omit Records` is equivalent to checking the `Omit` check box in a find request in Find mode. Finding records adds them to the current found set. Omitting records excludes them. As in Find mode, use multiple requests if it's necessary to both find and omit records in the course of a single stored search.
- **Find Records When** (or **Omit Records When**) shows a list of the fields in your current table. To construct a find request, begin by selecting a field from this list.

  To select a field from a related table, click the name of the current table at the top of the list and select the related table you want. Select a related field from this new list.

  Change the value in Repetition to specify a particular cell of a repeating field.

  Type the search criteria for the selected field in the Criteria area.

  Click Add to add criteria to the find request.

To change existing criteria, select the line containing the field and criteria from the top of the dialog box, and make the changes to the field and/or criteria. Click Change to store changes.

To delete existing criteria, select the line containing the field and criteria from the top of the dialog box and click Remove.

Description:

This script step places the system in Find mode and performs the search request(s) that have been designated for this step. If no find requests have been designated, the last find request(s) that the system performed is performed. If the system is in Find mode when Perform Find is executed, the currently entered find request is performed. This behavior is often used in conjunction with the Enter Find Mode step with the Pause option selected to allow a user to define a search request or group of search requests and then perform them. If FileMaker Pro doesn't find any records that match the find criteria when a script is performed, the script can be stopped, execution of the script can be resumed with zero records in the current found set, and the find criteria can be changed. With the Set Error Capture script step and the Get (LastError) function, a script to handle such situations can be written.

Examples:

```
Set Error Capture [On]
Perform Find [Restore]
#check for a "no records" error
If [Get (LastError) = 401]
  Show Custom Dialog ["Sorry, no records were found."; buttons ["ok"]]
End If
```

Perform Find/Replace 

Syntax:

Perform Find/Replace [No dialog; "<text to be found>"; "<replacement text>";
➥Find Next/Replace & Find/Replace/Replace All]

Options:

- **Perform Without Dialog** inhibits the display of the Find/Replace Summary dialog box at the end of the Find/Replace operation. This option also prevents display of the confirmation dialog box when a Replace All operation is executed.
- **Open Find/Replace** script step is used if it is desired that the user be able to enter find or replace criteria.
- **Specify** displays the Specify Find/Replace dialog box, where search options, as well as the type of find/replace operation to be performed, can be set.

Description:

This script step looks for the specified text in one or more fields and records of the current found set, and, if directed, replaces it with either literal text or the result of a calculation. The scope of the operation can be defined to be the current record or the entire found set. The Find/Replace can span all fields in a layout or just the current field. The operation can be defined to proceed forward or backward in the current found set (as sorted). Finally, options are available for the matching of whole words only instead of parts of words, and for the matching of case.

Examples:

```
Perform Find/Replace ["hte"; "the"; Replace All]
```

Perform Script

Syntax:

Perform Script ["<script name>"; Parameter: <parameter>]

Options:

- **Specify** allows you to choose the script from the list.
- Provide a script parameter using the optional script parameter choice. You can specify the parameter as text, or click Edit and specify the parameter by means of a calculation formula.

Description:

This script step performs a script either in the current file or in another FileMaker Pro file. Scripts can be as simple or as complex as required, but it is often more efficient to break larger scripts into smaller subscripts for ease of reuse, testing, and debugging.

Script parameters allow scripts to communicate with one another without having to use database fields or global fields. The script parameter may be accessed with the Get (ScriptParameter) function. It is important to note that script parameters exist only within a script into which they have been explicitly passed. For a subscript to have access to the parameter of the script that called it, it must, in turn, be passed into the subscript. For a subscript to pass data back to a calling script, Exit Script results may be specified as well. Script parameters exist for only as long as the script to which they are passed exists. Parameter strings can contain many pieces of information as long as they are properly separated. Carriage returns and separator characters are common ways to pass many pieces of information in a parameter string.

Examples:

```
Go to Layout ["Detail"]
Perform Script ["Find Contact"; Parameter: Contact::ContactID]
```

Print

Syntax:

Print [Restore; No dialog]

Options:

- **Perform Without Dialog** prevents a dialog box from displaying when the script step executes. Ordinarily, users would see a dialog box permitting them to use their own settings. When this option is selected, FileMaker Pro uses the print settings stored with the script step.
- **Specify Print Options** or **Specify** opens the Print dialog box and allows you to set generic printing options, including the printer, number of copies, and the pages to print. FileMaker Pro can also set printing options such as printing the current record, printing records being browsed, or printing a blank record.

Description:

This script step prints selected information from a FileMaker Pro file. This information can include field contents, reports based on database data, and field or script definitions. Print setup settings are stored with the script step but may be changed with the Print Setup script step. Multiple Print Setup steps may be used in a single script.

Printer settings generally do not transfer well between platforms. Unless your settings are generic, you will likely need to separate Print or Print Setup steps for each platform you intend to support. You may need to check the current user's platform with Get (SystemPlatform) and use separate print setups for each different platform.

Examples:

```
Go to Layout ["Detail View"]
Show All Records
Sort Records [Restore; No dialog]
Print Setup [Restore; No dialog]
Print []
```

Print Setup

Syntax:

Print Setup [Restore; No dialog]

Options:

- **Perform Without Dialog** prevents a dialog box from displaying when the script step that lets the user enter new printing options executes. When this option is selected, FileMaker Pro uses the print settings stored with the script step.

- **Specify Print Options** or **Specify** opens the Print dialog box and allows you to set generic printing options, including the printer, number of copies, and the pages to print. FileMaker Pro can also set printing options such as printing the current record, printing records being browsed, or printing a blank record.

Description:

This script step sets printing options such as the printer, print layout, number of copies, and so on, all of which can be saved within the script step. There is the option to allow the user to modify the print setup by presenting her with the Print Setup dialog box. Multiple Print Setup steps may be used in a single script.

Printer settings generally do not transfer well between platforms. Unless your settings are generic, you may need separate Print or Print Setup steps for each platform you intend to support. You may need to use Get (SystemPlatform) to check the current user's platform and use separate print setups for each different platform.

Examples:

```
Go to Layout ["Detail View"]
Show All Records
Sort Records [Restore; No Dialog]
Print Setup [Restore; No dialog]
Print []
```

Re-Login *

Syntax:

Re-Login [Account Name: <account name>; Password: <password>; No dialog]

Options:

- **Perform Without Dialog** prevents the Authentication dialog box from displaying when the script step executes. When this option is checked, FileMaker Pro uses the account and password information stored with the script step or derived from a calculation expression.
- **Specify** displays the Re-Login Options dialog box, where you can set the following options:
  - **Account Name** is the name of the account to be authenticated. This may be entered as literal text, or Specify can be clicked to derive an account name from a calculation.
  - **Password** is the password for this account. Literal text may be entered or Specify clicked to derive a new password from a calculation.

Description:

This script step allows a user to log in to the current database with a different account name and password. This does not require the database file to be closed or reopened.

Privileges assigned to the new account take effect immediately, including access to tables, records, layouts, scripts, and value lists. Users get five attempts to enter an account and password, unless the Set Error Capture script step is enabled. If the Set Error Capture script step is enabled, users get a single attempt to enter an account and password. If a user fails the allotted number of times, she must close and reopen the database file before she can try to access the database again.

When developing a system with several privilege sets, you'll want to test the system's functions with each set. It can save time to create Re-login scripts to allow you to instantly switch privileges without actually logging out of the file(s).

When programming for the Web, be sure to select Perform Without Dialog. Leaving the box unchecked is not web-compatible.

Examples:

```
Re-Login [Account Name:"User"; Password:"Password"; No dialog]
```

Recover File

Syntax:

Recover File [No dialog; "<filename>"]

Options:

- **Perform Without Dialog** prevents a dialog box from displaying after the script step completes. Ordinarily, users would see a dialog box that shows how many bytes of data were recovered, the number of records and field values skipped, and the number of field definitions recovered.
- **Specify Source File** or **Specify** displays a dialog box where you can select the file to be recovered. If you don't select a source file, the Open Damaged File dialog box displays when the script is run.

Description:

This script step recovers damaged FileMaker Pro files. In the recovery process, FileMaker Pro attempts to repair and recover as much of the information in a damaged file as is possible. It then creates a new file and saves it to the selected directory. The original file is not deleted or replaced. The new recovered file is named exactly as the damaged file except "Recovered" is appended to its filename, before any extenders. For example, the recovery of DataFile.fp7 would produce the file DataFile Recovered.fp7.

Recover File is an invasive process and is intended only to recover data from a corrupted file. It does not remove any corruption that may be present in the file, nor does it necessarily render the file fit for production use again. Try to avoid reusing a file that has been recovered. Import the extracted data into the most recent clean backup of the file and discard the recovered version.

FileMaker Server 9 includes an aggressive consistency check routine that can detect many forms of file corruption. Accordingly, FileMaker, Inc., has somewhat softened its long-standing advice against ever reusing a recovered file. If a file successfully passes the consistency check in FileMaker Server 9, the file may be deemed fit for production use; however, it is still recommended that recovered data be imported into a clean backup of your files.

Examples:

```
Recover File [No Dialog; "DataFile.fp7"]
```

Refresh Window 

Syntax:

Refresh Window

Options:

- **Flush cached join results** causes data for related records displayed in the current window to be refreshed. Choose this option if your script may have changed related data and you want to make sure the new data are visible after the screen refresh. If your script won't change related data, you may avoid a performance hit by leaving the option unchecked.
- **SQL data** causes any displayed data from an external SQL data source to be refreshed. The external SQL server will be queried for the current values of all displayed data. This is helpful if you want to make sure the user is viewing the latest data from the SQL source, including any updates or deletions that may have occurred since the SQL data was last refreshed.

Description:

This script step updates the active FileMaker Pro document window. Use Refresh Window after Freeze Window to update a window.

This step may also be used to force a portal to refresh after match fields (such as keys or other IDs) have been modified. It may also happen that complex related data is slow to refresh in a window, or user interaction—such as a mouse click—may be required to show the changed data. If you find such behavior, you may be able to cure it with an explicit Refresh Window step. (Note that for this application you must make sure to select the Flush cached join results option.)

Examples:

```
Freeze Window
Go to Record/Request/Page [First]
# Give everyone a 10% raise.
Loop
  Set Field [Employee::Salary; Employee::Salary * 1.1]
  Go to Record/Request/Page [Next; Exit after last]
End Loop
Refresh Window
```

Relookup Field Contents  *

Syntax:

Relookup Field Contents [No dialog; <table::field>]

Options:

- **Perform Without Dialog** prevents the display of a dialog box that prompts the user to confirm field information when the script step executes.
- **Go to Target Field** or **Specify** allows you to specify the field that is the match field of the relookup operation. FileMaker Pro moves the cursor to the field you specify. This must be the match field for the relationship upon which the lookup is based, not the lookup source or target field. If no field is selected, Relookup Field Contents returns an error code.

Description:

Use Relookup to "refresh" values that are copied from one place to another via the Lookup field option. It's important to realize that you must specify the field that's the *match field* for the lookup operation, rather than any of the fields that will receive the newly copied data. As an example, imagine that you have a system with a Customer table and an Invoice table. The two tables are related by a shared CustomerID. The Invoice table also has fields for Customer Name and Customer Address, which are defined to look up the corresponding fields from the related Customer record. To "refresh" the customer name and address information on one or more invoices, it would be necessary to specify the Customer ID field in Invoices, which is the match field that links the two tables, rather than specify either of the two fields intended to receive the refreshed data. Note that Relookup operates only on records in the current found set.

When programming for the Web, be sure to select Perform Without Dialog. Leaving the box unchecked is not web-compatible.

Examples:

```
Relookup Field Contents [No dialog, Invoice::Customer ID]
```

Replace Field Contents ⌘ ⊞ ⊕*

Syntax:

Replace Field Contents [No Dialog; <table::field>; Current contents/Serial ➥ numbers/Calculation results]

Options:

- **Perform Without Dialog** prevents display of the Replace Field Contents dialog box when the script step executes.
- **Go to Target Field** or **Specify** allows you to specify the target field for the replace operation.
- **Specify** displays the Replace Contents dialog box, where you can determine the settings required for the Replace Field Contents command so that they'll be stored in the script.
- **Replace with Current Contents** uses the current value in the specified field as the replacement value to place in that field in every other record in the current found set.
- **Replace with Serial Numbers** updates the field with new serial numbers in every record in the current found set.
- **Entry Options** causes FileMaker to consult the underlying database structure to determine how to serialize records. In particular, it causes the Replace step to use the database field settings for Next Value and Increment by, as stored in the field options for that field.
- **Custom Values** lets you enter a value to be used as a starting point for the serialization, as well as a value by which to increment each serialized field in the current found set.
- **Update Serial Number In Entry Options** resets the serial number value in the entry options for the field, so that the next serial number that is automatically entered follows the records you have reserialized with this script step. If this option is not used, the serial value in Entry Options is not changed and may not be in sequence with the newly reserialized records. This may lead to duplicated serial numbers or data validation errors.

  If the field to be replaced was set up for auto-entry of a serial number and Prohibit Modification of Value is not selected, FileMaker Pro still puts sequential numbers in the selected field, but does so starting with the next number to be automatically entered.
- **Replace with Calculated Result** displays the Specify Calculation dialog box, where you can enter a calculation to be used as the replacement value.

Description:

This script step replaces the contents of a selected field in the current record or every record in the found set with some value—the value of the field on the current record, a set of serial numbers, or a calculated result. This step can also be used to reserialize a field in every record in the found set. Note that if the specified field does not exist on the layout where the script is being performed, Replace Field Contents returns an error code that can be captured with the Get (LastError) function.

It may be helpful to think of this step as being akin to filling in multiple cells in a spreadsheet column. Replace is particularly powerful when used in conjunction with a calculation (a technique often known as a *calculated replace*). The calculation can reference fields, which refer to the field values in whichever is the current record.

Examples:

```
# Fill in full names
Replace Field Contents [No Dialog; Contacts::FullName; FirstName & " " & LastName]
```

Reset Account Password

Syntax:

Reset Account Password [Account Name: <account name>; New Password: <password>; Expire password]

Options:

- **Specify** displays the Reset Account Password Options dialog box.
- **Account Name** is the name of the account with the password to be reset. You can enter literal text or click Specify to derive an account name from a calculation.
- **New Password** is the new password for this account. Literal text may be entered or Specify clicked to derive a password from a calculation.
- **User Must Change Password on Next Login** forces users to change their password the next time they log in to the database.

Description:

This script step resets the account password for the selected account. The selected account must be existing. The Full Access privilege set is needed to perform this script step. The Run with Full Access Privileges option may be selected in the ScriptMaker dialog box to circumvent this restriction for all users.

Be aware that using User Must Change Password On Next Login does not work correctly when users log in to a solution via the Web. It's also important to make sure that any user with that restriction can modify his password (so take care, for example, when using this option with accounts that are externally authenticated).

Examples:

```
Reset Account Password [Account Name:"Guest User"; New Password:"guestpassword";
➥ Expire password]
```

Revert Record/Request

Syntax:

Revert Record/Request [No dialog]

Options:

- **Perform Without Dialog** inhibits the display of a confirmation dialog when the script step executes.

Description:

This script step discards changes made to a record and its fields, assuming the record has not been saved. After changes have been committed, such as through use of the Commit Records/Requests script step, they can no longer be reverted. This is also true if a user has clicked outside any field.

Note that record reversion applies not only to the current record on whatever layout is being viewed, but also to any records in related tables displayed in a portal on the current layout. If a user has edited one or more records in a portal, the Revert Record/Request script step, if carried out, undoes all uncommitted changes to portal records, as well as any uncommitted changes to the current record.

When programming for the Web, be sure to select Perform Without Dialog. Leaving the box unchecked is not web-compatible.

Examples:

```
Show Custom Dialog ["Do you want to save your changes?";
"Click 'Save' to save your changes, or 'Revert' to
return the record to its original state."]
#1 = Save, 2 = Revert
If [Get(LastMessageChoice) = 1]
    Commit Records/Requests
Else
    Revert Record/Request [No dialog]
End If
```

Save a Copy as

Syntax:

Save a Copy as ["<filename>"; copy/compacted/clone]

Options:

- **Specify Output File** displays the Specify Output File dialog box, which allows specification of the name and location of the resulting copy. If a save location is not specified in the script, FileMaker Pro displays a regular Save As dialog box so the user can specify copying options.

- **Specify** allows you to choose a save format: copy of current file, compacted copy (smaller), or clone (no records).

Description:

This script step saves a copy of the current file to the designated location. If no location is designated, a dialog box is presented to the user. Three types of copies are available. Copy creates an exact replica of the current file. Compressed also creates a copy of the current file, but the copy will be compressed to utilize space more efficiently. This sort of copy takes longer to create but is generally smaller than the original. Clone creates a file that's structurally identical to the current database but contains no data. This is useful for backup purposes because clones are compact.

Cloning a file naturally removes all of its record data, Perhaps less intuitively, it also wipes away any values in globally stored fields. If your solution uses globally stored fields for graphics or other sorts of system preferences, be aware that such data will be lost if the files are cloned.

Examples:

```
Save a Copy As ["Customers.bak"]
```

Save Records as Excel

Syntax:

Save Records As Excel [No dialog; "<output filename>"; Automatically open; Create email; Current records]

Options:

- **Perform Without Dialog** prevents certain dialog boxes from appearing as the script step executes. If you have specified a file and stored that information with the script step, no dialog boxes display. If you have not saved output file information with the script step, the Save Records as Excel dialog box will display (but the Excel options dialog still will not).
- **Specify Output File** allows you to save a file path with the script step. This file path will be used to determine where the new file should be saved. When specifying the output file you can also choose to Automatically open file, in which case the file will be opened when created, or choose Create email with file as attachment to create a new blank email, with the Excel file as an attachment, using the local machine's default email software.
- **Specify Options** allows you to set a number of useful properties of the output file, such as which database records should be included, whether the first row should contain field names, and worksheet properties such as title and author.

Description:

This script step allows you to save a set of records directly to an Excel spreadsheet. With appropriate selections of options, you can also automatically open the file or attach it to an email.

Note that the file path dialog accepts either a file path in text form or a variable ($local or $$global).

Examples:

```
Go to Layout ["Customer List"]
Show All Records
Save Records as Excel [No dialog; "Customer_List.xls"]
```

Save Records as PDF

Syntax:

Save Records As PDF [No dialog; "<output filename>"; Automatically open; Create email; Current records]

Options:

- **Append to Existing PDF** allows scripts to add additional pages to an existing PDF.
- **Perform Without Dialog** prevents certain dialog boxes from appearing as the script step executes. If you have specified a file and stored that information with the script step, no dialog boxes will display. If you have not saved output file information with the script step, the Save Records as PDF dialog box will display (but the PDF options dialog still will not).
- **Specify Output File** allows you to save a file path with the script step. This file path is used to determine where the new file should be saved. When specifying the output file you can also choose to Automatically Open File, in which case the file will be opened when created, or choose Create Email with File as Attachment to create a new blank email, with the PDF file as an attachment, using the local machine's default email software.
- **Specify Options** allows you to set a number of useful properties of the output file, such as which database records should be included, and a variety of properties, such as document author and PDF security settings.

Description:

This script step allows you to save a set of records as a PDF. With appropriate selections of options, you can also automatically open the file or attach it to an email. Developers have full control over security settings and document properties as well.

Note that the file path dialog accepts either a file path in text form or a variable ($local or $$global).

Examples:

```
Go to Layout ["Customer List"]
Set Variable[$path; "Get (DesktopPath) & "/myReport.pdf"]
Show All Records
Save Records as PDF [No dialog; $path]
```

Scroll Window

Syntax:

Scroll Window [Home/End/Page Up/Page Down/To Selection]

Options:

- **Specify** to choose a scrolling option.
- **Home**, **End**, **Page Up**, or **Page Down** scrolls the window to the beginning, to the end, up a page, or down a page.
- **To Selection** brings the current field into view (similar to tabbing into a field).

Description:

This script step scrolls a window to its top or bottom, up or down, or to a specified field.You may want to use this script step for rapid, easy scrolling within a window. For example, if you've had to design a layout that's wider than some users' screens, you can put dummy "scroll left/scroll right" fields at the far left and right sides of the layout. If you make the field small and forbid entry, the user will not notice them. Then a script like the following example scrolls quickly to the right side of the window (assuming the field is placed somewhere to the right).

Examples:

```
Go to Field[ "Scroll Right"]
Scroll Window [To Selection]
#The next step just makes sure we leave the "scroll to" field
Commit Records/Requests
```

Select All

Syntax:

Select All

Options:

None

Description:

This script step selects the entire contents of the current field.

Examples:

```
#place a contact person's statement on the clipboard
Go to Field [Contacts::Statement]
Select All
Copy []
```

Select Dictionaries

Syntax:

Select Dictionaries

Options:

None

Description:

This script step opens the Select Dictionaries dialog box. This is often used to give users access to the Select Dictionaries dialog box when access to the FileMaker Pro menus has been restricted.

Examples:

```
Select Dictionaries
Check Record
```

Select Window

Syntax:

Select Window [Current window or Name:<name of window>; Current file]

Options:

- **Current Window** brings the active window of the file that contains the script to the foreground.
- **Specify** also selects the window FileMaker Pro should bring to the foreground. The name may be typed as literal text, or derived from a calculation.
- **Current File Only** restricts the scope of window management script steps to consider only windows based on the current file.

Description:

This script step specifies a window by name and makes it the current, focal window. FileMaker Pro script steps are always performed in the foreground window and inherit context from that window's layout and associated table occurrence. Use this script step when working with scripts in multitable files to make sure that a script step is performed in the intended table. (You may also need to use a Go to Layout step to establish context correctly.) The Select Window script step does not open a window of a related file when the related file is open in a hidden state, such as when a file is opened, because it is the source file of a related field. The related file must be explicitly opened with the Open File script step before its windows are allowable targets for the Select Window step.

Examples:

Select Window [Name: "Contract Players"]

Send DDE Execute

Syntax:

Send DDE Execute [<topic text or filename>; <service name>]

Options:

- **Specify** displays the Send DDE Execute Options dialog box.
- **Service Name** is the name of the application that executes any specified commands. Refer to the documentation for the specified application to find the valid service name. The service name may be entered directly as text, or Specify can be clicked to create the service name from a calculation.
- **Topic** is a filename or text string that describes the topic on which the application executes the commands. Refer to the documentation for the application specified in the Service Name to determine valid topics. Enter the topic name directly as text, or click Specify to create the topic name from a calculation.
- **Commands** are calculated values or text strings that specify what the application does. Refer to the documentation for the application specified in the Service Name to determine valid commands and formats. Enter the commands directly as text or click Specify to create the commands from a calculation.

Description:

This script step sends a DDE (Dynamic Data Exchange) command to another DDE-aware application. FileMaker can send DDE commands but cannot receive them. When a FileMaker Pro script first establishes a DDE connection, the connection stays open to execute subsequent script steps for the same service name and topic. If the script includes another DDE Execute script step that specifies a different service name or topic, FileMaker Pro closes the current connection and opens another with the new service name and topic. All open connections close when the script is completed.

Examples:

Send DDE Execute [Service Name: "iexplore"; Topic: "WWW_OpenURL"; Commands:
➥"www.soliantconsulting.com"]

Send Event (Windows)

Syntax:

Send Event ["<aevt>"; "<event name>"; "<filename>"]

Options:

- **Specify** displays the Send Event Options dialog box.
- For **Send the *<Event Name>* Message**, select the following options:
  - **Open Document/Application** to tell FileMaker Pro to open a document file or application. The application that Windows has associated with the document's file type is used to open it.
  - **Print Document** to tell FileMaker Pro to print a document in another application.
- **File** or click **Specify** to specify a document/application to open or a document to print.
- **Calculation** or click **Specify** to create a message from a calculation.
- **Text** to manually enter text for the message to be sent.
- **Bring Target Application To Foreground** to activate the target application and display it on the screen. Displaying the target application can slow down the performance of a script. If Bring Target Application to Foreground is not selected, the event is performed in the background.

Description:

This script step communicates with other Windows applications. It can instruct them to either open or print a document in its associated application. Custom code written in a language such as C# or Visual Basic can be executed this way.

Examples:

```
#To launch the Notepad application, select the open document/application message, click File, and
➥specify notepad.exe. The following script step appears in the Script Definition dialog box:
Send Message ["NOTEPAD.EXE ", "aevt", "odoc"]
```

Send Event (Mac OS)

Syntax:

Send Event ["<Target Application>"; "<Event Class>"; "<Event ID>", "<Document or Calculation or Script Text>"]

Options:

- **Specify** to display the Send Event Options dialog box.
- **Send The <Value> Event With** offers a choice between the following:
  - **Open Application** tells FileMaker Pro to open an application. Click Specify Application to select the application.

  - **Open Document** tells FileMaker Pro to open a document in the target application. You can also specify a calculated value or script.
  - **Do Script** tells FileMaker Pro to perform a script in the language of the target application. Click Specify Application to select an application, and use Document to select the document to use with the target application. Or select Script Text and enter script text or type in the name of the script. (Make sure it is one that will be recognized by the target program.)
  - **Other** displays the Specify Event dialog box, where you can manually enter the Apple Event class and Event ID.
- **Document** or **Specify** allows you to select the document you want used with the target application.
- **Calculation** or **Specify** allows you to create a calculation that generates a value you want to send with the event.
- **Bring Target Application to Foreground** activates the target application and displays it on the screen. Displaying the target application can slow down the performance of a script. If Bring Target Application to Foreground is not selected, the event is performed in the background.
- **Wait for Event Completion Before Continuing** tells FileMaker Pro to wait until the event is finished before continuing. If you don't want to wait until the event is completed, deselect this option.
- **Copy Event Result to the Clipboard** copies the resulting events data to the Clipboard, from which it can later be retrieved. This option is disabled if Bring Target Application to Foreground is selected.
- **Specify Application** to display a dialog box where you can select the target application.

Description:

This script step sends an Apple Event to another Apple Event–aware application. The desired event is selected in the Send Event Options dialog box. When FileMaker Pro sends an Apple event, it sends text (not compiled) data. You must know what information the target application expects to receive with an event. Each Send Event script step sends one event. You can include more than one Send Event in a script.

Examples:

```
Send Event ["TextEdit", "aevt", "oapp"]
```

Send Mail

Syntax:

Send Mail [No dialog; To: <to>; CC: <CC>; BCC: <BCC>; Subject: <subject>; Message: <message>; "<attachment>"]

Options:

- **Perform Without Dialog** instructs FileMaker Pro to put the composed email message in the email application's Out box, ready to be sent. If this option is not selected, the composed message is left open in the email application so that it can be reviewed. In Microsoft Outlook Express or Microsoft Entourage on the Macintosh operating system, the new message is left in the Drafts folder.
- **Specify** displays the Specify Mail dialog box, where options for mail can be set. For each of the following options, one can enter text directly, or click > to enter values from an address book, field, or calculation:
  - **Specify Email Addresses** to select an email address from the email application's address book.
  - **Specify Calculation** to create an address (or subject or message text) from a calculation.
  - **Specify Field Name** to choose a single field that contains the desired value. If the Specify Field Name option is used to specify a value for the To:, CC:, or BCC: entries, one can also select Get Values from Every Record in Found Set to specify that all the values from this field in the current found set be used (to address a message to multiple recipients).
- **To** stores the address(es) of the recipient(s).
- **CC** stores the address(es) of the carbon copy recipient(s).
- **BCC** stores the address(es) of the blind carbon copy recipient(s).
- **Subject** indicates the title for the email message.
- **Message** indicates the text of the email message. The message may be typed as text, designated as a field value, or created by a calculation.
- **Attach File** allows you to select a file to send as an attachment to the mail message.

Description:

The Send Mail script steps allow you to send email to one or more recipients via a client-side email application. The following things are necessary to send mail from FileMaker:

- Windows—A [Mail] section in the Win.ini file, and Microsoft Exchange or another email application that is MAPI-compliant, installed and configured to work with an existing email account.
- Mac OS—Mac OS X Mail or Microsoft Entourage installed and configured as the default email application.

To send mail, you must have an Internet connection and a correctly configured email client (see the previous description section for Send Event for configurations). It's not possible to use the Send Mail step to send email directly via an SMTP server.

Examples:

```
Perform Find [Restore]
# Send the same email to everyone in the found set.
Send Mail [To: sContacts::email; Subject: "This is a test email"; Message:
➥"Testing..."]
```

Set Error Capture

Syntax:

Set Error Capture [<On or Off>]

Options:

- **On** suppresses most FileMaker Pro alert messages and some dialog boxes. If the error result is 100 or 803, certain standard file dialog boxes are suppressed, such as the Open dialog box.
- **Off** reenables the alert messages.

Description:

This script step suppresses or enables the FileMaker Pro error dialogs and messages. This provides the developer with the opportunity to write scripts to handle errors in a manner that is customizable and appropriate to the functions being performed. The Get (LastError) function, when used immediately after a script step is executed, gives the code of the error encountered, if an error was encountered.

Examples:

```
Perform Find [Restore]
Go to Record/Request/Page [First]
Open Record/Request
If [ Get(LastError) = 200 or Get(LastError) = 300]
  Show Custom Dialog ["An error has ocurred. This record is locked or you do
➥not have sufficient permission to access it."]
End If
```

Set Field

Syntax:

Set Field [<table::field>; <value or formula>]

Options:

- **Specify Target Field** or **Specify** allows you to specify the field whose contents you want to replace. If no field is specified and a field is already selected in Browse mode or Find mode, that field is used.

- **Specify** defines a calculation, the results of which replace the current contents of the target field.

Description:

This script step replaces the contents of the designated field on the current record with the result of the specified calculation. The result of the calculation must match the field type of the target field, or the results may be unexpected. If the result of the calculation doesn't match the target field type, and the Validate option for the field is set to Always, the field is not set, and an error code is returned (which can be captured with the Get (LastError) function).

When possible, the Set Field script step makes the record active and leaves it active until the record is exited or committed. Scripts that use a series of Set Field script steps should thus group these steps together if possible, so that subsequent Set Field script steps can act on the record without having to lock the record, synchronize data with the server, index the field, and so on, after each individual Set Field script step. Synchronization, indexing, and record-level validation are performed after the record has been exited or committed.

Unlike many other script steps that deal with field contents, Set Field does not require that the field being targeted be on the active layout. This script step should be used in almost every case that a developer wants to programmatically insert data into a database. It does not interfere with a user's Clipboard and is not dependent on layout objects.

Be sure to commit record data as appropriate after using the Set Field step to avoid leaving the record open and encountering a record lock error later.

Examples:

```
Freeze Window
Go to Record/Request/Page [First]
# Give everyone a 10% raise.
Loop
  Set Field [Employee::Salary; Employee::Salary * 1.1]
  Go to Record/Request/Page [Next; Exit after last]
End Loop
Refresh Window
```

Set Multi-User

Syntax:

Set Multi-User [On/On (Hidden)/Off]

Options:

- **On** allows network access via FileMaker Network Sharing. This is the same as enabling Network Sharing and selecting All Users in the FileMaker Network Settings dialog box.

- **On (Hidden)** allows network access but prevents the name of the shared database from appearing in the Open Remote File dialog box. This is the same as enabling Network Sharing and selecting the All Users and Don't Display in Open Remote File dialog options in the FileMaker Network Settings dialog box.
- **Off** disallows network access. This is the same as selecting No Users in the FileMaker Network Settings dialog box.

Description:

This script step allows or disallows network access to the current database. The Hidden option allows a file to be accessed by other files and in dialogs but not through the Open Remote dialog.

If FileMaker's Network Sharing is currently set to Off, both of this script step's On options will also enable network sharing. This could possibly enable sharing access to files other than just the one in which this script step is run. The converse is not true: The Off option to this script step does not also turn off FileMaker Network Sharing. It's sometimes helpful to have Set Multi-User On/Off script steps in all the files of a multifile solution. By means of a single master script in one of the files, all these individual files can execute their Set Multi-User On/Off scripts. This makes it possible to fully enable or fully disable multiuser access to a set of files with just a single script.

Examples:

```
If [Get (MultiUserState) = 0]
  Show Custom Dialog ["Would you like to enable network sharing?"]
  If [Get (LastMessageChoice) = 1]
    Set Multi-User [On]
  End If
End
```

Set Next Serial Value

Syntax:

Set Next Serial Value [<table::field>; <value or formula>]

Options:

- **Specify Target Field** or **Specify** allows you to specify the serial number field on which the script step is to operate. The field specified must be defined as an auto-entry serial number field.
- **Calculated Result**: Click **Specify** to enter the next serial value by hand or create a calculation to determine the next serial value.

Description:

This script step resets the next serial value for an auto-enter serial number field. This is especially useful to ensure that there are no duplicate serial numbers when a large number of records have been imported into a backup clone of a system. It is also useful for importing records when it is not desirable to allow auto-enter calculations. The calculated result always evaluates to a text result. Note this script step can operate on multiple files. If a field in another file is specified, FileMaker Pro attempts to update the serial number for the specified field in the other file. To specify a field in another file, define a relationship to that file and use Specify Target Field to select a field from that file. Also, if a serial number is not strictly a number, special care must be taken to ensure that the newly set serial number matches the format of the existing serial numbers.

This script step does not change any field data. Instead, it changes the definition of the target field that then controls data automatically entered for the next new record. Specifically, it changes the Next Serial Number you see in the Field Options dialog for that field.

Examples:

```
Find All
Set Next Serial Value [Contacts::ContactID; Contacts::MaxContactID + 1]
# Note: MaxContactID would be a summary field defined as the max of the serial field ContactID
```

Set Selection

Syntax:

Set Selection [Start Position: <n>; End Position: <n>]

Options:

- **Go to Target Field** or **Specify** by the check box to specify the field whose contents you want to select.
- **Specify** lets you set the starting and ending positions of a selection, either by entering the start and end numbers directly or by using a calculation to determine them.

Description:

This script step makes it possible to "select" some or all of a field's contents without direct user intervention. It's possible to specify the start and end positions (in terms of numbers of characters) for the new selection. These values may be entered literally or generated as the result of a specified calculation. This step does not operate on container fields. Data that is out of the visible portion of a layout or field is scrolled into view to show the newly selected contents. The start and end values must be integers between 1 and the number of characters in the target field. If the start position number is valid and the end position number is invalid, the selection goes from the start position number to the end of the field contents. If the start position number is invalid and the end position is valid, the cursor (or insertion point) is placed at the specified end position with no characters selected. If neither the start nor the end numbers are valid, the cursor is placed at the end of the field's contents.

You might use this script step to prepare additional operations that act on the current selection, such as cut or copy. You might also choose to transform the selection, for example by removing it and substituting a styled version of the same text.

Set Selection is one of a number of script steps that depend on the presence of specific fields on the current layout. Other script steps with the same limitations include Cut, Copy, and Paste.

Examples:

```
#select first 50 characters
Set Selection [Start Position:1; End Position:50]
```

Set Use System Formats

Syntax:

Set Use System Formats [On/Off]

Options:

- **On**
- **Off**

Description:

FileMaker Pro databases store date, time, and number format preferences. These are taken from the computer on which the database was created. These creation settings may differ from those in use on other machines on which the database may later be opened. This script step can be used to determine whether a file draws its time display settings from those stored in the file, or those in effect on the local machine.

If a FileMaker file is opened on a computer with different locale settings than those stored in the file, the user will see an alert that warns them of the difference. This script step can be used to automatically instruct the system to use the current locale settings when it starts up.

This script step does not change the locale settings stored in the file. It simply instructs FileMaker whether to use the locale settings on the current computer.

Examples:

```
If [Get (SystemLanguage) <> "English"]
   Set Use System Formats [On]
End If
```

Set Variable

Syntax:

Set Variable [<variable name> ([<Repetition number>]); Value: <value or formula>]

Options:

- **Specify** gives you access to a dialog where you can set the following variable options:
  - **Name** is the name you want to assign to the variable. Variables names are prefixed with $ (for local variables) or $$ (for global variables). With no prefix, $ is assumed.
  - **Value** is the value to which the variable will be set. You can specify some text manually, or enter a calculation.
  - **Repetition** is the repetition index you want to set within the variable. The default is 1.

Description:

Set a variable, or a repetition of a variable, with a specific value. If the variable is a local variable, the value will persist within the currently running script and that script only; the variable is not directly available to subscripts and ceases to exist when the script that created it stops executing. A global variable exists across all scripts and calculations, and continues to retain its value even when the script that created it stops executing.

A variable can hold data of any type, including text, number, date, time, timestamp, and container.

It's possible to set discontiguous variable repetitions. You can set $var[3] and $var[33] without defining or setting the other slots from 1 to 33.

Variables don't need to be declared or initialized, as in other languages. They are created implicitly the first time they are referred to.

Variables can also be set from within a Let statement:

```
Let ( [$$counter = $$counter + 1; result = "success]; result)
```

Examples:

```
# use a local variable
Set Variable [$loopCounter; Value: $loopCounter + 1]

# use a global variable
Set Variable [$$lastLoginTime; Value: Status(CurrentTime)]

# use a repetition index
Set Variable [$myArray[3]; Value: "Fred Smith"]

# use a dynamic repetition index
Set Variable [$$array; Value: ""]
Set Variable [$index; Value: 20]
Loop
   Set Variable[$$array[$index]; Value: $index]
   Set Variable [$index; Value: $index – 1]
   Exit Loop If[$index = 0]
End Loop
```

Set Window Title

Syntax:

Set Window Title [Current Window or Name: <name of window>; New Title: <new window name>]

Options:

- **Specify** sets any of the options for this script.
- **Window to Rename** tells FileMaker Pro which window to rename. Current Window renames the current window. You may also specify a different window, either by typing the window name in plain text or deriving the window name from a calculation.
- **Rename Window To** is the new title for the window. Here again, you can enter literal text or click **Specify** to derive a name from the result of a calculation.
- **Current File Only** causes FileMaker to search only within windows based on table occurrences from within the current file.

Description:

Set Window Title sets the name of the current window or the window specified by name.

Current File Only restricts the scope of window management script steps to consider only windows based on the current file.

Window names aren't case sensitive when you select them in this way, so be sure not to rely on case when designating names.

Examples:

```
Set Error Capture [On]
Allow User Abort [Off]
Perform Find [Restore]
Set Window Title [Get(FoundCount) &" Contacts Found"]
```

Set Zoom Level

Syntax:

Set Zoom Level [Lock; 25%. . . 400%/Zoom In/Zoom Out]

Options:

- **Lock** prohibits users from making changes to the zoom level.
- **Specify** lets you select a zoom level as follows:
  - Specific reduction values: 100%, 75%, 50%, or 25%.
  - Specific enlargement values: 150%, 200%, 300%, or 400%.
  - Zoom In: reduces the screen image by one zoom level.
  - Zoom Out: enlarges the screen image by one zoom level.

Description:

Set Zoom Level enlarges or reduces the image on the screen and optionally locks screen scaling. It is equivalent to using the magnification icons beneath the status area.

Examples:

```
Allow User Abort [Off]
Set Error Capture [On]
If[ // the screen resolution is too low// Get (ScreenHeight) < 600]
  Set Zoom Level [Lock; 100%]
Else
  Set Zoom Level [100%]
End
```

Show All Records 

Syntax:

Show All Records

Options:

None

Description:

Displays all the records in the current table and leaves the user on the current record. Show All Records is used in Browse mode or Preview mode. If you perform this step in Find mode or Layout mode, FileMaker Pro switches to Browse mode after the records have been found.

Examples:

```
Allow User Abort [Off]
Set Error Capture [On]
Enter Find Mode [Pause]
Perform Find []
If[Get(CurrentFoundCount) = 0] // no records were found
  Show Message ["No Records Found"; "Sorry, no records that match your find
  ➥criteria were found."]
  Show All Records [ ] // don't leave the user on an empty found set
```

Show Custom Dialog

Syntax:

Show Custom Dialog [<title>; <message text>; Table1::input field 1;. . .]

Options:

- **Specify** displays a dialog box where you can set the custom dialog box title, message text, and buttons, and specify up to three fields to use for input or display.
- **Title** lets you specify the title of the custom dialog box. You can enter literal text or click Specify to create the dialog box title from a calculation.
- **Message** lets you specify the message of the dialog box. You can enter literal text or click Specify to create the message text from a calculation.
- **Button Labels** let you specify how many buttons (up to three) to display in the custom dialog box and labels for these buttons. If you leave a button label blank, the button does not appear in the custom dialog box. If you leave all button titles blank, an OK button displays in the lower-right corner of the custom dialog box.

Input Field options (second tab of dialog):

- **Show input field <n>** activates an input field.
- **Specify** chooses the field for input. Each input area maps to one field.
- **Use Password Character (*)** masks text as it is entered, or as it is displayed from the database. This option obscures data being input into the custom dialog box or being displayed but does not alter the actual data as it is stored in the database.
- **Label** specifies a field label (the text that will identify this input to the user). You can enter literal text or create the label from a calculation.

Description:

Show Custom Dialog enables you to display a custom message dialog box. The dialog box is modal, with from one to three buttons, each with a custom title. The custom message window can also display up to three input fields, each with a custom label. Each of these input fields corresponds to a FileMaker data field. When the window is opened, each input area displays the most recent contents of the corresponding field. When the user closes the window, the button clicked can be determined by the Get (LastMessageChoice) function. A result of 1 represents the first button on the right, whereas 2 and 3 represent the middle and leftmost buttons if they were used. Button 1, the rightmost, is the default. It's also the only button that, when clicked, causes the data from any input fields to be written back to the corresponding FileMaker fields.

If values entered into any input fields don't match the field type of the underlying FileMaker field, a validation error message displays. The user must resolve validation errors before the dialog box can be closed. The fields you specify don't need to appear on the current layout. Show Custom Dialog input fields are independent of layouts, similar to the Set Field script step. And as with the Set Field script step, Show Custom Dialog bypasses the

Allow Entry Into Field formatting option. Data entry via the Show Custom Dialog script step is limited by any access privilege rules that may be in place. In other words, users can't use a custom dialog to edit data in fields that they can't normally change because of access restriction. If you select Run Script With Full Access Privileges, this restriction is lifted. On Windows, you can create a keyboard shortcut for a custom dialog box button by placing an ampersand before the shortcut key letter in the button label. For example, to create a keyboard shortcut D (Alt+D) for a button labeled Done, type the label **&Done**.

Examples:

```
Allow User Abort [ Off ]
Set Error Capture [ On ]
#
Show Custom Dialog [ Title: "Date Range"; Buttons: "OK", "Cancel";
Input #1: reportDate_start, "Start Date";
Input #1: reportDate_end, "End Date";
#
Perform Find []
```

Show Omitted Only

Syntax:

Show Omitted Only

Options:

None

Description:

Show Omitted Only "inverts" the found set to show records that are currently not displayed, and omits records that are currently displayed.

Examples:

```
// reduce found set to zero
Show All Records
Show Omitted Only
```

Show/Hide Status Area

Syntax:

Show/Hide Status Area [Lock; Show/Hide/Toggle]

Options:

- **Lock** prohibits the user from using the status area control button to manually show or hide the status area.

- **Show** tells FileMaker Pro to show the status area.
- **Hide** tells FileMaker Pro to hide the status area.
- **Toggle** switches between showing and hiding the status area (equivalent to clicking the status area control button).

Description:

Show/Hide Status Area allows for control of the display of the status area from scripts.

In databases where it's important to tightly control the user's navigation, it may be desirable to prevent users from using the status area either to page through records or to change layouts.

Examples:

```
Allow User Abort [Off]
Set Error Capture [On]
Go to Layout ["Invoice"]
Show/Hide Status Area [Lock; Show]
#show status area so the user can click continue
Enter Preview Mode [Pause]
Show/Hide Status Area [Lock; Hide]
#shut the status area back down again
Enter Browse Mode [ ]
Go to Layout [Original Layout]
```

Show/Hide Text Ruler 

Syntax:

Show/Hide Text Ruler [Show/Hide/Toggle]

Options:

- **Show** tells FileMaker Pro to show the text ruler.
- **Hide** tells FileMaker Pro to hide the text ruler.
- **Toggle** switches between showing and hiding the text ruler.

Description:

Hides or shows the text ruler. Choosing the Toggle option switches the current state of the ruler. The Text Ruler is used with text fields, and also to aid in design in Layout mode. It can be used to set tabs and indents for a text area. Hiding the text ruler is sometimes required to save screen space. Unless you have disabled access to menus, users generally can enable the text rulers by choosing View, Text Ruler, and it may later be desirable to disable the rulers again to save room.

Examples:

```
Allow User Abort [Off]
Set Error Capture [On]
If[ // the screen resolution to too low// Get (ScreenHeight) < 600]
  Show/Hide Text Ruler [Hide]
End
```

Sort Records

Syntax:

Sort Records [Restore; No dialog]

Options:

- **Perform Without Dialog** prevents display of a dialog box that lets the user enter a different set of sort instructions.
- **Specify Sort Order** or click the **Specify** button to create a sort order and store it with the script step. When Specify Sort Order is not selected, FileMaker Pro uses the most recently executed sort instructions.

Description:

Sort Records sorts the records in the current found set according to specified criteria. Be sure to perform any operations that might change the found set before calling Sort Records. If you sort a repeating field, FileMaker Pro sorts on only the first entry in that field. Sort criteria are saved with individual Sort Record script steps, so any number of sorts can be saved with a single script.

Note that saved sort criteria are relative to the current table context. If the table Contact was the active table when the sort criteria were entered, and fields from Contact are used in the sort order, that table must be active when the sort is executed. If your sort step makes field references that are not valid at the time the step is executed, the invalid field references are ignored. Table context is controlled by the current layout; to change table context, navigate to a layout that is used by the table in question.

The option to display a dialog box is compatible with Instant Web Publishing but is not compatible with Custom Web Publishing.

Examples:

```
Allow User Abort [Off]
Set Error Capture [On]
Perform Find [Restore] // find overdue invoices
Sort [Restore] // sort by due date and customer
Go to Layout ["Invoice"]
Enter Preview Mode [Pause]
Enter Browse Mode [ ]
Go to Layout [Original Layout]
Unsort
```

Speak

Syntax:

Speak [<text to be spoken>]

Options:

- **Specify** displays the Speak Options dialog box, where you can set the following options.

  You can enter the text to be spoken directly by hand, or draw the text from a calculation.
- **Use Voice** lets you select from the various voices available on your computer.
- **Wait for Speech Completion Before Continuing** tells FileMaker Pro to wait until the speech is completed before continuing with the next script step. If you leave this option unchecked, the script continues while the text is being spoken.

Description:

Speaks the specified text. You can specify which voice synthesizer to use and whether FileMaker Pro is to wait for the speech to be completed before continuing with the next script step. On a computer without speech capabilities, the script can still be edited, but only the default voice synthesizer is available. Speak script steps are not executed when the script is run on a computer without speech capability.

Examples:

```
Speak ["Hello"]
Speak[Get(CurrentDate)]
```

Spelling Options

Syntax:

Spelling Options

Options:

None

Description:

Opens the Spelling tab of the File Options dialog box. Use this script step to open the File Options dialog box for users if you have restricted their access to FileMaker Pro menus.

Examples:

```
# a button on a layout calls this script step directly:
Spelling Options
```

Undo

Syntax:

Undo

Options:

None

Description:

Undo acts the same as choosing Undo from the edit menu: The most recent edits to the record are reversed.

Examples:

```
Undo
```

Unsort Records 

Syntax:

Unsort Records

Options:

None

Description:

Unsort Records restores the found set to its natural order (the order in which records were created).

Examples:

```
Allow User Abort [Off]
Set Error Capture [On]
Enter Browse Mode []
Unsort Records
Go to Record/Request/Page [First]
```

Update Link

Syntax:

Update Link [<table::field>]

Options:

- **Go to Target Field** or **Specify** allows you to specify the field to be updated.

Description:

Update Link updates the OLE link in the specified container field. If the field does not contain an OLE link, Update Link returns an error. Both manual and automatic links are updated.

Examples:

```
Set Error Capture [On]
Allow User Abort [Off]
Update Link [Contact::Resume]
If [//an error occured// Get(LastError)]
 Show Message ["An error occurred updating the resume link"]
End If
```

View As

Syntax:

View As [Form/List/Table/Cycle]

Options:

- **View As Form** tells FileMaker Pro to display records page by page on the current layout, so that only one record at a time is shown.
- **View As List** tells FileMaker Pro to display records as records in a list, so that the user can see multiple records at once in a list.
- **View As Table** tells FileMaker Pro to display the records onscreen in a spreadsheetlike grid.
- **Cycle** switches from the current view type to the next type.

Description:

View As sets the view mode for the current layout. Note that Layout Setup can be used to limit which views are accessible via the View menu, but the View As script step can override those settings and enable you to view a layout in any of the three styles.

Examples:

```
Set Error Capture [On]
Allow User Abort [Off]
Go to Layout ["Contact List"]
View As [View As List
```

PART V

FileMaker Connectivity

CHAPTER 14

FileMaker XML Reference

About FileMaker and XML

XML (along with its companion technology, XSLT) is one of the driving technologies behind Custom Web Publishing (CWP) in FileMaker. FileMaker Server Advanced can serve out FileMaker data as XML for use in applications that require XML data. It can also transform the XML data extracted, using XSLT stylesheets, to output data in a variety of formats, such as HTML.

This section is a reference guide to FileMaker XML syntax. We cover the following areas:

- URL syntax for accessing FileMaker data over the Web
- Syntax of the various FileMaker XML grammars
- FileMaker URL query commands and query string parameters
- Important XML namespaces for use with Custom Web Publishing

We do not cover in detail all the XSLT extension functions available in Custom Web Publishing.

URL Syntax for Web Access to FileMaker Data

FileMaker can provide data in XML format in two ways: via the Export as XML feature in the regular FileMaker client, and via URL-based requests sent directly to databases hosted via FileMaker Server Advanced.

A URL designed to extract data from FileMaker Server Advanced has two components: a resource name and a query string. This section demonstrates the correct syntax for resource names within a URL. The query string is made up of potentially many commands and parameters: Subsequent sections discuss those in more detail.

URL Syntax for XML Access

To extract data from FileMaker Server Advanced in pure XML format, a URL of the following form is used:

```
<protocol>://<host>[:<port>]/fmi/xml/<grammar>.xml?<query string>
```

- <protocol> is either http (for regular HTTP access) or https (for secure HTTP access).
- <host> is the hostname or the IP address of the web server that's been configured with FileMaker Server Advanced. (Note that if the web server is on a different machine than the FileMaker Server, it's the address of the web server that must be used here, not that of the FileMaker Server machine.)
- <port> need only be specified if the web server has been configured to run on a port other than the default for the specified protocol (80 for HTTP, 443 for HTTPS).
- <grammar> is the name of one of the four valid FileMaker XML grammars, discussed in the next section.
- <query string> is a query string composed of some number of query parameters in combination with a query command. Specifics are discussed in upcoming sections.

Example:

```
http://my.filemakerserver.net:8080/fmi/xml/fmresultset.xml?-dbnames
```

This query will access a server running on port 8080 on the machine my.filemakerserver.net, and will request a list of all databases available for XML access on that server, with the results returned in the fmresultset grammar.

URL Syntax for Access to Container Objects

FileMaker Server Advanced has a special URL syntax for accessing data in container fields via the Web. Such a request causes the container data to be returned directly (much like clicking on a PDF link in a web page). The exact mechanism depends on whether the container data is stored directly in the database, or stored by reference. To extract container data stored directly in a FileMaker database, a URL of the following form is used:

```
<protocol>://<host>[:<port>]/fmi/xml/cnt/data.<extension>?<query string>
```

- <protocol>, <host>, <port>, and <query string> are as described in the previous section.
- <extension> is the file type extension for the container data being fetched (.jpg, .txt, and the like). This extension allows the web server to set the MIME type of the data correctly.

The query string must contain a –field query parameter with a fully qualified field name, meaning it must contain a repetition index number reference even if the field is not a repeating field.

Example:

```
http://my.filemakerserver.net/fmi/xml/cnt/data.gif?-db=Customers&-lay=web_search&-
field=photo[1]&-recid=303
```

This URL extracts container data from a specific field (called photo), from the record with recid 303. Even though photo is not a repeating field, the syntax photo[1] is still necessary. The web server returns this container data as GIF data, assuming the .gif suffix is correctly mapped to the GIF MIME type on the server.

For information on how to manage container data when the container data is stored only by reference, see the FileMaker Server Custom Web Publishing documentation.

URL Syntax for XSLT Access

When extracting XML data from FileMaker Server Advanced, it's also possible to apply an XSLT stylesheet to transform the XML into something else, such as an HTML page. The syntax for XSLT access is as follows:

```
<protocol>://<host>[:<port>]/fmi/xsl/<path>/<stylesheet>.xsl?<query string>
```

- <protocol>, <host>, <port>, and <query string> are as described in the previous sections.
- The <path> element is optional. Without it, the Web Publishing Engine looks for the specified stylesheet within the xslt-template-files directory on the web server. If you want to create additional directory structures within the xslt-template-files folder, the relative path to the stylesheet must be specified here. (You can't use stylesheets from outside the top level of the xslt-template-files directory.)
- <stylesheet> is the name of the stylesheet that will be applied to the XML data.

Example:

```
http://my.filemakerserver.net/fmi/xsl/customer-files/customer_list.xsl?-db=Customer&-
lay=list&-max=50&-findall
```

FileMaker XML Grammars

FileMaker can publish data in any of four XML *grammars*. Note that the grammar names are case-sensitive.

- FMPXMLRESULT—This grammar is available either via CWP or via Export as XML. It's a complete data export grammar but can be difficult to parse or read.

- FMPDSORESULT—Also a complete data export grammar, available via either CWP or export, but this grammar has been deprecated, and we recommend that you do not use it.
- fmresultset—This grammar was introduced with FileMaker Server 7 Advanced and is in some sense the "best" data export grammar, being rather easier to parse and read than FMPXMLRESULT. We recommend you use it where possible. It is available only via CWP using FileMaker Server Advanced, not via Export as XML.
- FMPXMLLAYOUT—A specialized grammar used for extracting information about a FileMaker layout. Only available via CWP.

Listings 14.1 through 14.4 contain a sample of each grammar.

Listing 14.1 FMPXMLRESULT

```
<?xml version="1.0" encoding="UTF-8" standalone="no"?>
<!DOCTYPE FMPXMLRESULT PUBLIC "-//FMI//DTD FMPXMLRESULT//EN"
➥"/fmi/xml/FMPXMLRESULT.dtd">
<FMPXMLRESULT xmlns="http://www.filemaker.com/fmpxmlresult">
 <ERRORCODE>0</ERRORCODE>
 <PRODUCT BUILD="4/11/2007" NAME="FileMaker Web Publishing Engine"
➥VERSION="9.0.1.54"/>
➥ <DATABASE DATEFORMAT="MM/dd/yyyy" LAYOUT="house_web" NAME="House"
RECORDS="14" IMEFORMAT="HH:mm:ss"/>
 <METADATA>
  <FIELD EMPTYOK="YES" MAXREPEAT="1" NAME="Address" TYPE="TEXT"/>
  <FIELD EMPTYOK="YES" MAXREPEAT="1" NAME="City" TYPE="TEXT"/>
  <FIELD EMPTYOK="YES" MAXREPEAT="1" NAME="State" TYPE="TEXT"/>
  <FIELD EMPTYOK="YES" MAXREPEAT="1" NAME="PostalCode" TYPE="TEXT"/>
  <FIELD EMPTYOK="YES" MAXREPEAT="1" NAME="LotSizeAcres" TYPE="NUMBER"/>
  <FIELD EMPTYOK="YES" MAXREPEAT="1" NAME="CountBedrooms" TYPE="NUMBER"/>
  <FIELD EMPTYOK="YES" MAXREPEAT="1" NAME="AskingPrice" TYPE="NUMBER"/>
 </METADATA>
 <RESULTSET FOUND="14">
  <ROW MODID="1" RECORDID="1">
   <COL>
    <DATA>12 Oak Lane</DATA>
   </COL>
   <COL>
    <DATA>Morten</DATA>
   </COL>
   <COL>
```

Listing 14.1 Continued

```
      <DATA>MO</DATA>
    </COL>
    <COL>
      <DATA>14231</DATA>
    </COL>
    <COL>
      <DATA>.65</DATA>
    </COL>
    <COL>
      <DATA>3</DATA>
    </COL>
    <COL>
      <DATA>265000</DATA>
    </COL>
  </ROW>
 </RESULTSET>
</FMPXMLRESULT>
```

Listing 14.2 FMPDSORESULT

```
<?xml version="1.0" encoding="UTF-8" standalone="no"?>
<!--This grammar has been deprecated - use fmresultset or FMPXMLRESULT
➥instead-->
<!--DOCTYPE FMPDSORESULT SYSTEM "/fmi/xml/FMPDSORESULT.dtd?-db=House&-
➥ilay=house_web"-->
➥<FMPDSORESULT xmlns="http://www.filemaker.com/fmpdsoresult">
 <ERRORCODE>0</ERRORCODE>
 <DATABASE>House</DATABASE>
 <LAYOUT>house_web</LAYOUT>
 <ROW MODID="1" RECORDID="1">
  <Address>12 Oak Lane</Address>
  <City>Morten</City>
  <State>MO</State>
  <PostalCode>14231</PostalCode>
  <LotSizeAcres>.65</LotSizeAcres>
  <CountBedrooms>3</CountBedrooms>
  <AskingPrice>265000</AskingPrice>
 </ROW>
</FMPDSORESULT>
```

Listing 14.3 fmresultset

```
<?xml version="1.0" encoding="UTF-8" standalone="no"?>
<!DOCTYPE fmresultset PUBLIC "-//FMI//DTD fmresultset//EN" "/fmi/xml/fmresultset.dtd">
<fmresultset xmlns="http://www.filemaker.com/xml/fmresultset" version="1.0">
 <error code="0"/>
 <product build="04/11/2007" name="FileMaker Web Publishing Engine" version="9.0.1.54"/>
 <datasource database="House" date-format="MM/dd/yyyy" layout="house_web "table="House"
➥time-format="HH:mm:ss" timestamp-format="MM/dd/yyyy HH:mm:ss" total-count="14"/>
 <metadata>
  <field-definition auto-enter="no" global="no" max-repeat="1" name="Address" not-empty="no"
➥result="text" type="normal"/>
  <field-definition auto-enter="no" global="no" max-repeat="1" name="City" not-empty="no"
➥result="text" type="normal"/>
  <field-definition auto-enter="no" global="no" max-repeat="1" name="State" not-empty="no"
➥result="text" type="normal"/>
  <field-definition auto-enter="no" global="no" max-repeat="1"
➥name="PostalCode" not-empty="no" result="text" type="normal"/>
  <field-definition auto-enter="no" global="no" max-repeat="1"
➥name="LotSizeAcres" not-empty="no" result="number" type="normal"/>
  <field-definition auto-enter="no" global="no" max-repeat="1"
➥name="CountBedrooms" not-empty="no" result="number" type="normal"/>
  <field-definition auto-enter="no" global="no" max-repeat="1"
➥name="AskingPrice" not-empty="no" result="number" type="normal"/>
 </metadata>
 <resultset count="14" fetch-size="1">
  <record mod-id="1" record-id="1">
   <field name="Address">
    <data>12 Oak Lane</data>
   </field>
   <field name="City">
    <data>Morten</data>
   </field>
   <field name="State">
    <data>MO</data>
   </field>
   <field name="PostalCode">
    <data>14231</data>
   </field>
   <field name="LotSizeAcres">
    <data>.65</data>
```

Listing 14.3 Continued

```
    </field>
    <field name="CountBedrooms">
      <data>3</data>
    </field>
    <field name="AskingPrice">
      <data>265000</data>
    </field>
  </record>
 </resultset>
</fmresultset>
```

Listing 14.4 FMPXMLLAYOUT

```
<?xml version="1.0" encoding="UTF-8" standalone="no"?>
<!DOCTYPE FMPXMLLAYOUT PUBLIC "-//FMI//DTD FMPXMLLAYOUT//EN"
➥"/fmi/xml/FMPXMLLAYOUT.dtd">
<FMPXMLLAYOUT xmlns="http://www.filemaker.com/fmpxmllayout">
 <ERRORCODE>0</ERRORCODE>
 <PRODUCT BUILD="04/11/2007" NAME="FileMaker Web Publishing Engine"
➥VERSION="9.0.1.54"/>
 <LAYOUT DATABASE="House" NAME="house_web">
  <FIELD NAME="Address">
   <STYLE TYPE="EDITTEXT" VALUELIST=""/>
  </FIELD>
  <FIELD NAME="City">
   <STYLE TYPE="EDITTEXT" VALUELIST=""/>
  </FIELD>
  <FIELD NAME="State">
   <STYLE TYPE="EDITTEXT" VALUELIST=""/>
  </FIELD>
  <FIELD NAME="PostalCode">
   <STYLE TYPE="EDITTEXT" VALUELIST=""/>
  </FIELD>
  <FIELD NAME="LotSizeAcres">
   <STYLE TYPE="EDITTEXT" VALUELIST=""/>
  </FIELD>
  <FIELD NAME="CountBedrooms">
   <STYLE TYPE="EDITTEXT" VALUELIST=""/>
  </FIELD>
```

Listing 14.4 Continued

```
  <FIELD NAME="AskingPrice">
   <STYLE TYPE="EDITTEXT" VALUELIST=""/>
  </FIELD>
 </LAYOUT>
 <VALUELISTS/>
</FMPXMLLAYOUT>
```

Query Parameters for XML/XSLT URL Requests

The FileMaker Web Publishing Engine delivers XML data in response to specially formatted URLs. The specific details of the request are contained in the *query string*, which is a specific portion of the URL. For example, the query string is highlighted in the following URL:

http://my.filemakerserver.net/fmi/xsl/customer-files/customer_list.xsl?**-db=Customer&-lay=list&-max=50&-findall**

The query string consists of a series of *name-value pairs*, in the form of name=value, separated by ampersands, and following a question mark within the URL.

Generally, a query string intended for the Web Publishing Engine consists of a single *query command*, representing the type of request being made, supported by additional query parameters that add specificity to the request. Continuing with the previous example, the request is –findall (find all records). Additional query parameters specify the database, the layout, and the maximum number of records to be returned.

Please note the following important points about URL queries:

- Each URL query string must contain one and only one query command (though it may contain many additional query parameters).
- Query commands and query parameters begin with a hyphen (-). Omitting the hyphen causes an error.
- A query command is expressed as a plain value, not as a name-value pair. Any supplied value will be ignored. (So you can say …&-findall=somevalue, but the =somevalue will be ignored.)
- The names of FileMaker fields, when included in the URL for purposes of searching, or for creating or editing records, do *not* require a hyphen.
- Most query commands have a minimum set of query parameters that *must* also be provided in the URL. These are noted in Tables 14.1 and 14.2.

Query Commands

This section lists the possible query commands. If the command requires certain specific additional parameters, those are listed in Table 14.1.

Table 14.1 Parameters for Query Commands

Command	Parameters Required	Description
-dbnames	None	Return a list of all databases on the given server that are enabled for XML or XSLT publishing.
http://my.server.com/fmi/xml/fmresultset.xml?-dbnames		
-delete	-db, -lay, -recid	Delete the record with the specified record ID from the specified database. (The affected table is determined by the specified layout.)
http://my.server.com/fmi/xml/fmresultset.xml?-db=Customer&-lay=web&-recid=303&-delete		
-dup	-db, -lay, -recid	Duplicate the record with the specified record ID from the specified database. (The affected table is determined by the specified layout.)
http://my.server.com/fmi/xml/fmresultset.xml?-db=Customer&-lay=web&-recid=303&-dup		
-edit	-db, -lay, -recid, field name(s)	Edit the record with the specified record ID from the specified database. (The affected table is determined by the specified layout.) Field names and associated field values determine what data gets written into the record.
http://my.server.com/fmi/xml/fmresultset.xml?-dbCustomer&-lay=web&-recid=303&name_first=Sarah&-edit		
-find	-db, -lay, field name(s)	Find a record in the specified database and table, with search criteria determined by the supplied field data.
http://my.server.com/fmi/xml/fmresultset.xml?-db=Customer&-lay=web&name_last=Smith&-find		
-findall	-db, –lay	Find all records in the specified database and table.
http://my.server.com/fmi/xml/fmresultset.xml?-db=Customer&-lay=web&-findall		
-findany	-db, -lay	Find a random record in the specified database and table.
http://my.server.com/fmi/xml/fmresultset.xml?-db=Customer&-lay=web&-findany		
-layoutnames	-db	Return a list of all layout names from the specified database.
http://my.server.com/fmi/xml/fmresultset.xml?-db=Customer&-layoutnames		
-new	-db, -lay	Create a new record in the specified database and table. If field names and field values are also supplied, these will create specific data values in the new record.
http://my.server.com/fmi/xml/fmresultset.xml?-db=Customer&-lay=web&name_first=Kai&name_last=Love&-new		

Table 14.1 Continued

Command	Parameters Required	Description
-process	-grammar	(XSLT only) This command instructs the Web Publishing Engine to process a stylesheet without performing any database transactions.
http://my.server.com/fmi/xsl/stylesheet.xsl?-grammar=fmresultset&-process		
-scriptnames	-db	Return a list of the names of all scripts in the specified database.
http://my.server.com/fmi/xml/fmresultset.xml?-db=Customer&-scriptnames		
-view	-db, -lay	Used with the FMPXMLLAYOUT grammar, -view retrieves layout information in the FMPXMLLAYOUT format. Used with the other grammars, it retrieves the database metadata and an empty result set.
http://my.server.com/fmi/xml/FMPXMLLAYOUT.xml?-db=Customer&-lay=web&-view		

Query Parameters

Each XML command requires one or more specific parameters, as shown in Table 14.1. Table 14.2 discusses each parameter in greater detail.

Table 14.2 Parameters

Parameter Name	Required Value(s)	Description
-db	Name of a database (without file extension)	Specify a database as a target of the URL command. Most commands require this parameter.
http://my.server.com/fmi/xml/fmresultset.xml?-db=Customer&-lay=web&name_first=Kai&name_last=Love&-new		
-encoding	US-ASCII, ISO-8859-1, ISO-8859-15, ISO-2022-JP, Shift_JIS, UTF-8	(XSLT only) Specify the text encoding for an XSLT request. This governs only the encoding of the request, not of the output page. Encoding for the output page is set within an XSL stylesheet using the encoding attribute of an <xml:output> element.
http://my.server.com/fmi/xsl/stylesheet.xsl?-grammar=fmresultset&-db=Company&-lay=detail&-encoding=ISO-8859-1&name=Beech%20Street&-new		
-field	Name of a container field	Specify a container field from which to extract data.
http://my.filemakerserver.net:8080/fmi/xml/cnt/data.tiff?-db=Customers&-lay=web_search&-field=photo[1]&-recid=303		

Parameter Required

Name	Value(s)	Description
<fieldname>	Name of a noncontainer field	Used to specify search parameters (with a –find command) or data values to be inserted (with the –edit and –new commands).
http://my.server.com/fmi/xml/fmresultset.xml?-db=Customer&-lay=web&name_first=Kai&name_last=Love&-new		
<fieldname>.op =	eq (equals) cn (contains) bw (begins with) ew (ends with) gt (greater than) gte (greater than or equal) lt (less than) lte (less than or equal) neq (not equal)	Specify a search comparison operator to use when searching on <fieldname>. Used with the –find command.
http://my.server.com/fmi/xml/fmresultset.xml?-db=Agent&-lay=web&commission=.3&commission.op=gte&-find		
-grammar	One of the four FileMaker XML grammars	(XSLT only) Specify the grammar in which the XML data should be passed to the XSL stylesheet.
http://my.server.com/fmi/xslstylesheet.xsl?-grammar=fmresultset&-process		
-lay	Name of a layout in the database specified by the –db parameter	Required by many commands. Note that the choice of layout also governs which table the command is performed against.
http://my.server.com/fmi/xml/fmresultsetxml?-db=Customer&-lay=web&name_first=Kai&name_last=Love&-new		
-lay.response	Name of a layout in the database specified by the –db parameter	You might want to return data from an alternate layout. For example, you might want to search on a particular field (in which case that field must be present on the layout specified by –lay), but not return that field in the result set (in which case you would return XML from the layout named in –lay.response, which would not contain the field in question).
http://my.server.com/fmi/xml/fmresultset.xml?-db=Customer&-lay=web&-lay.response=webresponse&-findall		
-lop	and or or	Specifies whether the criteria in a –find request represent an "and" search or an "or" search. (The default is "and").
http://my.server.com/fmi/xml/fmresultset.xml?-db=Customer&-lay=web&name_last=Smythe&hair_color=red&-lop=or&-find		
-max	A positive number, or the value "all"	For a –find or –findall request, specifies how many records to return. The default number of records returned is 50.
http://my.server.com/fmi/xml/fmresultset.xml?-db=Customer&-lay=web&name_last=Smythe&hair_color=red&-max=25&-find		

Table 14.2 Continued

Parameter Name	Required Value(s)	Description
-modid	A FileMaker modification ID	Use with the –edit command to specify a valid modification ID for the record being updated. If the –modid value does not match the target record's modification ID, the edit will be rejected. This is to ensure that the record has not been modified by someone else since the time it was fetched for a web user.
http://my.server.com/fmi/xml/fmresultset.xml?-db=Customer&-lay=web&name_last=Smythe&recid=10003&-modid13&-edit		
-recid	A FileMaker record ID	The –edit, -dup, and –delete commands need to know the ID of a specific record on which to operate. Generally this record ID will be extracted from the result of a previous request. The –recid parameter can also be used with the –find command.
http://my.server.com/fmi/xml/fmresultset.xml?-db=Customer&-lay=web&name_last=Smythe&recid=10003&-modid=13&-edit		
-script	The name of a script in the database specified by the –db parameter	Specifies a script to be run *after* the query and any sorting are performed. Make sure you understand the issue of web compatibility for scripts when using this parameter.
http://my.server.com/fmi/xml/fmresultset.xml?-db=Customer&-lay=web&-lay.response=web_response&-script=OmitDuplicates&-findall		
-script.param	Value of a script parameter to be passed to the script named in –script	The script named in –script may be passed a script parameter.
http://my.server.com/fmi/xml/fmresultset.xml?-db=Customer&-lay=web&-lay.response=web_response&-script=Omit&-script.param=3&-find		
-script.prefind	The name of a script in the database specified by the –db parameter	Specifies a script to be run *before* the specified query is run and sorted.
http://my.server.com/fmi/xml/fmresultset.xml?-db=Customer&-lay=web&-lay.response=web_response&-script.prefind=Omit&-script.prefind.param=3&-find		
-script.prefind.param	Value of a script parameter to be passed to the script named in –script.prefind	The script named in –script.prefind may be passed a script parameter.
http://my.server.com/fmi/xml/fmresultset.xml?-db=Customer&-lay=web&-lay.response=web_response&-script.prefind=Omit&-script.prefind.param=3&-find		
-script.presort	The name of a script in the database specified by the –db parameter	Specifies a script to be run *after* the specified query is run and *before* the results are sorted.
http://my.server.com/fmi/xml/fmresultset.xml?-db=Customer&-lay=web&-lay.response=web_response&-script.presort=Omit&-script.presort.param=3&-find		

Parameter Name	Required Value(s)	Description
-script.presort. param	Value of a script parameter to be passed to the script named in –script.presort	The script named in –script.presort may be passed a script parameter.
http://my.server.com/fmi/xml/fmresultset.xml?-db=Customer&-layweb&-lay. response=web_response&-script.presort=Omit&-script.presort.param=3&-find		
-skip	A number of records to skip	Based on this value, the Web Publishing Engine will skip some of the records normally returned by a query and begin returning records from later in the result set.
http://my.server.com/fmi/xml/fmresultset.xml?-db=Customer&-lay=web&-lay.response= web_response&-skip=20&-max=25&-find		
-sortfield. precedence	Name of a field to sort on, along with a sort precedence from 1 to 9	Using the values –sortfield.1 through –sortfield.9, it's possible to specify up to nine fields on which to sort. The precedence value is mandatory, even for a single sort criterion.
http://my.server.com/fmi/xml/fmresultset.xml?-db=Customer&-lay=web&-lay.response= web_response&-skip=20&-max=25&sortfield.1=name&-find		
-sortorder. precedence	ascend, descend, or a value list name	Specify a sort order for a specific sort field.
http://my.server.com/fmi/xml/fmresultset.xml?-db=Customer&-lay=web&-lay.response= web_response&-skip=20&-max=25&sortfield.1=name&-sortorder.1=descend&-find		
-stylehref	Path to a client-side stylesheet	This will cause the output document to contain XML processing instructions that link to a CSS or XSLT stylesheet. The stylesheet name must end in .css or .xsl. Used in conjunction with –styletype.
http://my.server.com/fmi/xsl/stylesheet.xsl?-grammar=fmresultset&-stylehref=/stylesheets/ display.css&-styletype=text/css&-process		
-styletype	text/css or text/xsl	Used in conjunction with –stylehref, specifies the MIME type of an associated client-side stylesheet.
http://my.server.com/fmi/xsl/stylesheet.xsl?-grammar=fmresultset&-stylehref=/ stylesheets/display.css&-styletype=text/css&-process		
-token. <token-name>	Any name for a token, plus the specific value to be assigned to the token of that name	(XSLT only) Tokens provide a means to pass information from one stylesheet to the next without using other session mechanisms.

http://my.server.com/fmi/xsl/stylesheet.xsl?-grammar=fmresultset&-token.name=Fred&-process

FileMaker XML and XSLT Namespaces

FileMaker's XML and XSLT publishing technologies use a number of XML namespaces. (We assume that if you're referring to this section, the concept of an XML namespace is a familiar one.) Each of the four XML grammars has its own namespace. In addition, a number of the XSLT features of Custom Web Publishing have their own namespaces as well. You generally need to concern yourself with namespaces only if you are writing XSLT stylesheets that transform FileMaker XML data.

Table 14.3 lists each namespace, along with its significance, and the conventional namespace prefix used to abbreviate it. The prefix is "conventional" in the sense that, in creating a stylesheet, you may choose any prefix you want for a namespace, but the ones listed in Table 14.3 are those used by FileMaker, Inc., in the official documentation.

Table 14.3 FileMaker XML Namespaces

Usage	Namespace	Prefix
FMPXMLRESULT grammar	http://www.filemaker.com/fmpxmlresult	fmp
FMPDSORESULT grammar	http://www.filemaker.com/fmpdsoresult	(*)
fmresultset grammar	http://www.filemaker.com/xml/fmresultset	fmrs
FMPXMLLAYOUT grammar	http://www.filemaker.com/fmpxmllayout	fml
Request query grammar	http://www.filemaker.com/xml/query	fmq
FileMaker XSLT extension functions	xalan://com.fmi.xslt.ExtensionFunctions	fmxslt

*Because the FMPDSORESULT grammar is deprecated, FileMaker makes no recommendation for a default prefix.

CHAPTER 15

FileMaker API for PHP

About the FileMaker API for PHP

The FileMaker API for PHP is a set of PHP libraries intended to allow developers to use the popular web development language PHP to access data in a FileMaker database. The API is packaged with FileMaker Server Advanced and may also be downloaded independently at http://www.filemaker.com/developers/resources/php/.

If you're an experienced PHP developer, there are a few things to note about FileMaker's PHP API:

- The API is based on an object-oriented design. You'll need some familiarity with object-oriented programming and design methods to make the most sense of it.
- Unlike much PHP code, the FileMaker API is not open source. Although you can inspect some of the PHP code in the library, key parts of the code are obscured. So you can't modify the base code directly, though you could write your own libraries that extend or incorporate the API.
- The FileMaker API for PHP does not directly expose any of the properties of its classes. All interactions with the API are performed via class methods.

Class Overview

The following UML-style diagram (see Figure 15.1) gives an overview of all the classes in the FileMaker API for PHP.

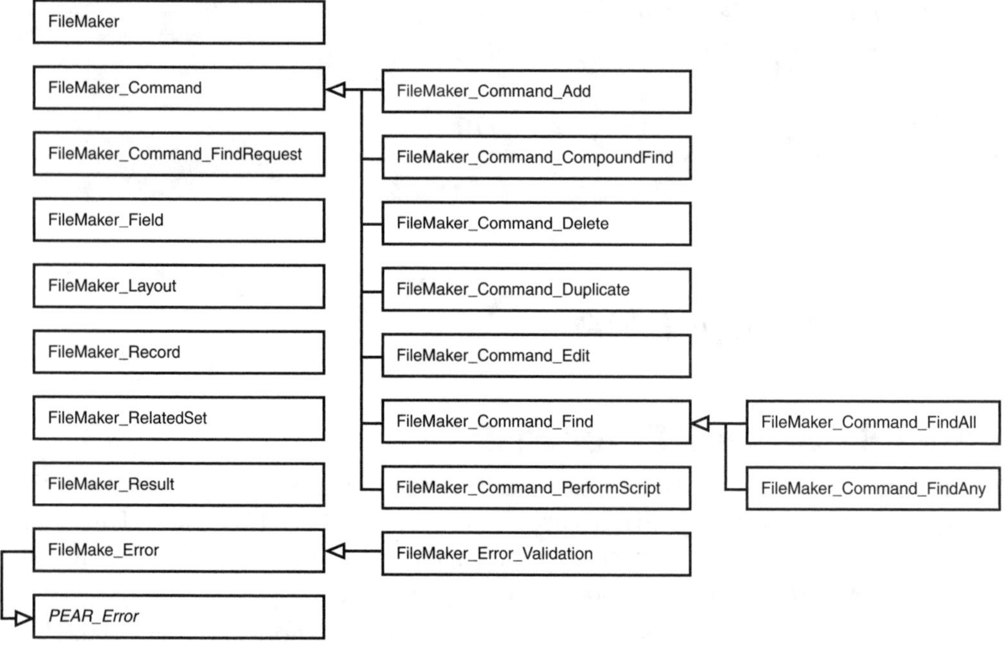

Figure 15.1

The FileMaker API for PHP consists of a set of related classes.

Classes and Methods

The following sections give an overview of each of the classes in the FileMaker API for PHP, as well as a listing of the method signatures for each class.

Static methods are denoted by a method name preceded by a class name and a double colon. For example, the static FileMaker class method isError is written as FileMaker::isError, which would also be the necessary syntax in PHP.

FileMaker

The FileMaker class is a bit of a hybrid class. It is responsible for managing general information about a FileMaker Server database connection and is also a *factory class* that's responsible for creating an instance of the various command classes (FileMaker_Command and its subclasses).

getAPIVersion

Syntax:

FileMaker::getAPIVersion()

Data type returned: string

Description:

Returns the current version of the FileMaker API for PHP.

getMinServerVersion

Syntax:

FileMaker::getMinServerVersion()

Data type returned: string

Description:

Returns the minimum version of FileMaker Server Advanced that will work with this version of the API.

isError

Syntax:

FileMaker::isError(mixed $variable)

Data type returned: boolean

Description:

Returns a boolean indicating whether $variable is an object of type FileMaker_Error.

FileMaker

Syntax:

new FileMaker([string $database], [string $hostspec], [string $username], [string $password])

Data type returned: FileMaker object

Description:

FileMaker object constructor. Returns a new instance of the FileMaker class.

createRecord

Syntax:

createRecord(string $layout, [array $fieldValues])

Data type returned: FileMaker_Record object

Description:

Returns a new FileMaker_Record object. Calling this method does not create a new database record. To do so, it's necessary to call the new FileMaker_Record object's commit() method.

getContainerData

Syntax:

getContainerData(string $url)

Data type returned: string

Description:

Returns the field data from a container field specified by $url.

getLayout

Syntax:

getLayout(string $layout)

Data type returned: FileMaker_Layout

Description:

Returns a FileMaker_Layout object corresponding to the layout specified by $layout, or a FileMaker_Error object if the specified layout can't be found.

getProperties

Syntax:

getProperties()

Data type returned: array

Description:

Returns an associative array containing entries for all properties of the current FileMaker object. Because the API in general doesn't allow direct inspection or manipulation of object properties, this method can be useful for gathering debugging information.

getProperty

Syntax:

getProperty(string $prop)

Data type returned: string

Description:

Returns a string corresponding to the value of a single named FileMaker property, $prop. (It may help to first call getProperties() to learn the names of all available properties.)

getRecordById

Syntax:

getRecordById(string $layout, integer $recordID)

Data type returned: FileMaker_Record

Description:

Returns a FileMaker_Record object corresponding to the record with a record ID of $recordID, from the table specified by $layout. If there's a problem accessing that record, getRecordById() returns a FileMaker_Error object.

listDatabases

Syntax:

listDatabases()

Data type returned: array

Description:

Returns an array containing the names of all databases known to this FileMaker object, or returns a FileMaker_Error object if the request fails.

listLayouts

Syntax:

listLayouts()

Data type returned: array

Description:

Returns an array containing the names of all layouts within the current database, or returns a FileMaker_Error object if the request fails.

listScripts

Syntax:

listScripts()

Data type returned: array

Description:

Returns an array containing the names of all scripts within the current database, or returns a FileMaker_Error object if the request fails.

Note

The next 10 methods are known as *factory methods* because their chief purpose is to create a new instance of some class. These functions all create new instances of various FileMaker command classes and subclasses. It's important to recognize that creating these objects will *not* result in the specified commands actually being executed. The command will not be executed until the command object's execute() method is called.

newAddCommand

Syntax:

newAddCommand(string $layout, [array $values])

Data type returned: FileMaker_Command_Add object

Description:

Returns a new FileMaker_Command_Add object capable of adding records on the layout specified by $layout.

newCompoundFindCommand

Syntax:

newCompoundFindCommand(string $layout)

Data type returned: FileMaker_Command_CompoundFind object

Description:

Returns a new FileMaker_Command_CompoundFind object capable of performing complex searches on the layout specified by $layout.

newDeleteCommand

Syntax:

newDeleteCommand(string $layout, integer $recordID)

Data type returned: FileMaker_Command_Delete object

Description:

Returns a new FileMaker_Command_Delete object capable of deleting the record with an ID of $recordID from the table specified by $layout.

newDuplicateCommand

Syntax:

newDuplicateCommand(string $layout, integer $recordID)

Data type returned: FileMaker_Command_Duplicate object

Returns a new FileMaker_Command_Duplicate object capable of duplicating the record with an ID of $recordID from the table specified by $layout.

newEditCommand

Syntax:

newEditCommand(string $layout, integer $recordID, [array $updatedValues], array $values)

Data type returned: FileMaker_Command_Edit object

Description:

Returns a new FileMaker_Command_Edit object capable of editing the record with an ID of $recordID from the table specified by $layout. The data values to be submitted are specified in the $values array. The $updatedValues array, if supplied, returns the new field values (this is significant if any of the fields are subject to auto-entry rules, in which case the updated values might be different from the submitted values).

newFindAllCommand

Syntax:

newFindAllCommand(string $layout)

Data type returned: FileMaker_Command_FindAll object

Description:

Returns a new FileMaker_Command_FindAll object capable of finding all records from the table specified by $layout.

newFindAnyCommand

Syntax:

newFindAnyCommand(string $layout)

Data type returned: FileMaker_Command_FindAny object

Description:

Returns a new FileMaker_Command_FindAny object capable of finding a random record from the table specified by $layout.

newFindCommand

Syntax:

newFindCommand(string $layout)

Data type returned: FileMaker_Command_Find object

Description:

Returns a new FileMaker_Command_Find object capable of finding records from the table specified by $layout.

newFindRequest

Syntax:

newFindRequest(string $layout)

Data type returned: FileMaker_Command_FindRequest object

Description:

Returns a new FileMaker_Command_FindRequest object capable of finding records from the table specified by $layout. These individual objects need to be added to a FileMaker_Command_CompoundFind object to actually perform a compound find.

newPerformScriptCommand

Syntax:

newFindCommand(string $layout, string $scriptName, [string $scriptParameters])

Data type returned: FileMaker_Command_PerformScript object

Description:

Returns a new FileMaker_Command_PerformScript object capable of performing the specified script (it's also possible to specify parameters for the script using the $scriptParameters parameter).

setLogger

Syntax:

setLogger(Log $logger)

Data type returned: void

Description:

Establish a PEAR Log object with which to log requests and responses.

setProperty

Syntax:

setProperty(string $prop, string $value)

Data type returned: void

Description:

Set the property $prop of the FileMaker object to the value $value.

FileMaker_Command

The FileMaker_Command class is the base class for seven other specific command classes capable of performing specific commands. This base class provides a set of methods common to, and inherited by, the various command subclasses.

execute

Syntax:

execute()

Data type returned: FileMaker_Result

Description:

Execute the object's underlying command and return a FileMaker_Result object.

setPreCommandScript

Syntax:

setPreCommandScript(string $scriptName, [string $scriptParameters])

Data type returned: void

Description:

Set a script to be run before performing the command or sorting the result set.

setPreSortScript

Syntax:

setPreSortScript(string $scriptName, [string $scriptParameters])

Data type returned: void

Description:

Set a script to be run after performing the command, but before sorting the result set.

setRecordClass

Syntax:

setRecordClass(string $className)

Data type returned: void

Description:

Individual records returned in a result set are instantiated by default as instances of the FileMaker_Record class. If you want the records to be instantiated as instances of some other class, use this function to establish that class name. Other record classes must provide the same interface as the FileMaker_Record class, either by extending it, or by implementing the necessary methods.

setRecordId

Syntax:

setRecordId(integer $recordID)

Data type returned: void

Description:

Set the specific record ID for this command to operate on. Certain commands, such as "add" and "find any," don't use a record ID and thus will ignore this command.

setResultLayout

Syntax:

setProperty(string $layout)

Data type returned: void

Description:

Set the layout to be used for returning the results of the command. You might use this if you wanted a different list of fields in your result set than were present on the layout used for the query.

setScript

Syntax:

setScript(string $scriptName, [string $scriptParameters])

Data type returned: void

Description:

Set a script to be run after the command is performed and the result set returned and sorted.

validate

Syntax:

validate([string $fieldName])

Data type returned: boolean

Description:

This method attempts to validate either a single field in a command, or an entire command if no specific field name is provided. Note that validate() does not actually execute the command against the server. It attempts to do as much validation as possible in the PHP layer. Validations such as strict data type, maximum data length, data ranges, and four-digit years can be validated by PHP without submitting a command to the database. Other types of validation, such as unique field values, or validation by calculation, cannot be tested using validate() but only by the actual execution of the command.

FileMaker_Command_Add

FileMaker_Command_Add is a subclass of FileMaker_Command. It's used to add new records to a database.

setField

Syntax:

setField(string $field, string $value, integer $repetition)

Data type returned: void

Description:

Set a new value for the named field and repetition ($repetition defaults to 1).

setFieldFromTimestamp

Syntax:

setFieldFromTimestamp(string $field, string $timestamp, integer $repetition)

Data type returned: void

Description:

This is a useful method that sets a new value for the named field and repetition ($repetition defaults to 1) from a UNIX-style Timestamp. The target field must be of type date, time, or Timestamp, or an error results. This allows the programmer to avoid worrying about complex conversions between UNIX Timestamps and the FileMaker date and time field types.

FileMaker_Command_CompoundFind

FileMaker_Command_CompoundFind is a subclass of FileMaker_Command. This class represents a set of find requests intended to be performed as a group.

add

Syntax:

add(integer $precedence, FileMaker_Command_FindRequest $findRequest)

Data type returned: void

Description:

Adds a specified FileMaker_Command_FindRequest object to the current find request set. The $precedence variable indicates the order in which the request is added to the set.

addSortRule

Syntax:

addSortRule(string $fieldName, integer $precedence, [mixed $order])

Data type returned: void

Description:

Adds a sorting rule to the compound find request, specifying a field name, a precedence from 1–9, and a sort order. Sort orders may be FILEMAKER_SORT_ASCEND, FILEMAKER_SORT_DESCEND, or a custom value list.

clearSortRules

Syntax:

clearSortRules()

Data type returned: void

Description:

Clear all sorting rules from this compound find request.

getRange

Syntax:

getRange()

Data type returned: array

Description:

Returns an associative array containing two keys. The skip key indicates at which record in the overall found set the result set will begin, whereas the max key indicates the maximum number of records that will be returned.

getRelatedSetsFilters

Syntax:

getRelatedSetsFilters()

Data type returned: array

Description:

Returns an associative array containing two keys. The relatedsetsfilter key returns the portal filter settings, whereas the relatedsetsmax key indicates the maximum number of related records that will be returned.

setRange

Syntax:

setRange(integer $skip, [integer $max])

Data type returned: void

Description:

Use setRange() to indicate that only part of a result set should be returned. The $skip parameter indicates how many records to skip over at the beginning of the result set, and the $max parameter indicates the maximum number of records that should be returned.

setRelatedSetsFilters

Syntax:

getRelatedSetsFilters(string $filter, string $max)

Data type returned: void

Description:

A related set filter can be thought of as the set of portal options that would apply to a portal showing a set of related records. Applicable settings include the initial row, number of rows to display, sort order, and whether a scrollbar is displayed. Use this method to specify whether to use the related set filtering present on this request's layout: Use a value of layout for the $filter parameter, or none if you don't intend to use the layout filter. Use the $max parameter to specify the maximum number of related records to return.

FileMaker_Command_Delete

This class represents a command intended to delete a single record. FileMaker_Command_Delete has no methods of its own; it inherits all its methods from its parent, FileMaker_Command.

FileMaker_Command_Duplicate

This class represents a command intended to duplicate a single record. FileMaker_Command_Duplicate has no methods of its own; it inherits all its methods from its parent, FileMaker_Command.

FileMaker_Command_Edit

FileMaker_Command_Edit is a subclass of FileMaker_Command. This class represents a command intended to edit a single record.

setField

Syntax:

setField(string $field, string $value, integer $repetition)

Data type returned: void

Description:

Set a new value for the named field and repetition ($repetition defaults to 1).

setFieldFromTimestamp

Syntax:

setFieldFromTimestamp(string $field, string $timestamp, integer $repetition)

Data type returned: void

Description:

This is a useful method that sets a new value for the named field and repetition ($repetition defaults to 1) from a UNIX-style Timestamp. The target field must be of type date, time, or Timestamp, or an error results. This allows the programmer to avoid worry about complex conversions between UNIX Timestamps and the FileMaker date and time field types.

setModificationID

Syntax:

setRange(integer $modificationID)

Data type returned: void

Description:

Use this method to set a new modification ID for the target record. (A modification ID is often used in web programming to determine whether a given record has been modified since it was last refreshed from the database.)

FileMakerCommand_Find

FileMaker_Command_Find is a subclass of FileMaker_Command. It represents a command intended to perform a search.

addFindCriterion

Syntax:

addFindCriterion(string $fieldName, string $testValue)

Data type returned: void

Description:

Add a single find criterion to this request. You need to specify the name of the field being tested and the value to test for.

addSortRule

Syntax:

addSortRule(string $fieldName, integer $precedence, [mixed $order])

Data type returned: void

Description:

Adds a sorting rule to the compound find request, specifying a field name, a precedence from 1–9, and a sort order. Sort orders may be FILEMAKER_SORT_ASCEND, FILEMAKER_SORT_DESCEND, or a custom value list.

clearFindCriteria

Syntax:

clearFindCriteria()

Data type returned: void

Description:

Clear all find criteria from this find request.

clearSortRules

Syntax:

clearSortRules()

Data type returned: void

Description:

Clear all sorting rules from this compound find request.

getRange

Syntax:

getRange()

Data type returned: array

Description:

Returns an associative array containing two keys. The skip key indicates at which record in the overall found set the result set will begin, whereas the max key indicates the maximum number of records that will be returned.

getRelatedSetsFilters

Syntax:

getRelatedSetsFilters()

Data type returned: array

Description:

Returns an associative array containing two keys. The relatedsetsfilter key returns the portal filter settings, whereas the relatedsetsmax key indicates the maximum number of related records that will be returned.

setLogicalOperator

Syntax:

setRange(integer $operator)

Data type returned: void

Description:

Use this method to specify that a search be run using logical AND or logical OR. The respective integer constants to use are FILEMAKER_FIND_AND and FILEMAKER_FIND_OR.

setRange

Syntax:

setRange(integer $skip, [integer $max])

Data type returned: void

Description:

Use setRange() to indicate that only part of a result set should be returned. The $skip parameter indicates how many records to skip over at the beginning of the result set, and the $max parameter indicates the maximum number of records that should be returned.

setRelatedSetsFilters

Syntax:

setRelatedSetsFilters(string $filter, string $max)

Data type returned: void

Description:

A related set filter can be thought of as the set of portal options that would apply to a portal showing a set of related records. Applicable settings include the initial row, number of rows to display, sort order, and whether a scrollbar is displayed. Use this method to specify whether to use the related set filtering present on this request's layout: Use a value of layout for the $filter parameter, or none if you don't intend to use the layout filter. Use the $max parameter to specify the maximum number of related records to return.

FileMaker_Command_FindAll

This class is a subclass of FileMaker_Command_Find. It represents a command intended to find all records from a given layout. FileMaker_Command_Find All has no methods of its own; it inherits all its methods from its ancestors, FileMaker_Command and FileMaker_Command_Find.

FileMaker_Command_FindAny

This class is a subclass of FileMaker_Command_Find. It represents a command intended to find a random record from a given layout. FileMaker_Command_Find Any has no methods of its own; it inherits all its methods from its ancestors, FileMaker_Command and FileMaker_Command_Find.

FileMaker_Command_FindRequest

Though the naming convention suggests otherwise, this class is *not* a child of FileMaker_Command. This class represents individual find requests that are intended to be grouped into a compound find by being added to a FileMaker_Command_CompoundFind object.

addFindCriterion

Syntax:

addFindCriterion(string $fieldName, string $testValue)

Data type returned: void

Description:

Adds a single find criterion to this request. You need to specify the name of the field being tested and the value to test for.

clearFindCriteria

Syntax:

clearFindCriteria()

Data type returned: void

Description:

Clear all find criteria from this find request.

setOmit

Syntax:

clearFindCriteria(boolean $value)

Data type returned: void

Description:

Specify whether this is an "omit" request.

FileMaker_Command_PerformScript

This class represents a command intended to perform a script. FileMaker_Command_Find Any has no methods of its own; it inherits all its methods from its parent, FileMaker_Command.

FileMaker_Error

FileMaker_Error is an extension of (child of) the PEAR_Error class, a generic error-handling class provided with the popular PEAR library (http://pear.php.net). In addition to all the methods it inherits from its parent (documented at http://pear.php.net/reference/PEAR-1.4.4/PEAR/PEAR_Error.html), FileMaker_Error has the following additional or overloaded methods.

FileMaker_Error

Syntax:

FileMaker_Error(FileMaker_Delegate $fm, [string $message], [integer $code])

Data type returned: FileMaker_Error

Description:

This is the class constructor. In general, you are more likely to find instances of FileMaker_Error being returned from various API methods, than you are to have to create instances of the class on your own.

getErrorString

Syntax:

getErrorString()

Data type returned: string

Description:

Returns the error string associated with this object. In the FileMaker implementation, the getMessage() method is a bit more generic than getErrorString() and can be used to extract error messages even when the underlying error is not a FileMaker XML error.

getMessage

Syntax:

getMessage()

Data type returned: string

Description:

Returns the textual error message for this error object.

isValidationError

Syntax:

isValidationError()

Data type returned: boolean

Description:

Returns a boolean value specifying whether this error is some sort of message from the server, or is instead a specific validation error.

FileMaker_Error_Validation

FileMaker_Error_Validation is a child of the FileMaker_Error class, with additional functionality pertaining specifically to validation errors. As with FileMaker error, as a programmer using the API you are more likely to consume these error objects than create and manage them.

The FileMaker API for PHP can recognize and enforce a certain number of FileMaker validation constraints. These constraints are referenced by integer constants, as shown in Table 15.1.

Table 15.1 FileMaker Validation Integer Constants

Validation Constraint	Integer Constant	Integer Value
Not empty	FILEMAKER_RULE_NOTEMPTY	1
Numeric only	FILEMAKER_RULE_NUMERICONLY	2
Maximum length	FILEMAKER_RULE_MAXCHARACTERS	3
4-digit year	FILEMAKER_RULE_FOURDIGITYEAR	4
Time of day	FILEMAKER_RULE_TIMEOFDAY	5
Timestamp	FILEMAKER_RULE_TIMESTAMPFIELD	6
Date	FILEMAKER_RULE_DATE_FIELD	7
Time	FILEMAKER_RULE_TIME_FIELD	8

Any references to validation rule numbers or validation constants refers to this set of values.

addError

Syntax:

addError(FileMaker_Field $field, integer $rule, string $value)

Data type returned: void

Description:

Use this method to add an error notification to this object, specifying the field, the number of the validation rule that was broken, and the offending field value.

getErrors

Syntax:

getErrors([string $fieldName])

Data type returned: array

Description:

Returns an array describing all the errors associated with this object. Each entry in the array is itself an indexed array. The first array element contains the field object for the field that failed validation, the second element contains an integer constant representing the validation rule that failed, and the third element contains the offending field value.

If you specify a field name, only errors pertaining to that field will be returned.

isValidationError

Syntax:

isValidationError()

Data type returned: boolean

Description:

Returns a boolean value specifying whether this error is some sort of message from the server, or is instead a specific validation error.

numErrors

Syntax:

numErrors()

Data type returned: void

Description:

Returns the number of validation errors referred to by this object.

FileMaker_Field

FileMaker_Field is a class representing a specific field as it appears on a specific layout.

FileMaker_Field

Syntax:

FileMaker_Field(FileMaker_Layout $layout)

Data type returned: FileMaker_Field

Description:

This is the class constructor. It's invoked by passing it a FileMaker_Layout object corresponding to the field's parent layout.

describeLocalValidationRules

Syntax:

describeLocalValidationRules()

Data type returned: array

Description:

This method returns an array of validation rule descriptors. Only validation rules that can be checked and enforced in PHP are included, so rules for validation criteria such as uniqueness, or validation by calculation, which can be evaluated only by FileMaker Server, are not included in the list. See the description of FileMaker_Error_Validation for a list of the possible rule values.

describeValidationRule

Syntax:

describeValidationRule(integer $validationRule)

Data type returned: array

Description:

For a specific validation rule on this field, this method returns additional information about the rule if necessary, such as a data range or a maximum number of characters. See the description of FileMaker_Error_Validation for a list of the possible rule values.

describeValidationRules

Syntax:

describeValidationRules()

Data type returned: array

Description:

Returns additional validation information for all validation rules defined on this field.

getLayout

Syntax:

getLayout()

Data type returned: FileMaker_Layout

Description:

Returns a FileMaker_Layout object representing the layout that contains this field.

getLocalValidationRules

Syntax:

getLocalValidationRules()

Data type returned: array

Description:

This function returns an array of integer constants representing the validation rules in place for this field. Only validation rules that can be checked and enforced in PHP are included, so rules for validation criteria such as uniqueness, or validation by calculation, which can be evaluated only by FileMaker Server, are not included in the list. See the description of FileMaker_Error_Validation for a list of the possible rule values.

getName

Syntax:

getName()

Data type returned: string

Description:

Returns a string representing the name of this field.

getRepetitionCount

Syntax:

getRepetitionCount()

Data type returned: integer

Description:

Returns an integer representing the number of repetitions defined for this field.

getResult

Syntax:

getResult()

Data type returned: string

Description:

Returns a string representing the data type or the result type of this field. (For "basic" FileMaker fields, this corresponds to the field's basic data type, whereas for calculations it corresponds to the data type that the calculation returns.)

getStyleType

Syntax:

getStyleType()

Data type returned: string

Description:

Returns a string representing the layout style of this field (for example, whether the field is formatted as a text edit box or a check box area).

getType

Syntax:

getType()

Data type returned: string

Description:

Returns a string representing the data type of this field. This is the field type you would find in the Manage Database dialog.

getValidationMask

Syntax:

getValidationMask()

Data type returned: integer

Description:

Returns an integer representing the sum of all the validation constants that apply to this field.

getValidationRules

Syntax:

getValidationRules()

Data type returned: array

Description:

This function returns an array of integer constants representing all the validation rules in place for this field. Unlike `getLocalValidationRules()`, this method returns information on all validation rules, not just those that can be evaluated by PHP.

getValueList

Syntax:

getValueList([integer $recid])

Data type returned: array

Description:

This function attempts to return an array of information representing any value list that might be associated with this field on the current layout. You may pass in the optional `$recid` parameter to specify a record from which the value list should be taken (this is useful in cases, such as with relational value lists, where the contents of the list may vary from record to record).

hasValidationRule

Syntax:

hasValidationRule(integer $validationRule)

Data type returned: boolean

Description:

This method tests to see whether this field has a validation rule corresponding to the integer constant passed to the method.

isAutoEntered

Syntax:

isAutoEntered

Data type returned: boolean

Description:

Returns a boolean value indicating whether this field has any auto-entry options set.

isGlobal

Syntax:

isGlobal()

Data type returned: boolean

Description:

Returns a boolean indicating whether this field uses global storage.

validate

Syntax:

validate(mixed $value, [FileMaker_Error_Validation $error])

Data type returned: boolean

Description:

This method returns a boolean TRUE if `$value` is a valid value for this field. Otherwise, the method returns a `FileMaker_Error_Validation` object describing the error.

If you are validating more than one field, you pass an existing `FileMaker_Error_Validation` object in as the `$error` parameter, and any validation errors will be added into that object.

FileMaker_Layout

FileMaker_Layout is a class representing an individual FileMaker layout. A FileMaker_Layout object, among other uses, is returned from a command along with a record result set.

FileMaker_Layout

Syntax:

FileMaker_Layout(FileMaker_Implementation $fm)

Data type returned: boolean

Description:

This is the class constructor. Pass it a FileMaker object. (FileMaker_Implementation is the hidden implementation class for a FileMaker object.)

getDatabase

Syntax:

getDatabase()

Data type returned: string

Description:

Returns a string with the name of the database in which this layout is found.

getField

Syntax:

getField($fieldName)

Data type returned: FileMaker_Field

Description:

Returns either a FileMaker_Field object corresponding to the name field, or a FileMaker_Error object if some error was encountered.

getFields

Syntax:

getFields()

Data type returned: array

Description:

Returns an associative array with information on all fields on the layout. The array keys are the names of individual fields, and each array value is an individual FileMaker_Field object.

getName

Syntax:

getName()

Data type returned: string

Description:

Returns the name of this layout as a string.

getRelatedSet

Syntax:

getRelatedSet($relatedSet)

Data type returned: FileMaker_RelatedSet

Description:

Returns the FileMaker_RelatedSet object referred to by $relatedSet, or a FileMaker_Error object if some error is encountered.

getRelatedSets

Syntax:

getRelatedSets()

Data type returned: array

Description:

Returns an associative array with the names of all related sets on the layout as keys. The value corresponding to each key is a FileMaker_RelatedSet object.

getValueList

Syntax:

getValueList($valueList, [integer $recid])

Data type returned: array

Description:

This method returns an array describing the values of the named value list on this layout. You can use the optional $recid parameter to specify a record from which the value list should be drawn.

getValueLists

Syntax:

getValueLists([integer $recid])

Data type returned: array

Description:

This method returns an associative array describing the values of all value lists on the layout. The keys are the names of individual value lists. Corresponding to each key is an array of the values in that value list. You can use the optional $recid parameter to specify a record from which the value list should be drawn.

listFields

Syntax:

listFields()

Data type returned: array

Description:

Returns an array of strings representing the names of each field on this layout. (Contrast with getFields(), which returns an array of FileMaker_Field objects).

listRelatedSets

Syntax:

listRelatedSets()

Data type returned: array

Description:

Returns an array of strings representing the names of each related set on this layout (contrast with getRelatedSets(), which returns an array of FileMaker_RelatedSet objects).

listValueLists

Syntax:

listValueLists()

Data type returned: array

Description:

Returns an array of strings representing the names of each value list on this layout (ccontrast with getValuelists(), which also returns the values in each value list).

FileMaker_Record

The FileMaker_Record class is the default class for representing each instance of a FileMaker record. You can provide your own record class as well, though it must either be a subclass of FileMaker_Record, or provide an identical interface. (Use the setRecordClass() method of FileMaker_Command and its subclasses to supply the name of your custom class.)

FileMaker_Record

Syntax:

FileMaker_Record(FileMaker_Layout $layout) or

FileMaker_Record(FileMaker_RelatedSet $relatedSet)

Data type returned: FileMaker_Record

Description:

This is the class constructor. It is called with either the FileMaker_Layout object or the FileMaker_RelatedSet object that contains this record.

commit

Syntax:

commit()

Data type returned: boolean

Description:

This method commits the record to the database. It returns boolean TRUE on success, or a FileMaker_Error object on failure.

delete

Syntax:

delete()

Data type returned: FileMaker_Result

Description:

This method deletes the record from the database. It returns a FileMaker_Result object on success, or a FileMaker_Error object on failure.

getField

Syntax:

getField(string $field, [integer $repetition])

Data type returned: mixed

Description:

This method returns the value from the specified field and repetition. The repetition defaults to 1 if not specified.

getFieldAsTimestamp

Syntax:

getFieldAsTimestamp(string $field, [integer $repetition])

Data type returned: integer representing a timestamp

Description:

This method returns the value from the specified field and repetition as a UNIX Timestamp. If the field specified is a data field, the Timestamp corresponds to midnight on that date. If the date specified is a time field, the Timestamp corresponds to that time on January 1, 1970. If the date specified is a FileMaker Timestamp, it is converted directly to a UNIX Timestamp. The method returns a FileMaker_Error object if the resulting Timestamp would be out of range, or if the underlying field is not a date, time, or Timestamp. The repetition defaults to 1 if not specified.

getFields

Syntax:

getFields()

Data type returned: array

Description:

This method returns an array of strings corresponding to the names of all the fields in this record.

getLayout

Syntax:

getLayout()

Data type returned: FileMaker_Layout

Description:

This method returns a FileMaker_Layout object corresponding to the layout this record is attached to.

getModificationID

Syntax:

getModificationID()

Data type returned: integer

Description:

Returns this record's modification ID.

getParent

Syntax:

getParent()

Data type returned: FileMaker_Record

Description:

If this record is a child record (in other words, this record is a part of a related set attached to another record), this method returns a FileMaker_Record object corresponding to the parent record.

getRecordID

Syntax:

getRecordID()

Data type returned: integer

Description:

Returns this record's record ID.

getRelatedSet

Syntax:

getRelatedSet(string $relatedSet)

Data type returned: array

Description:

This method, given the name of a portal corresponding to a related set, returns an array of FileMaker_Record objects corresponding to the records in the related set.

newRelatedRecord

Syntax:

newRelatedRecord(string $relatedSet)

Data type returned: FileMaker_Record

Description:

This method creates a new FileMaker_Record object in the portal named by $relatedSet.

setField

Syntax:

setField(string $field, string $value, [integer $repetition])

Data type returned: mixed

Description:

This method sets the given value into the specified field and repetition. The repetition defaults to 1 if not specified.

setFieldFromTimestamp

Syntax:

setFieldFromTimestamp(string $field, string $timestamp, integer $repetition)

Data type returned: void

Description:

This is a useful method that sets a new value for the named field and repetition ($repetition defaults to 1) from a UNIX-style Timestamp. The target field must be of type date, time, or Timestamp, or an error results. This allows the programmer to avoid worrying about complex conversions between UNIX Timestamps and the FileMaker date and time field types.

validate

Syntax:

validate([string $fieldName])

Data type returned: boolean

Description:

This method validates the entire record, using any validation rules that can be checked by PHP. Optionally, you may specify the name of just a single field to check. The method returns boolean TRUE if the validation tests succeed. Otherwise, the method returns a FileMaker_Error_Validation object describing the error.

FileMaker_RelatedSet

A FileMaker_RelatedSet object contains information about a single related set, which can generally best be thought of as a set of records displayed in a specific portal on a specific layout.

FileMaker_RelatedSet

Syntax:

FileMaker_RelatedSet(FileMaker_Layout $layout)

Data type returned: FileMaker_RelatedSet

Description:

This is the class constructor. It creates a new FileMaker_RelatedSet based on a specific FileMaker_Layout object.

getField

Syntax:

getField(string $fieldName)

Data type returned: FileMaker_Field

Description:

Returns a FileMaker_Field object corresponding to the named field, or a FileMaker_Error object if the request fails for some reason.

getFields

Syntax:

getFields()

Data type returned: array

Description:

Returns an associative array with information on all fields on the layout. The array keys are the names of individual fields, and each array value is an individual FileMaker_Field object.

getName

Syntax:

getName()

Data type returned: string

Description:

Returns the name of this layout as a string.

listFields

Syntax:

listFields()

Data type returned: array

Description:

Returns an array of strings representing the names of each field on this layout (contrast with getFields(), which returns an array of FileMaker_Field objects).

loadExtendedInfo

Syntax:

load_ExtendedInfo()

Data type returned: boolean

Description:

This method loads any additional extended information associated with the layout that contains this related set.

FileMaker_Result

This class represents a result returned by a FileMaker command. More often than not it contains a set of one or more records that were found or otherwise affected by the command.

FileMaker_Result

Syntax:

FileMaker_Result(FileMaker_Implementation $fm)

Data type returned: FileMaker_Result

Description:

This is the class constructor. Pass it a FileMaker object. (FileMaker_Implementation is the hidden implementation class for a FileMaker object.)

getFetchCount

Syntax:

getFetchCount()

Data type returned: integer

Description:

Returns the number of records in this result set. This count respects any range restraints placed on a search, such as a skip or max constraint.

getFields

Syntax:

getFields()

Data type returned: array

Description:

Returns an array of strings representing the names of each field in this result set. Unlike other methods named getFields, this method returns only the field names, not actual FileMaker_Field objects.

getFirstRecord

Syntax:

getFirstRecord()

Data type returned: FileMaker_Record

Description:

Returns a FileMaker_Record object representing the first record in the result set.

getFoundSetCount

Syntax:

getFoundSetCount()

Data type returned: integer

Description:

Returns the number of records in the entire found set of which this result set is a part. (This differs from the result of getFetchCount() if constraints such as skip and max are in effect.)

getLastRecord

Syntax:

getLastRecord()

Data type returned: FileMaker_Record

Description:

Returns a FileMaker_Record object representing the last record in the result set.

getLayout

Syntax:

getLayout()

Data type returned: FileMaker_Layout

Description:

Returns a FileMaker_Layout object representing the layout to which the result set belongs.

getRecords

Syntax:

getRecords()

Data type returned: array

Description:

Returns an array of objects representing all records in the result set. The objects will be of type FileMaker_Record, unless you have specified that a different class be used.

getRelatedSets

Syntax:

getRelatedSets()

Data type returned: array

Description:

Returns an array of strings representing the names of all related sets in this result set.

getTableRecordCount

Syntax:

getTableRecordCount()

Data type returned: integer

Description:

Returns the total number of records in the base table for this result set.

CHAPTER 16

JDBC/ODBC and External SQL Connectivity

About SQL-Based Data Exchange

A FileMaker system can act as a data source for external access via Open Database Connectivity (ODBC) or Java Database Connectivity (JDBC). Likewise, using the new External SQL Source (ESS) feature in FileMaker 9, FileMaker solutions can gain direct access to data in certain SQL-based database systems. FileMaker continues to support the ability to import records from an ODBC data source, and to execute SQL statements against remote data sources using the Execute SQL script step.

This chapter discusses how to make a FileMaker database available for external access from ODBC or JDBC. It also covers how to set up a Data Source Name (DSN) on both the Mac OS and Windows, for use with the ESS, Import ODBC, and Execute SQL features.

Setting Up Inbound ODBC and JDBC Connectivity

A FileMaker database has the capability to act as a data source for connections from ODBC and JDBC clients. If the database is accessed locally (not via FileMaker Server), it can serve data to ODBC and JDBC clients on the same local machine (for example, Microsoft Excel can be used as an ODBC client to access data in a FileMaker file that's open on the same machine as the Excel application).

To serve FileMaker data to remote ODBC and JDBC clients (where the files will not be open on the same machine as the ODBC/JDBC client), you'll need to use FileMaker Server Advanced, which provides remote ODBC/JDBC connectivity.

Configuring a Database for ODBC/JDBC Access

To make a file's data accessible to external ODBC and JDBC clients, the appropriate extended privileges must first be set. ODBC/JDBC access is controlled via the [fmxdbc] extended privilege. You can enable this privilege directly, for various privilege sets, via the Extended Privilege area under File, Manage, Accounts and Privileges, as shown in Figure 16.1.

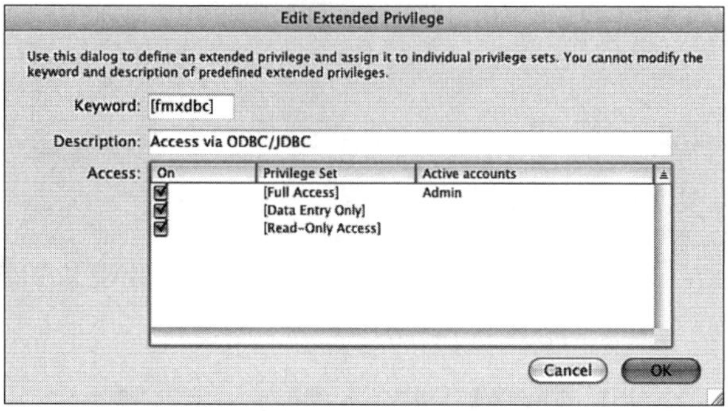

Figure 16.1

You must enable the [fmxdbc] *extended privilege in a database to share it via ODBC or JDBC.*

As an alternative, you can choose File, Sharing, ODBC/JDBC. The lower half of that dialog box, pictured in Figure 16.2, is simply a more convenient way of managing the same extended privileges.

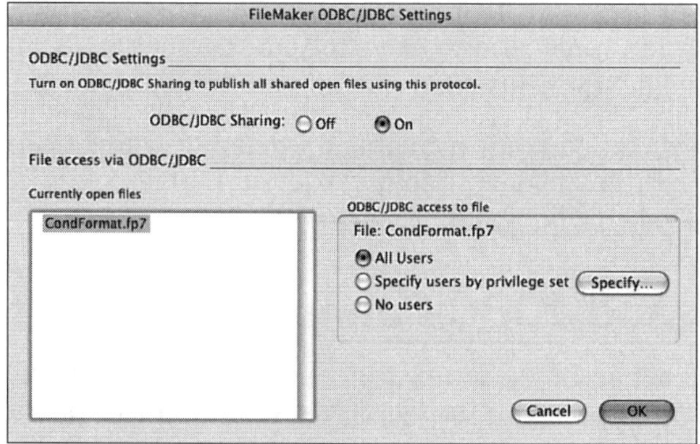

Figure 16.2

The FileMaker ODBC/JDBC Settings dialog provides an alternative way to set the [fmxdbc] *extended privilege in one or more open files.*

If no privilege set has the [fmxdbc] extended privilege set enabled, OBDC and JDBC clients will not be able to access any data in the file.

Enabling ODBC/JDBC Access in FileMaker Pro

FileMaker data can be shared via ODBC/JDBC in either of two ways. In the first method, a copy of FileMaker Pro or FileMaker Pro Advanced acts as the data provider. In this case, the data is available only to other applications running on the same computer. ODBC/JDBC clients on a different computer won't be able to access data when FileMaker Pro is the data provider. (For security reasons, FileMaker Pro and Advanced only allow access from processes running on the same machine.)

To enable ODBC/JDBC access from FileMaker Pro or FileMaker Pro Advanced, choose File, Sharing, ODBC/JDBC; then make sure that ODBC/JDBC Sharing is set to On in the upper area of the dialog, as shown previously in Figure 16.2.

Enabling ODBC/JDBC Access in FileMaker Server Advanced

You can share FileMaker data to remote ODBC/JDBC clients if you are using FileMaker Server Advanced. The files you want to make accessible must be hosted by FileMaker Server Advanced (and of course have the [fmxdbc] extended privilege enabled). The only other prerequisite is that FileMaker Server Advanced must have its ODBC/JDBC access enabled. This is done using the FileMaker Server Admin Console, as shown in Figure 16.3.

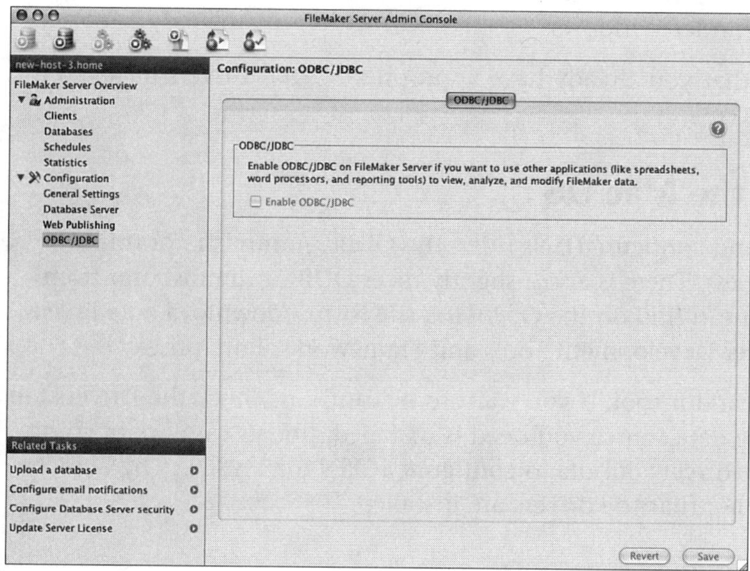

Figure 16.3

The Enable ODBC/JDBC setting in FileMaker Server Advanced must be enabled to allow remote ODBC/JDBC access to hosted files.

Setting Up a DSN for External SQL Connectivity

FileMaker has several means for requesting data from remote data sources via ODBC:

- ODBC Import (choose File, Import, ODBC Data Source)
- Execute SQL script step
- External ODBC data source (choose File, Manage, External Data Sources)

To use any of these methods of interacting with a remote ODBC source, you will need to have one or more Data Source Names (DSN) configured. For ODBC Import and the Execute SQL script step, the DSNs need to be configured on the same computer as the specific copy of FileMaker Pro that performs the access. The new External SQL (ODBC) Source feature is unique in that, for files hosted under FileMaker Server, the DSNs may be configured on the FileMaker Server machine instead. This can save a great deal of time and bother, as it avoids the need to configure identical DSNs on each client computer that will use the files.

Note

No additional configuration is necessary on the FileMaker Server machine: If the DSNs are present, FileMaker Server automatically finds them and uses them without additional setup.

The following sections illustrate how to set up a DSN for MySQL under Mac OS, and a DSN for Microsoft SQL Server under Windows.

Both demonstrations assume that you already have appropriate ODBC drivers installed for the data source you want to access.

Setting Up a DSN for the Mac OS

On the Mac OS, you manage and configure DSNs using the ODBC Administrator utility (located in /Applications/Utilities). There is also a slightly nicer ODBC Administrator from OpenLink software, which you can find on the OpenLink site (http://download.openlinksw.com/download/?p=m_os) under Development Tools and Frameworks: Enterprise.

First, open the ODBC Administrator tool. If you want to be cautious, check the Drivers tab to make sure the driver for the data source you need is installed. In this case, we're going to use the Actual Open Source drivers bundle to configure a DSN for MySQL. The Drivers tab, shown in Figure 16.4, shows that the drivers are installed.

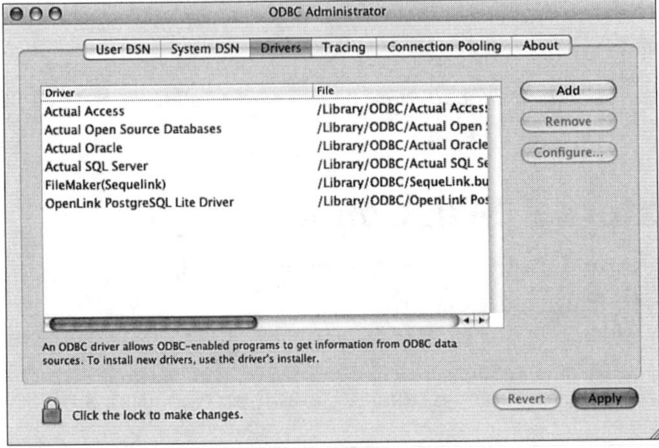

Figure 16.4

The Drivers tab of the Mac OS ODBC Administrator shows all installed ODBC drivers.

Switch to the System DSN tab, which shows a list of all system-level DSNs currently configured on this computer. (A *system DSN* may be used by anyone on the computer, whereas a *user DSN* may be used only by a specific user. In general, it's probably a good idea to stick with system DSNs.) Figure 16.5 shows the System DSN tab.

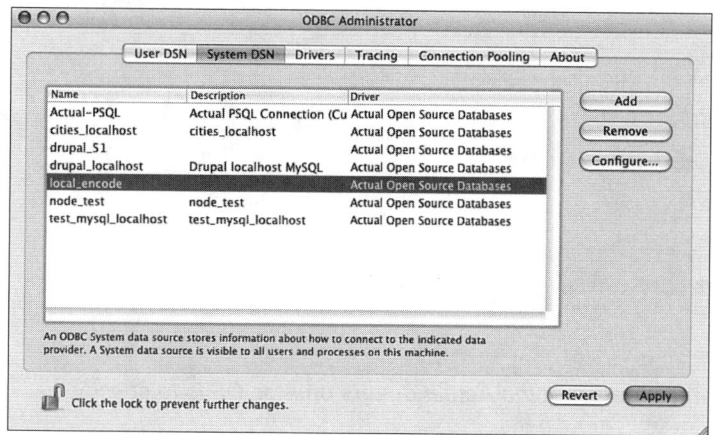

Figure 16.5

The System DSN tab of the Mac OS ODBC Administrator allows you to manage system-level DSNs.

Click the Add button, and then choose your driver (in this case, Actual Open Source Databases). This brings up a configuration wizard for the driver you've chosen. In this example, you might be creating a DSN for a MySQL server running on a host called mysql.someplace.net, to access a customer database. You would need to configure the DSN's description, hostname, and database name, along with some other optional parameters, as shown in Figures 16.6, 16.7, and 16.8.

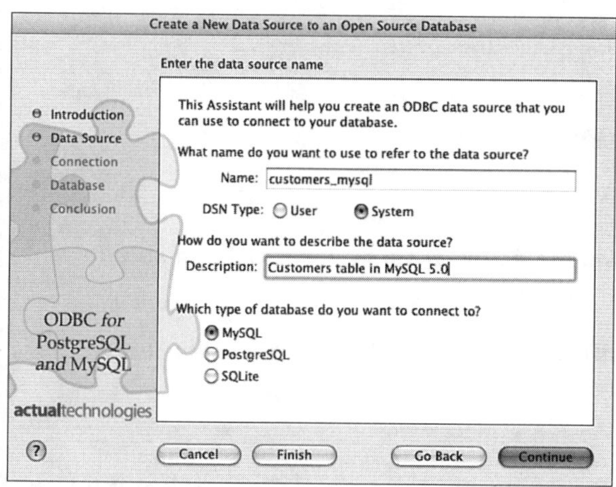

Figure 16.6

When configuring a MySQL connection using the Actual drivers on Mac OS, you'll first need to name your DSN and choose which type of database you are connecting to.

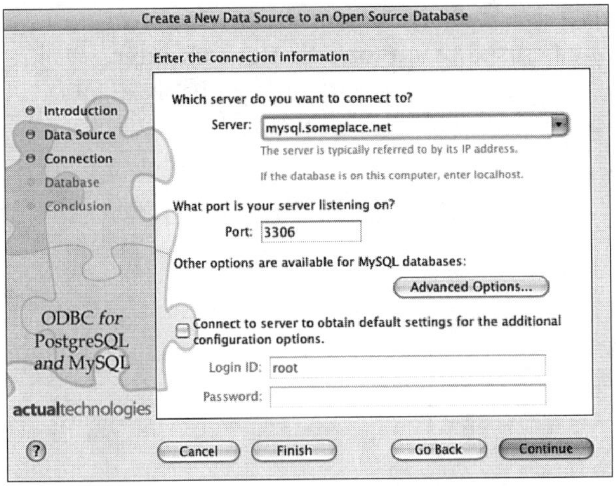

Figure 16.7

The next step in creating a MySQL connection using the Actual drivers on Mac OS is to specify a host configuration.

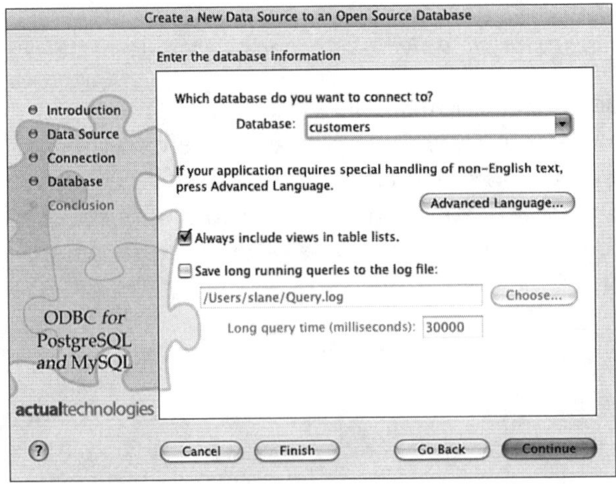

Figure 16.8

The last step in creating a MySQL connection using the Actual drivers on Mac OS is to specify a database name.

At the end of the wizard, click the Done button and the new DSN is ready for use.

Setting Up a DSN in Windows

Setting up a DSN on Windows is conceptually similar to setting up a DSN for the Mac OS: Use your system's ODBC administration tool to check that your driver is loaded and to kick off the DSN configuration process.

The procedure demonstrated is for Windows XP: The procedure for creating a DSN in Windows 2000 is virtually identical.

Begin by choosing the Windows ODBC administration tool (Start, Control Panel, Administrative Tools, Data Sources [ODBC]). Check the Drivers tab to make sure a driver for the data source you want to work with is installed, as shown in Figure 16.9.

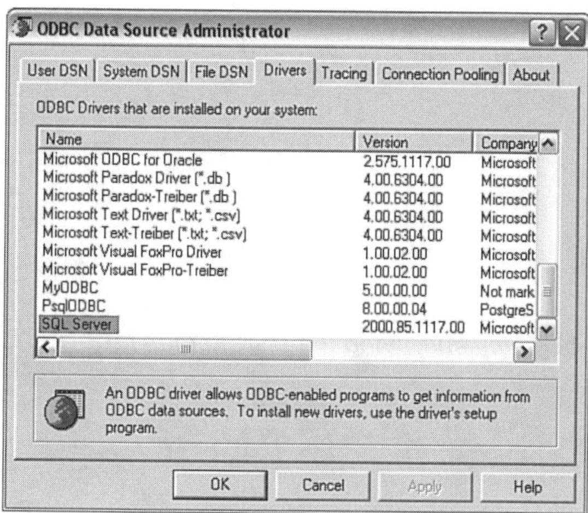

Figure 16.9

The Windows ODBC Data Source Administrator also has a Drivers tab showing all installed drivers.

Switch to the System DSN tab and click Add; and then choose the appropriate driver from the Create New Data Source window, as shown in Figure 16.10.

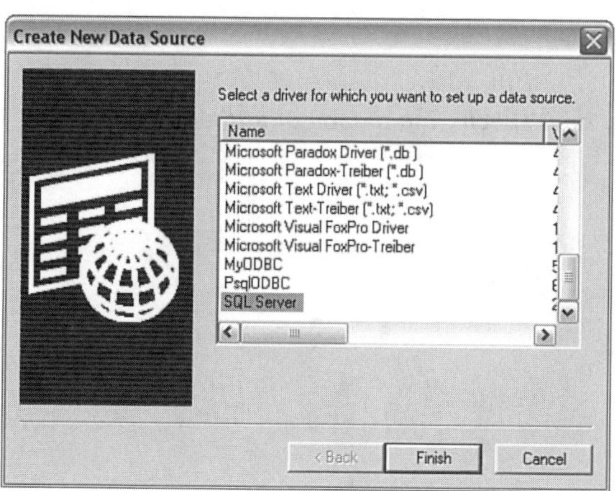

Figure 16.10

On Windows, choose from among the available drivers to create a new SQL Server DSN.

The next steps run through several configuration screens in which you enter specifics for the data source you're working with, as shown in Figures 16.11 through 16.14. After you've filled in the appropriate information in the screens, the new DSN is ready for use.

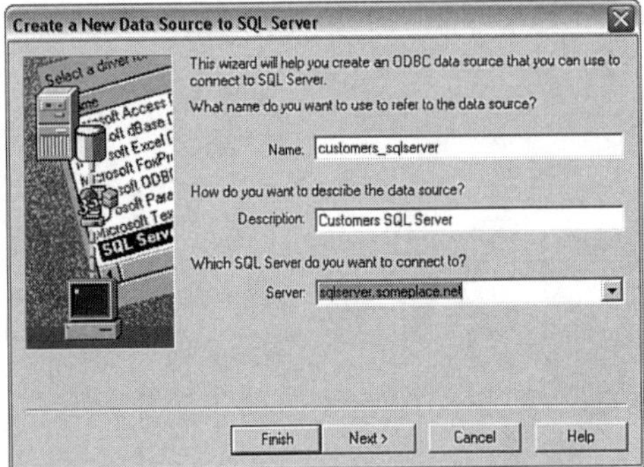

Figure 16.11

When creating a new SQL Server DSN on Windows, begin by specifying the DSN name and hostname.

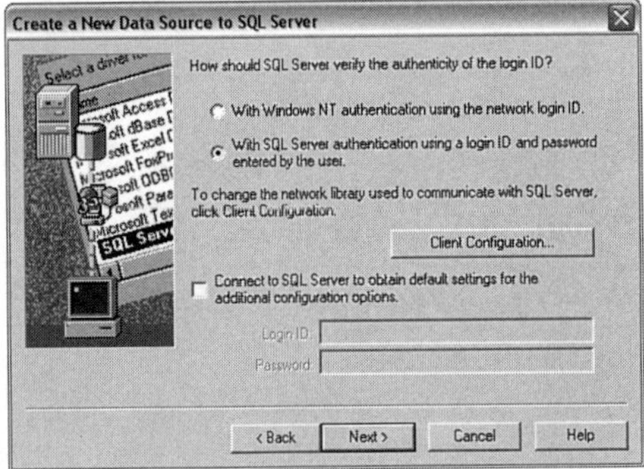

Figure 16.12

When creating a new SQL Server DSN on Windows, next specify the means of authentication.

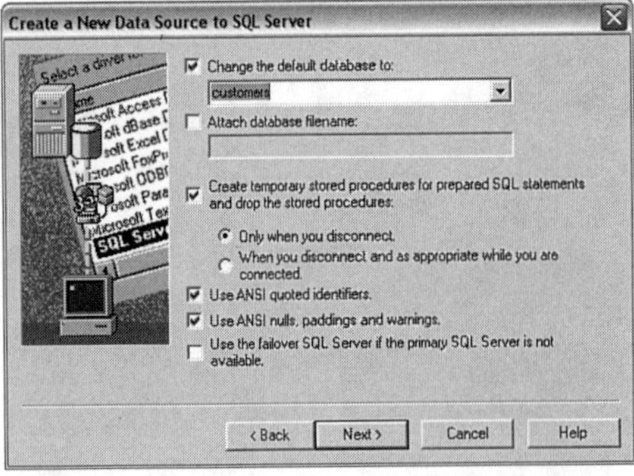

Figure 16.13

When creating a new SQL Server DSN on Windows, next specify the database name.

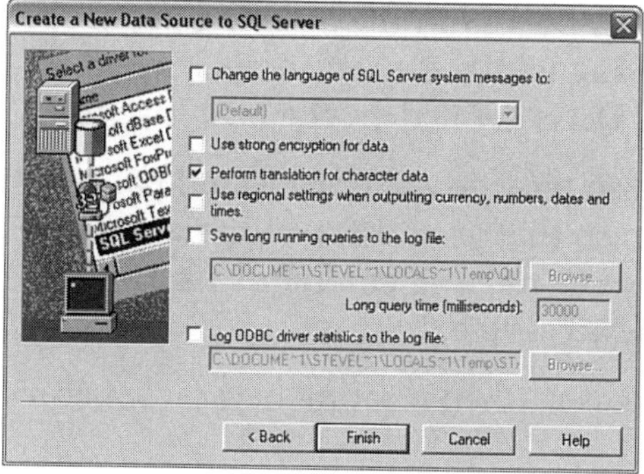

Figure 16.14

The configuration of an SQL Server DSN on Windows concludes with a set of miscellaneous configuration options.

Using an External Data Source from Within FileMaker

After you've defined a DSN, it is available for use from within FileMaker. A new DSN can be used immediately with the Import from ODBC Source command and the `Execute SQL` script step. To use the new External SQL (ODBC) Data Source feature, one more step is necessary:

1. Choose File, Manage, External Data Sources.
2. On the Manage External Data Sources screen, choose New.
3. On the Edit Data Source screen (shown in Figure 16.15), choose ODBC for the data source type.

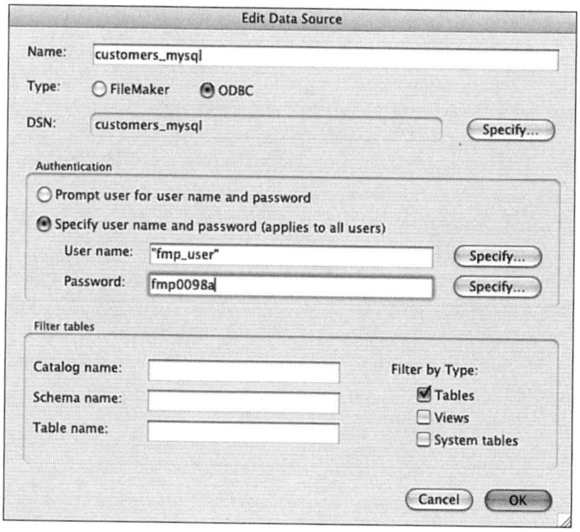

Figure 16.15

In FileMaker 9, choose File, Manage, External Data Sources to create and configure a new External SQL (ODBC) Data Source.

4. For the DSN, choose Specify, and then select your DSN from the resulting list of DSNs defined on this machine. (If you are working with a file served via FileMaker Server, you'll be choosing instead from a list of DSNs defined on the host machine.)
5. As part of setting up the data source, you can also provide a username and password to be used when accessing the remote database (so that your users don't have to remember another password), as well as apply some filtering criteria to limit which tables and views from the remote source will be accessible.
6. After the new data source is set up, you can access it when creating new table occurrences in the Relationships Graph.

CHAPTER 17

AppleScript Integration

Understanding AppleScript

AppleScript is a scripting language built into the Mac OS X operating system and is configured and ready to run on Apple computers right out of the box. In addition to providing users with a macro-like ability to manipulate files and other aspects of the Mac OS X and the Finder, AppleScript also has the capability to automate and integrate applications that have been engineered to be "scriptable."

FileMaker is one such application, and users can use AppleScript both to manipulate FileMaker and to allow FileMaker to control and communicate with other applications. For instance, developers can embed the following script in FileMaker to get the name, title, and image of the first selected contact in the OS X Address Book and use that data to create and populate a new record in the Personnel Records database:

```
-- control the Address Book application...
tell application "Address Book"
    -- get the selected contacts...
    set sel_people to the selection
    -- get the first selected contact...
    set first_per to first item of sel_people
    -- get the name, title, and image of the first selected contact...
    set {per_lst_nm, per_fst_nm, per_title, per_img} to {last name of first_per, ¬
        first name of first_per, job title of first_per, image of first_per}
end tell
(*
temporarily save Address Book TIFF format picture because setting the data
of container fields is not supported in FileMaker's AppleScript support.
The TIFF import is done at the end with a call to a special ScriptMaker
script...
*)
-- control the Address Book application...
tell application "Address Book"
```

```
   -- get the selected contacts...
   set sel_people to the selection
   -- get the first selected contact...
   set first_per to first item of sel_people
   -- get the name, title, and image of the first selected contact...
   set {per_lst_nm, per_fst_nm, per_title, per_img} to ¬
      {last name of first_per, first name of first_per, ¬
         job title of first_per, image of first_per}
end tell
(*
temporarily save Address Book TIFF format picture because setting the data
of container fields is not supported in FileMaker's AppleScript support.
The TIFF import is done at the end with a call to a special ScriptMaker
script...
*)
tell application "System Events"
   -- set up file path for the temp tiff file...
   set tif_path to "/var/tmp/tempic.tiff"
   -- open a file reference...
   set file_ref to open for access ¬
      ((POSIX file tif_path) as reference) with write permission
   -- clear all data if file exists...
   set eof of file_ref to 0
   -- write the TIFF data...
   write per_img to file_ref as TIFF picture
   -- close the file reference...
   close access file_ref
end tell
-- control FileMaker Pro...
tell application "FileMaker Pro Advanced"
   tell database "Personnel Records"
      -- create new personnel record...
      set new_rec to create new record
      -- populate the new record with data from Address Book...
      tell new_rec
         show
         set {cell "First Name", cell "Last Name", cell "Title"} to {per_fst_nm, per_lst_nm, per_title}
         -- call the ScriptMaker script that inserts TIFF into container field...
         do script "insertTempTiff"
      end tell
   end tell
end tell
```

This script illustrates AppleScript's capabilities as an integration tool. In the first section, AppleScript takes control of the Address Book application and acquires data from that application. In the last section it instructs FileMaker Pro to create a new record in the Personnel Records database, populates the fields with Address Book text data, and then calls a ScriptMaker script, which imports the contact's TIFF image from its temporary location on disk.

The AppleScript Interface

AppleScript code executes from the script step `Perform AppleScript`, which allows developers to embed AppleScript code in their FileMaker scripts.

As shown in Figure 17.1, FileMaker's Perform AppleScript Options dialog presents two options for embedding AppleScript within ScriptMaker scripts:

- Calculated AppleScript gives developers the ability to programmatically derive AppleScript from a calculation expression, as shown in Figure 17.2. Note that the 30,000 character restriction in the calculation dialog limits how much code one can generate dynamically.
- Native AppleScript accepts a block of text code, up to 30,000 characters.

→ *For more information about using the Specify Calculation dialog,* ***see*** *"The Calculation Function Interface" in Chapter 7, "Calculation Primer."*

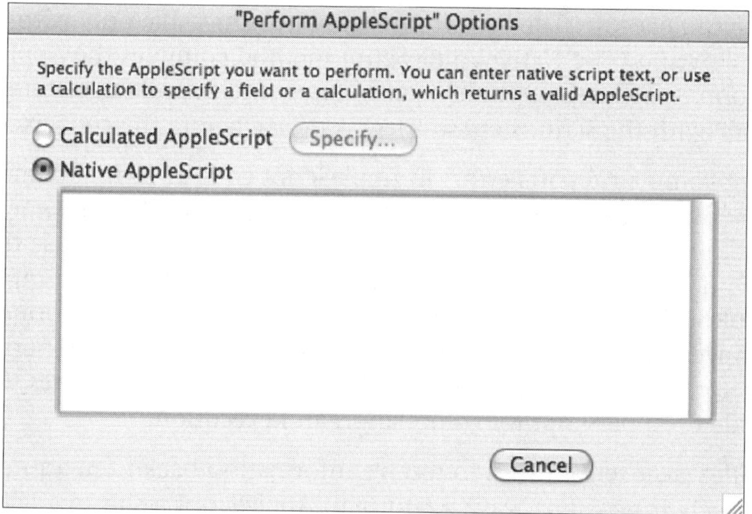

Figure 17.1

The "Perform AppleScript" Options dialog.

→ For more information about using the Specify Calculation dialog, **see** "The Calculation Function Interface" in Chapter 7, "Calculation Primer."

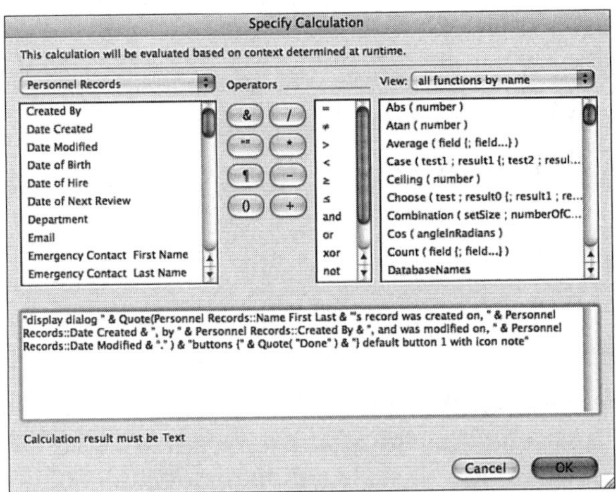

Figure 17.2

Defining AppleScript code with a calculation.

AppleScript code must be compiled by the system before it is executed, which means that performance may be somewhat slower with Calculated AppleScript code because the calculation must first be evaluated by FileMaker and the result compiled by AppleScript before the code can execute. The lag will probably be noticeable only with large Calculated AppleScripts. The Native AppleScript method compiles the AppleScript code when the Perform AppleScript Options dialog closes, and ScriptMaker stores the compiled AppleScript code with the script step, so there is no lag before the code executes.

The AppleScript compiler reports errors in AppleScript code at compile time, so this means that the two methods of Perform AppleScript report errors at different times. The Native AppleScript method reports errors in the code when you attempt to close the "Perform AppleScript" Options dialog, because that's the time that AppleScript compiles the code. Calculated AppleScript reports any errors in the calculation syntax or formatting when you close the Specify Calculation dialog but does not report AppleScript errors until the ScriptMaker script runs because that is the time that FileMaker Pro passes the Calculated AppleScript code to AppleScript for compilation and execution.

Sometimes a FileMaker script needs to receive information back from an AppleScript, but unfortunately there is no direct way to return an AppleScript result to a FileMaker script. Because the `Perform AppleScript` step does not return a result, AppleScript cannot set FileMaker variables, nor can AppleScript pass a parameter to a ScriptMaker script via the `do script` command. Instead, the three most common ways to return AppleScript results to a FileMaker script are indirect:

- **FileMaker fields**—AppleScript can set one or more FileMaker fields with return values:

```
set short_date to ((month of (current date) as number) & "/" & day of ¬
   (current date) & "/" & year of (current date)) as text
tell application "FileMaker Pro Advanced"
   tell database "Personnel Records"
      tell current record
         set field "First Name" to "John"
         set field "Last Name" to "Smith"
         set field "Date of Hire" to short_date
      end tell
   end tell
end tell
```

- **The Clipboard**—AppleScript can place return values on the Clipboard for FileMaker scripts to retrieve with the Paste script step. In cases that require multiple return values, the result should be structured in such a way that it can be parsed by a FileMaker script. Using a carriage return to delimit separate field values, for instance, can be parsed using the FileMaker function MiddleValues():

```
set the clipboard to "John" & return ¬
   & "Smith" & return ¬
   & ((month of (current date) as number) & "/" & day of (current date) ¬
   & "/" & year of (current date)) as text
```

- **A file in a common disk location**—A FileMaker script can use an Import script step to read result data that AppleScript has written to a file in a common location on disk:

```
-- after performing some process...
set AS_result to the result
set result_path to "/var/tmp/ASResult.txt" -- set up file path for the temp text file...
set file_ref to open for access ((POSIX file result_path) as reference) with write permission
set eof of file_ref to 0 -- clear any previous data from the file...
write AS_result to file_ref
close access file_ref
```

About the AppleScript Object Model

AppleScript is an object-oriented scripting language, which means that AppleScript can query and control objects that have been exposed to AppleScript within a "scriptable" application. To use AppleScript to manipulate FileMaker data, you need to be familiar with its object containment hierarchy. For instance, the following AppleScript queries a series of objects, starting with the application itself (FileMaker Pro, in this case):

```
tell application "FileMaker Pro Advanced"
   tell document "Personnel Records"
      tell layout "Form View"
         tell record 2
            return field "Employee ID"
         end tell
      end tell
   end tell
end tell
```

There's an implied hierarchy in this code example, which begins with application as the top-level object (sometimes referred to as the *parent*). Document is an element of application (sometimes referred to as the *child*), whereas layout is an element of document, and so on.

Sometimes the terms *object* and *class* are used interchangeably, but in traditional object-oriented programming (OOP), a *class* is a template that defines the object structure and is used simply to create or instantiate an object of that particular class. So you may have objects A, B, and C, which are three separate objects, but they can all be of the same class.

Database and table objects, concepts familiar to FileMaker Pro developers, belong to a different branch of FileMaker's object hierarchy. A script that has the same result as the previous script, but using the database branch would look like this:

```
tell application "FileMaker Pro Advanced"
   tell database "Personnel Records"
      tell record 2
         return cell "Employee ID"
      end tell
   end tell
end tell
```

The reason for the difference is that FileMaker Pro's object hierarchy has two sides: the user interface side, in which the "document" contains objects such as "window" and "layout," and then there's the underlying "database," which contains objects such as "table" and "FileMaker Script." It's important to understand the containment hierarchy of the application being scripted because the objects called by the script determine the scope of the data that the script can access. Figure 17.3 illustrates FileMaker Pro's containment hierarchy.

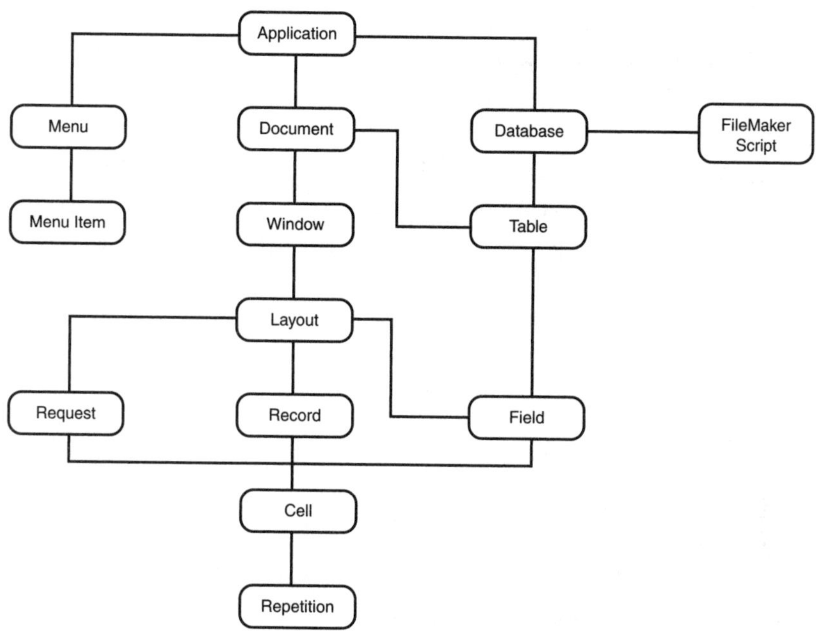

Figure 17.3

FileMaker Pro's containment hierarchy.

Understanding the Application Dictionary

The application dictionary documents the containment hierarchy of an application's object model, along with the commands and properties of the object model that are available for AppleScript to control. Viewing an application dictionary can be a good way to familiarize oneself with the AppleScript capabilities within a given application.

View an application's dictionary by dragging and dropping the application's icon onto the AppleScript Editor icon, which is in the /Applications/AppleScript/ folder on the startup hard drive. The Open Dictionary command in the File menu of the Script Editor will also open the Application Dictionaries for study. Every scriptable application must have a dictionary; if the dictionary window will not open, the application is not scriptable. The application dictionary appears in a dictionary window like the one shown in Figure 17.4.

The dictionary window provides three different ways to browse the classes, commands, and properties within the object model:

- **Suite View**—This view shows the classes, commands, and properties organized into functional "suites." Typically there will be a *Required suite*, which is the base set of commands, classes, and properties required by all scriptable applications. Next will be the *Application suite*, which shows all the classes, commands, and properties that pertain specifically to the parent application. Additionally, there may be additional suites from the system or from AppleScript itself that the application lists in its dictionary because those suites pertain to the application's operation.

- **Containment View**—This view shows the parent/child relationship between objects.
- **Inheritance View**—In OOP, child objects can "inherit" properties and commands from the parent object; this view shows the object inheritance hierarchy.

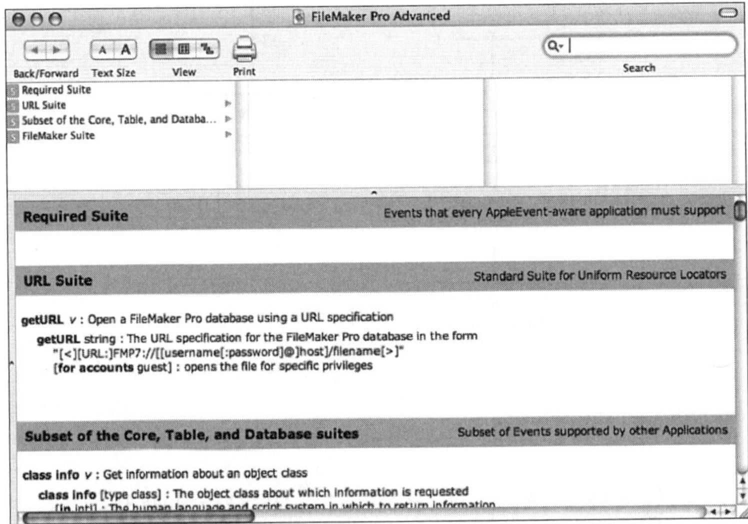

Figure 17.4

The application dictionary window.

The dictionary window denotes the type of object it displays using the following icons:

Suites—Functional groups of classes, commands, properties, and elements.

Commands—Directives that instruct the application to perform an action. Examples of commands include, Open, Close, Copy, and Paste. In some cases a command is actually a function; that is, it returns a value as the result of its operation. For those commands that return a result, the last line of the dictionary definition begins with → string, which indicates that the command returns a text value as its result.

Classes—Classes list the objects that AppleScript can "tell" to do something; as in, tell application 'FileMaker Pro', tell layout 'Form View', and so on.

Properties—Properties, sometimes also referred to as *attributes*, are simply class variables that store information about a particular instance of a class. For example, the FileMaker Pro field class has the property choices, which stores the value list associated with the field instance on a particular layout.

E **Elements**—Classes often contain one or more elements, which typically contain a specific type of data. Elements, in most cases, are also classes, so they may also be referred to as child objects. For instance, the FileMaker field class contains the cell class as an element, so field is the parent object whose child object is cell.

AppleScript Examples

The following examples illustrate some other AppleScript possibilities with FileMaker:

- **Showing records/creating found sets**—This AppleScript shows any record in the Personnel Records database where the Date of Hire is in the year 2007:

```
tell application "FileMaker Pro Advanced"
   tell database "Personnel Records"
      tell table "Personnel Records"
         show (every record whose cellValue of cell "Date of Hire" ends with 2007)
      end tell
   end tell
end tell
```

- **Getting the current state of objects**—This AppleScript gets FileMaker's current View state. If the Browse Mode, View as Form, and Status Area items of the View menu are checked, this script sets the view_status variable to a list containing three text strings: {"Browse Mode","View as Form","Status Area"}.

```
tell application "FileMaker Pro Advanced"
   set view_state to name of every menu item of menu "View" whose checked is true
end tee
```

- **Getting an inventory of elements**—This AppleScript sets a variable to list properties for every field on a particular layout:

```
tell application "FileMaker Pro Advanced"
   tell document "Personnel Records"
      tell layout "Form View"
         set layout_fields to ¬
            {name of every field, ¬
               default type of every field, ¬
               access of every field, ¬
               formula of every cell}
      end tell
   end tell
end tell
```

Other Resources

The following list provides website addresses that give more information about programming with AppleScript:

- **AppleScript Language Guide**: http://developer.apple.com/techpubs/macosx/Carbon/interapplicationcomm/AppleScript/AppleScriptLangGuide/index.html
- **Apple AppleScript Users List**: http://www.lists.apple.com/mailman/listinfo/applescript-users
- **MacScripter's Forums**: http://bbs.applescript.net/
- **AppleScript Resources**: http://www.apple.com/macosx/features/applescript/resources.html

PART VI

Quick Reference

CHAPTER 18

FileMaker Error Codes

Error Codes in FileMaker

FileMaker can generate a number of possible errors in the course of a script. In fact, FileMaker generates errors at various times, such as during normal use of the application—but in general these errors are reported directly to the user via a dialog box. It's only during scripting, or during certain interactions with the Web Publishing Engine, that you are in a position to trap and examine the error codes FileMaker generates. To do so requires that Error Capture be set to On during the script, and that the script developer use the Get(LastError) function to inspect any possible errors.

Remember that the FileMaker error results that occur during scripts are transient. You must check for an error immediately after a script step executes. If script step A produces an error, and a subsequent script step B executes with no error, the error from script step A will be "forgotten" after script step B executes. Hence the name of the Get(**Last**Error) function: It reports only the last error code, even if that error code is 0 (no error). (Note, though, that the error code from the last script step will be retained even after the script has stopped executing, until it is replaced by another script. Further, the script steps Exit Script and Halt Script do *not* clear the previous error code.)

Changes to the Script Debugger introduced in FileMaker Pro 9 Advanced provide another tool for determining whether any errors occurred during the execution of a script. As shown in Figure 18.1, the Script Debugger automatically tells you the error code generated by the last executed script step. Further, the option to Pause on Error allows you to quickly test a script for errors without stepping through it line by line.

Table 18.1 lists the errors that can arise during normal operation of FileMaker or during ODBC access. The errors listed in Table 18.2 are those generated by the FileMaker Server Command Line Interface. Finally, Table 18.3 lists errors generated by the Web Publishing Engine.

Error codes 951 through 958 are returned only by databases being accessed via the Web.

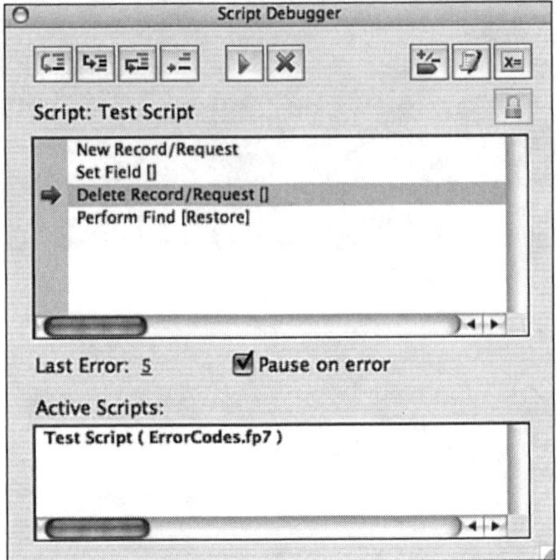

Figure 18.1

The Script Debugger in FileMaker Pro 9 Advanced shows the error code generated by each script step as it executes.

Table 18.1 FileMaker Error Codes

Code	Error Description
-1	Unknown error.
0	No error.
1	User canceled action.
2	Memory error.
3	Command is unavailable (for example, wrong operating system, wrong mode, and so on).
4	Command is unknown.
5	Command is invalid (for example, a Set Field script step does not have a calculation specified).
6	File is read-only.
7	Running out of memory.
8	Empty result.
9	Insufficient privileges.
10	Requested data is missing.
11	Name is not valid.
12	Name already exists.
13	File or object is in use.
14	Out of range.
15	Can't divide by zero.
16	Operation failed, request retry (for example, a user query).
17	Attempt to convert foreign character set to UTF-16 failed.

Code	Error Description
18	Client must provide account information to proceed.
19	String contains characters other than A-Z, a-z, 0-9 (ASCII).
100	File is missing.
101	Record is missing.
102	Field is missing.
103	Relationship is missing.
104	Script is missing.
105	Layout is missing.
106	Table is missing.
107	Index is missing.
108	Value list is missing.
109	Privilege set is missing.
110	Related tables are missing.
111	Field repetition is invalid.
112	Window is missing.
113	Function is missing.
114	File reference is missing.
115	Specified menu set is not present.
116	Specified layout object is not present.
117	Specified data source is not present.
130	Files are damaged or missing and must be reinstalled.
131	Language pack files are missing (such as template files).
200	Record access is denied.
201	Field cannot be modified.
202	Field access is denied.
203	No records in file to print, or password doesn't allow print access.
204	No access to field(s) in sort order.
205	User does not have access privileges to create new records; import will overwrite existing data.
206	User does not have password change privileges, or file is not modifiable.
207	User does not have sufficient privileges to change database schema, or file is not modifiable.
208	Password does not contain enough characters.
209	New password must be different from existing one.
210	User account is inactive.
211	Password has expired.
212	Invalid user account and/or password. Please try again.
213	User account and/or password does not exist.

continues

Table 18.1 Continued

Code	Error Description
214	Too many login attempts.
215	Administrator privileges cannot be duplicated.
216	Guest account cannot be duplicated.
217	User does not have sufficient privileges to modify administrator account.
300	File is locked or in use.
301	Record is in use by another user.
302	Table is in use by another user.
303	Database schema is in use by another user.
304	Layout is in use by another user.
306	Record modification ID does not match.
400	Find criteria are empty.
401	No records match the request.
402	Selected field is not a match field for a lookup.
403	Exceeding maximum record limit for trial version of FileMaker Pro.
404	Sort order is invalid.
405	Number of records specified exceeds number of records that can be omitted.
406	Replace/Reserialize criteria are invalid.
407	One or both match fields are missing (invalid relationship).
408	Specified field has inappropriate data type for this operation.
409	Import order is invalid.
410	Export order is invalid.
412	Wrong version of FileMaker Pro used to recover file.
413	Specified field has inappropriate field type.
414	Layout cannot display the result.
415	One or more required related records are not available.
416	Primary key required from data source table.
417	Database is not supported for ODBC operations.
500	Date value does not meet validation entry options.
501	Time value does not meet validation entry options.
502	Number value does not meet validation entry options.
503	Value in field is not within the range specified in validation entry options.
504	Value in field is not unique as required in validation entry options.
505	Value in field is not an existing value in the database file as required in validation entry options.
506	Value in field is not listed on the value list specified in validation entry option.
507	Value in field failed calculation test of validation entry option.
508	Invalid value entered in Find mode.
509	Field requires a valid value.

Code	Error Description
510	Related value is empty or unavailable.
511	Value in field exceeds maximum number of allowed characters.
512	Record was already modified by another user.
513	Record must have a value in some field to be created.
600	Print error has occurred.
601	Combined header and footer exceed one page.
602	Body doesn't fit on a page for current column setup.
603	Print connection lost.
700	File is of the wrong file type for import.
706	EPSF file has no preview image.
707	Graphic translator cannot be found.
708	Can't import the file or need color monitor support to import file.
709	QuickTime movie import failed.
710	Unable to update QuickTime file reference because the database file is read-only.
711	Import translator cannot be found.
714	Password privileges do not allow the operation.
715	Specified Excel worksheet or named range is missing.
716	A SQL query using `DELETE`, `INSERT`, or `UPDATE` is not allowed for ODBC import.
717	There is not enough XML/XSL information to proceed with the import or export.
718	Error in parsing XML file (from Xerces).
719	Error in transforming XML using XSL (from Xalan).
720	Error when exporting; intended format does not support repeating fields.
721	Unknown error occurred in the parser or the transformer.
722	Cannot import data into a file that has no fields.
723	You do not have permission to add records to or modify records in the target table.
724	You do not have permission to add records to the target table.
725	You do not have permission to modify records in the target table.
726	There are more records in the import file than in the target table. Not all records were imported.
727	There are more records in the target table than in the import file. Not all records were updated.
729	Errors occurred during import. Records could not be imported.
730	Unsupported Excel version. (Convert file to Excel 7.0 [Excel 95], Excel 97, 2000, or XP format and try again.)
731	The file you are importing from contains no data.
732	This file cannot be inserted because it contains other files.
733	A table cannot be imported into itself.
734	This file type cannot be displayed as a picture.

continues

Table 18.1 Continued

Code	Error Description
735	This file type cannot be displayed as a picture. It will be inserted and displayed as a file.
736	Too much data to export to this format. It will be truncated.
800	Unable to create file on disk.
801	Unable to create temporary file on System disk.
802	Unable to open file.
803	File is single user or host cannot be found.
804	File cannot be opened as read-only in its current state.
805	File is damaged; use `Recover` command.
806	File cannot be opened with this version of FileMaker Pro.
807	File is not a FileMaker Pro file or is severely damaged.
808	Cannot open file because access privileges are damaged.
809	Disk/volume is full.
810	Disk/volume is locked.
811	Temporary file cannot be opened as FileMaker Pro file.
813	Record Synchronization error on network.
814	File(s) cannot be opened because maximum number is open.
815	Couldn't open lookup file.
816	Unable to convert file.
817	Unable to open file because it does not belong to this solution.
819	Cannot save a local copy of a remote file.
820	File is in the process of being closed.
821	Host forced a disconnect.
822	FMI files not found; reinstall missing files.
823	Cannot set file to single-user, guests are connected.
824	File is damaged or not a FileMaker file.
900	General spelling engine error.
901	Main spelling dictionary not installed.
902	Could not launch the Help system.
903	Command cannot be used in a shared file.
905	No active field selected; command can be used only if there is an active field.
906	Current file must be shared to use this command.
920	Can't initialize the spelling engine.
921	User dictionary cannot be loaded for editing.
922	User dictionary cannot be found.
923	User dictionary is read-only.
951	An unexpected error occurred (web).
954	Unsupported XML grammar (web).

Code	Error Description
955	No database name (web).
956	Maximum number of database sessions exceeded (web).
957	Conflicting commands (web).
958	Parameter missing (web).
1200	Generic calculation error.
1201	Too few parameters in the function.
1202	Too many parameters in the function.
1203	Unexpected end of calculation.
1204	Number, text constant, field name, or "(" expected.
1205	Comment is not terminated with "*/".
1206	Text constant must end with a quotation mark.
1207	Unbalanced parenthesis.
1208	Operator missing; function not found or "(" not expected.
1209	Name (such as field name or layout name) is missing.
1210	Plug-in function has already been registered.
1211	List usage is not allowed in this function.
1212	An operator (for example, +, -, *) is expected here.
1213	This variable has already been defined in the Let function.
1214	AVERAGE, COUNT, EXTEND, GETREPETITION, MAX, MIN, NPV, STDEV, SUM, and GETSUMMARY: Expression found where a field alone is needed.
1215	This parameter is an invalid Get function parameter.
1216	Only Summary fields allowed as first argument in GETSUMMARY.
1217	Break field is invalid.
1218	Cannot evaluate the number.
1219	A field cannot be used in its own formula.
1220	Field type must be normal or calculated.
1221	Data type must be number, date, time, or Timestamp.
1222	Calculation cannot be stored.
1223	The function is not implemented.
1224	The function is not defined.
1225	The function is not supported in this context.
1300	The specified name can't be used.
1400	ODBC driver initialization failed; make sure the ODBC drivers are properly installed.
1401	Failed to allocate environment (ODBC).
1402	Failed to free environment (ODBC).
1403	Failed to disconnect (ODBC).
1404	Failed to allocate connection (ODBC).
1405	Failed to free connection (ODBC).

continues

Table 18.1 Continued

Code	Error Description
1406	Failed check for SQL API (ODBC).
1407	Failed to allocate statement (ODBC).
1408	Extended error (ODBC).
1409	Error (ODBC).
1413	Failed communication link (ODBC).

Table 18.2 FileMaker Server Command Line Error Messages

Code	Error Description
10001	Invalid parameter.
10502	Host was unreachable.
10504	Cannot disconnect administrator..
10600	Schedule is missing.
10604	Cannot enable schedule.
10606	Invalid backup destination for schedule.
10801	Locale was not found.
10900	Engine is offline.
10901	Too many files are open.
10902	File is not open.
10903	File by the same name is already open.
10904	File for this operation was not found.
11000	User specified an invalid command.
11001	User specified invalid options.
11002	Command is invalid as formatted.
11005	Client does not exist.
20302	Unknown Universal Path Type.
20400	File operation canceled.
20401	End of file.
20402	No permission.
20404	File is not open.
20405	File not found.
20406	File exists.
20407	File already open.
20500	Directory not found.
20600	Network initialization error.

Table 18.3 Web Publishing Engine Error Codes

Code	Error Description
10000	Invalid header name.
10001	Invalid HTTP status code.
10100	Unknown session error.
10101	Requested session name is already used.
10102	Session could not be accessed—maybe it does not exist.
10103	Session has timed out.
10104	Specified session object does not exist.
10200	Unknown messaging error.
10201	Message formatting error.
10202	Message SMTP fields error.
10203	Message "To Field" error.
10204	Message "From Field" error.
10205	Message "CC Field" error.
10206	Message "BCC Field" error.
10207	Message "Subject Field" error.
10208	Message "Reply-To Field" error.
10209	Message body error.
10210	Recursive mail error—attempted to call send_email() inside an email XSLT stylesheet.
10211	SMTP authentication error—either login failed or wrong type of authentication provided.
10212	Invalid function usage—attempted to call set_header(), set_status_code(), or set_cookie() inside an email XSLT stylesheet.
10213	SMTP server is invalid or is not working.

CHAPTER 19

FileMaker Keyboard Shortcuts

Working Quickly, Saving Time

FileMaker is a rapid application development (RAD) tool. As with any tool, how "rapid" it really is depends to a great degree on a developer's mastery of the tool. It's one thing to know how to get something done—another to know how to get it done quickly. There are many aspects to knowing how to work quickly in FileMaker, from using the Copy Table/Field/Script step commands in FileMaker Pro Advanced, to using custom functions and script parameters to abstract and automate frequently used logic. But we have also observed over the years that the fastest users of the tool tend to be those who also heavily use keyboard shortcuts.

Like any modern software application, FileMaker has many keyboard shortcuts hidden under the hood—probably about 400 by our count, though that number is not exact. Of those, we'd list a couple dozen or so as being critical to working quickly in FileMaker, and perhaps another dozen as desirable to master.

This chapter is divided into two broad areas. In the first, we examine a number of important areas of FileMaker development and discuss the shortcuts we feel are most important in each area. The second section is a comprehensive listing of keyboard shortcuts for menu items.

Note

With the advent of FileMaker Pro Advanced and its Custom Menus feature, it became possible to alter the landscape of FileMaker keyboard shortcuts almost beyond recognition. For this reason the About FileMaker dialog box now includes the words Custom Menus Active in the Info section if you're working in a file that has a custom menu set active. (If you're trying to provide phone help to someone, and her copy of FileMaker doesn't respond to "normal" commands, you can have her check this dialog to see whether custom menus may be in effect.) So just be advised that all information in this chapter assumes that the standard FileMaker menu set is in effect.

Essential Shortcuts by Group

In this section we'll call out shortcuts we believe are essential in each of a number of areas. We'll also delve into some more specialized or lesser-known shortcuts in each area as well.

Keyboard Essentials

Shortcuts in this section should be required knowledge for all FileMaker Pro developers. If you haven't mastered these, you need to spend more time with FileMaker Pro!

Working with Modes

Function	Mac Key	Windows Key
Browse Mode	⌘-B	Ctrl+B
Layout Mode	⌘-L	Ctrl+L
Find Mode	⌘-F	Ctrl+F
Preview Mode	⌘-U	Ctrl+U

Working with Files

Function	Mac Key	Windows Key
Open (File)	⌘-O	Ctrl+O
Open Remote (File)	Shift-⌘-O	Ctrl+Shift+O
Force a password dialog to display when opening a file	Hold down the Option key while opening the file.	Hold down the Shift key while opening the file.

Working with Records

Function	Mac Key	Windows Key
New Record/Request/Layout	⌘-N	Ctrl+N
Delete Record/Request/Layout	⌘-E	Ctrl+E
Duplicate Record/Request	⌘-D	Ctrl+D
Omit Record	⌘-T	Ctrl+T
Show All Records	⌘-J	Ctrl+J
Sort Records	⌘-S	Ctrl+S

Developer Essentials

Function	Mac Key	Windows Key
Manage Accounts and Privileges		Alt+F+G+A
Manage Fields	Shift-⌘-D	Shift+Ctrl+D
Manage Custom Functions		Alt+F+G+C
Manage Value Lists		Alt+F+G+V
ScriptMaker	Shift-⌘-S	Shift+Ctrl+S

When using keyboard shortcuts, keep the following in mind:

- It's possible to hold down the Option key (Mac) or Shift key (Windows) to skip a confirmation dialog when deleting an item, be it a record, a field, a script step, or the like. The sole exception concerns deleting a layout: FileMaker always prompts you for confirmation before deleting a layout.
- The only available shortcuts for Manage Custom Functions and Manage Value Lists are Windows Alt+key combinations. This is unfortunate because these tools form an integral part of at least our own development processes, so we'd love to see a single shortcut working on both Mac and PC for each of these items.

Navigation

The shortcuts in this section are concerned not only with moving around between records but also moving around between layouts and among found sets of records.

Function	Mac Key	Windows Key
Next/Previous Record	Ctrl-up/down arrow	Ctrl+up/down arrow
Next/Previous Layout	Ctrl-up/down arrow	Ctrl+up/down arrow
Next/Previous Request	Ctrl-up/down arrow	Ctrl+up/down arrow
Next/Previous Page	Ctrl-up/down arrow	Ctrl+up/down arrow
Hide/Unhide Status Area	⌘-Opt-S	Ctrl+Alt+S
Zoom/Unzoom Window	⌘-Opt-Z	Alt+V+I/O
Omit Multiple Records	Shift-⌘-M	Ctrl+Shift+T

When using shortcuts for navigation, keep the following in mind:

- The Ctrl+up/down arrow shortcut has a different meaning in each mode: in Browse mode it moves between records, in Layout mode between layouts, in Find mode between find requests, and in Preview mode between different pages of the output.
- To omit all records from the current record to the end of the found set, perform the Omit Multiple Records command and choose a large number of records to omit. FileMaker responds that it can omit only a certain number of records and fill in the correct number of remaining records. You can then go ahead and omit these without needing to calculate the exact number yourself.

Data Entry and Formatting

The shortcuts in this section have to do with the mechanics of putting data into fields and with formatting data after it's been entered into a field.

Function	Mac Key	Windows Key
Select All	⌘-A	Ctrl+A
Cut, Copy, Paste	⌘-X, C, V	Ctrl+X, C, V
Copy Current Record (When Not in a Field)	⌘-C	Ctrl+C
Copy All Records	⌘-Opt-C	Ctrl+Shift+C
Paste Without Text Styles	⌘-Opt-V	Ctrl+Shift+V
Plain Text	Shift-⌘-P	Ctrl+Shift+P
Bold Text	Shift-⌘-B	Ctrl+Shift+B
Italic Text	Shift-⌘-I	Ctrl+Shift+I
Underline Text	Shift-⌘-U	Ctrl+Shift+U
Left-Justify Selected Text	⌘-[	Ctrl+[
Center Selected Text	⌘-\	Ctrl+\
Right-Justify Selected Text	⌘-]	Ctrl+]
Increase/Decrease Font Size	Shift-⌘->/<	Ctrl+Shift+>/<
Insert Current Date	⌘-<hyphen>	Ctrl+<hyphen>
Insert Current Time/Timestamp	⌘-;	Ctrl+;
Insert Nonbreaking Space into Text	Opt-space	Ctrl+space
Insert Tab Character into Text	Opt-tab	Ctrl+tab

Be aware of the following when using keyboard shortcuts for data entry and formatting:

- Using Ctrl+C or ⌘-C in Browse mode when you're not in any field of the current record copies the entire record as tab-delimited text. Using ⌘-Opt-C or Ctrl+Shift+C copies all records in the found set, again as a tab-delimited text block.
- Using Shift-⌘->/< or Ctrl+Shift+>/< to increase or decrease font sizes normally moves the font size up or down through the list of "standard" font sizes. If you hold down Shift (Windows) or Option (Mac), the changes occur in one-point increments instead.
- The ⌘/Ctrl+; shortcut inserts the current time if the selected field is of type text, time, or number, but inserts the current Timestamp if the current field is of type Timestamp.

Managing Fields

The shortcuts in this section work only within the Fields tab of the Manage Database dialog.

Function	Mac Key	Windows Key
Manage Database	Shift-⌘-D	Ctrl+Shift+D
Text Data Type	⌘-T	Ctrl+T
Number Data Type	⌘-N	Ctrl+N
Date Data Type	⌘-D	Ctrl+D
Time Data Type	⌘-I	Ctrl+I
Timestamp Data Type	⌘-M	Ctrl+M
Container Data Type	⌘-R	Ctrl+R
Calculation Data Type	⌘-L	Ctrl+L
Summary Data Type	⌘-S	Ctrl+S
Field Options	Shift-⌘-O	Alt+N
Reorder Tables or Fields in a List	⌘-<up/down arrow>	Ctrl+<up/down arrow>

Working with the Relationships Graph

Many keyboard shortcuts and techniques apply to the Relationships Graph. The following is a selection of the most useful: Consult the online help for a full listing.

Function	Mac Key	Windows Key
New Table Occurrence	Shift-⌘-T	Ctrl+Shift+T
New Relationship	Shift-⌘-R	Ctrl+Shift+R, Insert
Edit Relationship	Shift-⌘-R	Ctrl+Shift+R
New Text Note	Shift-⌘-N	Ctrl+Shift+N
Duplicate Selected Items	⌘-D	Ctrl+D
Select All Table Occurrences Directly Related to the Current Table Occurrence	⌘-Y	Ctrl+Y
Select All Table Occurrences with the Same Source Table as the Current Table Occurrence	⌘-U	Ctrl+U
Toggle the Display Mode of Selected Table Occurrences	⌘-T	Ctrl+T

Following are some additional shortcuts to be aware of:

- The Up, Down, Left, and Right arrows can be used to cycle through the elements of the Graph (table occurrences, relationships, notes), selecting each one in turn. After an item has been selected, other keyboard shortcuts can open the item for editing.
- Typing on the keyboard selects objects containing text that matches what is being typed.
- Using the Control/Shift key in conjunction with the arrow keys moves any selected table occurrences.
- Using Ctrl+Shift in combination with the arrow keys resizes any selected table occurrences.

Working with Layouts

Layout mode is where FileMaker's famously quick-to-develop GUIs (graphical user interfaces) get built. A thorough knowledge of important layout shortcuts is a must-have for a FileMaker developer.

Function	Mac Key	Windows Key
Group	⌘-R	Ctrl+R
Ungroup	Shift-⌘-R	Ctrl+Shift+R
Lock	Opt-⌘-L	Ctrl+Alt+L
Unlock	Shift-Opt-⌘-L	Ctrl+Alt+Shift+L
Bring Forward	Shift-⌘-[	Ctrl+Shift+[
Bring to Front	Opt-⌘-[	Ctrl+Alt+[
Send Backward	Shift-⌘-]	Ctrl+Shift+]
Send to Back	Opt-⌘-]	Ctrl+Alt+]
Align Left, Right, Top, Bottom	Opt-⌘-<left, right, up, down arrow>	Ctrl+Alt+<left, right, up, down arrow>
Field Control Setup	Opt-⌘-F	Ctrl+Shift+F
Field Control Behavior	Opt-⌘-K	Ctrl+Shift+K
Field Control Borders	Opt-⌘-B	Ctrl+Shift+B
Insert Merge Field	Opt-⌘-M	Ctrl+Shift+M
View Object Info		Alt+V+N
Select Similar Objects	Opt-⌘-A	Ctrl+Shift+A

When working with layouts, the following may also be of some value:

- In Layout mode, ⌘-dragging or Ctrl+dragging causes all objects touched by the selection rectangle to be selected. This can be easier than dragging a selection rectangle that fully encloses the desired objects.
- Use Opt-⌘-A/Ctrl+Shift+A to select all objects of the same type as the currently selected objects. You can use this technique to select all text labels, for example.
- As in many graphical layout applications, the arrow keys can be used to move selected layout objects a pixel at a time in any direction.
- The Object Info window is useful for exact positioning of objects. We usually set the measurement units to pixels. Unfortunately, the only shortcut to this feature at present is an Alt+key combination on Windows.
- Shift-dragging restricts the movement of selected objects to a horizontal or vertical direction.
- Ctrl+/Opt-dragging creates a duplicate of the selected objects.
- Shift-dragging, combined with the Opt or Ctrl key, drags a duplicate of selected objects along a horizontal or vertical axis.

- Double-clicking a layout tool in the status area "locks" the tool, causing it to remain selected through multiple uses. Pressing Esc or Enter "unlocks" and deselects the tool, selecting the Pointer tool instead (the default). Pressing Enter when the Pointer tool is selected reselects the most recently used layout tool.
- Any object formatting options chosen while no layout object is selected will become the defaults for any new objects. If you ⌘-click (Mac) or Ctrl+click (Windows) an existing object, its attributes become the default.

Scripting

A number of useful shortcuts pertain to ScriptMaker.

Note that functions marked with an (A) are available only in FileMaker Pro Advanced.

Function	Mac Key	Windows Key
Open ScriptMaker	⌘-Shift-S	Ctrl+Shift+S
Scroll Through Script List	Up/Down arrows	Up/Down arrows
Move Selected Script Up or Down in the List	⌘-Up/Down arrows	Ctrl+Up/Down arrows
Toggle Check box to Include Selected Script in Scripts Menu	Space	Space
Select a Script by Name (When Scripts List Is Active)	Begin typing script name	Begin typing script name
Select All Scripts	⌘-A	Ctrl+A
Copy Selected Scripts (A)	⌘-C	Ctrl+C
Paste Copied Script(s) (A)	⌘-V	Ctrl+V
Navigate Up or Down Through Available Script Steps	Up/Down arrows	Up/Down arrows
Select a Script Step by Name (When Script Steps List Is Active)	Begin typing script step name	Begin typing script step name
Insert Selected Script Step into Script	Return/Enter or Space	Enter
Select All Script Steps	⌘-A	Ctrl+A
Copy Selected Script Steps (A)	⌘-C	Ctrl+C
Paste Copied Script Steps (A)	⌘-V	Ctrl+V
Move Selected Script Step Up or Down in the List	⌘-Up/Down arrows	Ctrl+Up/Down arrows
Delete Selected Script Steps	Delete	Backspace/Delete

When editing a script step that has options accessible via a Specify button, pressing the spacebar on the Mac is generally equivalent to clicking the Specify button. On Windows, Alt+F accomplishes the same thing.

Navigating the FileMaker Interface

A number of shortcuts can help you navigate through the FileMaker interface itself. Using keyboard commands, you can trigger buttons, move between elements of a dialog box, and scroll quickly though pop-up lists and menus.

Function	Mac Key	Windows Key
Move Between Tabs in a Dialog Box		Ctrl+Tab
Move Backward and Forward Between Items/Areas Within a Dialog	Shift-Tab/Tab	Shift+Tab/Tab
Move Up and Down Within a Pop-up List or Menu	Up/Down arrow	Up/Down arrow
Move to Beginning or End of a Pop-up List or Menu	Home/End	Home/End
Cancel a Dialog	Esc	Esc
Submit a Dialog (Choose the Default Button)	Enter	Enter

The Mac OS has weaker support for tabbing through and activating elements in a dialog box. For those dialogs where it's possible to do this on the Mac OS, only a few of the elements are accessible via the keyboard. In Windows, by contrast, virtually every aspect of a dialog can be selected and triggered via the keyboard.

Menu Reference

The following table presents a list of all of the menu items in FileMaker Pro and FileMaker Pro Advanced. We list the Mac and Windows keyboard shortcuts, as well as the Windows Alt+key equivalents.

We consider certain commands essential knowledge for FileMaker developers. We've marked these with an asterisk (*).

File Menu

Menu Item or Submenu	Mac OS Key	Windows Key	Windows Alt
New Database			Alt+F+N
*Open	⌘-O	Ctrl+O	Alt+F+O
*Open Remote	Shift-⌘-O	Ctrl+Shift+O	Alt+F+M
Open Recent			Alt+F+T+item number
*Close	⌘-W	Ctrl+W	Alt+F+C
Manage			
*Database	Shift-⌘-D	Ctrl+Shift+D	Alt+F+G+D
Accounts and Privileges			Alt+F+G+A
Value Lists			Alt+F+G+V

Menu Item or Submenu	Mac OS Key	Windows Key	Windows Alt
Scripts	⌘-Shift-S	Ctrl+Shift+S	Alt+F+G+S
External Data Sources			Alt+F+G+E
Custom Functions			Alt+F+G+C
Custom Menus			Alt+F+G+M
Sharing			Alt+F+H
FileMaker Network			Alt+F+H+N
ODBC/JDBC			Alt+F+H+O
Instant Web Publishing			Alt+F+H+W
File Options			Alt+F+F
Change Password			Alt+F+W
Print Setup			Alt+F+S
Print	⌘-P	Ctrl+P	Alt+F+P
Import Records			Alt+F+I
File			Alt+F+I+F
Folder			Alt+F+I+D
XML Data Source			Alt+F+I+X
ODBC Data Source			Alt+F+I+O
Export Records			Alt+F+E
Save/Send Records As			
Excel			Alt+F+R+E
PDF			Alt+F+R+P
Send Mail			Alt+F+L
Send Link			Alt+F+K
Save a Copy As			Alt+F+Y
Recover			Alt+F+V
*Exit (Windows only)		Ctrl+Q	Alt+F+X

FileMaker Pro/Advanced Menu (Mac OS Only)

Menu Item or Submenu	Mac OS Key	Windows Key	Windows Alt
Preferences	⌘-,		
*Quit	⌘-Q		
Sharing			
FileMaker Network			
Instant Web Publishing			
ODBC/JDBC			

Edit Menu

Menu Item or Submenu	Mac OS Key	Windows Key	Windows Alt
*Undo	⌘-Z	Ctrl+Z	Alt+E+U
Redo	⌘-Y	Ctrl+Y	Alt+E+R
*Cut	⌘-X	Ctrl+X	Alt+E+T
*Copy	⌘-C	Ctrl+C	Alt+E+C
*Paste	⌘-V	Ctrl+V	Alt+E+P
Paste Special			Alt+E+S
*Clear	Del	Del	Alt+E+E
*Duplicate		Ctrl+D	Alt+E+D
*Select All	⌘-A	Ctrl+A	Alt+E+A
Find/Replace			
Find/Replace	Shift-⌘-F	Ctrl+Shift+F	Alt+E+L+F
Find Again	⌘-G	Ctrl+G	Alt+E+L+A
Replace and Find Again	Shift-⌘-G	Ctrl+Alt+G	Alt+E+L+R
Find Selected	Shift-⌘-H	Ctrl+Alt+H	Alt+E+L+S
Spelling			
Check Selection			Alt+E+N+S
Check Record			Alt+E+N+R
Check Layout (L)			Alt+E+N+L
Check All			Alt+E+N+A
Correct Word	Shift-⌘-Y	Ctrl+Shift+Y	Alt+E+N+W
Select Dictionaries			Alt+E+N+D
Edit User Dictionary			Alt+E+N+U
Object (Windows Only)			
Links			Alt+E+O+L
Show Objects			Alt+E+O+S
Convert			Alt+E+O+C
Export Field Contents			Alt+E+X
Preferences (Windows Only)			Alt+E+F

View Menu

Note that items marked with (L) are available only in Layout mode.

Menu Item or Submenu	Mac OS Key	Windows Key	Windows Alt
*Browse Mode	⌘-B	Ctrl+B	Alt+V+B
*Find Mode	⌘-F	Ctrl+F	Alt+V+F
*Layout Mode	⌘-L	Ctrl+L	Alt+V+L

Menu Item or Submenu	Mac OS Key	Windows Key	Windows Alt
*Preview Mode	⌘-U	Ctrl+U	Alt+V+P
Go to Layout			Alt+V+Y
View as Form			Alt+V+M
View as List			Alt+V+S
View as Table			Alt+V+E
Toolbars			
Standard			Alt+V+T+S
Text Formatting			Alt+V+T+F
Arrange (L)			Alt+V+T+A
Align (L)			Alt+V+T+G
Tools (L)			Alt+V+T+T
Status Bar (Windows Only)			Alt+V+U
Status Area	Opt-⌘-S	Ctrl+Alt+S	Alt+V+A
Text Ruler			Alt+V+X
Zoom In			Alt+V+I
Zoom Out			Alt+V+O
Page Margins (L)			Alt+V+M
Graphic Rulers (L)			Alt+V+G
Ruler Lines (L)			Alt+V+R
T-Squares (L)	⌘-T	Ctrl+T	Alt+V+Q
Object Info (L)			Alt+V+N
Show			
Buttons (L)			Alt+V+S+B
Sample Data (L)			Alt+V+S+S
Text Boundaries (L)			Alt+V+S+T
Field Boundaries			Alt+V+S+F
Sliding Objects			Alt+V+S+O
Non-Printing Objects			Alt+V+S+N
Tooltips			Alt+V+S+P

Insert Menu

Note that items marked with (L) are available only in Layout mode.

Menu Item or Submenu	Mac OS Key	Windows Key	Windows Alt
Picture			Alt+I+P
QuickTime			Alt+I+Q
Sound			Alt+I+S

Menu Item or Submenu	Mac OS Key	Windows Key	Windows Alt
File			Alt+I+F
Object (Windows Only)			Alt+I+O
Current Date	⌘-<minus>	Ctrl+<minus>	Alt+I+D
Current Time	⌘-;	Ctrl+;	Alt+I+T
Current User Name	Shift-⌘-N	Ctrl+Shift+N	Alt+I+U
(Insert) From Index	⌘-I	Ctrl+I	Alt+I+I
(Insert) from Last Visited	⌘-'	Ctrl+'	Alt+I+L
Record			
Field (L)			Alt+I+F
Part (L)			Alt+I+A
Graphic Object (L)			
Text (L)			Alt+I+G+T
Line (L)			Alt+I+G+L
Rectangle (L)			Alt+I+G+R
Rounded Rectangle (L)			Alt+I+G+U
Oval (L)			Alt+I+G+O
Field/Control (L)			Alt+I+O
Portal (L)			Alt+I+P
Tab Control (L)			Alt+I+B
Web Viewer (L)			Alt+I+V
Button (L)			Alt+I+N
Object (L, Windows Only)			Alt+I+J
Picture (L)			Alt+I+C
Date Symbol (L)			Alt+I+E
Time Symbol (L)			Alt+I+I
User Name Symbol (L)			Alt+I+S
Page Number Symbol (L)			Alt+I+Y
Record Number Symbol (L)			Alt+I+R
*(Insert) Merge Field (L)	Shift-⌘-M	Ctrl+M	Alt+I+M

Format Menu

Note that items marked with (L) are available only in Layout mode.

Menu Item or Submenu	Mac OS Key	Windows Key	Windows Alt
Font			
Configure/More Fonts (Windows Only)			Alt+M+F+F
Size			
Custom			Alt+M+Z+C
Style			
*Plain Text	Shift-⌘-P	Ctrl+Shift+P	Alt+M+S+P
*Bold	Shift-⌘-B	Ctrl+Shift+B	Alt+M+S+B
*Italic	Shift-⌘-I	Ctrl+Shift+I	Alt+M+S+I
*Underline	Shift-⌘-U	Ctrl+Shift+U	Alt+M+S+U
Word Underline			Alt+M+S+W
Double Underline			Alt+M+S+D
Condense			Alt+M+S+C
Extend			Alt+M+S+E
Strikeout			Alt+M+S+K
Small Caps			Alt+M+S+M
Uppercase			Alt+M+S+A
Lowercase			Alt+M+S+L
Title Case			Alt+M+S+T
Superscript	Shift-⌘-<plus>		Alt+M+S+S
Subscript	Shift-⌘-<minus>		Alt+M+S+R
Align Text			
*Left	⌘-[	Ctrl+[	Alt+M+G+L
*Center	⌘-\	Ctrl+\	Alt+M+G+C
*Right	⌘-]	Ctrl+]	Alt+M+G+R
Full	Shift-⌘-\	Ctrl+Shift+\	Alt+M+G+F
Top			Alt+M+G+T
Center			Alt+M+G+E
Bottom			Alt+M+G+B
Line Spacing			
Single			Alt+M+L+S
Double			Alt+M+L+D
Custom			Alt+M+L+C
Orientation			
Horizontal			Alt+M+E+H
Sideways (Asian text only)			Alt+M+E+S

Menu Item or Submenu	Mac OS Key	Windows Key	Windows Alt
Text Color			Alt+M+R
Text (L)			Alt+M+X
Number (L)			Alt+M+N
Date (L)			Alt+M+D
Time (L)			Alt+M+M
Graphic (L)			Alt+M+H
Conditional (L)			Alt+M+A
Field/Control (L)			
*Setup (L)	Shift-Opt-⌘-F	Ctrl+Alt+F	Alt+M+C+S
*Behavior (L)	Shift-Opt-⌘-K	Ctrl+Alt+K	Alt+M+C+H
*Borders (L)	Shift-Opt-⌘-B	Ctrl+Alt+B	Alt+M+C+B
Portal Setup (L)			Alt+M+P
Tab Control Setup (L)			Alt+M+B
Web Viewer Setup (L)			Alt+M+V
Button Setup (L)			Alt+M+U
Format Painter (L)			Alt+M+O
Set Sliding/Printing (L)			Alt+M+I
Set Tooltip (L)			Alt+M+T

Layouts Menu (Layout Mode Only)

Menu Item or Submenu	Mac OS Key	Windows Key	Windows Alt
*New Layout/Report	⌘-N	Ctrl+N	Alt+L+N
Duplicate Layout			Alt+L+U
*Delete Layout	⌘-E	Ctrl+E	Alt+L+D
Go to Layout			
Next (Layout)	Ctrl-<up arrow>	Ctrl+<up arrow>	Alt+L+G+N
Previous (Layout)	Ctrl-<down arrow>	Ctrl+<down arrow>	Alt+L+G+P
Specify			Alt+L+G+S
Layout Setup			Alt+L+Y
Part Setup			Alt+L+A
Set Layout Order			Alt+L+O
Set Tab Order			Alt+L+T
Set Rulers			Alt+L+R
Save Layout	⌘-S	Ctrl+S	Alt+L+S
Revert Layout			Alt+L+E

Records Menu

Menu Item or Submenu	Mac OS Key	Windows Key	Windows Alt
*New Record	⌘-N	Ctrl+N	Alt+R+N
*Duplicate Record	⌘-D	Ctrl+D	Alt+R+A
*Delete Record	⌘-E	Ctrl+E	Alt+R+D
Delete Found/All Records			Alt+R+T
Go to Record			
Next (Record)	Ctrl-<down arrow>	Ctrl+<down arrow>	Alt+R+G+N
Previous (Record)	Ctrl-<up arrow>	Ctrl+<up arrow>	Alt+R+G+P
Specify			Alt+R+G+S
Refresh Window		Ctrl+Shift+R	Alt+R+H
*Show All Records	⌘-J	Ctrl+J	Alt+R+W
Show Omitted Only			Alt+R+I
*Omit Record	⌘-T	Ctrl+T	Alt+R+O
Omit Multiple	Shift-⌘-T	Ctrl+Shift+T	Alt+R+M
*Modify Last Find	⌘-R	Ctrl+R	Alt+R+F
*Sort Records	⌘-S	Ctrl+S	Alt+R+S
Unsort			Alt+R+U
*Replace Field Contents	⌘-=	Ctrl+=	Alt+R+E
Relookup Field Contents			Alt+R+K
Revert Record			Alt+R+R

Requests Menu (Find Mode Only)

Menu Item or Submenu	Mac OS Key	Windows Key	Windows Alt
*Add New Request	⌘-N	Ctrl+N	Alt+R+N
*Duplicate Request	⌘-D	Ctrl+D	Alt+R+U
*Delete Request	⌘-E	Ctrl+E	Alt+R+D
Go to Request			
Next	Ctrl-<down arrow>	Ctrl+<down arrow>	Alt+R+G+N
Previous	Ctrl-<up arrow>	Ctrl+<up arrow>	Alt+R+G+P
Specify			Alt+R+G+S
Show All Records	⌘-J	Ctrl+J	Alt+R+W
Perform Find	Enter	Enter	Alt+R+P
Constrain Found Set			Alt+R+C
Extend Found Set			Alt+R+E
Revert Request			Alt+R+R

Arrange Menu (Layout Mode Only)

Menu Item or Submenu	Mac OS Key	Windows Key	Windows Alt
*Group	⌘-R	Ctrl+R	Alt+A+G
*Ungroup	Shift-⌘-R	Ctrl+Shift+R	Alt+A+U
*Lock	Opt-⌘-L	Ctrl+Alt+L	Alt+A+L
*Unlock	Shift-Opt-⌘-L	Ctrl+Alt+Shift+L	Alt+A+K
Bring to Front	Opt-⌘-[	Ctrl+Alt+[	Alt+A+F
Bring Forward	Shift-⌘-[	Ctrl+Shift+[	Alt+A+W
Send to Back	Opt-⌘-]	Ctrl+Alt+]	Alt+A+B
Send Backward	Shift-⌘-]	Ctrl+Shift+]	Alt+A+C
Rotate	Opt-⌘-R	Ctrl+Alt+R	Alt+A+R
Align			
*Left Edges	Opt-⌘-<left arrow>	Ctrl+Alt+<left arrow>	Alt+A+N+L
Centers			Alt+A+N+C
*Right Edges	Opt-⌘-<right arrow>	Ctrl+Alt+<right arrow>	Alt+A+N+R
*Top Edges	Opt-⌘-<up arrow>	Ctrl+Alt+<up arrow>	Alt+A+N+T
Middles			Alt+A+N+M
*Bottom Edges	Opt-⌘-<down arrow>	Ctrl+Alt+<down arrow>	Alt+A+N+B
Distribute			
Horizontally			Alt+A+D+H
Vertically			Alt+A+D+V
Resize To			
Smallest Width			Alt+A+S+S
Smallest Height			Alt+A+S+M
Smallest Width & Height			Alt+A+S+A
Largest Width			Alt+A+S+L
Largest Height			Alt+A+S+H
Largest Width & Height			Alt+A+S+W
Object Grids	⌘-Shift-Y	Ctrl+Shift+Y	Alt+A+O

Scripts Menu

Menu Item or Submenu	Mac OS Key	Windows Key	Windows Alt
*ScriptMaker	Shift-⌘-S	Ctrl+Shift+S	Alt+S+C
Save Script†	⌘-S	Ctrl+S	Alt+S+S
Save All Scripts†	Opt-⌘-S	Ctrl+Alt+S	Alt+S+A
Revert Script†			Alt+S+R

†Note that the last three commands in this list are available only if an Edit Script window is in the foreground and unsaved script changes are present.

Tools Menu (FileMaker Pro Advanced Only)

Menu Item or Submenu	Mac OS Key	Windows Key	Windows Alt
Script Debugger			Alt+T+D
Debugging Controls			
Step	F5	F5	Alt+T+E+S
Step Into	F6	F6	Alt+T+E+T
Step Out	F7	F7	Alt+T+E+O
Run	F8	Alt+F8	Alt+T+E+R
Halt Script	⌘-F8	Ctrl+F8	Alt+T+E+H
Set Next Step	⌘-Shift-F5	Ctrl+Shift+F5	Alt+T+E+N
Set Breakpoint	⌘-F9	Ctrl+F9	Alt+T+E+B
Remove Breakpoints	⌘-Shift-F9	Ctrl+Shift+F9	Alt+T+E+M
Edit Script	⌘-F10	Ctrl+F10	Alt+T+E+E
Pause on error			Alt+T+E+P
Data Viewer			Alt+T+V
Custom Menus			
Manage Custom Menus			Alt+T+C+M
Database Design Report			Alt+T+G
Developer Utilities			Alt+T+U
File Maintenance			Alt+T+A
Launch PHP Assistant			Alt+T+P

Window Menu

Note

All the window commands (except for New Window) now also act on open scripting windows.

Menu Item or Submenu	Mac OS Key	Windows Key	Windows Alt
New Window			Alt+W+N
Show Window			Alt+W+S+item number
Hide Window			Alt+W+H
Minimize Window	⌘-H		Alt+W+M
Tile Horizontally		Shift+F4	Alt+W+T
Tile Vertically			Alt+W+V
Cascade Windows		Shift+F5	Alt+W+C
Arrange Icons			Alt+W+I
More Windows (W)			Alt+W+M

Help Menu

Menu Item or Submenu	Mac OS Key	Windows Key	Windows Alt
FileMaker Help	⌘-?	F1	Alt+H+H
Keyboard Shortcuts			Alt+H+K
Learning Center			Alt+H+L
Product Documentation			Alt+H+P
User's Guide			Alt+H+P+U
Tutorial			Alt+H+P+T
Customizing Starter Solutions			Alt+H+P+C
Development Guide			Alt+H+P+D
Instant Web Publishing Guide			Alt+H+P+I
ODBC and JDBC Guide			Alt+H+P+O
More Documentation			Alt+H+P+M
Deactivate			Alt+H+A
Downloads and Updates			Alt+H+D
Register Now			Alt+H+R
Send Us Your Feedback			Alt+H+S
About FileMaker Pro Advanced (W)			Alt+H+F

CHAPTER 20

FileMaker Network Ports

About Network Ports

A network *port* may sound like a physical connection of some kind, like the USB ports on the back (or front or side) of your computer. In network terminology, though, a port is most often a logical or virtual concept, part of a network transport protocol (TCP/IP, for example, or UDP). In this sense, a port is a logical destination on a specific host, that is identified with some particular service or listener. Port 21, for example, is often used for FTP servers.

Ports are most often significant to FileMaker administrators who administer or otherwise encounter firewalls. Many firewalls do port-based blocking or filtering of traffic. If traffic to or from a particular port is not permitted across a firewall, services may be disrupted or blocked. For example, if port 21 is blocked on a firewall, an FTP server behind that firewall will be unreachable. If port 5003 is blocked on a firewall, a FileMaker server behind the firewall will be unreachable.

The bulk of these port numbers are set internally by the FileMaker products in question and cannot be changed or overridden. The one exception, noted in Table 20.1, is the web publishing port (80 by default).

Note

For an extensive listing of port numbers, see the list maintained by IANA at http://www.iana.org/assignments/port-numbers. Some of the FileMaker network ports are registered; others are not, though this has little practical significance for FileMaker administrators.

Table 20.1 FileMaker Network Ports

Port	Service
80	The default port for web publishing. (This port can be freely changed in the configuration for the web server being used to serve FileMaker data, so make sure you're aware of whether a non-default port is being used.)
2399	Port used for ODBC and JDBC access to FileMaker Server Advanced. In addition to enabling ODBC/JDBC on the server and in the privilege sets of individual files, traffic must be able to flow to port 2399 on the master server machine from any ODBC/JDBC clients.
5003	Port used for network access to hosted FileMaker databases. To open hosted FileMaker databases, traffic must be able to flow to port 5003 on the server from any FileMaker clients on the network.
16000 16001 16004	These ports are used by the FileMaker Server Admin Console.
16006 16008 16010 16012 16014 16018	These ports are used by the Web Publishing Engine in FileMaker Server Advanced.
50003 50006	These ports are used locally, on the master machine in a FileMaker Server configuration, by the core FileMaker Server services.

CHAPTER 21

FileMaker Server Command Line Reference

Administering FileMaker Server from the Command Line

In addition to administering FileMaker Server using the FileMaker Server Admin Console, it's also possible to administer the server using a command line tool called fmsadmin. The fmsadmin tool is installed along with FileMaker Server itself and can be used to administer instances of FileMaker Server running on the same machine.

The fmsadmin tool behaves like any other command line utility or tool in the Mac OS X or Windows operating systems. It can be invoked directly from the command line (Mac OS X Terminal, Windows Command Prompt). It can also be invoked from within any command line script, and as such can form part of a variety of automated administrative processes.

To invoke fmsadmin from the command line, you'll need to know where the tool is located. As long as the install location is in your system path, simply issuing the command fmsadmin (plus necessary options) is sufficient. The default install locations are as follows:

Mac OS X:

```
/Library/FileMaker Server/Database Server/bin/fmsadmin
```

Windows Server 2003:

```
C:\Program Files\FileMaker\FileMaker Server\Database Server\fmsadmin.exe
```

On Mac OS X, a symbolic link to fmsadmin is created within /usr/bin, which is in the default system path, so you should be able to invoke it without any additional configuration. On Windows, you'll either need to reference it by the full install path, or add C:\Program Files\FileMaker\FileMaker Server\Database Server to your system path.

To issue instructions to FileMaker Server from the command line, you'll need to supply three pieces of information:

- The name of the tool itself (fmsadmin, assuming it is accessible by an existing path; otherwise, the full path to the tool must be specified.
- The name of a particular command to invoke, such as backup to back up files or close to close files.
- You might need one or more options that give further specificity to the command. An example would be

```
fmsadmin close –m "All files closing" –t 120
```

This command closes all files on the server after a 2-minute (120-second) grace period and sends all connected clients a message saying "All files closing."

FileMaker Server Command Line Reference

In the reference that follows, we list the name of each command, along with a description, a general usage template, one or more examples, and explanations of any applicable options. Some of the options are specific to only one or two commands, but most are applicable across several commands.

Note

See Chapter 18, "FileMaker Error Codes," for a list of the errors that may be returned when issuing command line instructions.

backup

Syntax:

fmsadmin backup [file...] [path...] [-dopuw]

Options:

- **-d PATH, --dest PATH**—Specify a destination path for a backup.
- **-o, --offline**—Perform an offline backup.
- **p pass, --password pass**—Password to use to authenticate with the server.
- **u user, --user user**—Username to use to authenticate with the server.
- **-w seconds, --wait seconds**—Specify time in seconds for command to time out.

Description:

The backup command can be used to back up either a single specified file, all the files in a directory, or all the files hosted by a single instance of FileMaker Server. If no destination path is specified, the backup will be created in the directory specified by the Default Backup Folder preference for the specified FileMaker Server.

The backup command can be used alone, in which case it performs a "live" or "hot" backup of the specified files. It can also be used in conjunction with the pause and resume commands. Though this method will interfere with user access to the files, it will also allow the backup to complete more quickly. The pause-backup-resume usage mimics the backup behavior of FileMaker Server 5.5.

Examples:

```
fmsadmin backup Products
fmsadmin backup /Products -d E:\FileMaker_Backups
```

close

Syntax

fmsadmin close [file...] [path...] [-mptuwy]

Options:

- **-m message, --message message**—Specify a text message to send to clients.
- **-p pass, --password pass**—Password to use to authenticate with the server.
- **-t, --grace-time**—Specify time in seconds before clients will be forcibly disconnected.
- **-u user, --user user**—Username to use to authenticate with the server.
- **-w seconds, --wait seconds**—Specify time in seconds for command to time out.
- **-y, --yes**—Automatically answer "yes" to all prompts.

Description:

This command closes one or more database files. It can be used to close a specific file, all the files in a directory, or all files on the server. You can reference a file by its ID rather than its filename; use the command fmsadmin list files -s to get a list of files with their IDs.

Examples:

```
fmsadmin close
fmsadmin close 3 -y
fmsadmin close -y Products.fp7
fmsadmin close -y "Invoice Items.fp7"
```

disable

Syntax:

fmsadmin disable type [schedule #] [-puw]

Options:

- **-p pass, --password pass**—Password to use to authenticate with the server.
- **-u user, --user user**—Username to use to authenticate with the server.
- **-w seconds, --wait seconds**—Specify time in seconds for command to time out.

Description:

This command is used to disable schedules. Schedules are referenced by number. The numbers can be determined by using the fmsadmin list schedules command.

Example:

```
fmsadmin disable schedule 1
```

disconnect

Syntax:

fmsadmin disconnect client [client #] [-mpuwy]

Options:

- **-m message, --message message**—Specify a text message to send to clients.
- **-p pass, --password pass**—Password to use to authenticate with the server.
- **-u user, --user user**—Username to use to authenticate with the server.
- **-w seconds, --wait seconds**—Specify time in seconds for command to time out.
- **-y, --yes**—Automatically answer "yes" to all prompts.

Description:

This command is used to disconnect a specific client. Clients are referenced by client number. Client numbers can be determined by using the LIST CLIENTS command. A specific message can be sent to the client(s) as well.

If no client number is provided, all clients will be disconnected.

Examples:

```
fmsadmin disconnect client 13 -y
fmsadmin disconnect client 12 -m "It's time for lunch, Sarah" -y
```

enable

Syntax:

fmsadmin enable type [schedule #] [-puw]

Options:

- **-p pass, --password pass**—Password to use to authenticate with the server.
- **-u user, --user user**—Username to use to authenticate with the server.
- **-w seconds, --wait seconds**—Specify time in seconds for command to time out.

Description:

This command is used to enable schedules. Schedules are referenced by number. The numbers can be determined by using the fmsadmin list schedules command.

Example:

```
fmsadmin enable schedule 3 –u fred –p mypassword
```

help

Syntax:

fmsadmin help [command]

Options:

None

Description:

This command displays help information on the command line commands and syntax.

Examples:

```
fmsadmin help options
fmsadmin help commands
fmsadmin help resume
```

list

Syntax:

fmsadmin list type [-psuw]

Options:

- **-p pass, --password pass**—Password to use to authenticate with the server.
- **-s, --stats**—Return additional detail about clients or files.
- **-u user, --user user**—Username to use to authenticate with the server.
- **-w seconds, --wait seconds**—Specify time in seconds for command to time out.

Description:

This command can be used to obtain a list of clients, files, plug-ins, or schedules from the server. Among other things, this command returns ID numbers that are necessary for other commands such as enable schedule and similar commands.

Examples:

```
fmsadmin list clients --s
fmsadmin list schedules
fmsadmin list files --s
fmsadmin list plugins
```

open

Syntax:

fmsadmin open [file...] [path...] [-puwy]

Options:

- **-p pass, --password pass**—Password to use to authenticate with the server.
- **-u user, --user user**—Username to use to authenticate with the server.
- **-w seconds, --wait seconds**—Specify time in seconds for command to time out.
- **-y, --yes**—Automatically answer "yes" to all prompts.

Description:

This command is used to open databases. Like the close command, it can be used to open all files on the server, all files within a single directory, or a single named file. If no file or directory is specified, the open command opens all database files in the default and additional database folders.

You can reference a file by its ID rather than its filename; use the command fmsadmin list files -s to get a list of files with their IDs.

Examples:

```
fmsadmin open Clinic.fp7
fmsadmin open --y
fmsadmin open 3 18 34
fmsadmin open /ClinicFiles
```

pause

Syntax:

fmsadmin pause [file...] [path...] [-puw]

Options:

- **-p pass, --password pass**—Password to use to authenticate with the server.
- **-u user, --user user**—Username to use to authenticate with the server.
- **-w seconds, --wait seconds**—Specify time in seconds for command to time out.

Description:

This command is used to pause databases. Like the open and close commands, it can be used to affect all files on the server, all files within a single directory, or a single named file.

You can reference a file by its ID rather than its filename; use the command fmsadmin list files -s to get a list of files with their IDs.

Examples:

```
fmsadmin pause 3
fmsadmin pause myFile
fmsadmin pause --wait 30
```

resume

Syntax:

fmsadmin resume [file...][path...] [-puw]

Options:

- **-p pass, --password pass**—Password to use to authenticate with the server.
- **-u user, --user user**—Username to use to authenticate with the server.
- **-w seconds, --wait seconds**—Specify time in seconds for command to time out.

Description:

This command is used to resume databases that have been paused. Like the open and close commands, it can be used to affect all files on the server, all files within a single directory, or a single named file.

You can reference a file by its ID rather than its filename; use the command fmsadmin list files -s to get a list of files with their IDs.

Examples:

```
fmsadmin resume
fmsadmin resume "Clinic.fp7"
```

run

Syntax:

fmsadmin run schedule [schedule #] [-puw]

Options:

- **-p pass, --password pass**—Password to use to authenticate with the server.
- **-u user, --user user**—Username to use to authenticate with the server.
- **-w seconds, --wait seconds**—Specify time in seconds for command to time out.

Description:

This command is used to run a schedule, specified by number. Schedule numbers can be obtained by using the list schedules command.

Examples:

```
fmsadmin run schedule 3
```

send

Syntax:

fmsadmin send [-cmpuw] [client #] [file...] [path...]

Options:

- **-c, --client**—Used to specify a client number.
- **-m message, --message message**—Specify a text message to send to clients.
- **-p pass, --password pass**—Password to use to authenticate with the server.
- **-u user, --user user**—Username to use to authenticate with the server.
- **-w seconds, --wait seconds**—Specify time in seconds for command to time out.

Description:

This command can be used to send a text message to the specified clients. Messages can be sent to all clients connected to the server, or be limited to just those clients connected to files in a specific path, or to a single specific file, or to a single client specified by number. Unlike other commands, you must use the -c option when specifying a client number.

Examples:

```
fmsadmin send -m "The server will shut down for maintenance in 15 minutes."
fmsadmin send -c 17 -m "Fred, it's time to go home."
fmsadmin send "Clinics.fp7" -m "The Clinics file will shut down in 5 minutes."
```

start

Syntax:

fmsadmin start server

Options:

- **-w seconds, --wait seconds**—Specify time in seconds for command to time out.

Description:

This command instructs FileMaker Server to start. This works only if the FileMaker Server Helper is already running.

Examples:

```
fmsadmin start server
```

status

Syntax:

fmsadmin status type [-puw] [id #] [file]

Options:

- **-p pass, --password pass**—Password to use to authenticate with the server.
- **-u user, --user user**—Username to use to authenticate with the server.
- **--w seconds, --wait seconds**—Specify time in seconds for command to time out.

Description:

This command is used to determine the status of a client or a file.

Examples:

```
fmsadmin status file ""Invoice Items.fp7"
fmsadmin status client 30
```

stop

Syntax:

fmsadmin stop [-fmptuwy]

Options:

- **-f, --force**—Close databases or shut down the server forcefully, without waiting for clients to disconnect gracefully.
- **-m message, --message message**—Specify a text message to send to clients.

- **-p pass, --password pass**—Password to use to authenticate with the server.
- **-t, --grace-time**—Specify time in seconds before clients will be forcibly disconnected.
- **-u user, --user user**—Username to use to authenticate with the server.
- **-w seconds, --wait seconds**—Specify time in seconds for command to time out.
- **-y, --yes**—Automatically answer "yes" to all prompts.

Description:

This command stops the server process. All connected users have 30 seconds to close their open files. This grace period can be changed using the -t option.

Examples:

```
fmsadmin stop
fmsadmin stop -f
fmsadmin stop -t 120 -m "The server will shut down in two minutes."
```

PART VII

Appendix

APPENDIX A

Additional Resources

General Information on Relational Databases

The relational model was first conceived by E. F. Codd and presented in the paper "A Relational Model of Data for Large Shared Data Banks." This paper started the entire relational database industry. Originally published in 1970 in CACM 13, No. 6, this paper is now available online as a PDF file through the ACM Digital Library:

http://doi.acm.org/10.1145/362384.362685

If you'd like to read up on the roots of the relational model (set theory and predicate logic), a pretty readable math book is *Discrete Mathematics* by Richard Johnsonbaugh (ISBN: 0-130-89008-1). We have found it to be succinct on the topics of set theory and predicate logic.

An Introduction to Database Systems by C. J. Date (now in its eighth edition, ISBN: 0-321-19784-4) is a classic overview of database systems with an emphasis on relational database systems. You should consider it essential reading if you want to know your craft well.

Date's main book is dense, not to mention expensive. Though it's certainly a definitive work on database theory, if you find it rough going you may want to try his *Database in Depth: Relational Theory for Practitioners* (ISBN: 0-596-10012-4).

Data Modeling and Database Design

Data Modeling for Information Professionals by Bob Schmidt (ISBN: 0-130-80450-9) gets into much more than just data modeling, but the content is great.

The Data Modeling Handbook by Michael Reingruber and William Gregory (ISBN: 0-471-05290-6) goes further into the data modeling design process.

Handbook of Relational Database Design by Candace Fleming and Barbara von Halle (ISBN: 0-201-11434-8) provides full coverage of design methodologies.

Project Management, Programming, and Software Development

Software Project Survival Guide by Steve McConnell (ISBN: 1-572-31621-7) is a great place to start with project management methodologies if your work still has a bit of the Wild West flavor to it. McConnell's work is all-around excellent...you can't go wrong with anything he writes.

Agile Software Development: The Cooperative Game by Alistair Cockburn (ISBN: 0-321-48275-1) is not prescriptive in the way McConnell's work is. Cockburn provides a useful summary of the more "lean" or "agile" software development methods. If you're looking for a step-by-step guide to improving your methods, this may not be the book for you. If you're looking for big ideas and broad concepts to guide you, this is one of the best books out there.

Code Complete by Steve McConnell (second edition—ISBN: 0-735-61967-0) is the latest edition of the more than ten-year-old, fundamental book on good programming practices. This new edition is thoroughly updated. It's oriented toward structured languages such as C and Java but includes plenty of useful information for developers in any language. You might also try his more recent *Rapid Development* (ISBN: 1-556-15900-5) or *Professional Software Development* (ISBN: 0-321-19367-9).

While we're at it, we have to mention McConnell's latest book, *Software Estimation: Demystifying the Black Art* (ISBN: 0-735-60535-1), an outstanding book on estimating techniques and the ideas that guide them.

Practical Software Requirements by Benjamin L. Kovitz (ISBN: 1-884-77759-7) is an extremely useful and readable book about developing requirements for software, including plenty of information useful to database developers. The book offers helpful discussions of data modeling, among many other topics.

The Pragmatic Programmer: From Journeyman to Master by Andrew Hunt (ISBN: 0-201-61622-X) is a masterful selection of compact, easy-to-digest precepts about the craft of programming. This book will benefit any software developer, regardless of the tools he uses.

Joel on Software by Joel Spolsky (ISBN: 1-590-59389-8) provides an assorted collection of incisive and often irreverent essays on various topics in software development. If you don't feel like buying the book, the essays can be read from the archives of Spolsky's website, www.joelonsoftware.com.

Running a FileMaker Consulting Practice

Managing the Professional Service Firm by David H. Maister (ISBN: 0-684-83431-6) is an essential book if you run or work in a consulting company. This book will open your eyes as it explores every aspect of running a service firm.

The Trusted Advisor by David H. Maister, Charles H. Green, and Robert M. Galford (ISBN: 0-743-21234-7) is more conceptual than the other book but still offers plenty of food for thought for database consultants.

General Resources for Tips and Tricks

Soliant Consulting: http://www.soliantconsulting.com/

Soliant Consulting, the company the authors founded and manage, offers some materials on its site.

FileMaker Pro Advisor: http://filemakeradvisor.com/

For years, FileMaker Advisor has been the place to look for product announcements, news about upcoming FileMaker conferences, product reviews, and tips and tricks.

ISO FileMaker Magazine: http://www.filemakermagazine.com/

ISO Productions has been publishing tips and tricks longer than just about anyone. This site has two levels of content: one for the general public and one for subscribers only.

Database Pros: http://www.databasepros.com/index.html

Database Pros has the largest collection of FileMaker templates and technique examples on the Internet. Especially if you're still learning FileMaker Pro, you should bookmark this site.

FileMaker TechInfo database: http://www.filemaker.com/support/techinfo.html

FileMaker, Inc., publishes its own technical support database online. It contains thousands of articles to help you troubleshoot problems and to help you learn the important details about seldom-visited corners of FileMaker Pro's feature set.

Data Concepts Tips: http://www.dwdataconcepts.com/dwdctips.htm

Don Wieland has created dozens of tips in the form of free downloadable example files. He has separate versions for Windows and Mac.

FM Forums: http://www.fmforums.com

FM Forums hosts an active community of message board participants, exchanging information on working with FileMaker.

FileMaker World Web Ring: http://l.webring.com/hub?ring=fmpring

This web ring links together more than 150 websites with FileMaker-themed content.

FileMaker Developers: http://www.filemaker.com/solutions/find/consultants.html

Trying to find a FileMaker developer or trainer in your part of the world? This site lists consultants and trainers in more than 20 different countries.

Hosting FileMaker Databases on the Web

FileMaker ISPs: http://www.filemaker.com/support/isp.html

After you've created a FileMaker-based web solution, you need to host it on a server that's connected to the Internet. If you or your client doesn't have such a server, you may be able to find a FileMaker Pro web hosting provider at this link.

FileMaker News Sources

FileMaker Newsletters: http://www.filemaker.com/company/newsroom/news/newsletter_signup.html

FileMaker, Inc., offers several newsletters on FileMaker topics, including general news, the latest Knowledge Base articles, and security news.

FMPro.org: http://www.fmpro.org/

The Hot FileMaker Pro News section lists FileMaker-related product announcements and user group meetings.

Plug-ins

FileMaker Plug-in Directory: http://solutions.filemaker.com/solutions/index.jsp

or:

http://solutions.filemaker.com/solutions/search_results.jsp?developer=plug-in&status=Plug-In

FileMaker's own site has the most complete listing of available plug-ins. If you need to find out whether a specialized plug-in even exists, this is the place to start. Although there are many plug-in developers, the following publishers have some of the largest selections.

New Millennium Communications: http://www.nmci.com

- DialogMagic: Allows for enhanced control of standard FileMaker Pro dialogs.
- ExportFM: Enables developers to export images, sound, and movie files in their native formats. (This tool is due to be replaced by a new product known as Media Manager).
- SecureFM: This tool allows extensive customization of the FileMaker menu and command system.

Troi Automatisering: http://www.troi.com/

- Troi Activator Plug-in: Controls scripts on different computers, includes scheduling capabilities.
- Troi Coding Plug-in: Adds capability to use DES encryption to encrypt and decrypt fields.

- Troi Dialog Plug-in: Allows use of dynamic dialogs, including calculation-based progress bars and up to nine input fields.
- Troi File Plug-in: Works with files from within a database. Enables saving and reading of files and the capability to use file and folder information.
- Troi Serial Plug-in: Adds the capability to read and write to serial ports.
- Troi Text Plug-in: Includes XML parsing and a variety of powerful text manipulation tools.
- Troi URL Plug-in: Fills in web forms and retrieves raw data from any HTTP URL.
- Troi ClipSave Plug-in: Saves and restores the Clipboard.
- Troi Grabber Plug-in: Records images and video from a video camera and puts them in container fields.
- Troi Graphic Plug-in: Adds color container creation, screen shot capture, and thumbnail creation.
- Troi Number Plug-in: Adds Dynamic Balance Functions.
- Troi Ranges Plug-in: Generates date and number ranges between endpoints.

Scodigo: http://www.scodigo.com

SmartPill: SmartPill is a powerful plug-in that embeds the popular scripting language PHP into your FileMaker solution.

Worq Smart (formerly Waves in Motion): http://www.worqsmart.com

eAuthorize: Allows users to authorize credit cards securely from within FileMaker.

Events: Triggers scripts based on specified scheduling.

24U Software: http://www.24usoftware.com/plugins.php

- 24U SimpleTalk Plug-in: SimpleTalk enables FileMaker to communicate with other FileMaker Pro clients and other applications across TCP/IP.
- 24U SimpleFile Plug-in: SimpleFile allows you to create and delete files and perform other file-system operations from within FileMaker Pro.
- 24U FMTemplate: This template file assists in developing plug-ins for FileMaker.
- 24U SimpleDialog Plug-in: Allows you to display progress bars and complex dialog boxes.
- 24U SimpleSound Plug-in: Allows you to record and play custom sounds from with FileMaker Pro.
- 24U Virtual User Plug-in: Allows you to record and simulate user actions such as mouse clicks and keystrokes.

Developer Tools

FMNexus: http://www.fmnexus.com

Inspector: Inspector is a powerful tool that allows you to analyze a FileMaker solution and document all of its problems and dependencies.

Chaparral Software: http://www.chapsoft.com/

Brushfire: Creates an easy-to-read HTML document illustrating script relationships, designed to aid in refactoring. Aids in migration from FileMaker 6 to FileMaker 7.

EZxslt: Produces Microsoft Word documents by generating XSLT stylesheets based on templates. Allows for a better way to do mail merges, contracts, and more.

Visio: http://www.microsoft.com/office/visio/prodinfo/default.mspx

Visio, published by Microsoft, is a Windows-only technical diagramming tool that does a great job on entity-relationship (ER) diagrams.

OmniGraffle: http://www.omnigroup.com/applications/omnigraffle/

OmniGraffle, published by The Omni Group, is a Mac OS X–based diagramming and charting tool that also does a great job on ER diagrams.

New Millennium: http://www.nmci.com/

MetadataMagic, published by New Millennium, is an outstanding database analysis tool. The File Reference Fixer feature is an essential tool for assisting with migration of pre-FileMaker 7 databases to the FileMaker 7 format.

FMrobot, also published by New Millennium, allows the easy moving of tables, fields, custom functions, value lists, and privilege sets among files.

Web Programming

If you're going to venture into web deployments of FileMaker, you'll find it beneficial to be well read on web programming technologies. Even if you're using only Instant Web Publishing, it helps to be familiar with how the Web works. A good—though very exact and technical—discussion is *HTTP: The Definitive Guide* by David Gourley, Brian Totty, et al. (ISBN: 1-565-92509-2).

If you're getting into custom web publishing, you'll likely be well served by a solid reference library on the fundamental web technologies: HTML, JavaScript, and CSS. In general, we've found the books from O'Reilly Press (http://www.oreilly.com) to be impeccable. Sams also has a strong lineup in this area. You can also sign up for a nifty e-book subscription service, Safari (http://www.safaribooksonline.com), to take these and other hefty volumes for a test drive.

XML/XSL

XML.com: http://www.xml.com/. This site gives access to a wide range of XML resources.

Jeni Tennison's site: http://www.jenitennison.com/xslt/. Jeni Tennison is a sharp XML author and consultant, and her personal pages contain many useful links, documents, and references.

We find a lot of the books from Wrox Press (now defunct, but many titles are still alive under the Apress label) to be quite good. You might want to look into *Beginning XML* by David Hunter, et al. (ISBN: 0-764-54394-6) as well as *Professional XML* by Mark Birbeck, et al. (ISBN: 1-861-00311-0), and *Beginning XSLT* by Jeni Tennison (ISBN: 1-590-59260-3).

After you get further into XSLT you might also look at *XSLT 2.0 Programmer's Reference* by Michael Kay (ISBN: 0-764-56909-0).

These books, even the beginning ones, are meaty and do presume some hands-on experience with some form of web programming, such as HTML, or similar experience and familiarity with web technology. Out of all of these, Jeni Tennison's XSLT book may be the best starting point. She's extremely knowledgeable about the subject and an effective writer. A number of the Wrox books are out of print but widely available on the used market. The other Wrox books, especially the multiauthor ones, tend to mingle generally useful chapters with more specialized ones. As a reference work, though not a tutorial, you might consult *The XML Companion* by Neil Bradley (ISBN: 0-201-77059-8). The same goes for *Definitive XSLT and XPath* by G. Ken Holman (ISBN: 0-130-65196-6). For a tour of the esoteric power of XSLT, check out *XSLT and XPath On The Edge* by Jeni Tennison (ISBN: 0-764-54776-3).

PHP

For complex web development, we make heavy use of PHP. There's an embarrassment of riches as far as PHP books and resources go.

PHP main website: http://www.php.net

This is the official PHP project website, home to tutorials, the annotated online manual (a great resource), the PHP software itself, and links to many other useful sites and resources.

Zend: http://www.zend.com

Zend is a commercial entity, founded by some of the core authors and developers of PHP, that sells a number of tools for working with and enhancing PHP.

For books, you might look at *Learning PHP 5* by David Sklar (ISBN: 0-596-00560-1). As your learning progresses, you'll definitely want to look at *Advanced PHP Programming* by George Schlossnagle (ISBN: 0-672-32561-6).

ODBC/JDBC

Actual Technologies: http://www.actualtechnologies.com/

Actual Technologies is probably the best current source for Mac ODBC drivers. It offers drivers for all the SQL data sources supported by the new External SQL Source feature.

OpenLink Software: http://www.openlinksw.com

OpenLink offers a wide variety of ODBC and JDBC drivers.

Sun's JDBC site: http://java.sun.com/products/jdbc/index.jsp

JDBC is Sun's Java-based cross-platform database access technology. Sun's main JDBC page gives a nice overview of the technology. You'll also find a link to Sun's driver database. It lists available JDBC drivers for dozens of different databases.

INDEX

Symbols

A

B

C

F

G

H

I

J–K

L

M

N

O

P

Q–R

U

V

W

X–Z

THIS BOOK IS SAFARI ENABLED

INCLUDES FREE 45-DAY ACCESS TO THE ONLINE EDITION

The Safari® Enabled icon on the cover of your favorite technology book means the book is available through Safari Bookshelf. When you buy this book, you get free access to the online edition for 45 days.

Safari Bookshelf is an electronic reference library that lets you easily search thousands of technical books, find code samples, download chapters, and access technical information whenever and wherever you need it.

TO GAIN 45-DAY SAFARI ENABLED ACCESS TO THIS BOOK:

- Go to **http://www.quepublishing.com/safarienabled**
- Complete the brief registration form
- Enter the coupon code found in the front of this book on the "Copyright" page

If you have difficulty registering on Safari Bookshelf or accessing the online edition, please e-mail customer-service@safaribooksonline.com.